dBASE III PLUS™:
POWER USER'S GUIDE

Edward Jones

Osborne-McGraw Hill
Berkeley, California

Osborne **McGraw-Hill**
2600 Tenth Street
Berkeley, California 94710
U.S.A.

For information on translations and book distributors outside of the U.S.A., please write
to Osborne **McGraw-Hill** at the above address.

A complete list of trademarks appears on page 433.

dBASE III PLUS™: POWER USER'S GUIDE

1234567890 DODO 898

ISBN 0-07-881317-4

dBASE III PLUS™:
POWER USER'S GUIDE

To Judie
who has, for over a decade, shared in my hopes

Contents

Acknowledgments

A number of people and companies deserve my thanks for helping this comprehensive work reach the market. Sincere thanks to Nancy Carlston of Osborne/McGraw Hill, who conceived the idea of an advanced dBASE work that could be aimed at more than just a small subset of dBASE users, and who juggled schedules amidst a hectic autumn to guide this project to completion. Thanks for the vital task of manuscript preparation go to Lindy Clinton. And a note of thanks goes to Stuart Ozer, whose dBASE knowledge and in-depth technical suggestions added much to the final product.

On the corporate side, thanks to PC's Limited for the use of the PC's Limited 386 (the raw speed did come in handy), and thanks also to C. Itoh for the loan of the Jet/Setter laser printer, which has spoiled me for other lasers forever.

Finally, as a consultant and writer who, like many others, earns a living from dBASE, I would like, for once, to thank Ashton-Tate for making such successes possible in the first place.

Introduction

dBASE, in all its flavors, has established itself as a major force in the database management area. But more than that, it has fostered a language standard, along with all the add-on products, competing database programs, magazines, books, and small army of supporting consultants. The program's popularity has ensured it a place in microcomputer history; and its continuing use by so many means that more than a few individuals are eager to get the most out of dBASE.

Like all things in this world, dBASE is not perfect. It does an admirable job of database management. Inside that broad specification, there are things that it does well, and things that it does not so well. This book is aimed at helping you fine-tune your dBASE practices and procedures so that dBASE excels in what it does, even if the things that you do often fall into the "not-so-well" category.

This book assumes a comfortable working knowledge of dBASE. Also, it is written to provide a wide range of helpful hints and tools in all working areas of dBASE use, for programmers and nonprogrammers alike. Many advanced dBASE books on the market assume that all power users are programmers, but experience in working with dBASE users proves that this is not always the case. From the start, this book was written to provide useful information, whether you prefer to write your own code or to perform all or nearly all of your dBASE work from the dot prompt. For those who are interested in such things, the book was written using a PC's Limited 386 with a 151-megabyte hard disk and an EGA monitor. Many of the speed tests listed in the book were performed using this combination of hardware.

WHAT YOU'LL FIND IN THIS BOOK

Chapter 1 covers an assortment of topics that can help you get greater performance from your overall use of dBASE. Areas such as dBASE's interaction with DOS, hard disk interleave factors, and the use of ram disks are included. In Chapter 2, tips are provided on how the actual mechanics of database layout can be changed to increase dBASE performance. Chapter 3 covers the myriad ways you can put data into dBASE, with an emphasis on uncovering the best method for your particular tasks.

Chapter 4 delves into various tricks that can improve performance when you use file management commands. In Chapter 5, the best ways to utilize the power of index files are covered in detail. Maximizing the relational powers inherent (and often ignored) in dBASE is the subject of Chapter 6, while Chapter 7 provides hints on how you can handle the more complex and unusual types of screen display needs.

Books like this one can be written on the science of database management, but it all boils down to one need: that of information retrieval. Chapters 8 and 9 both focus on this all-important need. Chapter 8 will be of interest to programmers who use the dBASE Report Generator, but the chapter was written primarily for nonprogrammers who depend heavily on the Report Generator for their reports. The chapter shows how to use the Report Generator to produce reports that are often thought to be beyond the limits of the Report Generator. Chapter 9 shows how program code can be used to handle complex and varied reporting needs. The more unusual subjects that often present reporting challenges, like handling columnar listings and dealing with large text fields, are included in this chapter.

Chapter 10 provides techniques for implementing security and backup procedures. In Chapter 11, useful tools for dealing with foreign files are detailed; you will also find specialized hints on moving data into WordPerfect, the number one word processor at the time of this writing. Chapter 12 offers an examination of the wide array of add-on products that support the dBASE marketplace, including compilers, report generators, and programmer's utilities.

Chapter 13 provides useful tricks and techniques for users of the dBASE Administrator, the local-area network version of dBASE. In Chapter 14, you will find a potpourri of unusual techniques that can come in handy for those rare situations when the common commands don't do the job. Chapter 15 provides hints for programmers on creating highly modularized program code that can be used in a variety of applications with minimal change. Finally, in Chapter 16, a complete database system is offered for your use or for modification to suit your purposes.

Appendixes A and B contain listings of the dBASE III PLUS commands and functions. In Appendix C is a sample of end-user documentation, in the hope that providing an example that can be copied and modified will leave some of the world's end users with better documentation for those in-house systems. Appendix D contains a resource listing for products that are mentioned in various chapters of the book.

The program files in this book, including the complete database system described in Chapter 16 and the generic end-user documentation in Appendix C, are also available on diskette. The complete cost of the diskette package is $15.00, which covers the costs of duplication, postage, and handling. (Add $3.00 for Canadian or $5.00 for other foreign orders.) To order the diskette package, use the form on the following page.

Please send me the diskette package that accompanies *dBASE III PLUS: Power User's Guide*. My payment of $15.00 ($18.00 Canadian or $20.00 foreign) is enclosed.

Name _____

Address _____

City _____ State _____ ZIP _____

Send payment to:

J.E.J.A. Software, Inc.
P.O. Box 1834
Herndon VA 22070-1834

This offer is solely the responsibility of J.E.J.A. Software, Inc. Osborne/McGraw-Hill takes no responsibility for the fulfillment of this offer.

1: Turbocharged dBASE

Since the first release of dBASE II (perhaps known as Vulcan to those who have been around PCs for a long time), power users have been searching for ways to coax more speed out of dBASE. Major improvements in performance have come in both hardware and software. dBASE II, which was agonizingly slow in sorting and indexing, made a quantum leap with the development of dBASE III. And the 8-bit CP/M systems that ran with a memory that now seems to have had little more than the capacity of an ordinary notepad have given way to machines based on 80386 processors with hard disks in excess of 100 megabytes. Yet still we crave more speed, and we work at tweaking dBASE to gain a few seconds of performance here and there.

To a large extent, speed is relative. A 30,000-record database running under dBASE seems slow until you compare it with the manual system it replaced. Searches that took days or weeks with a manual system now take 12 minutes, and we complain about how slow dBASE is!

Still, reminders of relativity don't help when you are twiddling your thumbs waiting for dBASE to search a massive database for one record. However, you can improve the performance of dBASE, and you'll find many ways to do so described in this chapter. Some tips on improving the speed of dBASE relate directly to how you manage your database and index files; hints in these areas are covered in Chapter 3. Finally, some methods for improving the performance of dBASE require going slightly outside the dBASE environment to make use of dBASE-compatible products such as compilers. These techniques are the subject of Chapter 12.

FINE-TUNING DOS

Too many dBASE users ignore the effects of the operating system, or DOS, on the operation of dBASE. DOS makes a specified number of files and buffers available for use by the applications software, and the performance of dBASE can be either improved or adversely affected by the number of available DOS files and buffers. These numbers can be changed by modifying the CONFIG.SYS file in the root directory of the system's startup disk. If the system lacks a CONFIG.SYS file in the startup disk's root directory, it doesn't take long to encounter major performance problems in dBASE. And regardless of the standard settings of FILES = 20 and BUFFERS = 15, you may be able to coax more performance from your application by modifying these settings. To modify or create CONFIG.SYS, use any word processor that lets you edit and save files as ASCII text. Or use the dBASE word processor by entering **MODIFY COMMAND C:\CONFIG.SYS** at the dot prompt (assuming your hard disk is drive C).

About Files

The FILES = n setting in the CONFIG.SYS file controls the number of DOS file handles provided for file access. Most applications software, dBASE III PLUS included, use file handles to open, read, write, and close files. DOS must provide a file handle for every file that dBASE uses, in addition to some handles needed for DOS' own overhead. If no CONFIG.SYS file is on the startup disk, the default value for files is eight. Of these, five files are used by DOS for handling the screen, keyboard, and printer data transfer. That leaves three for your application, and dBASE needs two files just to get started (one for the main program and one for the overlay, DBASE.OVL). That leaves room for *one* file, which explains why attempting to accomplish much of anything without a CONFIG. SYS file on the startup disk results in the "too many files are open" error message.

Although the FILES parameter in the CONFIG.SYS file will accept any value between 8 and 255, DOS versions 2.0 through 3.3 will provide a maximum of only 20 files to each application. Since DOS uses five of those files for overhead and dBASE uses two to operate, you are limited in practice to 13 available files. (Keep this limit in mind when developing complex applications.) For example, the following ten lines in a program would reach the limit of 13 files:

```
SELECT 1
USE STOCKS INDEX STOCKS, NAMES
SET FORMAT TO STOCKS
SELECT 2
USE CUSTOMER INDEX CUSTOMER, LASTNAME
SET FORMAT TO CUSTOMER
SELECT 3
USE TRANSACT INDEX TRANSACT, DATES
SET FORMAT TO TRANSACT
DO REPORT1
```

Each database, index file, and format file counts as an open file under DOS. So does another program, called with the command DO REPORT1. If the called program tries to open another file, dBASE crashes with a "too many files are open" error. The only solution is to design your applications so that you avoid taxing this limitation. (Ashton-Tate's dBASE Programmers Utilities package includes a utility that lets users open 5 additional files for a total of 18 user files. The utility can be used with DOS versions 3.0 and higher.)

Even when you have the room to do so, however, opening a large number of files can adversely affect dBASE performance. The results become noticeable in machines with severe memory constraints, such as 256K systems. While each open file increases DOS overhead by only 48 bytes, the contents of the file also require memory overhead. With databases, which are swapped partially in and out of memory by dBASE, that overhead can become significant. A database with 128 fields and 4000 records requires roughly 80K of available memory. dBASE III PLUS will use all available memory up to the 640K limit. In a system with just 256K of memory, it is quite possible to open so many files that dBASE slows to a crawl. The same problem occurs in systems with more memory when you load multiple memory-resident packages, like Side-Kick, into RAM. You can engineer your way around such a limitation by opening fewer files, or you can add more memory to the machine.

About Buffers

DOS also makes use of *disk buffers,* which are temporary storage areas in memory for disk reads and writes. During disk read operations, DOS typically places data read from the disk into buffers. When dBASE tells DOS to look for a record, DOS does not immediately read the disk. Instead, DOS first looks in the available buffers to see if the data is there from a prior read operation. If DOS finds the data, it passes it over to dBASE, and no disk access is necessary. If the desired data is not in the buffer, DOS must perform a disk access to read the data.

The default value for the BUFFERS setting is 2 on the PC and XT and 3 on the AT. Both settings provide poor performance with dBASE, which typically needs at least ten buffers available for satisfactory results. On the other hand, it is easy to get carried away by specifying too many buffers, which can actually degrade the performance of dBASE. Every two buffers use 1K of available RAM; you can eat into your available memory by specifying a large number of buffers in the CONFIG.SYS file. And DOS takes time to search all the buffers that you specify prior to each disk access. Make the value large enough, and you would actually be better off performing a hard disk access rather than searching through all the buffers. Table 1-1 shows the effects of various

Table 1-1.

Effects of Buffers Settings

Index 2000-record file on lastname, firstname, and department fields

No. Buffers	Time To Index
2	1 minute, 51 seconds
15	1 minute, 39 seconds
99	1 minute, 58 seconds

Sort same 2000-record file on same fields

No. Buffers	Time to Sort
2	2 minutes, 27 seconds
15	2 minutes, 25 seconds
99	2 minutes, 36 seconds

buffers settings on sorts and index operations on a 2000-record file, with the structure of the database shown here. The hardware used was an 80386-based system running at 16 mHz; times would be slower and differences more pronounced on slower PC-compatibles based on the 8088 processors.

```
Structure for database: D:testfile.dbf
Number of data records:      2002
Date of last update   : 08/16/87
Field  Field Name  Type       Width    Dec
    1  LASTNAME    Character     20
    2  FIRSTNAME   Character     20
    3  DEPARTMENT  Character     12
    4  BIRTH_DATE  Date           8
    5  HOURLY_SAL  Numeric        5      2
    6  INSURED     Logical        1
    7  COMMENTS    Memo          10
** Total **                     77
```

The effects of an optimal buffers setting are more dramatic for indexing than for sorting. Since sorting requires dBASE to read and write multiple records back and forth in temporary and permanent files, the high rate of disk access means that dBASE is going to take time to finish the job no matter what you put in the CONFIG.SYS file. Still, having the optimal settings can clearly impact dBASE performance, and with very large files, the differences can be significant. Keep in mind that some settings of buffers may adversely affect the performance of other software that you may be using; you may have to find a middle ground between what is best for dBASE and what is best for your other software.

THE CHALLENGE OF dBASE IN A 256K MACHINE

If you are forced into the unenviable task of using dBASE on a 256K system, you should do some things differently. Ashton-Tate alludes to this in the booklet *Getting Started: dBASE III PLUS* supplied with the dBASE software. The booklet recommends that you use two files supplied on System Disk #1, CONFI256.SYS and CONFI256.DB. These files should replace, respectively, the CONFIG.SYS file, usually in the root directory or on the start-up disk, and the CONFIG.DB file, normally in the same directory as the dBASE program files. The replacement is recommended because 256K is barely enough memory to run dBASE and therefore you need all the help that fine-tuning your configuration can offer. Also, a 256K limit assumes that you are using a version of DOS below 3.0. If you are using DOS version 3.0 or above, you cannot use dBASE III PLUS on a system equipped with 256K of memory.

The CONFI256.SYS file provided by Ashton-Tate contains the statements FILES = 20 and BUFFERS = 4. You can modify your existing CONFIG.SYS to contain the same parameters, or copy the file from the dBASE System Disk #1 to your startup disk or root directory and rename it to CONFIG.SYS.

You will also want to copy the CONFI256.DB file into the same directory that contains the dBASE program files and rename this file to CONFIG.DB. This file, which is read by dBASE on startup, contains the following operating parameters:

```
COMMAND = ASSIST
STATUS = ON
BUCKET = 1
GETS = 35
MVARSIZ = 3
HISTORY = 10
TYPEAHEAD = 10
```

These settings will reduce the amount of memory that dBASE will need to operate. You should be particularly aware of the limits these changes bring to the BUCKET, GETS, and MVARSIZ settings. The BUCKET = 1 statement limits dBASE to 1024 bytes (1K) of available RAM for any picture and range clauses used with the @...SAY...GET commands. The GETS = 35 statement limits the CREATE SCREEN command to a single screen with a maximum of 35 GETS. This limitation can be a real problem if you are accustomed to creating multiple-page entry screens with Screen Painter. The only reasonable option is more memory. Finally, the MVARSIZ = 3 statement cuts the usual default of 6K for memory variables in half, setting aside 3K instead.

With these changes, you will get by with 256K of RAM, but don't be surprised to encounter problems if your uses of dBASE grow complex. Many operations will tax the limits of the system, and dBASE will complain by displaying an "insufficient memory" message. Although you can close files to get around the message, the best solution is to add memory to the machine.

HARDWARE VERSUS SOFTWARE

One solution to sluggish performance too often overlooked is to change the hardware. Business micros have experienced major gains in computational power at least four times in the space of their ten-year history: from the 8-bit machines that ran dBASE II under CP/M operating systems, to the 16-bit address/8-bit data bus 8088-based IBM-compatibles, to the true 16-bit 80286 based IBM AT compatibles, to the latest 80386-based machines. If the application is becoming bogged down because of overwhelming size, it may be time to ask if the hardware is sufficient to handle the task. You can spend time structuring your commands in a more efficient manner, recoding program loops to minimize unnecessary repetition, and fine-tuning the CONFIG.SYS file, and you may pick up a 25% to 50% performance increase. On the other hand, by adding a speedup board to your existing PC, or by moving the application to a faster machine such as an AT or an 80386-based machine, you can easily double or triple the performance of dBASE. Table 1-2 illustrates the striking differences that hardware can have on the operating speed of dBASE.

In this case, a 6000-record database was sorted on lastname, firstname, and birth—date fields. The sort was performed on three different machines: an IBM-compatible using an 8088 processor and an 80-millisecond hard disk, an AT-compatible with an 80286 processor and a 35-millisecond hard disk, and an 80386-based PC with a 28-millisecond hard disk.

```
Structure for database: D:bigfile.dbf
Number of data records:      6010
Date of last update   : 08/16/87
Field   Field Name  Type        Width      Dec
    1   LASTNAME    Character     20
    2   FIRSTNAME   Character     20
    3   DEPARTMENT  Character     12
    4   BIRTH_DATE  Date           8
    5   HOURLY_SAL  Numeric        5         2
    6   INSURED     Logical        1
    7   COMMENTS    Memo          10
     Total **                    77
```

Table 1-2.

Hardware Speed Tests

8088-based IBM PC-compatible	8 minutes, 30 seconds
80286-based AT-compatible	1 minute, 56 seconds
80386-based PS/2-compatible	1 minute, 25 seconds

CHANGING THE INTERLEAVE FACTOR

A little-known setting called the *hard disk interleave factor* (HDIF) is actually not dBASE specific, but it affects every application you work with. Its important impact on system performance, including that of dBASE, makes it well worth discussing. The HDIF setting controls how your hard disk reads data. If it isn't optimized for your hard disk (and often it isn't), your machine can plod along at well under 50% of the speed it is normally capable of.

Before you get excited and think you have found a way to turn your PC into an AT, be forewarned that optimizing your HDIF is not as simple as changing the parameters of the CONFIG.SYS file. First, many hard disk configuration programs require the HDIF to be set prior to a low-level format procedure, which means erasing your hard disk. If you decide to change the HDIF, be prepared to back up the disk onto floppy or tape, and restore all the files. Second, no two hard disk manufacturers seem to use the same program to change the HDIF. You will need to dig out your hard disk owner's manual and the installation software that came with the hard disk to determine how to go about changing your machine's HDIF. If, after all this, you are still willing to give it a try, it may prove to be time well spent.

To understand how an ideal HDIF can boost the performance of dBASE (and your other software as well), a discussion of hard disk technology is in order. Hard disks, like floppies, store data on concentric tracks, which are divided into sectors. Figure 1-1 is an illustration of the sectors that make up the tracks of a hard disk.

As the disk spins underneath a magnetic read/write head, the disk controller card and hard disk electronics send signals to the head to write magnetic data into the sectors and to read data from the sectors. Most data gets written and read in sequential sectors, sectors that follow one another. Because the sectors are sequential, the read/write head inside the hard disk does not have to go searching all over the hard disk to find information. This system works well, except for one small problem: once the computer places the read/write head over a track, it is physically impossible for the system to actually read or write adjacent sectors. The disk is simply moving too fast for the combination of mechanics and electronics to keep up.

To get around this problem, the hard disk separates sequential sectors on the same track by interspersing a given number of other sectors in between them. The number of sectors that fall between consecutive sectors of data on the hard disk determines the hard disk interleave factor. For example, if the disk reads every other sector that goes by, the HDIF is set to a 1:2 ratio. If the disk reads every third sector that goes by, the ratio is 1:3. If the disk reads every fourth sector that goes by, the ratio is 1:4, and so on. Eventually, all the sectors that occupy a track are written to or read, but not in the order of adjacent sectors. Figure 1-2 illustrates this point.

Figure 1-2 shows sectors on a hard disk that were written using a 1:3 interleave factor. With this ratio, the PC skips two sectors for every sector that it reads from or writes to the disk. Most software packages used to install hard disks let you change the HDIF; if yours doesn't, your dealer's service shop should be able to supply you with a disk that will change the ratio.

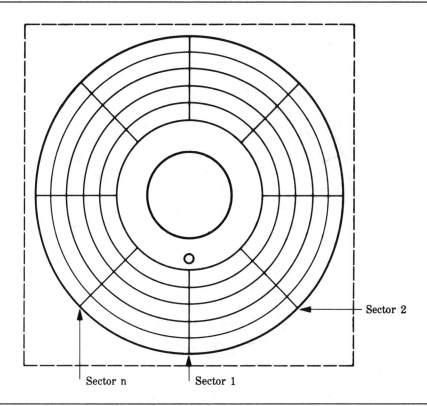

Figure 1-1.

Sectors of a disk (reprinted from
DOS: The Complete Reference by
Kris Jamsa. Berkeley, Calif.:
Osborne/McGraw-Hill, 1987)

Changing the HDIF can provide dBASE with a dramatic performance boost because an annoyingly large number of hard disk machines are shipped with less than optimal HDIF ratios. Often, they are set at a default value of 1:6, which is about the worst value you could choose. The hard disk must wait for the disk platter to make six revolutions before it

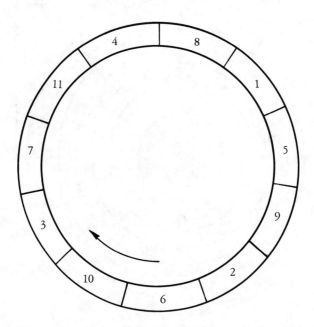

Figure 1-2.

Disk sectors written with 1:3 hard
disk interleave

can attempt to read another disk sector. Most hard disks can manage
quite well with a 1:4 or 1:3 ratio; some high-performance hard disks can
get by with a 1:2 ratio. If you have software that lets you change your
HDIF, and if you have backed up your hard disk, try adjusting the ratio
downward, one digit at a time. After each new setting, install DOS if
necessary, load dBASE, copy a database file with a few thousand records,

and perform a sort while timing the results. As you lower the HDIF ratio toward 1:1, performance will improve with each step until you reach a point where performance takes a drastic step backward. The setting *prior to that setting* is the one at which you want to leave your hard disk.

USING RAMDISKS

Another way to significantly increase the speed of dBASE, and one that may cost relatively little, is to use a sizeable ramdisk for sorting tasks and for reports that call for a large amount of random-access disk activity. You are probably concerned about putting data in a disk that would vanish if the machine lost power. But in any serious dBASE application, you will encounter times when files that are not critical to the long-term health of the application must be created. A prime example is a file sorted on a date field to provide a chronological report. If you don't want to maintain a date index becuase of the size of the database file and the resulting slowness during editing operations, you will probably take the alternative approach of sorting or indexing only when that specific report is needed. Build the index file or the sorted file in a ramdisk, and you will find that dBASE does the job in half the time or less. This advantage becomes particularly evident with large sorts because sorting files is probably one of the most disk-intensive applications that dBASE performs. Table 1-3 shows one example, sorting a 1000-record database by lastname field to both a high-speed hard disk and to a ramdisk. The database structure was identical to the structure used for the tests described earlier in the chapter, and the computer used was an 80386-based PS/2-compatible, equipped with a 28-millisecond hard disk.

A very large database file does not have to preclude the use of a ramdisk. If the file is sizable, you can still use a ramdisk by using a memory card that supports the Intel expanded memory specification; such cards allow you to designate up to 2 megabytes of on-board memory as one giant ramdisk. Perform all of your sorting and index tasks in the ramdisk, and base your reports or searches on the files in the ramdisk.

Table 1-3.

Hard Disk Versus Ramdisk
Comparison

Hard Disk	Ramdisk
1:07 seconds	0:17 seconds

If you are still nervous about working with files in a ramdisk, you can use the hard disk for entering and updating data files and still save time by sorting and indexing them in the ramdisk. The files can be copied back to the hard disk when you complete the desired tasks. Consider the commands in the following example, which uses a hard disk as drive C and a ramdisk as drive D:

```
CLOSE DATABASES
RUN COPY MAINFILE.DBF D:
RUN D:
USE MAINFILE
INDEX ON LASTNAME + FIRSTNAME TO NAMES
USE
RUN COPY NAMES.NDX C:
RUN C:
USE MAINFILE INDEX NAMES
.
.
.
```

With these commands, in the dot prompt mode or in a program, the indexing is performed entirely in the ramdisk. Once the indexing is completed, the RUN command is used to copy the index file back to the hard disk. (Note that the RUN command is used in place of the dBASE COPY FILE command because performing a file copy from DOS is generally much faster than the dBASE COPY FILE command, which copies in 512-byte blocks.) If your database files are relatively small (on the order of a thousand records or less), the effort is probably not worthwhile. With small databases, changing directories and copying files usually takes more time than you are likely to save in sorting. But when your databases number in the thousands of records, you will notice significant savings in time by taking this approach. Software for creating ramdisks is readily available; it is supplied free with most multifunction cards for the PC, as well as with most expanded memory cards. Also, a device driver for creating a ramdisk, called VDISK.SYS, is supplied with DOS 3.0 and all higher versions of DOS. See your DOS manual for details.

FAST SETTING OF ENVIRONMENTAL VARIABLES WITH SET

One dBASE command is somewhat like the popular comedian who complains that he "gets no respect." The SET command is generally ignored by programmers, who would rather keep all menus under complete control of the program being written. The command is also treated rather superficially in most dBASE texts, since it is primarily a menu-driven way to duplicate the SET (PARAMETER) TO (STATUS) commands. It's a shame that SET doesn't get more use than it does, because the command affords a fast way to change a large number of environmental variables inside dBASE, and it just may save you some programming if you include it as a part of any programs that you may write. The SET command results in the appearance of a full-screen menu, shown in Figure 1-3.

The Set menu offers seven choices: Options, Screen, Keys, Disk, Files, Margin, and Decimals. Each choice corresponds to a different pull-down menu, which displays the various commands associated with that menu.

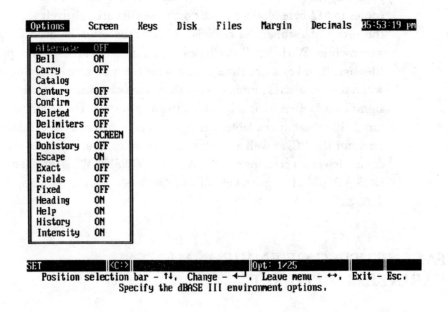

Figure 1-3.

Set menu

Most set commands that affect the environmental variables in dBASE can be reached via the Options menu, shown in Figure 1-3. The set commands that affect screen display colors and intensity are available from the Screen menu.

The Keys menu lists the function keys that can be readily changed; selecting any of the keys F2 through F10 under this menu is equivalent to using the SET FUNCTION X TO command within dBASE. However, an advantage of the use of the SET command to change the keys is that you can assign values to all nine keys at once, instead of being forced to use nine different SET commands within dBASE to program nine different keys.

The Disk and Files menus let you select default disk drives and paths that dBASE will search for a file, and the format file, index file, and alternate file (for text output with SET ALTERNATE ON) desired. The Margin menu lets you set the default left margin for a report, as well as the display width of a memo field. Finally, the Decimals menu lets you change the default number of decimal places displayed for numeric data.

The SET command offers programmers a relatively simple way to provide users of a program with the ability to change the environmental settings. As a fast means of data entry, for example, users will often want to reprogram a function key to represent a commonly entered city or ZIP code. You can write program code to reassign text strings to the function keys, or you can simply include one line of text in the program that accesses the SET command. When the user finishes selecting options from the menu and presses the ESC key, your program continues where it left off. You can include detailed explanations, if desired, as illustrated in the following example of a portion of a program:

```
ACCEPT "Set function keys, screen colors? Y/N:" TO ANS
IF UPPER(ANS) = "Y"
   CLEAR
   ? "Use arrow keys to select desired menu."
   ? "Use Keys Menu to set function keys."
   ? "Use Screen Menu to change screen colors."
   ? "Press ESCAPE key when finished."
   WAIT
   SET
ENDIF
   .
   .
   .
```

Anyone who has written a few dozen lines of program code to give the users of a program the ability to change colors and function keys will save considerable time by using this approach. The only disadvantage to this approach is that the users of the program will have access to some environmental variables that programmers would just as soon see left alone, such as disk drive paths and files in use. If the users of the program can be trusted to not change things that shouldn't be changed, this access should not present a major problem.

2: Building Better Databases

Before you ask "What on earth is a chapter on creating databases doing in this book?", rest assured that this chapter is *not* going to tell you how to create a database. If you don't know how, you are reading the wrong book. What this chapter will emphasize is how to design a database so that dBASE does not have to work so hard in dealing with it.

Both the size and the layout of a database can affect dBASE performance. It is well known that the more fields in a database, the longer dBASE will take to work with the data. What is not so obvious is that the actual layout of the fields in the database structure can have an advantageous or detrimental effect on performance. The effect isn't incredibly dramatic, because dBASE uses a highly efficient algorithm to keep track of field positions in a database and to look directly at those positions when retrieving data; but small, noticeable differences in performance can occur, depending on how the database fields are arranged. Consider this example: a personnel recruiting agency maintains a database with highly detailed information on college graduates it is seeking to place in the corporate world. Among the data are three complete addresses: a school, a home, and a work address. Which of the two structures works better for the proposed database — A or B, or is it an even match?

Example A   Example B

```
LASTNAME                     LASTNAME
FIRSTNAME                    FIRSTNAME
SCHOOL_ADD                   SCHOOL_ADD
HOME_ADD                     SCHOOLCITY
WORK_ADD                     SCHOOLSTAT
SCHOOLCITY                   SCHOOLZIP
HOMECITY                     HOME_ADD
WORKCITY                     HOMECITY
SCHOOLSTAT                   HOMESTAT
HOMESTAT                     HOMEZIP
WORKSTAT                     WORK_ADD
SCHOOLZIP                    WORKCITY
HOMEZIP                      WORKSTAT
WORKZIP                      WORKZIP
```

An answer requires a little knowledge of how dBASE stores data within a database file. The structure of a database can be readily seen by using DOS DEBUG to examine the contents of a file. If you open a file by entering a command like DEBUG JUNK.DBF and then repeatedly issue the DEBUG DUMP command by pressing D, you can see the data stored within the fields, represented in hex format. Such a display will resemble this:

SAMPLE DEBUG DUMP

(For those unfamiliar with DEBUG, you can get back to the DOS prompt by pressing Q to issue the QUIT command.) The listing of the file under DEBUG shows the sequential arrangement of data in a dBASE file. dBASE keeps track of the position of each field by remembering that field's *offset* (in effect, distance) from the beginning of each record. Once a record is in memory, dBASE knows where a particular field begins or ends and can perform calculations based on the offset to find the required data, thus greatly reducing the amount of time dBASE must spend looking in a given record for a particular field. Fields placed far from where they are needed, or in a random order, don't help dBASE in its efforts.

The question of which of the two database structures would provide the better results becomes easier to answer: unless the data is stored and retrieved in an unusual manner, the second example is the more efficient. Time-consuming tasks like reporting are likely to match the way the data is stored in structure B. A report that displays the permanent address, city, state, and ZIP in consecutive rows wouldn't need to find the data all in a row if the structure is laid out as in the second example. If the structure follows example A, dBASE must respond to widely varying calculations of its offsets to collect the required data.

Consider an actual example to see the possible differences in performance. The hardware used was an IBM XT-compatible, with an 8088 processor at 4.77 mHz, 10 megabyte, 80-millisecond hard disk, and 512K of memory. The database structure is shown in the following two examples:

```
Structure for database: C:bigfile.dbf
Number of data records:     1500
Date of last update     : 01/02/80
Field   Field Name   Type        Width   Dec
    1   COMMENT20    Character      50
    2   COMMENT19    Character      50
    3   COMMENT18    Character      50
    4   COMMENT17    Character      50
    5   COMMENT16    Character      50
    6   COMMENT15    Character      50
    7   COMMENT14    Character      50
    8   COMMENT13    Character      50
    9   COMMENT12    Character      50
   10   COMMENT11    Character      50
   11   COMMENT10    Character      50
   12   COMMENT9     Character      50
   13   COMMENT8     Character      50
   14   COMMENT7     Character      50
   15   COMMENT6     Character      50
   16   COMMENT5     Character      50
   17   COMMENT4     Character      50
   18   COMMENT3     Character      50
   19   COMMENT2     Character      50
   20   COMMENT1     Character      50
   21   SOC_SEC      Character      11
   22   BIRTH_DATE   Date            8
   23   HOURLY_SAL   Numeric         5     2
   24   INSURED      Logical         1
   25   COMMENTS     Memo           10
   26   LASTNAME     Character      20
   27   FIRSTNAME    Character      20
** Total **                       1076
```

The second example, of better database design, lists the commonly reported fields, LASTNAME, FIRSTNAME, and SOC__SEC at the top of the database:

```
Structure for database: C:bigfile.dbf
Number of data records:    1500
Date of last update    : 01/01/80
Field  Field Name   Type        Width    Dec
    1  LASTNAME     Character      20
    2  FIRSTNAME    Character      20
    3  SOC_SEC      Character      11
    4  COMMENT20    Character      50
    5  COMMENT19    Character      50
    6  COMMENT18    Character      50
    7  COMMENT17    Character      50
    8  COMMENT16    Character      50
    9  COMMENT15    Character      50
   10  COMMENT14    Character      50
   11  COMMENT13    Character      50
   12  COMMENT12    Character      50
   13  COMMENT11    Character      50
   14  COMMENT10    Character      5C
   15  COMMENT9     Character      50
   16  COMMENT8     Character      50
   17  COMMENT7     Character      50
   18  COMMENT6     Character      50
   19  COMMENT5     Character      50
   20  COMMENT4     Character      50
   21  COMMENT3     Character      50
   22  COMMENT2     Character      50
   23  COMMENT1     Character      50
   24  BIRTH_DATE   Date           8
   25  HOURLY_SAL   Numeric        5       2
   26  INSURED      Logical        1
   27  COMMENTS     Memo          10
** Total **                     1076
```

Except for the location of the fields, the contents of the two databases used in the tests were identical. Performance differences appeared in the areas of listing and reporting data with the LIST and REPORT FORM commands as well as with the LOCATE command, both with and without filters set across the database. Table 2-1 shows the results of the tests. Although the differences are not that dramatic, and this test represents an extreme case of a large number of large fields, the times do show that exercising forethought in planning the layout of fields can help the performance of dBASE.

These hints can be summarized in our first rule of better database design: *let the structure imitate the storage and retrieval order.* For screen-oriented operations like displaying a single record, the difference in speed will be so small that users won't notice any improvement. But when they are cranking out those long reports, the layout of the database can make a difference.

Table 2-1.

Results of Tests

	First Database Design	Second Database Design
LOCATE command, on lastname field, where record is approx. 1/3 into the database	2 min. 56 sec.	2 min. 32 sec.
GO to record 500, LIST NEXT 300, fields LASTNAME, FIRSTNAME, COMMENT19	1 min. 54 sec.	2 min. 01 sec.
GO to record 500, REPORT FORM NEXT 500 using a report format that includes the LASTNAME, FIRSTNAME, SOC_SEC, and COMMENT19 fields	2 min. 37 sec.	2 min. 46 sec.
SET FILTER across an indexed file, GO TOP, and LIST NEXT 300 with fields of LASTNAME, FIRSTNAME, and COMMENT19	4 min 28 sec.	5 min. 05 sec.

Another quiz: you are designing a database for a law firm embroiled in a suit over an auto maker's liability for faulty brakes. The law firm has taken statements from thousands of witnesses, and each statement constitutes one record in a witness facts database. The fields will include a unique character field that stores a document number. This field, called DOCNO, will contain a different number for each record, but, since no calculations are performed, the field is a character field. Also needed in the file are date fields for the date of the statement (STATED) and the date of the incident described by the witness (OCCURRED); and character fields for the witness' name (WITNESS) and the other persons involved (PERSONS). Finally, a large character field will be needed for a summary of the witness' comments. The lawyers will routinely want to search the COMMENTS field for a particular string of text. (It should not be a memo field; memo fields can't be searched within dBASE.) Most edits to existing records will be done by finding a record with the proper document number. Occasionally, a search or a report will be performed using the name of the witness. Given these design constraints, which of the following database structures is the better design?

Example A

```
DOCNO/character/6
STATED/date
OCCURRED/date
WITNESS/character/30
PERSONS/character/100
COMMENTS/character/254
```

Example B

```
COMMENTS/character/256
DOCNO/character/6
WITNESS/character/30
PERSONS/character/100
STATED/date
OCCURRED/date
```

Although many designers would out of habit build a database resembling the first example, with the large COMMENTS field at the bottom of the structure, in this case the second example is the better design. The attorneys have said that the primary use for this database will be to search the COMMENTS field for evidence that will help them win the case. In the more typical design of the first example, where the COMMENTS field is at the bottom of the database, dBASE must search through all the fields to get to the last field. If 80% of the reports and the queries are based on the contents of the COMMENTS field, then a structure like the first means that dBASE must go to the bottom of each record 80% of the time. Our second rule of better database design, then, is to *place the fields most often used at the top of the structure.* In the second example, the DOCNO and WITNESS fields follow the COMMENTS field because these fields are the second and third most likely fields to be used for searching and reporting operations.

One last question, and then no more quizzes—at least not in this chapter. You are asked to design a database with a large number of fields, about a hundred or so. The database is for a hospital's patient records; each record contains data for one patient. Included in the fields are the patient's vital statistics, attending physicians' names, and other medical facts. Like most users, the hospital staff needs all of the fields occasionally, so you cannot trim this monster down without losing desirable capabilities. However, the staff admits that most of the time the data that they will need will be in the first ten fields shown in the example structures. Under the circumstances, which is better: example A, which places the data in more than one database, and uses SET RELATION to link the files, or example B, which puts all the data in a single file?

```
Example A              Example B

(database 1)           (database)
PATIENTID              PATIENTID
PATIENT                PATIENT
INSURER                INSURER
INS_CODE               INS_CODE
ROOMNUMB               ROOMNUMB
STAFF_DR               STAFF_DR
PRIVATE_DR             PRIVATE_DR
STAFF_NURS             STAFF_NURS
ILLNESS                ILLNESS
BLOODTYPE              BLOODTYPE
                       <field 11>
(database 2)           <field 12>
PATIENTID              <field 13>
<field 11>             <fields 14...100>
<field 12>
<field 13>
<fields 14...100>
```

The answer to the question depends on who is doing the asking: you or dBASE. While example B is less work for you if you are the designer of the database, example A will be less work for dBASE. It is easy to overlook the usefulness of the relational power of dBASE in this kind of an application. The database embodies a simple, one-to-one relationship: one patient, one large set of facts for that patient. So, why build two (or more) databases for one complete set of facts? Because dBASE will thank you for your efforts. dBASE does not care for databases with dozens of fields. It puts up with them, but it gets slow and piggish, and overall performance suffers considerably. Example A shows how you can achieve better results by splitting one file into two or more related files. You can use the SET RELATION command to link the files on the basis of the patient ID number. When adding or editing records, open both files, link them with SET RELATION, and use your preferred methods of data entry or editing to store the necessary data. When retrieving data in response to a query or a report request, you'll only need to open the smaller file most of the time, and dBASE won't get so lethargic when responding to an inquiry. Our third rule of better database design is *never use one large structure when you can do the job better with more than one smaller structure.*

CHANGING EXISTING FIELDS

In an existing database, you can use the MODIFY STRUCTURE command to move fields around to make the data retrieval process more efficient. For example, if an existing file has a key field or an often-searched field at the bottom of the database, you can rearrange the database by entering the MODIFY STRUCTURE command, deleting the field at the present location, and adding the same field at the desired new location. dBASE will rearrange the database structure with no loss of data as long as you use the exact same field name and field type. To be on the safe side, make a backup copy of any existing database before using MODIFY STRUCTURE. If you make a typo that results in the loss of an entire field of data, you'll still have something to work with.

When changing field names, sizes, or field characteristics, you can usually perform such changes without loss of existing data, provided you follow a sequence that won't confuse dBASE too badly. If field sizes need changes, perform those changes separately from field name and field type modifications. Change field names separately also; when you change one or more field names while leaving the order of the fields alone, dBASE will ask if you wish to append data from all fields when you press CTRL-END at the end of the structure modification. Answer Y, and dBASE will copy the data from the fields with the old names into the corresponding fields with the new names. The most difficult change is changing a field type. dBASE will do its best to avoid loss of the data, but in some cases it can't be helped. Contents of a numeric field will appear in a character field as digits when changing from numeric to character, and numbers stored in a character field will transfer to a number field (obviously, any nonnumeric characters are lost). Date fields can be particularly tricky; changing a character field to a date field without a loss of data requires that the entries in the character field be of the proper length and in the proper format. Memo fields are a virtual lost cause because of the way dBASE stores data in a separate memo text file. If you change the structure of a field from memo to character or from character to memo, don't expect any existing entries to be carried over. dBASE will simply discard the existing data.

Finally, any movement of the order of the fields should also be done separately from any other changes. In a worst-case scenario, you may have to use MODIFY STRUCTURE three separate times to accomplish all of the changes that you want, but at least you will have all of your data intact.

3: Getting Data into dBASE

Of the seven different ways to get data into a dBASE III PLUS database file, you are probably using one method most, if not all, of the time. But each method has its advantages and disadvantages. All of the ways you can enter data are worth looking into because a method that you haven't tried may be faster and more effective than one you are currently using.

If you are adding data from the dot prompt mode of dBASE, you are probably doing so with either

```
APPEND
```

or something like

```
SET FORMAT TO MyFile
APPEND
```

You go merrily along adding records to the database until you press the CTRL-END key combination to terminate the data-entry process. This method is fast, easy to implement (no programming required), and can even be done from the ASSIST mode — and let's face it, there aren't many things that can be done from the ASSIST mode. Also, memo fields can be accessed from the same screen used to edit the other fields. Many other methods of editing dBASE files don't permit direct editing of the contents of a memo field.

The disadvantages of this method are significant, however. First, the database is open the entire time you are adding data, thus violating a safety rule endorsed by many who have worked with dBASE: open databases only when you need to, and close them as soon as you can. Databases that remain open for long periods of time are more susceptible to possible corruption or damage from power outages, machine lockup, or accidental rebooting than those opened and closed less often. Another disadvantage is that to validate the data, you are limited to whatever controls can be put in a format file with picture clauses. In the append mode, it is also all too easy to wind up with unwanted blank records if, for example, the data-entry operator chooses Append from the Assist menu or selects Add Record from a program menu and then decides that it is time to go to lunch, pressing the CTRL-END key combination on the way out the door. Unless the data-entry personnel specifically remember (a) to press CTRL-END while still in the last record entered, or (b) to press ESC if they want to exit from a new blank record, numerous blank records will accumulate over a period of time. These will have to be deleted to avoid gaps of white space at the top of your reports.

A second method of entering data, easily done from the dot prompt mode, isn't well known but has its strong points. It is to use the INSERT command to insert one record in the database. From the dot prompt you could enter something like

```
INSERT
```

or

```
SET FORMAT TO MyFile
INSERT
```

An advantage of this command is that it maintains the order of a file if you take the time to insert the record in the desired location. A significant disadvantage of this method of data entry is the time dBASE spends to save the record when you press CTRL-END. Because INSERT maintains the order of the file, dBASE must move around what may be a large number of records, rather than simply tack on a record at the end of the file. If you are going to use INSERT, use it only with small files.

A third, slightly more complicated, approach with a similar result is to use the APPEND BLANK command to add a single record to the end of the database and then use a combination of a format file and a READ command to edit the record. This approach uses commands like these:

```
USE MyFile
SET FORMAT TO MyFile
APPEND BLANK
READ
```

The second and third methods are somewhat better than the first as far as database integrity is concerned because the operator has access to just one record and not to the entire database. They can be done from the dot prompt, but they have the disadvantage of requiring that the commands (at least, the INSERT or the APPEND BLANK and the READ) be executed each time a record is added. The overall advantages: they are almost as fast and painless as the first method. You are also less likely to wind up with extra blank records than with the first method. A disadvantage: the database is open, and susceptible to possible damage, until you close it. A tip if the third of these methods interests you: you can get away with a READ command here because you are using a format file. If you do not use a format file, you can't use this method because dBASE will show you nothing but a blank screen when you enter the READ command.

The fourth method calls for some programming. It uses the @...SAY...GET commands and the READ command to store data directly in the fields of a database. Such a program looks like this:

```
USE NAMES INDEX NAMES
APPEND BLANK
a 3, 5 SAY " LAST NAME:" GET LASTNAME
a 4, 5 SAY "FIRST NAME:" GET FIRSTNAME
a 8, 5 SAY "ADDRESS:" GET ADDRESS
a 10, 5 SAY "  CITY:" GET CITY
a 10, 35 SAY "STATE:" GET STATE
a 10, 45 SAY "ZIP CODE:" GET ZIP
READ
```

This method provides more control over the user's options, while being relatively simple to implement.

The fifth method, extremely common among programmers, is the program approach, which moves data from memory variables to fields. This method uses a program that resembles the following:

```
*create memory variables.
CLEAR
MLAST = SPACE(30)
MFIRST = SPACE(20)
MADDRESS = SPACE(40)
MCITY  = SPACE(20)
MSTATE = SPACE(2)
MZIP = SPACE(10)
*display prompts, store data to variables.
a 3, 5 SAY " LAST NAME:" GET MLAST
a 4, 5 SAY "FIRST NAME:" GET MFIRST
a 8, 5 SAY "ADDRESS:" GET MADDRESS
a 10, 5 SAY "  CITY:" GET MCITY
a 10, 35 SAY "STATE:" GET MSTATE
a 10, 45 SAY "ZIP CODE:" GET MZIP
READ
*open database, make new record, store variables.
USE NAMES INDEX NAMES
APPEND BLANK
REPLACE LASTNAME WITH MLAST, FIRSTNAME WITH MFIRST,;
ADDRESS WITH MADDRESS, CITY WITH MCITY,;
STATE WITH MSTATE, ZIP WITH MZIP
```

Such a command file has three main parts. The first consists of a series of commands that create memory variables; the memory variables precisely match the field types and field lengths. The second portion of the file uses @...SAY...GET commands to display prompts at the desired screen locations, along with data entry fields for the desired data. The final portion of the file opens the database, uses an APPEND BLANK command to add one blank record to the end of the database, and uses the REPLACE command to move the data from the variables into the database fields. Once all of the required records have been added, the database can be closed. The code described above is often enclosed within a DO WHILE .T. loop, with a conditional prompt added just before the ENDDO that matches the DO WHILE command. The loop might look like this:

```
WAIT "Add another record? Y/N:" TO ANSWER
IF UPPER(ANSWER) = "N"
     CLOSE DATABASES
     EXIT
ENDIF
```

If the data-entry operator enters N in response to the prompt, the program ends. One significant advantage of this method is *database integrity;* the database is open only during the append process and not necessarily throughout the entire application, thus minimizing the chances of damage. Another is ease of validation; since the data is stored in memory variables and later moved to the fields of the actual database, all sorts of program code can be added to see if the data is valid before it is moved to the database. Programmers can make data entry easier by storing default values in the memory variables. For example, if 80% of the addresses stored in an order database are in San Diego, the programmer can store the text string as "San Diego", along with the required number of spaces following the string to fill the field to the memory variable for the city field. The variable will then appear by default in the entry screen, and the user can overtype the entry to enter the name of another city.

And now, the disadvantage: this approach gets deeply into programming, like it or not. Anyone who has written an entry routine like this one for a 60-field database will tell you that typing all the lines of code is no fun; you will require two pages just to create the variables. The coding effort is enough to make you wonder whether database integrity is all that important, or whether you can get by with a format file and a full-screen EDIT command. Also, you cannot use this method to edit the contents of memo fields. (Ways around this limitation will be discussed later in this chapter.)

The sixth method of entering data is to use the BROWSE command, a method that shares advantages and disadvantages with the first method. Operators can make major changes to a database when in BROWSE, whether the programmer wants that to happen or not. In fact, BROWSE probably offers the least possible number of safeguards since you can't validate any data with picture or range clauses when using the BROWSE command.

The seventh and final method is to use a small file as a temporary holding area for newly added records and to append the records to the primary database at a later time. While programmers may be more familiar with this method than nonprogrammers, it can be done inside or outside a program. From the dot prompt, the user enters commands like these:

```
USE MyFile
COPY STRUCTURE TO TEMP
USE TEMP
APPEND
```

The user then adds as many records as desired to the temporary file. When the data-entry process is complete, the records are added to the primary file with commands like these:

```
USE MyFile
SET INDEX TO Names
APPEND FROM TEMP
```

This method of data entry provides a reasonable amount of data integrity because the user is working with a temporary copy of the main database and not the main database itself. Once the temporary database has been created, data entry can be as fast as the operator; because the operator is working with a small file, dBASE will not lag behind as it does when files grow large and have many indexes open. Blank records can be filtered from the temporary database before its contents are added to the primary database; commands as simple as

```
DELETE ALL FOR LASTNAME = " "
PACK
```

may be all that's needed. Any similar command that tests for a blank field where the field should always have an entry would also work. If the thought of using dozens of memory variables within a program does not appeal to you, this method lets you use a format file, which you can easily create with the dBASE III PLUS Screen Painter. If a format file already exists for the primary database, you can use the same format file for the temporary database with some modifications since the structures are identical. The format file will contain the database prefix along with the filename, in a format like this:

```
RECRUITS->LASTNAME
```

You can use your word processor's search-and-replace feature to strip the database prefix from every line of the format file, leaving only the fieldnames.

A disadvantage of using a temporary file is the time required to append the records from the temporary file to the primary database. In addition, you must either keep empty copies of the primary database on disk or create a new temporary one each time data is to be added.

Which of the seven methods is best? None of them. They all work, and each method is suited to different uses. If you are not a programmer, you can't use methods four and five. If you are a programmer, methods four, five, and seven are probably the ones that you consider when working with dBASE. If you are spending increasing amounts of time working with large files or with medium-to-large files that have multiple indexes open, then there is much to be said in favor of method seven. dBASE gets annoyingly slow when working with large files, and multiple open index files only complicate the problem. You can neatly and effectively sidestep this limitation by using small temporary files for adding data.

VALIDATING DATA

Making sure that correct data is entered into the database is of prime importance since a database full of corrupt data can be worse than none at all. It is necessary to validate your data to avoid the extra work that often results if data is not validated. You can do this in dBASE in a number of ways. You can use picture and range clauses, validation choices, memory tables, or databases as lookup files.

The picture and range clauses are simple to implement, yet are powerful performers. Also, these tools are usable by programmers and nonprogrammers alike. Dot prompt power users can validate data with picture and range clauses supplied by Screen Painter during the design of a format file. Programmers who want to save time and effort can use the same technique, later using the format file created by Screen Painter alone, or reading it into a program. (Nonprogrammers should already be aware of the benefits of Screen Painter, since it is the only way in dBASE III PLUS to create format files for an attractive screen display without writing program code.) This book will not describe the complete use of Screen Painter since it is a fairly basic feature of dBASE III PLUS. However, if you are a programmer and you aren't using Screen Painter, you are overlooking a dBASE feature that can write significant portions of your data-entry and edit code for you.

To invoke Screen Painter, use the command CREATE SCREEN *filename,* and the Screen Painter menu will appear (Figure 3-1).

To build a data-entry form, use the Select Database File and Load Field options from the Set Up menu to open a database file (if one is not already in use) and load the required fields; then press F10 to switch to the Screen Painter Blackboard, the area used to lay out the location of the desired fields (Figure 3-2).

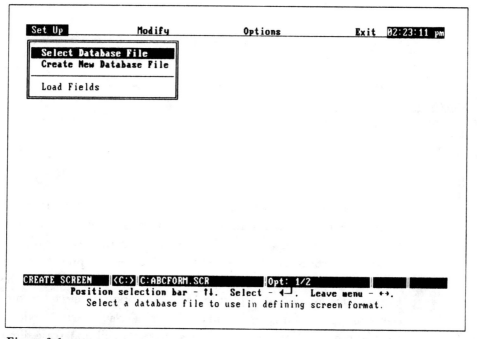

Figure 3-1.

Screen Painter menu

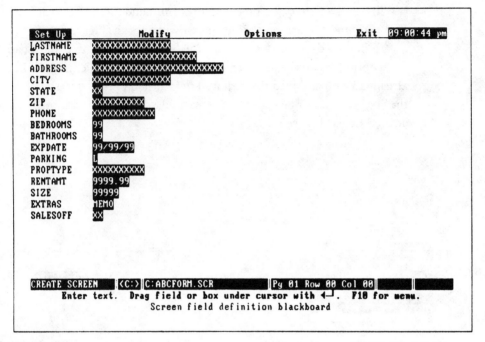

Figure 3-2.

Example of Screen Painter
Blackboard

You can use the usual dBASE cursor and editing keys to make changes on the Blackboard. To add validation through picture and range clauses when designing a form, place the cursor anywhere in the desired field while in the Screen Painter form design screen, and press F10 to get to the Screen Painter menus. From the Modify menu, either use the Picture Function option or Picture Template option to select a picture clause or use the Range option to enter a range clause. Screen Painter lets you use the clauses to make alpha characters all uppercase, limit numeric entry to a range of numbers, limit logical entries to Y or N, or limit alphanumeric entries to match a specific pattern of your choosing. Table 3-1 shows the picture clauses available as functions (affecting all of the entry) or as templates (affecting single characters).

Table 3-1.

Available Picture Clauses from
Screen Painter

	Functions
Symbol	**Meaning**
!	Converts letters to uppercase
A	Displays alphabetic characters only
D	Displays American date format
E	Displays European date format
S	Allows horizontal scrolling of characters
R	Allows entry into a field without overwriting special characters contained in an associated picture template
	Templates
Symbol	**Meaning**
A	Allows only letters
L	Allows only logical data (true/false, yes/no)
N	Allows only letters and digits
X	Allows any character
Y	Allows Y or N
#	Allows only digits, blanks, periods, and signs
9	Allows only digits for character data, or digits and signs for numeric data
!	Converts letters to uppercase
other	Used to format the entry, such as with hyphens and parentheses to format a phone number [example: (999)999-9999]

When you exit from Screen Painter and save the data-entry form, two files are always created: one with an .SCR extension, used by Screen Painter to design the form, and one with an .FMT extension, which is the conventional "format" file used for full-screen editing with dBASE. If your approach to adding and editing records is to use this format file with commands like

```
SET FORMAT TO Fancy
EDIT
```

then you may want to retain the .SCR file created by Screen Painter because dBASE will need it if you ever want to change the design of the screen form. If you use the format file created by Screen Painter as part of your program coding, it probably makes sense to delete the .SCR file because you are likely to make any changes to the entry screens by tweaking the program code.

If you come from the school that says that real programmers don't use code generators of any sort and you insist on writing six dozen @...Say...GET commands by hand, just tack on the picture and range clauses at the end of your @...SAY...GET commands, where necessary, to validate your data. The following example shows how to use picture and range clauses to check for a number of different types of invalid data:

```
a 5, 8 SAY "State: " GET STATE PICTURE "!!"
a 5, 9 SAY "Zip: " GET ZIP PICTURE "99999-9999"
a 5,10 SAY "Age: " GET AGE RANGE 18, 65
a 5,11 SAY "Hire Date: " GET HIRED RANGE;
CTOD("02/05/75"),DATE()
```

The first line of code uses the picture clause to force uppercase entry, which can save you frustration later in trying to qualify records for a search (besides being standard postal format). The second line uses a picture clause to ensure that data gets entered in a desired format (five numbers, a hyphen, then four numbers). The third line uses a range clause to limit a numeric entry to a specific age group, while the last line limits a data entry to a range between a set date and the date stored in the PC's system clock.

Of all the picture clauses mentioned in Table 3-1, the A, !, and 9 are probably used most often. The A formats the data into the GET field as character data only. If the user tries to enter any other type of data, the cursor refuses to move. In a similar fashion, the 9 template will not allow character data; only numerals will be accepted at the position represented by the 9 template. When formatting a field for data with this symbol for the entry of ZIP codes, social security numbers, phone numbers, and the like, you will also want to include literal characters so they will appear automatically within the field when it is displayed. In the following example, the parentheses and hyphens in the template for the phone number are considered "literal" characters, and although they are stored in the field along with the numbers that make up the phone number, the user does not need to type them in for each record.

```
a 5,20 SAY "Phone number? "
a 5,35 GET M_PHONE PICTURE "(999)-999-9999"
```

When you use literals in a picture template, remember that the field must be long enough to store the data *plus* the literals. In the preceding example, a ten-digit phone number would require a 14-character-wide field to store the entire number.

Obviously, you can't catch all bad data with picture and range clauses. Misspellings will get by; so will things like part numbers that don't exist. Those kinds of validation call for programming. But effective use of picture and range clauses can reduce possible data-entry errors.

Using Choices and Lookup Tables

Another common method of data validation is to compare what is input to a group of valid choices. This can be done in a straightforward manner with a conditional IF...ENDIF statement, as shown in this example:

```
DO WHILE .T.
    CLEAR
    <...various a...SAY...GET commands...>
    a 5, 14 SAY "Commission code?" GET M_CCODE PICTURE "!"
    READ
    IF M_CCODE = "A" .OR. M_CODE = "B" .OR. M_CODE = "C"
        APPEND BLANK
        REPLACE CCODE WITH M_CCODE...
        <...other REPLACE statements...>
    ELSE
        a 5,20 SAY "INVALID COMMISSION CODE! ENTER A,B,C"
        WAIT " "
        LOOP
    ENDIF
    <...>
ENDDO
```

This portion of the program code would be part of an "add records" routine written using the memory-variables-to-fields approach described earlier in this chapter. The contents of the memory variable are tested after the user has responded. If the variable matches the available choices, the REPLACE statement moves the data from the variable into the database file. If no match is found, the ELSE command within the IF...ENDIF structure causes an error message to appear; after the user presses a key in response to the WAIT command, the LOOP command causes the routine to allow reentry of the data.

A similar coding approach can be used to validate records against the contents of a lookup table in memory. For this approach, the substring search capability comes in handy, as shown in this example:

```
DO WHILE .T.
CLEAR
<...various a...SAY...GET commands...>
a 5, 14 SAY "Department?" GET M_DEPART
READ
IF M_DEPART $ "Admin Sales Service Manufacturing
Shipping"
    APPEND BLANK
    REPLACE DEPARTMENT WITH M_DEPART, <...other
    replacements...>
ELSE
    a 5,20 SAY "NO SUCH DEPARTMENT!"
    WAIT " "
    LOOP
ENDIF
ENDDO
```

The coding is nearly identical to that of the previous example, the only significant difference being the use of the substring search ($) character. The substring search character tells dBASE to search the text string enclosed in quotes, looking for a match for what was stored to the memory variable. If a match is found, the data is stored to the field; if not, an error message is provided to the user.

Using Databases as Lookup Files

You can carry the lookup table approach a step further and store the matching data in another database. This method may be the only practical way to validate data when you have a large number of possibilities. Perhaps you want to make sure that a particular city is in a list of approved cities before your database of orders will accept an order from a sales rep for product installation in that city. The valid cities could be stored in a small database, and the data-entry code could check that database before allowing a record to be added to the order database, using a code something like this:

```
DO WHILE .T.
SELECT 1
USE ORDERS
<...>
@ 5, 14 SAY "City ?" GET M_CITY
READ
SELECT 2
USE CITIES INDEX CITIES
SEEK M_CITY
IF FOUND()
     SELECT 1
     APPEND BLANK
     REPLACE CITY WITH M_CITY, <..other replacements..>
ELSE
     SELECT 1
     @ 5,20 SAY "WE CAN'T INSTALL IN THAT CITY YET!"
     WAIT " "
     LOOP
ENDIF
<...>
ENDDO
```

The program opens a second work area, opens the smaller database, and does a lookup of the data entered in the memory variable. If a match is found, the program selects the work area of the orders database and proceeds to add the data to the record. Again, if no match is found, an appropriate error message is produced, and the data is not added to the record.

DATA ENTRY
IN MEMO FIELDS

When you must work with memo fields, your possible options are severely limited. You cannot move data between memory variables and memo fields in a manner similar to that used with other fields. The only way to add and edit records in a memo field is to use a full-screen command like EDIT or CHANGE. For those who work with dBASE from the dot prompt, this limitation is no problem; in a browse or append mode, the screen will be visible as a part of the structure. Memo fields become more of a challenge when you control data entry through a program. Since the use of variables is out, you are left with little choice but to use some variation of a full-screen command along with the rest of the commands used to add or edit the record. The CHANGE command works well since it puts you in an interactive editing mode but limits its use to the current record if you specify NEXT 1 along with the name of the memo field with the command. For example, a program used to add new records might contain code like the following. In this example, the memo field is named COMMENTS.

```
USE PERSONNEL INDEX EMPLOYEE
DO WHILE .T.
    *create memory varaiables.
    CLEAR
    MLAST = SPACE(30)
    MFIRST = SPACE(20)
    MEMPCODE = SPACE(4)
    *display prompts, store data to variables.
    @ 3, 5 SAY " LAST NAME:" GET MLAST
    @ 4, 5 SAY "FIRST NAME:" GET MFIRST
    @ 5, 5 SAY "EMPLOYEE ID CODE:" GET MEMPCODE
    READ
    *open database, make new record, store variables.
    APPEND BLANK
```

```
        REPLACE LASTNAME WITH MLAST, ;
        FIRSTNAME WITH MFIRST, EMPCODE WITH MEMPCODE
        CHANGE NEXT 1 FIELD COMMENTS
        CLEAR
        WAIT "Add another? Y/N:" TO ANS
        IF UPPER(ANS) = "N"
            CLOSE DATABASES
            EXIT
        ENDIF
ENDDO
```

When the program runs, the data-entry screen will display entry fields for the name and employee number. Once the data has been entered, the APPEND BLANK command causes a new record to be added, and the REPLACE statements store the contents of the variables in the record. Then, the CHANGE statement causes a full-screen display of just the memo field, called COMMENTS, and the scope (NEXT 1) limits the editing to the current record. The user can press CTRL-PG DN to get into the memo field and CTRL-END to save the contents. The user can employ a command like CHANGE NEXT 1 FIELD *memo field-name* regardless of whether he or she is in a data-entry routine or in an editing routine.

Another way to accomplish the same result is to create a format file just for the memo field and use a SET FORMAT TO *filename* command, followed by a full-screen command like READ, to edit the contents of the field. The program code that follows is designed to add records in a database and provides the user with an option for editing a comments field that is a memo field.

```
*Testfile.PRG
USE YourFile INDEX YourInx
DO WHILE .T.
    CLEAR
    MLAST = SPACE(20)
    MFIRST = SPACE(20)
    MSOC_SEC = SPACE(11)
    MSAL = 00.00
    @  1,  1  TO 14, 52
    @  4,  3  SAY "LASTNAME" GET MLAST
    @  5,  3  SAY "FIRSTNAME" GET MFIRST
    @  7,  3  SAY "SOCIAL SECURITY NO:" GET MSOC_SEC
    @  9,  3  SAY "HOURLY SALARY:" GET MSAL
    READ
    APPEND BLANK
    REPLACE LASTNAME WITH MLAST, FIRSTNAME WITH MFIRST,;
    SOC_SEC WITH MSOC_SEC, HOURLY_SAL WITH MSAL
    CLEAR
```

```
      SET FORMAT TO MEMO
      READ
      CLEAR
      WAIT "Add another? Y/N:" TO ANS
      IF UPPER(ANS) = "N"
            CLOSE DATABASES
            EXIT
      ENDIF
ENDDO
RETURN
*end of testfile.prg.
```

For the memo field, you create a format file that contains only the memo field. The result is an extra disk file, but an advantage is that you can add helpful user messages to the memo-field editing screen by including the desired @ . . . SAY statements in the format file, as shown in the next example:

```
*memo.fmt*
@ 3,3 TO 7,50 DOUBLE
@ 7,5 SAY "Control-PgDn to enter, Return to proceed."
@ 5,20 SAY "Comments:" GET COMMENTS
```

With either method, the end results are the same. The user sees a field containing the word MEMO and, by pressing CTRL-PG DN, is placed in the memo field. After the edits are made and CTRL-END is pressed to save the contents to the memo field, dBASE continues executing the rest of the program.

FINDING WHAT YOU WANT

The process of editing and deleting records obviously requires finding the records that you wish to edit or delete; after all, you can't change what you can't find. In dBASE, finding desired records is not a difficult task, but finding them *quickly* may be a challenge.

You can use four commands to search for items in dBASE: LOCATE, CONTINUE, FIND, and SEEK. The LOCATE and CON-TINUE commands perform a sequential search and will work with any database. The FIND and SEEK commands perform a random-access search but work with indexed files *only*. And dBASE approaches the two sets of commands very differently.

In a sequential search, dBASE starts with a record, usually the first one in the database or the first one in the order of the index (if an index is open). It checks to see if that is the record you are looking for. If it is, dBASE stops the search and provides you with the result, and everyone is happy. If the record is not the one that you are looking for, dBASE moves the record pointer to the next record (or the next one in order of the index) and tests to see if that is the desired record. dBASE goes on doing this for every record in the database, until it finds a match, a slow but effective process. Note that LOCATE does not find *all* matches or even the second match; it finds only the first match. Its companion command, CONTINUE, is used to continue the search as many times as desired if the first record found was not the one you really wanted. LOCATE and CONTINUE will carry on a sequential search until (a) a record is found, or (b) the end of the database is reached. If you are at the dot prompt and LOCATE or CONTINUE is unsuccessful, you get the message, "End of LOCATE scope." In a program, the end-of-file condition is set to true, FOUND() is set to false, and the program handles that condition in accordance with the wishes of its designer.

FIND and SEEK work very differently from LOCATE and CONTINUE. Both FIND and SEEK make use of index files to perform a very fast search. (dBASE may not find anything, but you will know about it very quickly!) Either a record matching the condition supplied is found, or the end of the database is reached. Here is a simplified example of how dBASE does its magic with FIND or SEEK (Figure 3-3 illustrates the example). Let's say you are searching for the last name "Smith" in an indexed database. dBASE looks in the index file, jumps to the halfway point of the index, and examines the record marked by that point — in this case, "Miller". This isn't the desired record, so dBASE asks itself, "Is the desired record before or after this record?" The answer is "after" because Smith comes after Miller in an alphabetical index. So dBASE divides the lower half of the index in half again, jumping halfway between "Miller" and the end of the index. This time, it finds "Thompson". Still not the right record, but getting closer. dBASE again asks itself, "Is the desired record before or after this record?" This time, the answer is "before," so dBASE divides the half of the index between

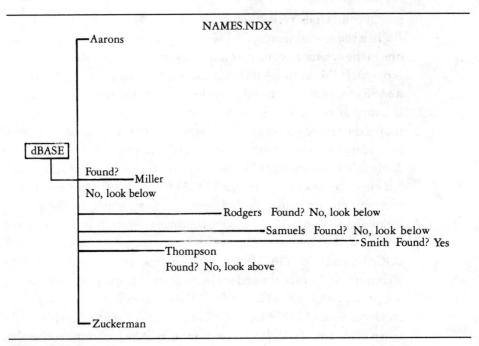

NAMES.NDX

Aarons

dBASE

Found? — Miller
No, look below

Rodgers   Found? No, look below

Samuels   Found? No, look below

Smith   Found? Yes

Thompson
Found? No, look above

Zuckerman

Figure 3-3.

Concept of indexed search

"Miller" and "Thompson" in half, and jumps to that point, finding "Rodgers". dBASE keeps cutting the index in half and jumping directly to records until it finds what it is looking for.

The actual mechanics behind the search are more complex than the explanation suggests because dBASE does the search using binary algorithms. But the illustration demonstrates the difference between this type of search and a sequential search, where dBASE must qualify every record. This type of search is common with database management software; it is popular because it is extremely fast. Even with a very large database, dBASE can usually find a record in this manner in well under two seconds when a hard disk is used. By comparison, the time that a LOCATE command takes grows progressively longer as the database grows in size. Consider a comparison of search times, using a 300-record database containing 40 fields, and keep in mind that these times are only a one-case example. Actual results will vary depending on the hardware, the database structure and size, and where in the database the record is located. In this case, the name used for the LOCATE was about three-quarters of the way into the database, so dBASE clearly had to spend much time checking records before it found the desired one.

```
LOCATE FOR LASTNAME = "Smith" .AND. FIRSTNAME = "Renee"
time required: 17 seconds

FIND "Smith     Renee"
time required: 0.5 seconds
```

If FIND and SEEK are usually so much faster than LOCATE, why aren't FIND or SEEK used in every case? Simplicity sometimes plays a part. First, remember that none of these commands is guaranteed to find what you really want. In many cases, it is easier for novice users to get close with LOCATE and CONTINUE than with FIND or SEEK, because FIND and SEEK will find only the first record that matches. If you're searching for "Jim Smith" in a 12,000-name mailing list with 75 Jim Smiths, a FIND command will find the first one. It's then up to you to figure out how to find the one you want. This can be done by using a WHILE qualifier along with the LOCATE command, which will then tell dBASE to start its search at the current position in the database. As an example, you could use commands like these, assuming that the database is indexed by last names:

```
FIND "Smith"
LOCATE WHILE LASTNAME = "Smith" FOR FIRSTNAME = "Jim" ;
.AND. CITY = "New York"
```

These commands will help you narrow the search down to the desired record without wasting a great deal of time. An inherent advantage of LOCATE and CONTINUE is that these commands will find *every* matching record and therefore, sooner or later, the desired one.

Another problem with FIND and SEEK is the index file requirement. For reasons of efficiency, you want to index your files on some logical element. The problem arises when the user wants to search using a different element. You index by social security number as well as by a combination of last and first name, and you pride yourself on being efficient. Then the user comes along and wants to find "this customer I spoke with last week, and I can't remember her name, and I don't know the social security number, but the person lives somewhere on Myterra Avenue." Your index files are fairly worthless when given this information because dBASE could spend ten minutes on a command like

```
LOCATE ALL FOR ADDRESS = "Myterra Ave"
```

while you mutter under your breath, thinking there must be a better way. This example emphasizes one point: Ashton-Tate put those commands in there because there would be times you would need them. There are times you will need FIND and SEEK, and there are times you may need LOCATE and CONTINUE (although with good planning, you can minimize those times). Knowing how to use the commands effectively will reduce the amount of time that dBASE must spend searching for your data.

The secret to the quick find, insofar as one can be said to exist, is to use an index file, and a FIND or SEEK rather than a LOCATE. This secret may seem elementary to some, but it is surprising how many applications still use LOCATE when it isn't necessary. When you are indexing on one field, using FIND or SEEK is rarely a problem. If, for example, a personnel list is indexed by last names, and you are looking for Ms. Samuels, you simply use

```
FIND "Samuels"
EDIT
```

and unless the database is a sizable one, you are probably at the record, or close enough to use PG DN to get to the desired record. For dot prompt users, the problem arises when you have large databases and you index on multiple fields to get a more precise match. Let's say you are working with a large mailing list, and you index on a combination of LAST-NAME + FIRSTNAME + CITY. The lastname and firstname fields are each 15 characters long and the records in the index get stored like this:

```
Smith          Art            Raleigh
Smith          Louise         Tampa
Smith          Louise         Washington
Sodelski       Thomas         St. Louis
```

The contents of the index precisely match the structure of the field, spaces and all. To use FIND or SEEK from the dot prompt with such an index and be assured of finding the correct record, you would have to enter something like

```
FIND "Smith          Louise         Washington"
```

while including the exact number of spaces to match the index; otherwise, you get a "no find." No wonder dot prompt users are so fond of LOCATE and single-field indexes. In a program, this limitation is less of a problem. You can create memory variables of the exact length needed by storing dummy values to the variables, using @ . . . SAY . . . GET and READ commands, and combining the results into a search expression.

Back to our example. If the lastname and firstname fields are 20 characters long and the city field is 15 characters, you can use code like

```
STORE SPACE(20) TO M_LNAME
STORE SPACE(20) TO M_FNAME
STORE SPACE(15) TO M_CITY
a 5,7 SAY "Last name?" GET M_LNAME
a 6,7 SAY "First name?" GET M_FNAME
a 7,7 SAY "City?" GET M_CITY
READ
STORE M_LNAME + M_FNAME + M_CITY TO FINDER
SEEK FINDER
```

As long as the spaces stored in the memory variables when they are created match the length of the fields that make up the index expression, the program will find what you need. In very large databases, you may need to base your index file on a complex expression resulting from a combination of multiple fields, but you can structure the program to use as many fields as necessary to ensure finding a precise match.

Removing the Blanks

Dot prompt users must still enter all those spaces in the index expression along with a FIND or SEEK. Fortunately, a little known but effective solution to this problem exists: you can build an index file that places all the blanks at the end of the index expression, instead of between the fields. To do this, simply use a minus sign instead of the more common plus sign between the field names when creating an index. If you were to index a database on the lastname, firstname, and city fields in the conventional manner, you would use a command like

```
USE MAILING
INDEX ON LASTNAME + FIRSTNAME + CITY TO ORDER
```

and the contents of the index file would look like this:

```
Smith          Art          Raleigh
Smith          Louise       Tampa
Smith          Louise       Washington
Sodelski       Thomas       St. Louis
```

But if you instead use commands like

```
USE MAILING
INDEX ON LASTNAME - FIRSTNAME - CITY TO ORDER
```

the contents of the index file would then look like this:

```
SmithArtRaleigh
SmithLouiseTampa
SmithLouiseWashington
SodelskiThomasSt. Louis
```

All the blank spaces are stored at the end of the last field. You could then do a near-instantaneous search for a record by entering a command like

```
FIND "SmithLouiseWashington"
```

This command beats counting spaces to enter precisely matched search commands. As with all SEEK and FIND operations, you do not need to enter the full expression to find a record. In the preceding example, if there is only one Louise Smith in the database, entering FIND "Smith-Louise" would be enough to pin down the precise record. One warning if you use this method: you must preserve the upper- and lowercase syntax of the individual names that make up the index expression. You should not use the UPPER or LOWER functions to force all entries into upper- or lowercase with this method of indexing. As an example, if you indexed a database with all the names stored in the index as uppercase letters, a name stored in the index as "SMITHERSALAN" would precede a name stored as "SMITHIRENE", even though Alan Smithers alphabetically falls after Irene Smith.

Even if you're a fan of the BROWSE command (with all its inherent dangers), you can index the database in this manner and enter the find expression from the browse mode. Just enter **BROWSE**, press F10 to bring up the optional Browse menu, and choose Find. In response to the "expression" prompt that appears, enter all or a uniquely sufficient part of the desired expression, and the record will appear within the browse mode.

Avoid the Trimmed Index Trap

When running into the problem of needing precise expressions to search through a complex index key, some dBASE users index on a character field trimmed with a TRIM function, as in a command like this one:

```
INDEX ON TRIM(LASTNAME) + TRIM(FIRSTNAME) + CITY
```

This solution is safe if you are using dBASE III PLUS version 1.1 or later. If you are using version 1.0, however, do not be tempted to try this solution. It is inherently dangerous in that, although it will work *most* of the time, some of the time (and you never know exactly when) you will get inconsistent results with FIND or SEEK when searching such an index.

When you create an index file with the earlier version of dBASE, dBASE must put aside a set number of characters as the length of the key expression in the index file. If you build an index file with TRIM() as a part of the key expression, dBASE uses the results of the TRIM() on the *first record* in the database. On all other records, if the key expression is shorter or no longer than that of the first record, a FIND or SEEK operation will find the data with no problems. But if the key expression for the record you want is *longer* than the key expression for that first record in the database, you may not be able to find precisely what you are looking for. All versions of dBASE III PLUS above version 1.0 allot the sum of the untrimmed field lengths to the index, and therefore this problem does not occur in those versions.

More on Sequential Versus Random Access

The discussion earlier in the chapter on commands that use sequential and random access when looking for records made clear that sequential access consumes a great deal of dBASE time. Sequential access requires considerably more disk access, and disk drives are inherently slow mechanical devices. All dBASE commands that result in the record pointer being moved are either sequential or random in nature. Here is a partial listing:

Sequential in Nature	Random in Nature
LOCATE	FIND
CONTINUE	GO
AVERAGE	GOTO
COPY (TO)	SKIP
COUNT	SEEK

DISPLAY
LIST
LABEL (FORM)
REPORT (FORM)
SORT
SUM
TOTAL
UPDATE

The secret to speed is to avoid every dBASE command that is sequential in nature. That's easy, you say, until you must search for a nonindexed item or until you need a count or a sum or an average. No, when you need sequential access, you obviously need sequential access. But there are ways to speed up what looks like a sequential process.

There's just not much you can do about LOCATE. It's slow and it will always be slow. But many other commands that are basically sequential in nature can be speeded up significantly with the aid of a few well-placed index files and a few WHILE commands. In particular, the COUNT, SUM, AVERAGE, REPORT, and LABEL commands often benefit by finding the first applicable record in an index and then using the WHILE command instead of the FOR command to find and process the desired records. Instead of using a command like

```
LIST FOR <condition>
```

you use commands like these:

```
FIND <expression>
LIST WHILE <condition>
```

As an example, consider a 300-record database, with 40 fields per record. Performing the command

```
LIST FOR LASTNAME = "Smith"
```

causes dBASE to spend a total of 19 seconds on an 80386-based PS/2 compatible to complete the list. On the other hand, the commands

```
FIND "Smith"
LIST WHILE LASTNAME = "Smith"
```

take dBASE a total of three seconds. Compare these times with the same database on the same hardware generating a group of mailing labels:

```
LABEL FORM NADS FOR LASTNAME = "Smith"        21 seconds

FIND "Smith"
LABEL FORM NADS WHILE LASTNAME = "Smith"       5 seconds
```

In both cases, the commands doing the work (such as LIST and LABEL FORM) are sequential-access commands. What saves the time is the use of the FIND command with the index along with the WHILE command, which works differently than FOR. The WHILE command says, "Do it for as long as the condition still exists." With the FIND command, dBASE jumps directly to the first record in the group that meets the criteria. Then, the WHILE command sequentially processes the data only until the criteria are no longer met. By comparison, if only the FOR command is used, the entire database is scanned. As an option, you can use FOR and WHILE together to process the same subset of records that fall within a WHILE range. When both FOR and WHILE are used in the same command, you avoid scanning the entire database. Only the portion defined by the WHILE statement is scanned, and all records meeting the FOR condition are selected.

Even the math commands can benefit if you can narrow down the qualifying records with an index. With a large database, it will take considerably less time to count a group of employee records for all sales reps with commands like

```
USE PERSONNEL INDEX DEPARTMENT
FIND "Sales"
SUM Salary WHILE DEPARTMENT = "Sales"
```

than it would take if you simply entered the commands

```
USE PERSONNEL
SUM Salary FOR DEPARTMENT = "Sales"
```

In many cases, even when all you want to do is edit records from the dot prompt, you can find the records faster with these techniques. For example, having dBASE perform the commands

```
USE MAILING
FIND "Roberts"
LIST LASTNAME, FIRSTNAME WHILE LASTNAME = "Roberts"
```

may take 12 seconds to display a dozen names, along with the record numbers for each record. You find the record you want, enter **EDIT** *X* (where *X* is the record number), and you are at the record. By contrast, a LOCATE on the same record might take 30 seconds or more.

Finding What You Want Under Program Control

If the search for a record is part of an edit routine for a program, you can build the program around the described hints and techniques, using @...SAY...GETs to store user responses to memory variables, and using search logic to find the responses in the appropriate index file. The basic design behind an edit routine as part of a program is

```
open database, index files
DO-WHILE-TRUE loop (until finished)
  prompt user for variables to search by
  FIND variable in index file
  IF NOT FOUND
    show error message, exit routine
  ELSE
    store database fields into memory variables
    paint data edit screen with @...SAY...GETs
    ask user if data should be edited
        if not, see if next record is same name
        and should be edited
    read variables, and validate if desired
    store variables to database fields
  ENDIF
ENDDO the loop
CLOSE DATABASES
```

Some aspects of your code's design may differ; you may, for example, decide to use a format file and a full-screen command instead of the fields-to-memory-variables approach. But the basics will be similar. Following is an example of such a routine for a program. The program assumes that the database, called STOCKS, is indexed by lastname and firstname.

```
*EDITOR.PRG EDITS STOCKS RECORD
*LAST UPDATE 8/11/87
CLEAR
MLAST = SPACE(40)
MFIRST = SPACE(40)
a 5, 6 SAY [LAST NAME ?] GET MLAST
a 6, 6 SAY [FIRST NAME ?] GET MFIRST
READ
FINDIT = MLAST + MFIRST
USE STOCKS INDEX STOCKS
SEEK FINDIT
IF .NOT. FOUND()
     CLEAR
     a 5, 5 SAY [CAN'T FIND THAT NAME. CHECK SPELLING.]
     a 6, 5 SAY [CHECK THAT CAPITALIZATION IS SAME AS;
     IN RECORD.]
     WAIT
     CLOSE DATABASES
     RETURN
ENDIF
CLEAR
DO WHILE .NOT. EOF()
STORE "N" TO EDITANS
CLEAR
a 3, 2 TO 17,70
a 5, 5 SAY [LASTNAME]
a 5, 16 SAY LASTNAME
a 6, 5 SAY [FIRSTNAME]
a 6, 17 SAY FIRSTNAME
a 7, 5 SAY [ADDRESS]
a 7, 15 SAY TRIM(ADDR1)+ " " + ADDR2
a 8, 5 SAY TRIM(CITY)+ " "+TRIM(STATE)+ " " + ZIP
a 9, 5 SAY [DATE TRADED]
a 9, 20 SAY TRADED
a 10, 5 SAY [SHARES]
a 10, 15 SAY SHARES
a 11, 5 SAY [BUY/SELL]
a 11, 16 SAY ACTION
a 11, 20 SAY [PRICE]
a 11, 29 SAY PRICE
a 15, 5 SAY "IS THIS THE DESIRED RECORD TO EDIT? Y/N;
or C to Cancel"
a 15, 62 GET EDITANS
READ
DO CASE
```

```
    CASE UPPER(EDITANS) = "C"
         EXIT

    CASE UPPER(EDITANS) = "Y"
         CLEAR
         MLAST = LASTNAME
         MFIRST = FIRSTNAME
         MADDR1 = ADDR1
         MADDR2 = ADDR2
         MCITY = CITY
         MSTATE = STATE
         MZIP = ZIP
         MTRADED = TRADED
         MSETTLED = SETTLED
         MSHARES = SHARES
         MACTION = ACTION
         MPRICE = PRICE
         @ 0, 1 TO 20, 75 DOUBLE
         @ 1, 4 SAY [STOCK TRACKING DATA ENTRY SCREEN]
         @ 3, 5 SAY " LAST NAME:" GET MLAST
         @ 4, 5 SAY "FIRST NAME:" GET MFIRST
         @ 6, 5 SAY "ADDRESS:" GET MADDR1
         @ 7, 14 GET MADDR2
         @ 8, 5 SAY "    CITY:" GET MCITY
         @ 8, 35 SAY "STATE:" GET MSTATE PICTURE "!!"
         @ 8, 45 SAY "ZIP CODE:" GET MZIP
         @ 10, 5 SAY "TRADE DATE:" GET MTRADED
         @ 10, 30 SAY "SETTLED:" GET MSETTLED
         @ 12, 5 SAY "NO. SHARES:" GET MSHARES
         @ 12, 28 SAY "ACTION (B/S):" GET MACTION
         @ 12, 46 SAY "PRICE:" GET MPRICE
         READ
         REPLACE LASTNAME WITH MLAST, FIRSTNAME WITH MFIRST;
         ADDR1 WITH MADDR1, ADDR2 WITH MADDR2;
         CITY WITH MCITY, STATE WITH MSTATE, ZIP WITH MZIP;
         TRADED WITH MTRADED, SETTLED WITH MSETTLED;
         SHARES WITH MSHARES, ACTION WITH MACTION;
         PRICE WITH MPRICE
         CLEAR
         EXIT

    CASE UPPER(EDITANS) = "N"
         SKIP
         IF FINDIT <> LASTNAME + FIRSTNAME
             CLEAR
             @ 5, 5 SAY "Sorry...no more records;
             by that name."
             WAIT "Press a key to return to menu."
             EXIT
         ENDIF
ENDCASE
ENDDO
CLOSE DATABASES
RETURN
```

If you are going to be coding applications, add a similar routine for deleting unwanted records. This routine is too often left out of a system's design, as if users always want to add but never want to delete records from a database. The logic is similar to a search routine because in both cases you have to find the record first. The design of your routine to delete a record may look like this:

```
DO-WHILE-TRUE loop (until finished)
   prompt user for variables to search by
   open database, index files
   FIND variable in index file
   IF NOT FOUND
      show error message, exit routine
   ELSE
      show record to user with @...SAY commands
      ask user for confirmation to delete record
      IF confirmation is given
         DELETE the record
      IF no confirmation
         move to next record to see if it is same name
         if it is same name, request confirmation
      ENDIF
   ENDIF
ENDDO the loop
```

The fastest way to build such a routine is probably to copy your edit routine, remove the lines of code that allow for changing the fields, add lines of code that ask for confirmation, and proceed to delete the record. Shown here is an example:

```
*ERASER.PRG DELETES STOCKS RECORD
*LAST UPDATE 8/12/87
CLEAR
MLAST = SPACE(40)
MFIRST = SPACE(40)
@ 5, 6 SAY [LAST NAME ?] GET MLAST
@ 6, 6 SAY [FIRST NAME ?] GET MFIRST
READ
FINDIT = MLAST + MFIRST
USE STOCKS INDEX STOCKS
SEEK FINDIT
IF .NOT. FOUND()
   CLEAR
   ?CHR(7)
   @ 5, 5 SAY "CAN'T FIND THAT NAME. CHECK SPELLING."
   @ 6, 5 SAY "CHECK THAT CAPITALIZATION IS SAME;
   AS IN RECORD."
```

```
        WAIT
        CLOSE DATABASES
        RETURN
ENDIF
CLEAR
DO WHILE .NOT. EOF()
        STORE "N" TO DELANS
        CLEAR
        a 3, 2 TO 17,70
        a 5, 5 SAY [LASTNAME]
        a 5, 16 SAY LASTNAME
        a 6, 5 SAY [FIRSTNAME]
        a 6, 17 SAY FIRSTNAME
        a 7, 5 SAY [ADDRESS]
        a 7, 15 SAY TRIM(ADDR1)+ " " + ADDR2
        a 8, 5 SAY TRIM(CITY)+ " "+TRIM(STATE)+ " " + ZIP
        a 9, 5 SAY [DATE TRADED]
        a 9, 20 SAY TRADED
        a 10, 5 SAY [SHARES]
        a 10, 15 SAY SHARES
        a 11, 5 SAY [BUY/SELL]
        a 11, 16 SAY ACTION
        a 11, 20 SAY [PRICE]
        a 11, 29 SAY PRICE
        a 15, 5 SAY "ERASE THIS RECORD? Y/N or C to Cancel"
        a 15, 62 GET DELANS
        READ
        DO CASE
        CASE UPPER(DELANS) = "C"
                RETURN

        CASE UPPER(DELANS) = "Y"
                DELETE
                EXIT

        CASE UPPER(DELANS) = "N"
        SKIP
        IF FINDIT <> LASTNAME + FIRSTNAME
                CLEAR
                a 5, 5 SAY "Sorry...no more records;
        by that name."
                WAIT "Press a key to return to menu."
                EXIT
        ENDIF
ENDCASE
ENDDO
CLOSE DATABASES
RETURN
```

Of course, the topic of deletions brings up the question of whether
you pack the database or not. Most systems provide the user with an
option to pack the file at some point. It probably isn't wise to pack the
file too often, nor is it necessary since you can use SET DELETED ON to

hide the deleted records. Given that a PACK is going to be time-consuming with all but the smallest of databases, this option should be performed at the user's discretion. Many systems provide a Pack option in the form of a question that the user sees on the screen just before exiting the system. Here is an example:

```
CLEAR
ACCEPT "  ==PACK database now? Y/N: " TO PACKANS
IF UPPER(PACKANS) = "Y"
      CLEAR
      a 5,5 SAY "Please wait...do NOT interrupt!"
      SET TALK ON
      USE STOCKS INDEX STOCKS
      PACK
      SET TALK OFF
ENDIF
QUIT
```

This question gives the user, who may not want to spend the time at that particular instant, the option of performing or not performing the PACK.

4: A Potpourri of File Management Commands

As you know, dBASE has its share of commands for the manipulation of files. The more common uses of commands like COPY, DISPLAY, LIST, SORT, INDEX, SUM, and TOTAL are familiar to most dBASE users and described in enough introductory books to make their description unnecessary here. But some of these commands offer options that aren't commonly known and used. Many of these options can come in handy for unusual tasks, so it is worth taking a look at them.

SELECTIVE USE OF COPY TO AND APPEND FROM

The COPY TO command often comes in handy for moving data between files. The command, which creates another database file based on all or part of the structure of an existing file, uses this syntax:

```
COPY TO <filename> [<scope>][FIELDS <fields list>] [FOR
<condition>] [WHILE <condition>] [TYPE SDF/WKS/SYLK/DIF/DELIMITED
[<WITH delimiter>]]
```

As with most file management commands, you can use FOR and
WHILE qualifiers to limit the operation to a subset of records. This use
of the COPY TO and the APPEND FROM commands becomes useful
when you need to split portions of a file or merge two similar files into
one file. For example, consider a national sales database with the
following structure:

```
Structure for database: A:SALES.dbf
Number of data records:    253
Date of last update   : 01/04/80
Field  Field Name  Type      Width   Dec
    1  CONTACT     Character    25
    2  FIRM        Character    35
    3  ADDRESS1    Character    30
    4  ADDRESS2    Character    20
    5  CITY        Character    15
    6  STATE       Character     2
    7  ZIP         Character    10
    8  PHONE       Character    12
    9  RECRUITER   Character    25
** Total **                   175
```

If two smaller databases containing only the names and addresses of the
firms in the national file are needed, you might use commands like

```
USE NATIONAL
COPY TO CAL FIELDS FIRM, ADDRESS1, ADDRESS2, CITY,;
STATE, ZIP FOR STATE = "CA"
COPY TO TEXAS FIELDS FIRM, ADDRESS1, ADDRESS2, CITY,;
STATE, ZIP FOR STATE = "TX"
```

to create the smaller files — in this instance, one for Texas and one for
California. In each case, the file will contain only those fields listed in the
command. If you omit the list of fields, dBASE assumes that you want all
the fields in the original database to be a part of the new one.

The APPEND FROM command performs a similar operation but in
reverse order: it will read the contents of one file into another. The
syntax for the command is

```
APPEND FROM <filename> [FOR <condition>] [TYPE
SDF/WKS/SYLK/DIF/DELIMITED [WITH delimiter]]
```

You can use APPEND FROM to selectively append records using a FOR
qualifier. Unlike COPY TO, you cannot use a list of fields with the

APPEND command. The Type options, which can be used with both the COPY TO and the APPEND FROM commands, let you move data between dBASE and foreign files in a number of formats, including Lotus 1-2-3, SDF, and Delimited. Those unfamiliar with these options will find more on the subject in Chapter 9.

One point that may not be initially obvious is that the database structures of the two files need not be a perfect match. If one file has fields that aren't in the other file, dBASE will transfer the data where the fields match and discard the data where the fields don't match. For example, consider two database files with these structures:

```
    PERSONNL.DBF                          ASSIGNED.DBF
Name       Type        Width       Name       Type        Width
EMPLOYEE   Character      4         LASTNAME   Character     20
LASTNAME   Character     20         FIRSTNAME  Character     20
FIRSTNAME  Character     20         EMPLOYEE   Character      4
ADDRESS    Character     20         POSITION   Character     10
CITY       Character     15         HIRED      Date           8
STATE      Character      2         SALARY     Numeric      6/2
ZIP        Character      5         DEPT       Character     15
POSITION   Character     10         LAST_EVAL  Date
HIRED      Date           8
SEX        Character      1
MINORITY   Logical        1
```

Note that all the fields are not common to the two files, and where the fields are common, they are not in matching order. dBASE doesn't care; if you were to enter commands like

```
USE ASSIGNED
APPEND FROM PERSONNL
```

the new records added to the second database would contain data from those fields in the first database that had the same name. Where matching fields do not exist in the second database, data will not transfer.

In those instances where fields do not match but you nevertheless need to move the data between files, you can use the Type option to copy the data to a foreign file, then read it back into the second database from the foreign file. As an example, consider two databases like those shown in Table 4-1. If you try to use the second file and append directly from the first, only the ADDRESS and CITY fields will come across because they

Table 4-1.

Dissimilar Databases

ABCLIST.DBF			XYZLIST.DBF		
Name	Type	Width	Name	Type	Width
LASTNAME	Character	20	LAST	Character	25
FIRSTNAME	Character	20	FIRST	Character	25
CUST_ID	Character	10	ACCT_NO	Numeric	10
HIGH_CR	Character	20	MAXCREDIT	Numeric	8/2
ADDRESS	Character	15	ADDRESS	Character	25
CITY	Character	2	CITY	Character	20
STATE	Character	5	ST	Character	2
ZIP	Numeric	8/2	ZIPCODE	Character	10

are the only matching fields. Instead, you could use commands like

```
USE ABCLIST
COPY TO TEMP TYPE SDF
USE XYZLIST
APPEND FROM TEMP TYPE SDF
```

and for each record, dBASE will place the first field of the foreign file into the first field of the database in use, the second field of the foreign file into the second field of the database in use, and so on. This transference works rather painlessly if the overall field types are in matching order, as in the example. If they don't match, you can use the fields clause of the COPY TO command to specify the order in which you want the fields to appear in the foreign file originally created with the COPY TO command.

AVOIDING THE UNWANTED:
DEALING WITH BLANKS
AND DUPLICATES

Duplicate records are the bane of the data-entry world. Like them or not, they will probably creep into your files if you aren't careful. And blank records can also multiply because of carelessness on the part of the data-entry operators or poor program design or both. However, you can take steps to minimize blank records and duplicate records, and there are ways to get rid of such records once they exist.

To avoid duplicates, dBASE does offer one powerful command, SET UNIQUE, that's useful in a dot prompt mode. This command lets you build an index that has no duplicates. For example, you may have created a database of current and prospective clients, and you've indexed it by firm name. You are reasonably sure that no two firms in your database have the same name. You can tell dBASE to build an index file based on firm name and to weed out any possible duplicates in the firm name field. To do so, you could use the commands

```
USE CLIENTS
SET UNIQUE ON
INDEX ON FIRM TO CLIENTS
```

Another way to enter the same command is

```
USE CLIENTS
INDEX ON FIRM TO CLIENTS UNIQUE
```

The results in either case will be an index file with a unique entry for every firm name in the database. If the database by accident contains two records for a single firm named "Thompson, Sampson & Delilah, P.C.," the index will include the first such record in the database, but not the second. Whenever you use the database along with the unique index, the duplicate record may still exist in the database, but it won't appear in any operations because it isn't a part of the index file.

However, the fact that the duplicate record is still in the database means that what SET UNIQUE does is something of an illusion. The command should be used only if you are confident that the *first* record of any duplicate pair contains correct or current information. You may prefer to make the effects of SET UNIQUE permanent with a single-pass filtering of deleted records. You can do so by using the database along with the unique index file, copying the records to another file, and then renaming that file, with commands like

```
USE CLIENTS
INDEX ON FIRM TO CLIENTS UNIQUE
COPY TO TEMP
CLOSE DATABASES
ERASE CLIENTS.DBF
RENAME TEMP.DBF TO CLIENTS.DBF
```

If you like, the commands could be included as a part of a program option for deleting possible duplicates. Again, the danger with using SET UNIQUE is that the second record of any duplicate pair may contain more current information, such as a new address. It may be better to have a user visually compare suspected duplicates before purging records from a database. You have to know when using SET UNIQUE will do more good than harm. For example, it would not be put to good use in a mailing list indexed by names, where you would expect multiple entries to have the same name. If you build the index on a combination of fields that results in each entry in the index being different, however, you can safely use SET UNIQUE to filter the duplicates.

The best way to avoid duplicates is to prevent them from getting into the database in the first place, which can be effectively done by searching the index for a possible match before allowing the entry of a new record. Possible duplicates should be found before using the APPEND BLANK command to add a blank record, and you can effectively make this search no matter how you add records to a database by asking the user for just enough information to search the index. Consider this example:

```
*Routine to add records and test for duplicates first.*
Do While .T.
CLEAR
STORE SPACE(20) TO MLAST
STORE SPACE(20) TO MFIRST
a 5,5 SAY " Last Name? " GET MLAST
a 6,5 SAY " First Name? " GET MFIRST
READ
STORE MLAST + MFIRST TO FINDIT
SEEK FINDIT
IF FOUND()
        CLEAR
        a 2,1 TO 14,60 DOUBLE
        a 3,2 Say [Last Name]
        a 3,16 Say LASTNAME
        a 5,2 Say [First Name ]
        a 5,16 Say FIRSTNAME
        a 9,2 Say [Address 1]
        a 9,16 Say ADDRESS1 FUNCTION "S25"
        a 10,2 Say [Address 2]
        a 10,16 Say ADDRESS2 FUNCTION "S25"
        a 11,2 Say [City]
        a 11,16 Say CITY
        a 11,25 Say [State]
        a 11,32 Say STATE PICTURE '!!'
        a 12,2 Say [ ZIP Code]
        a 12,16 Say ZIP Picture "99999-9999"
        ? CHR(7)
        a 14,20 SAY "This name is already on file!"
        a 15,2
        ACCEPT "Add new name anyway? Y/N:" TO ADDANS
        IF UPPER(ADDANS) = "N"
            EXIT
        ENDIF
ENDIF
<...Append Blank and a...SAY...GET commands here...>
ENDDO
```

The database used in this routine is indexed on a combination of last and first names, so the first thing that the routine does is to ask for the last and first names of the new person to be added to the database. The responses are stored within variables, and a SEEK command is used to search for a possible duplicate. If a record with the same name is found, enough vital statistics concerning that record are displayed to allow the user to decide whether the new record should be entered or not.

The more distinctive the index, the more efficient this type of duplicate prevention can be. If a database uses a highly distinctive field (like employer ID or social security number) to identify each record, do a SEEK on that field. If a record with a matching value is found, you can immediately reject the attempted new entry and display an error message.

Avoiding Blanks

Blank records also have a way of turning up in databases. If the data entry is being performed with something as straightforward as an APPEND command, then a blank record will appear each time someone presses CTRL-END without entering any data in a new record. The only way to avoid the blank record during the entry process is to press ESC, and not CTRL-END, to exit the append mode from a blank record. The empty record will not be saved if you press ESC.

If you press CTRL-END while in the final field of a record containing data, that record is stored, and you exit the append mode without adding a blank record. The problem, particularly for data entry done with the APPEND command, occurs when the last field fills with data. Any cursor movement then causes dBASE to move to a new, blank record, whether you want one or not.

One way of reducing this problem is to issue a SET CONFIRM ON command. The SET CONFIRM ON command tells dBASE to require a confirmation of each field entry. With SET CONFIRM ON, you will have to press ENTER to move to the next field (and to the next record, if the cursor is in the last field). The down side of this method is that it requires a return keypress on each field, which sometimes draws complaints from the data-entry people.

Once blank records exist in the database, it is easy enough to get rid of them. Pick a field that should always have an entry, and use a DELETE command with a FOR qualifier to delete all blank records. As an example, if a database has a character field called COMPANY (20 characters in length), and you are certain that any record with nothing in the field is a blank record, you can enter a command like

```
DELETE FOR COMPANY = SPACE(20)
```

Similarly, if you are using a numeric field to store employee identification numbers, you can enter a command like

```
DELETE FOR EMPDI = 0
```

to delete the blank records. One thing that you don't want to do is make the assumption that you can delete all records where a required entry in a character field is equivalent to a null string, as with the command

```
DELETE FOR LASTNAME = ""
```

Using the null string (no space between the quotes) might seem a logical choice because a field with data in it is not equivalent to a null string. Unfortunately, dBASE sees things differently, and will proceed to delete every record in the database. You can always use RECALL ALL to get them back, but you will also recall every record that was intended for deletion. If you include at least one space between the quotes, the command will work properly. However, such a command will also delete any records that were erroneously entered with a leading space, and you might want to keep and correct such errors rather than reenter them. Using a command like DELETE FOR LASTNAME = SPACE(20) ensures that you will only delete records that are truly blank.

Under program control, your options are more precise. Avoiding blanks within a routine for adding records is a relatively trivial matter. One basic technique is similar to that used from the dot prompt: pick a field containing the required entry. If the data to be placed in that field is blank, reject the record. If you are using the memory-variables-to-fields method of data entry, you can include commands like these within the DO-WHILE loop used to add records:

```
DO WHILE .T.
      CLEAR
      a <co-ordinates> SAY "Last name:" GET MLAST
      a <co-ordinates> SAY "First name:" GET MFIRST
      <...more a...SAY...GET commands...>
      READ
      IF LEN(TRIM(MLAST)) = 0
            CLEAR
            a 5,1 SAY "Name fields MUST have entries!"
            WAIT "-press C to cancel, any other key;
            to continue." TO ANS
            IF UPPER(ANS)="C"
                  EXIT
            ELSE
                  LOOP
            ENDIF
      ENDIF
      <...Append Blank and REPLACE commands follow...>
ENDDO
```

Even if you are using the simple approach of setting a format file and using APPEND in a program, you can add a few lines of code to delete immediately any blank record that is accidentally added at the end of the append process. The following example shows such an addition to a program originally created with the dBASE Applications Generator.

```
CASE Selectnum = 1
    * DO add records.
    SET FORMAT TO SALES
    APPEND
    SET FORMAT TO
    SET CONFIRM OFF
    IF LASTNAME = SPACE(20)
          DELETE
    ENDIF
    STORE ' ' TO wait_subst
    a 23,0 SAY "Press a key to continue." GET wait_subst
    READ
    SET CONFIRM ON

CASE Selectnum = 2
    <...more commands...>
```

Also added at the start of the program is a SET DELETED ON statement that will hide any blank records from view.

SELECTIVE USE OF BROWSE

It is a rare user of dBASE who is not familiar with the BROWSE command, which displays a full-screen columnar display used for multiple edits of records. There may be debate on whether you should use the command or not. Many feel that because BROWSE lets you make major changes to a database with no error trapping or verification, it should remain out of the hands of all but accomplished programmers. On the other hand, there are power dot prompt users who swear by this command. Instead of taking sides on this issue the discussion here will point out some lesser-known options that you should know about if you're going to use BROWSE.

First, it doesn't seem to be common knowledge that the Browse menu, accessed by pressing F10 when in browse mode, offers an additional useful option for finding records *if* you have an index file open. Figure 4-1 shows the Browse menu when an index file is open. The Find option, which appears at the far right side of the screen, does not appear when a database is open but an index file is not open.

This option makes finding records in a large file while in the browse mode relatively easy if you know enough characters in the index expression to find a record that is close enough to the one you want. Choose the option, and dBASE prompts for a search string (which is a novice's way of saying index expression). Enter an expression that matches the way your index is designed, and dBASE will find the desired record. If the find is unsuccessful, dBASE displays the error message "Not found" at the bottom of the screen.

All of the remaining menu options (and some others that aren't provided on the menu) can also be set from the dot prompt or in a

Bottom	Top	Lock	Record No.	Freeze	01:17:31 pm

LASTNAME------------	FIRSTNAME----------	SOC_SEC----	BIRTH_DATE	HOURLY_SAL
Williamson	Frank	829-56-6861	08/30/50	7.75
Smith	Steven	324-57-6371	01/12/52	7.75
Roberts	Cynthia	425-58-6481	10/04/51	7.75
Atkins	Gerald	526-59-6591	06/26/51	7.75
Jones	Wendy	627-52-6621	01/07/49	7.75
Walker	Renee	728-53-6731	09/29/48	7.75
Jackson	Nancy	829-54-6841	06/21/48	7.75
Curtis	Lynn	324-55-6351	11/03/49	7.75
Clay	Carol	425-56-6461	07/26/49	7.75
Sampson	Fred	526-57-6571	04/17/49	7.75
Williamson	Richard	627-58-6681	01/07/49	7.75
Smith	Nancy	728-59-6791	09/29/48	7.75
McNiell	Phyllis	829-52-6821	04/13/46	7.75
Atkins	Carol	324-53-6331	08/26/47	7.75
Carter	Frank	425-54-6441	05/18/47	7.75
Rhodes	Richard	526-55-6551	02/07/47	7.75
Baker	Cynthia	627-56-6661	10/30/46	7.75

BROWSE	<D:> BIGFILE	Rec: 4429/6008		

Position selection bar with ↔. Select with ↵.
Go to end of the file.

Figure 4-1.

Browse menu

program as a part of the BROWSE command. The complete syntax for the command, which is

```
BROWSE [FIELDS<list of fields>] [LOCK<n>] [FREEZE<field>]
[NOFOLLOW] [NOMENU] [WIDTH<n>] [NOAPPEND]
```

gives an idea of the options available. The Width option can be useful because most databases have more fields than will ever fit on the width of a single screen. The Width option limits the number of characters displayed in any field; by entering a command like

```
BROWSE WIDTH 10
```

you limit all fields in the display to a ten-character width. Fields larger than the limit will become scrolling fields, and the left and right arrow keys can then be used to move around in the field. Unfortunately, there is no way to set a selective width to specific columns; the width you specify will apply to every field shown with the BROWSE command. You can further limit the amount of information shown on the screen by specifying a list of fields along with the Fields option. For example, entering the command

```
BROWSE FIELDS LASTNAME, FIRSTNAME, AGE
```

would show only those fields listed, regardless of the number of fields in the database.

The Nofollow option corrects what is for some users a visually annoying trait of dBASE's. If you are working with an indexed file in BROWSE and you move a field that is part of the index, dBASE not only moves the record to its proper place in the index, it moves you along with it. If you are editing a group of records, you may find yourself at a different location in the database from where you began, and you then have to get back to the original spot to continue editing in that group. You can avoid this annoyance with

```
BROWSE NOFOLLOW
```

When you make a change to a record within a field that is part of the index, the record may go elsewhere, but you won't go along with it.

The Top, Bottom, and Recno options are fairly mundane, used to move the record pointer to the top, bottom, or to a specific record number of the database, respectively. Those who want to use BROWSE in a program environment but want to maintain some semblance of user safety may be interested in the Noappend, Lock, and Freeze options. The Noappend option limits the use of BROWSE to editing only; new records cannot be added to the database when this option is selected. The Lock option, followed by a number or a numeric expression, tells dBASE to lock a set number of columns; those columns will remain in view while the others scroll in the usual fashion. The Freeze option, followed by a fieldname, will allow editing in only the named field. All other fields will be visible, but editing will not be allowed in them.

The options for the BROWSE command can be combined in any order. As an example, the command

```
BROWSE FIELDS LAST, FIRST, AGE, SALARY WIDTH 10 NOFOLLOW NO;
APPEND FREEZE SALARY
```

will tell dBASE to show the file in use, in browse mode, with all fields limited to a width of ten characters. Only the LAST, FIRST, AGE, and SALARY fields will show, no appending will be permitted, the Nofollow option will be on, and editing will be allowed in the SALARY field only.

SET FILTER: THE GOOD, THE BAD, AND THE UGLY

The SET FILTER command will never suffer from lack of use. Used often both outside of programs and within them, SET FILTER makes it possible to solve a lot of data selecting and reporting needs that would otherwise call for a number of time-consuming commands. However, the use of SET FILTER sometimes severely taxes dBASE performance. And often, a decline in performance isn't noticeable until the database starts working with a significant number of records. A problem may not become apparent until users start complaining about how long dBASE takes to find a record or to generate a particular report.

SET FILTER hides records that do not meet the condition described. The syntax for the command is

```
SET FILTER TO <condition>
```

Once the command is entered, other database commands that would normally use records from the entire database will instead use only those records that meet the condition specified by the filter. In effect, this lets you work with a subset of a database as though it were the entire database. A command like

```
SET FILTER TO CITY = "Washington" .AND. STATE = "DC"
```

limits a mailing list database to those records located in Washington, D.C. One point sometimes overlooked is that when you set a filter, the current record is not immediately affected by the filter. The filter does not take effect until you move the record pointer. If the next command causes the record pointer to move before data is displayed or printed, fine. If not, you may wind up with a record you don't really want. This problem can be illustrated by a large personnel database containing a last name field. When the following commands are entered, note the result, shown in Figure 4-2.

```
SET FILTER TO LASTNAME = "Roberts"
BROWSE
```

The first name in the display isn't Roberts. The first name shown was the current record when the BROWSE command was entered. Once any action that moves the record pointer is taken, the invalid record disappears. You will have to think about whether the commands you use immediately after the SET FILTER command will move the record pointer before displaying any data. The REPORT FORM and LABEL FORM commands will move the pointer to the top of the database before printing any reports or labels, so you will get the proper results if

```
LASTNAME------------  FIRSTNAME-----------  SOC_SEC----  BIRTH_DATE HOURLY_SAL
Sampson              Jerry                  111-11-1111  04/23/52        7,50
Robertson            Jean                   343-37-7372  04/09/43        5,50
Roberts              Peggy                  748-35-7752  09/12/59        5,50
Robertson            Christine              546-37-7572  05/30/56        7,50
Roberts              Michael                849-38-7882  05/22/50        8,50
Robertson            Donna                  829-58-6881  02/15/53        8,50
Roberts              Monica                 324-55-6351  02/07/47        6,75
Roberts              Cynthia                728-57-6771  07/13/40        6,75
Roberts              Steven                 425-58-6481  10/17/37        6,75
Robertson            Henry                  829-58-6881  06/04/59        9,20
Roberts              Phyllis                324-55-6351  05/30/56        7,50
Roberts              Martin                 728-57-6771  02/15/53        7,50
Roberts              Renee                  425-58-6481  10/04/51        7,75
Robertson            Richard                324-55-6351  04/09/43        8,50
Roberts              Sheryl                 425-52-6421  08/13/38        6,75
Robertson            Douglas                829-58-6881  06/04/59        9,20
Roberts              Peggy                  324-55-6351  05/30/56        7,50



BROWSE            <D:>BIGFILE              Rec: 1/6008
```

View and edit fields,

Figure 4-2.

Results of Browse command

no next or while clauses are included in the REPORT FORM or LABEL
FORM command. Similarly, a LIST command will normally move the
pointer before a display of data, but it won't if you include a NEXT or
WHILE scope along with the command. Try a command like LIST
NEXT 20 immediately after a SET FILTER command, and you will get

19 records that meet the condition and one that may not. Likewise, if you try this:

```
SET FILTER TO SOC_SEC = "094-55-6370"
EDIT
```

you may be surprised to see a record that is not what you wanted. The solution, simple enough, is to move the record pointer with a GO TOP command immediately after the SET FILTER command. This will move the record pointer to the first record meeting the filter condition, and you can then use the desired commands.

Now for the bad news. The SET FILTER command appears to perform a rapid sequential qualification of every record in the database, starting from record one and moving to the highest record number. Because dBASE performs a rapid internal search during this process, no problems occur if the record numbers happen to be in sequential order (in other words, no index files are open). If an index file is open, and one usually is, dBASE examines each record sequentially in index order. Since this examination involves checking both the index and the database for each record, any operation that uses SET FILTER can become terribly slow with a large, indexed database. In the world of dBASE programming, you may occasionally see programs written to edit or delete records with search routines like this one:

```
ACCEPT "Enter last name:" TO LN
ACCEPT "Enter first name:" TO FN
SET FILTER TO LASTNAME = LN .AND. FIRSTNAME = FN
GO TOP
SET FORMAT TO FANCY
EDIT
```

For good reason, SET FILTER should *never* be used to select a single record, as the preceding code attempts to do. Unless your database is never going to grow past a few hundred records or you never use index files, don't waste your time with this kind of coding. Those who have tried it with indexed files of over 500 records know how slow it can be. Those who haven't can see the problem with a simple demonstration. Get into dBASE, and open a database with a thousand records or more, preferably one that contains a field for name or last name. If you don't have one, create one with a series of commands similar to the following:

```
USE YourFile
COPY NEXT 100 TO JUNK
USE JUNK
COPY NEXT 100 TO JUNK2
APPEND FROM JUNK2
APPEND FROM JUNK2
APPEND FROM JUNK2
APPEND FROM JUNK2
APPEND FROM JUNK2
APPEND FROM JUNK2
APPEND FROM JUNK2
APPEND FROM JUNK2
```

Once you have a database of around 1000 records, index the file on the name field with a command like

```
INDEX ON LASTNAME TO JUNK
```

then enter APPEND to add a record to the database, and enter the name "Miller". Then, get back to the dot prompt, and enter

```
SET FILTER TO LASTNAME = "Miller"
GO TOP
EDIT
```

You will see the problem as soon as you try to move the record pointer with the GO TOP command. dBASE has to set the filter across an indexed file, an annoyingly slow process on a hard disk, and an agonizing crawl on a floppy-based system. The times, using the following database file, with just over 1000 records, on an 8088-based PC with a 10MB hard disk, worked out to 31 seconds for the GO TOP command to take effect, during which time the PC's hard disk sounded like it was performing an advanced aerobic workout.

```
Structure for database: D:BIGFILE.dbf
Number of data records:    1008
Date of last update    : 09/24/87

Field   Field Name  Type         Width   Dec
    1   LASTNAME    Character      20
    2   FIRSTNAME   Character      20
    3   SOC_SEC     Character      11
    4   BIRTH_DATE  Date            8
    5   HOURLY_SAL  Numeric         5     2
    6   INSURED     Logical         1
    7   COMMENTS    Memo           10
** Total **                       76
```

The combination of a medium-to-large database, one or more open index files, and a filter condition is deadly to dBASE performance. And changing the execution order of the commands does not solve the problem. If you try something like the following:

```
USE BigFile
SET FILTER TO DEPARTMENT = "Marketing"
SET INDEX TO Names
```

then dBASE will set the filter quickly, but take an inordinate amount of time to open the index file. The performance difference if you do not open any index files is extreme. Using the same material described previously but with the index file closed, dBASE took one second to perform the GO TOP command.

Understandably, the larger the database, the longer the wait with an indexed file gets. With the same hardware and the same database structure described above, but with 6000 records indexed on a combination of last and first names, dBASE took 3 minutes and 50 seconds to perform a GO TOP immediately after a SET FILTER. With no index file open, dBASE took 2 seconds to perform the same task. "Don't open any index files," you say? That's fine if you don't mind the problems of trying to keep the indexes updated after changes have been made. And what happens when you want a report with an odd selection of certain records? You probably want it in some kind of sorted order, and the alternative of sorting the database and then setting a filter is about as appealing as the slow index.

The solution, like so many things in life, is a compromise. When using indexes, stay away from filters wherever possible; and when using filters, stay away from indexes wherever possible. If you want to find records for editing and updating, don't use filters. Open indexes, and use the FIND or the SEEK command instead. Save the SET FILTER command for showing lists of data and for reporting needs. It is less annoying to see a delay during reporting; most users turn on the printer, choose the report, and go off to do something else while dBASE does all the work. Also, in reporting needs, often a large percentage of your records may meet the filter criterion, and performance improves as more records match the criteria outlined with the SET FILTER command.

Doing the Two-Step

An approach that will often save time in reporting selective records is to set a filter without an index file open, copy the selective records out to a temporary file, and then use the temporary file for the reporting. If the file needs to be in a particular order, you can create the temporary file and sort or index the file in much less time than it would take to set a filter across the indexed version of the larger file. Consider again the example of the 6000-record database of names: suppose someone wants a report of everyone whose last name is Jackson and whose salary is $8.00 per hour or more. The list must be in alphabetical order, so you will need the index file open during the use of the LIST command or the report generation. It would be great to do a SEEK on the first occurence of "Jackson" and then use a command like LIST WHILE LASTNAME = "Jackson", but that would give you all the Jacksons, and you only want the ones with salary levels above a certain value. You could do this at least two ways with SET FILTER. The first method uses the main file alone and sets a filter while an index based on the combination of last and first names is open. You might use commands like these:

```
USE BigFile INDEX Names
SET FILTER TO LASTNAME = "Jackson" .AND. Hourly_sal > 8.00
LIST
```

You will eventually get the results you are seeking. In the tests using a
6000-record file with approximately 120 "Jacksons" meeting the specified condition, dBASE took 3 minutes, 17 seconds to perform the
commands shown above. The second method, which creates a temporary file, uses commands like these:

```
USE BigFile
SET FILTER TO LASTNAME = "Jackson" .AND. Hourly_sal > 8.00
COPY TO TEMP
USE TEMP
INDEX ON LASTNAME + FIRSTNAME TO TEMP
LIST
```

With the same hardware (an 80386-based system) and the same database, dBASE took a total of 26 seconds, including the time for the screen
display of data, to perform the commands shown above. The second
example follows the suggestion of not mixing filters with indexed files,
while demonstrating that with some planning you can nevertheless
achieve the results of using both indexes and filters.

Using SET FILTER in a Program

For reporting needs, SET FILTER can save development time. Because
reporting needs can be so varied, the SET FILTER command lets you
cover all the possibilities; with some planning, it can provide users with
selective reports based on conditions they may not have dreamed would
ever come up. You can probably use SET FILTER dozens of ways in a
program, but for purposes of simplicity, consider three general ways:
one simple and easy to use, one slightly more complex and relatively
easy on the users, and one very complex and hard to use, but offering the
ultimate in capability.

Our first method is to present a menu with a series of choices, and,
depending on the user's selection, set a different filter condition. The
user can then go on to generate the desired report. The command file
shown here illustrates this technique.

```
***Report1.PRG prints Applicant database.***
*Last update 10/22/86*
PUBLIC SIFTERS, SIFTERS1, SIFTERS2
CLEAR
@ 2, 2 TO 18,78 DOUBLE
@ 3, 5 SAY "Enter filter condition, if any, for report."
@ 6,10 SAY "1. All Applicants (no filter in effect)"
@ 7,10 SAY "2. By School Name"
@ 8,10 SAY "3. By Year of Graduation"
@ 9,10 SAY "4. By School Name AND Year of Graduation"
@ 10,10 SAY "5. By State"
@ 11,10 SAY "6. Prior To Or Equal To A Date Received"
@ 19, 5
INPUT "      Enter a selection (1-6): " TO SIFTIT
CLEAR
DO CASE
     CASE SIFTIT = 1
          SET FILTER TO
          *no filter used.
     CASE SIFTIT = 2
          STORE SPACE(20) TO SCH_NAME
          @ 5,5 SAY "School name: " GET SCH_NAME
          READ
          STORE UPPER(SCH_NAME) TO SIFTERS
          SET FILTER TO UPPER(SCHOOL) = SIFTERS
     CASE SIFTIT = 3
          STORE 88 TO SCH_YEAR
          @ 5,5 SAY "Year of graduation: " GET SCH_YEAR
          READ
          STORE SCH_YEAR TO SIFTERS
          SET FILTER TO GRADYEAR = SIFTERS
     CASE SIFTIT = 4
          STORE SPACE(20) TO SCH_NAME
          STORE 88 TO SCH_YEAR
          @ 5,5 SAY "School name: " GET SCH_NAME
          @ 7,5 SAY "Year of graduation: " GET SCH_YEAR
          READ
          STORE UPPER(SCH_NAME) TO SIFTERS1
          STORE SCH_YEAR TO SIFTERS2
          SET FILTER TO UPPER(SCHOOL) = SIFTERS1 ;
          .AND. GRADYEAR = SIFTERS2
     CASE SIFTIT = 5
          STORE SPACE(2) TO M_STATE
          @ 5,5 SAY "State: " GET M_STATE
          READ
          STORE UPPER(M_STATE) TO SIFTERS
          SET FILTER TO UPPER(STATE) = SIFTERS
     CASE SIFTIT = 6
          STORE DATE() TO M_DAY
          @ 5,5 SAY "Cutoff Date: " GET M_DAY
          READ
          STORE M_DAY TO SIFTERS
          SET FILTER TO RECEIVED <= SIFTERS
     CASE SIFTIT > 6
          RETURN

ENDCASE
*generate report.
WAIT "Turn on printer, press a key..."
REPORT FORM YourFile TO PRINT
```

This approach is the simplest of the three, although it does not necessarily require creating the least amount of program code. Its simplicity lies in its user interface; most users won't need documentation, or even a detailed explanation, to figure out how to make a selection. When the program runs, the user sees a menu offering various filter choices, such as all records where the student attends a particular school, or all records submitted before a particular date. When the desired choice is selected, the appropriate choice in the series of CASE statements causes a corresponding filter to be set. An advantage of declaring the memory variables public, as is done in the third line of the program, is that one universal "filter menu" can be used for all reports based on that database. Instead of placing the REPORT FORM or other report-generating commands at the end of a filter-setting program, the user can place a RETURN statement there and call the routine before generating reports. For example, assuming the filter routine is named FILTERS.PRG, the portion of the program that generates a report might resemble the following:

```
CLEAR
? "Include all records (A) or selected (S) by filter?"
ACCEPT "Enter A or S: " TO ANS
IF UPPER(ANS) = "S"
    DO FILTERS
ENDIF
REPORT FORM APPLY1 TO PRINT
<...more commands...>
```

The second method complicates things somewhat for the end user, but it uses about the same amount of program code as the first method. This method presents the user with a screen with various options for all the desired fields, and the user selects the conditions. The advantage over the first method is that the user has the added flexibility of creating filter conditions that may not have been provided in a menu of limited options, as in the first method. A program accomplishing this type of filter could resemble the following:

```
*Setter.PRG is for selective filtering of records.*
USE BigFile INDEX Names
SET CONFIRM ON
CLEAR
*create variables for components of filter.
PUBLIC FILTERS, MLAST, MFIRST, MSOCSEC, MSAL, MBDATE
STORE " " TO FILTERS
STORE SPACE(20) TO MLAST
STORE SPACE(20) TO MFIRST
STORE SPACE(11) TO MSOCSEC
STORE 0.00 TO MSAL
STORE CTOD("01/01/01") TO MBDATE
STORE " =" TO VAR1, VAR2, VAR3
STORE " >" TO VAR4, VAR5
*get filter conditions from user.
@ 0, 0  TO 15, 55 DOUBLE
@ 13, 25  SAY "REPORT SELECTION CRITERIA"
```

```
@ 14, 24   SAY "Press Control-END when done."
@  2,  4   SAY "Last name:" GET VAR1
@  2, 20   GET   MLAST
@  4,  3   SAY "First name:" GET VAR2
@  4, 20   GET   MFIRST
@  6,  9   SAY "Soc Sec:" GET VAR3
@  6, 23   GET   MSOCSEC PICTURE "999-99-9999"
@  8,  8   SAY "Salary:" GET VAR4
@  8, 21   GET   MSAL
@ 10,  5   SAY "Date of Birth:" GET VAR5
@ 10, 24   GET   MBDATE
READ
*Build the filter macro.*
IF MLAST <> " "
       Filters = "UPPER(Lastname) &VAR1 UPPER(TRIM(MLAST)) .AND. "
ENDIF
*
IF MFIRST <> " "
       Filters = Filters + "UPPER(Firstname) &VAR2 ;
       UPPER(TRIM(MFIRST)) .AND. "
ENDIF
*
IF MSOCSEC <> " "
       Filters = Filters + "SOC_SEC &VAR3 MSOCSEC .AND. "
ENDIF
*
IF MSAL > 0
       Filters = Filters + "HOURLY_SAL &VAR4 MSAL .AND. "
ENDIF
IF DTOC(MBDATE) > "01/01/01"
       Filters = Filters + "Birth_Date &VAR5 MBDATE .AND. "
ENDIF
*Trim trailing .And.*
Filters = SUBSTR(Filters, 1 , LEN(Filters) - 6)
*Set the filter.*
SET FILTER TO &Filters
RETURN
*End of Setter.PRG*
```

When the program is run, the user is presented with a fill-in screen (Figure 4-3) containing variables representing the desired fields. The user can then fill in the blanks where necessary to build a filter applicable to the desired report. In Figure 4-3, the entries chosen will set a filter that selects all records with last names from Johnson through Z, with salaries above $9.00 per hour.

An analysis of the code reveals how the program works. After memory variables that will represent the desired fields are created, a series of @...SAY...GET commands is used to get the user responses that will indicate what conditions are a part of the filter. Included among the possible user responses are the "less-than," "greater-than," and "equal" symbols. The variables that contain these responses, labeled VAR1 through VAR5 in the example, provide the user with the option of building filters for fields equal to or greater or less than the values entered.

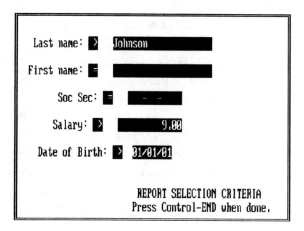

Figure 4-3.

Example of filter screen

Once the READ statement is used to store all of the variables to
memory, a series of IF...ENDIF statements is used to build the filter,
using macro substitution. Finally, the SET FILTER command is used to
set the filter to the expression denoted by the macro.

From a programmer's standpoint, this method is more elegant than
the first method. However, users will need training in how to fill in the
screen with the correct symbols, or they may get improper results.

The third method is to allow the user to create a dBASE query file
while under program control. Programmers are often not familiar with

the dBASE query file because they are used to writing filter selections in the program code. The advantage of using a query file is that the user can build a filter for any imaginable desired condition. By way of review, if you enter the command CREATE QUERY <filename>, you are presented with the Query menu (Figure 4-4). You can then proceed to use the pull-down menus to build a filter condition, as described in the dBASE documentation on the use of the Query menu. As an example, Figure 4-5 shows a completed Query menu that will result in a filter for all records in a database that contain "VA" in the State field.

Once you use the Save option from the Exit menu to save the query, dBASE stores the filter condition outlined in the query in a file with a

```
 Set Filter           Nest          Display        Exit  12:26:52 pm
┌─────────────────────────────────────────────────────┐
│ Field Name                                           │
│ Operator                                             │
│ Constant/Expression                                  │
│ Connect                                              │
│─────────────────────────────────────────────────────│
│ Line Number          1                               │
└─────────────────────────────────────────────────────┘

┌──────┬────────┬──────────────┬─────────────────────┬──────────┐
│ Line │ Field  │ Operator     │ Constant/Expression │ Connect  │
├──────┼────────┼──────────────┼─────────────────────┼──────────┤
│ 1    │        │              │                     │          │
│ 2    │        │              │                     │          │
│ 3    │        │              │                     │          │
│ 4    │        │              │                     │          │
│ 5    │        │              │                     │          │
│ 6    │        │              │                     │          │
│ 7    │        │              │                     │          │
└──────┴────────┴──────────────┴─────────────────────┴──────────┘

 CREATE QUERY      <C:> VAHOMES.QRY          Opt: 1/2
      Position selection bar - ↑↓.  Select - ←┘.  Leave menu - ↔.
             Select a field name for the filter condition.
```

Figure 4-4.

Query menu

.QRY extension. You can then proceed to use that file to set a filter by using this variation of the SET FILTER command:

```
SET FILTER TO FILE <query filename>
```

To use this in a program, the basic commands might be something like

```
ACCEPT "Name of file for filter?" TO ANS
CREATE QUERY &ANS
SET FILTER TO FILE &ANS
REPORT FORM YourFile TO PRINT
```

The example may be brief, but it shows the concept. Ideally, you would also want to have error-trapping that would check to make sure

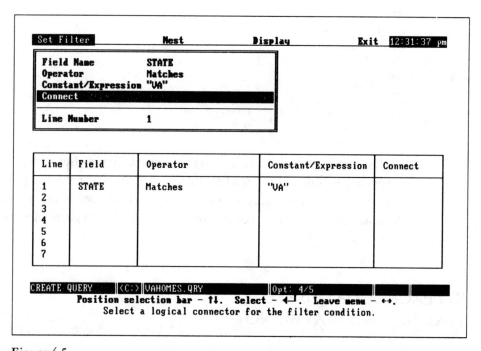

Figure 4-5.

Completed Query menu

the user had not entered an invalid filename or decided the Query menu
was too complicated and pressed ESC, in which case dBASE would have
tried to open a query file that did not exist. An example of a more
thorough way to let users build a custom filter is shown here.

```
*Custom.PRG lets user design a custom filter for report.*
CLEAR
ACCEPT "Enter name for new Filter file (NO EXTENSION):" TO QNAME

**check to see if DOS filename was entered properly.
IF LEN(QNAME) > 8
      WAIT "You MUST use filenames of 8 characters or less!"
      RETURN
ENDIF
*Now check for spaces in filename.
IF AT(' ',QNAME) > 0
      WAIT "DO NOT include SPACES in a FILENAME!"
      RETURN
ENDIF
*Now check for accidental inclusion of extension.
IF AT('.',QNAME) > 0
      WAIT "Use FILENAME ONLY!  DO NOT include ANY extension!"
      RETURN
ENDIF
*Filename looks OK, so create a query file by that name.
CREATE QUERY &QNAME
STORE QNAME + ".QRY" TO QNAME
*check to be sure user didn't just escape from Query menu.*
IF FILE("&QNAME")
      SET FILTER TO FILE &QNAME
ELSE
      RETURN
ENDIF
*Filter file in effect, so do the desired report.
WAIT "Turn on printer, press a key..."
REPORT FORM YourFile TO PRINT
*End of Custom.PRG*
```

Like most programs, this is not foolproof. If the user enters a
filename containing an invalid character other than a space, the program will not catch the mistake. But it will catch most user errors, and it
demonstrates how you can code a similar application to guard against
user errors.

TO PACK A DATABASE:
MAYBE, AND MAYBE NOT

Another well-known command that may someday get you into hot
water is PACK. Many experienced dBASE users either avoid PACK
altogether or use it rarely, preferring to make effective use of SET

DELETED ON instead. Entering the SET DELETED ON command will cause dBASE to hide all records marked for deletion from view. dBASE commands, whether in a dot prompt mode or in a program, will ignore these records until you enter a SET DELETED OFF command.

Assuming you use SET DELETED ON, the only thing you have to gain from doing a PACK is disk space. On a system running on floppies, that may be necessary, but dBASE on floppy-based systems is becoming the exception rather than the rule. On a system with a hard disk, the minor amount of disk space freed may not be worth the amount of time it takes to perform a PACK. Worse yet is the havoc that can occur if something goes wrong with the hardware during the pack operation. If a power failure, parity check error, or other system error fatal to DOS occurs near the end of the pack, any number of records marked for deletion may mystically reappear, minus the deletion markers. dBASE will have no record of which ones were marked for deletion and which ones weren't. And the poor users must go through the deletion process all over again. If index files were open when the system crashed, the index files are probably corrupted and will need rebuilding. And if the failure occurs at a critical moment close to the end of the pack, the database file will be corrupted with premature end-of-file markers, rendering the database nearly useless without the aid of some advanced file-recovery techniques. These are good reasons for avoiding a pack or performing a backup approach, since there are safer alternatives.

One alternative is to create a new file with the COPY TO command, build the indexes for the new file, then erase the old file. From either the dot prompt or in a program it works the same, with commands like these:

```
USE OldFile
SET DELETED ON
COPY TO NewFile
USE
RUN ERASE OldFile.DB*
RUN RENAME NewFile.DB* OldFile.DB*
USE OldFile
INDEX ON SOC_SEC TO SOCIAL
```

In this example, the RUN command is suggested for erasing and renaming the files for an important reason. If the database contains any memo fields, then there are two files on disk for the database, one with the .DBT extension. Using the asterisk as a DOS wildcard along with the DOS versions of the erase and rename commands takes care of the database and the memo field file in one pass. If your database doesn't use memo fields, use the dBASE ERASE and RENAME commands, which are slightly faster than the equivalent DOS commands.

Another advantage of this approach is that the PACK command does not release disk space back to DOS, but the COPY command does. Also, the COPY command will remove deleted space from any memo (.DBT) files, freeing still more disk space. Each time a memo field is edited, a great deal of old, unused data accumulates in the .DBT file. The PACK command has no effect on this, but the COPY command frees this space and can make a database full of heavily-used memo fields much more compact.

If this seems like a lot of work for something you feel isn't likely to happen, a less complex alternative is to simply make a backup copy of the file before doing a PACK, with commands like these:

```
USE
RUN COPY OLDFILE.DBF OLDFILE.BAK
USE OLDFILE INDEX SOCIAL
PACK
```

If the machine ever failed in the midst of a PACK, you would at least have a copy of the database to work with. The temporary backup could always be erased later, if necessary, to free disk space.

5: Maintaining
Order

The mechanics of maintaining order are handled with the SORT and INDEX commands. Unless told otherwise, dBASE will put data into a database in what is known as *natural order,* or *FIFO* (first in, first out). In this order, the oldest records are at the top of the database. New records get tacked onto the bottom of the file. The user changes this order with SORT or INDEX.

Many people avoid SORT, but it can be useful. At times you will find it difficult to get the same results from indexing, and at other times you will want the advantage of working with a database arranged in something close to the natural order; indexes can greatly slow you down. The trick in maintaining speed and power is in knowing when to use SORT and INDEX, and in knowing whether to use INDEX rather than SORT. If you accept the proposition that dBASE exists so that you can (a) put data into a computer, (b) organize that data, and (c) get organized data out of a computer, then sorting and indexing offer one-third of the capabilities needed for the basic task of database management.

THE MECHANICS OF SORTING

When dBASE sorts, it creates another file, identical in size to the initial file, with the records in the database arranged in the order specified by the SORT command. "Elementary," you say. But the objective here is not to repeat what you already know, which is how to enter a SORT command; the point is to emphasize *natural order.* This point provides a basis for the view that the SORT command has a worse reputation than it deserves. In the days of dBASE II, when sorting was a painfully slow process, many dBASE users avoided sorting altogether. The truth is that sorting is usually not necessary, and in most applications it makes little sense to sort on a regular basis. However, an occasional sort can speed up performance with medium-to-large databases because the sort puts the database back in the natural order. As an example, consider a file with the following database structure:

```
Structure for database: D:JUNK.DBF
Number of data records:    6008
Date of last update   : 09/23/87
Field  Field Name  Type       Width   Dec
    1   LASTNAME    Character     20
    2   FIRSTNAME   Character     20
    3   SOC_SEC     Character     11
    4   BIRTH_DATE  Date           8
    5   HOURLY_SAL  Numeric        5     2
    6   INSURED     Logical        1
    7   COMMENTS    Memo          10
** Total **                       76
```

The file contained just over 6000 records, in a random order such that when indexed by a combination of last and first names, less than 2% of the records were in natural order. To perform a sequential operation of listing the names in alphabetical order based on the index, the following commands were used:

```
USE JUNK INDEX JUNK
LIST LASTNAME, FIRSTNAME, SOC_SEC, BIRTH_DATE
```

taking a total of 4 minutes, 27 seconds to execute. Also, when the BROWSE command was used with the index file open, visual delays were evident while the user moved from screen to screen. To put the database back in a natural order, the following commands were used:

```
COPY TO TEMP
USE
RUN DEL JUNK.DBF
RUN DEL JUNK.DBT
RUN RENAME TEMP.DBF JUNK.DBF
RUN RENAME TEMP.DBT JUNK.DBT
```

When the same commands were used to list the data

```
USE JUNK
INDEX ON LASTNAME + FIRSTNAME TO JUNK
LIST LASTNAME, FIRSTNAME, SOC_SEC, BIRTH_DATE
```

the result took 3 minutes, 31 seconds to execute, an approximate 20% increase in execution time. The delays evident with the use of BROWSE were no longer present when the database was used in the natural order. How often you will need to do this depends on how often fields containing key index data are changed in your records. If records are updated often, you may want to design a procedure for re-sorting that is performed every few months.

THE MECHANICS OF INDEXING

When dBASE builds an index file based on an index expression, it creates a separate file that contains only two items for each record: the record number and the key expression of that record. The key expression is limited to 100 characters, so you cannot, for example, attempt to index on all of a 254-character text field (although you can use the SUBSTR( ) function as a part of the index expression). Because index files let you quickly FIND or SEEK a particular record, index files are great at random access of a database. In contrast to sorting, index files maintain the indexed sequence of a database as new records are added or changed — as long as the index file is used every time the database file is opened. Sorting, on the other hand, must be performed again whenever data is added or key fields changed if the ordered sequence of the database is to be maintained. This limitation can be unwieldy with large databases.

Index files are not so useful when performing sequential operations; an open index file will slow down sequential operations to some degree. The delays can be minimized by performing routine maintenance on indexes, a topic covered later in this chapter.

ON SORT VERSUS INDEX

It's no secret that you can order a database on a collection of more than one field. With the SORT command, you use

```
SORT ON FIELD1, FIELD2, FIELD3 TO SORTFILE
```

while with the INDEX command, you use

```
INDEX ON FIELD1 + FIELD2 + FIELD3 TO INDXFILE
```

But do the two commands accomplish the same result? Usually, but not always. The SORT command is not particular about field types and will work on any combination of fields except logical and memo fields. However, sorting only operates on combinations of whole fields, and not on arbitrary expressions. When necessary, indexing can be based on arbitrary expressions, which can be quite complex. The INDEX command will give different results depending on the field types, and the user must in any case convert the fields to a common expression if those fields are of different types.

With SORT and INDEX, creating an order based on multiple

character fields yields the same results, as shown in the following examples:

```
USE CSALES
SORT ON STORE, CUSTNAME TO STORES
USE STORES
LIST STORE, CUSTNAME, CUSTNUMB, BALANCE

STORE         CUSTNAME      CUSTNUMB BALANCE
Collin Creek  Artis, K.     1008        0.00
Collin Creek  Jones, J.L.   1004     1850.00
Collin Creek  Williams, E.  1010        0.00
Downtown      Jones, J.     1011      875.00
Downtown      Walker, B.    1006     1167.00
Galleria      Johnson, L.   1002      675.00
Oak Lawn      Jones, C.     1003      350.00
Prestonwood   Allen, L.     1005      312.00
Prestonwood   Smith, A.     1001      788.50
Prestonwood   Smith, A.M.   1009      220.00
Six Flags     Keemis, M.    1007        0.00
```

```
USE CSALES
INDEX ON STORE + CUSTNAME TO ISTORES
LIST STORE, CUSTNAME, CUSTNUMB, BALANCE

STORE         CUSTNAME      CUSTNUMB BALANCE
Collin Creek  Artis, K.     1008        0.00
Collin Creek  Jones, J.L.   1004     1850.00
Collin Creek  Williams, E.  1010        0.00
Downtown      Jones, J.     1011      875.00
Downtown      Walker, B.    1006     1167.00
Galleria      Johnson, L.   1002      675.00
Oak Lawn      Jones, C.     1003      350.00
Prestonwood   Allen, L.     1005      312.00
Prestonwood   Smith, A.     1001      788.50
Prestonwood   Smith, A.M.   1009      220.00
Six Flags     Keemis, M.    1007        0.00
```

The results are the same in both cases. With multiple numeric fields, however, the results are not always quite the same because of the way dBASE builds an index expression. Consider the same database used to prepare a mailing to target customers who have high credit lines, low account balances, and are therefore likely prospects for heavy spending. You would like to get an idea of who these customers are, so you prepare a report to show records sorted by high credit amounts. Where the high credit amounts are the same, you would like to order the records by outstanding balance. You use the INDEX command to do something like

```
USE CSALES
INDEX ON HIGHCREDIT + BALANCE TO CSALES
LIST STORE, CUSTNAME, CUSTNUMB, HIGHCREDIT, BALANCE
```

STORE	CUSTNAME	CUSTNUMB	HIGHCREDIT	BALANCE
Collin Creek	Artis, K.	1008	1200.00	0.00
Oak Lawn	Jones, C.	1003	900.00	350.00
Galleria	Johnson, L.	1002	1200.00	675.00
Six Flags	Keemis, M.	1007	2000.00	0.00
Collin Creek	Williams, E.	1010	2000.00	0.00
Prestonwood	Smith, A.M.	1009	2000.00	220.00
Prestonwood	Allen, L.	1005	2000.00	312.00
Downtown	Walker, B.	1006	1300.00	1167.00
Prestonwood	Smith, A.	1001	2000.00	788.50
Downtown	Jones, J.	1011	2000.00	875.00
Collin Creek	Jones, J.L.	1004	2000.00	1850.00

Rather than concatenating the credit and the balance, dBASE has added them and indexed in the order of the sum, which may not be what you had in mind. The plus symbol means different things to dBASE for numeric expressions as opposed to string expressions. The plus symbol adds numbers but concatenates character expressions. If you instead use the SORT command, with commands like the following

```
USE CSALES
SORT ON HIGHCREDIT,BALANCE TO SALES1
USE SALES1
LIST STORE, CUSTNAME, CUSTNUMB, HIGHCREDIT, BALANCE
```

STORE	CUSTNAME	CUSTNUMB	HIGHCREDIT	BALANCE
Oak Lawn	Jones, C.	1003	900.00	350.00
Collin Creek	Artis, K.	1008	1200.00	0.00
Galleria	Johnson, L.	1002	1200.00	675.00
Downtown	Walker, B.	1006	1300.00	1167.00
Six Flags	Keemis, M.	1007	2000.00	0.00
Collin Creek	Williams, E.	1010	2000.00	0.00
Prestonwood	Smith, A.N.	1009	2000.00	220.00
Prestonwood	Allen, L.	1005	2000.00	312.00
Prestonwood	Smith, A.	1001	2000.00	788.50
Downtown	Jones, J.	1011	2000.00	875.00
Collin Creek	Jones, J.L.	1004	2000.00	1850.00

what you get is what was expected—a file in numeric order by high credit and, where high credit is the same, in order of the outstanding balance.

The unexpected results when using INDEX occur because the INDEX command, when used with multiple fields, depends on a math expression. In this case, dBASE is adding the amounts, building the index on a value that is the sum of the amounts. To index on the combined numeric fields, you must first convert the numeric expressions into string values, and then use the plus symbol to concatenate the string values, a topic covered in more detail under the next heading. In the preceding example, you could issue a command like

```
INDEX ON STR(HIGHCREDIT) + STR(BALANCE) TO CSALES
```

to accomplish the same result as the SORT command.

INDEXING ON FIELDS
OF DIFFERENT TYPES

In dBASE, you usually need to base the order of the database on fields of dissimilar types, such as a combination of character and numeric fields, or on a numeric and a date field, or on a combination of all three types. (Indexing on memo fields is not possible, and indexing on a logical field takes a tricky use of the IIF( ) function.) You cannot directly combine dissimilar fields with the INDEX command as you can with the SORT command, but since you can index on an expression, the solution is simple: use functions to convert one or more of the fields so that the index uses a uniform type of expression, either character or numeric. A date expression can be converted to a character expression with the DTOC( ) function, and a numeric field can be converted to a character field with the STR( ) function. If you have a character field containing numbers and you want to use it as part of an index expression that mathematically combines one or more numeric fields, you can convert the contents of the character field to a numeric value with the VAL( )

function. As an example, perhaps a department store's list of customers needs to be in order of high credit and, for each group of customers with the same high credit, ordered alphabetically. A simple task is to use the STR( ) function to convert the high credit field to a character string and combine that field with the contents of the name field, as shown in the following example:

```
INDEX ON STR(HIGHCREDIT) + CUSTNAME TO CUSTLIST
LIST CUSTNAME, HIGHCREDIT

Record#   CUSTNAME        HIGHCREDIT
      3   Jones, C.          900.00
      8   Artis, K.         1200.00
      2   Johnson, L.       1200.00
      6   Walker, B.        1300.00
      5   Allen, L.         2000.00
      4   Jones, J.L.       2000.00
     11   Jones, J.         2000.00
      7   Keemis, M.        2000.00
      1   Smith, A.         2000.00
      9   Smith, A.M.       2000.00
     10   Williams, E.      2000.00
```

In this case, the STR( ) function is used to convert what is normally a numeric value, the contents of the HIGHCREDIT field, into its character equivalent. That character equivalent can then be combined with the CUSTNAME field, a character field, to produce a valid index expression.

INDEXING ON LOGICAL FIELDS

Although the dBASE III PLUS manual says that it is not possible to index on a logical field, you can perform this so-called impossibility with a creative use of the immediate IIF( ) function. You can use this function as a part of the index expression to convert the contents of a logical field into a character string that gets stored in the index file along with the rest of the character expression. The syntax for this variation of the INDEX command is

```
INDEX ON IIF(<logical field>,<expression 1>,<expression2>) TO LOGIC
```

In this example, if the logical field evaluates as true, dBASE returns the value specified in the first expression. Otherwise, dBASE returns the value specified in the second expression. In the following example, the expressions are character equivalents of logical "true" and logical "false," and it is these characters that are stored in the index file:

```
INDEX ON IIF(INSURED,"T","F") TO INS
```

Expressions like these can be combined with any character-based expression to build a more complex index. For example, if you wished to define an index by a combination of a logical field (INSURED) and a character field (PATIENT), you might use commands like these, with the results shown.

```
USE PATIENT
INDEX ON IIF(INSURED,"T","F") + PATIENT TO INS
LIST

PATIENT              SOCIAL_SEC   DIAGNOSED  ADMITTED  INSURED
Artis, K.            890-55-4325  04/19/86   05/20/86  .F.
Johnson, L.          122-33-4522  03/06/85   04/15/85  .F.
Smith, A.M.          560-23-4501  02/03/86   05/20/86  .F.
Walker, B.           671-00-5460  05/16/86   05/20/86  .F.
Allen, L.            987-33-4567  05/12/86   05/20/86  .T.
Jones, C.            450-33-6790  02/08/85   04/15/85  .T.
Jones, J.            232-90-3355  06/13/86   06/22/86  .T.
Jones, J.L.          121-09-0557  03/02/85   04/15/85  .T.
Keemis, M.           455-23-8625  02/23/86   05/20/86  .T.
Smith, A.            121-33-4545  03/17/85   04/05/85  .T.
Williams, E.         123-45-6789  06/01/86   06/14/86  .T.
```

If you happen to be working in an environment where dBASE III and dBASE III PLUS coexist and you want to use the commands or program code with both versions of the program, you can't use this technique because dBASE III does not support the immediate IIF( ) function. You can get around this loss by adding another field to the database — character type, one character in width — and filling that field with character equivalents of the logical field with REPLACE commands. Finally, you sort on the character field. Assuming you added a field called EXTRA, and the logical field was named GRADUATE, you could use commands like

```
REPLACE ALL EXTRA WITH "F"
REPLACE ALL EXTRA WITH "T" FOR GRADUATE
INDEX ON EXTRA TO GRADS
```

This technique works, but it is clearly a kludge, and an upgrade to dBASE III PLUS along with the use of IIF( ) is a preferable alternative.

INDEXING IN DESCENDING ORDER

According to the "Command" reference in the dBASE III PLUS documentation, indexing is always in ascending order, but it is possible to index in descending order. The trick to indexing in descending order is to use an index key that always results in negative values. As an example, consider these commands and the results:

```
USE CSALES
INDEX ON -(BALANCE) TO DUEDEBTS
LIST CUSTNAME, BALANCE

Record#   custname        balance
      4   Jones, J.L.     1850.00
      6   Walker, B.      1167.00
     11   Jones, J.        875.00
      1   Smith, A.        788.50
      2   Johnson, L.      675.00
      3   Jones, C.        350.00
      5   Allen, L.        312.00
      9   Smith, A.M.      220.00
      7   Keemis, M.         0.00
      8   Artis, K.          0.00
     10   Williams, E.       0.00
```

Another way of accomplishing the same result would be to index on an expression that subtracts the value from some arbitrarily large value. To do this, you use a command like

```
INDEX ON 10000-BALANCE TO DUEDEBTS
```

As long as no customer has an account balance of over $10,000, you are fine. Since dBASE always builds an index in ascending order, and negative numbers in ascending order resemble a descending order to humans, you get an index that is arranged in descending order. Be aware that this method works well for generating lists of values in descending order, not so well for finding records with FIND and SEEK. Since the index in the first example is built on negative values, you would need to enter something like

```
FIND -58.50
```

to find a balance in the amount of $58.50. If you used the second method described, you would be in worse shape; you would need to enter something like

```
FIND 9941.50
```

because 10,000—58.50 provides the actual index entry value of 9,941.50. This is not often a problem since most users don't want to find a record based purely on the cost of an item. If you need to search on a combination of fields within an index created in this manner, remember to include the necessary expressions to make the search on the negative values present in the index.

Descending Indexes on Character Fields

With character fields, descending indexes get much trickier. You cannot use a negative expression on a character field. Assuming that a field called LASTNAME is a character field, an expression like

```
INDEX ON -(LASTNAME) TO CNAMES
```

would result in nothing more than a data type mismatch error. You can use the ASC( ) function to convert part of a character string to its ASCII equivalent and index on a numeric equivalent of that value. As an example, commands like the following provide the results shown:

```
USE TEMP
INDEX ON -ASC(LASTNAME) TO CNAMES
LIST LASTNAME, FIRSTNAME

   1   Smith        Allen
   9   Smith        Allen M.
   7   Keemis       Martin
   2   Johnson      Lonnie
   3   Jones        Charisse
   4   Jones        Judie Lynn
  11   Jones        Judith
   5   Allen        Larry
   8   Artis        Kelvin
```

By using the ASC( ) function, you build an index in descending order, based on the first character of the LASTNAME field, but the resulting index is not a very orderly one. You should probably ask yourself whether you would not be better off using the descending option of the SORT command. You could create an index based on a character field in descending order by doing a sort and building the index file based on the natural order of the records.

```
USE CSALES
SORT ON LASTNAME /D, FIRSTNAME /D TO TEMP
USE
RUN ERASE CSALES.DBF
RUN RENAME TEMP.DBF CSALES.DBF
USE CSALES
```

When used, the new database will contain the records in descending order, based on lastname, then firstname. This works well for reporting, but not so well for editing and updating; to maintain the order, you would need to do another SORT after any updating. Fortunately, the reverse-order alphabetic index is a rare requirement.

USING FUNCTIONS TO STANDARDIZE CASE

Frequent use is made of the UPPER (and less frequently, the LOWER) functions to avoid problems arising because of the case-sensitive nature of dBASE. The functions can also be used as part of an index expression, resulting in an index containing characters that are all uppercase (or lowercase, if the LOWER function is used). The problem that can arise when the data-entry people are not consistent with methods of data entry is shown in the following example:

```
USE TEMP2
INDEX ON NAME TO NAMES
LIST

Record#  NAME              AGE
      1  Addison, E.        32
      2  Addison, a.        28
      3  Carlson, F.        45
      6  McDonald, M.       25
      4  McLean,R.          28
```

```
   5   Mcdonald, s.          47
   7   Smith, S.             55
   8   Smith, b.             37
  10   adams, j.q.           76
   9   edelstien, m.         22
```

Unless told otherwise, dBASE puts lowercase letters after uppercase letters in the index, and the results are probably not what you had in mind. If you use the UPPER function to build the index, you get acceptable results, as shown by the following commands:

```
USE TEMP2
INDEX ON UPPER(NAME) TO NAMES
LIST

Record#   NAME                 AGE
    10    adams, j.q.          76
     2    Addison, a.          28
     1    Addison, E.          32
     3    Carlson, F.          45
     9    edelstien, m.        22
     6    McDonald, M.         25
     5    Mcdonald, s.         47
     4    McLean,R.            28
     8    Smith, b.            37
     7    Smith, S.            55
```

To find such records in the index, simply use the same function along with the FIND or SEEK command. The following code shows such a use of the UPPER function:

```
MNAME = SPACE(20)
CLEAR
@ 5,5 say "Name? " GET MNAME
READ
MNAME = UPPER(MNAME)
SEEK MNAME
IF FOUND()
    EDIT
ENDIF
```

CREATING SORTED FILES FROM INDEXES

One trick that can save time is to use an existing index to create a sorted file. Sometimes, for reasons already mentioned, you want a file sorted in the same order as an existing index. Perhaps you need a subset of the file for a selective report; the index already exists, but you want to set a filter and you don't want the delay of setting a filter with an index file open. You can create a sorted file based on the contents of the existing index with the COPY TO command. For example, if a file is sorted by cost,

```
USE SALES INDEX COSTS
COPY TO TEMPFILE
```

the new database file, named TEMPFILE, is identical in order to the indexed file you would have created by using the commands

```
USE SALES
SORT ON COSTS TO TEMPFILE
```

The advantage is felt when the index file already exists, as it does in this example. The COPY TO command will always be faster than a comparable SORT command; dBASE will spend up to 40% less time to COPY than to SORT. You also save the disk space needed by the two temporary files created during the sort process.

INDEXING ON A DATE FIELD

When you need a chronological index, dBASE can present a bit of a challenge. It's no problem when you want to see the database in order by just one date field. You can use commands like these, with the results shown:

```
USE PATIENT
INDEX ON ADMITTED TO DATESIN
LIST PATIENT, ADMITTED

Record#  PATIENT          ADMITTED
      1  Smith, A.        04/05/85
      2  Johnson, L.      04/15/85
      3  Jones, C.        04/15/85
      4  Jones, J.L.      04/15/85
      5  Allen, L.        05/20/86
      6  Walker, B.       05/20/86
      7  Keemis, M.       05/20/86
      8  Artis, K.        05/20/86
      9  Smith, A.M.      05/20/86
     10  Williams, E.     06/14/86
     11  Jones, J.        06/22/86
```

As shown, you get a database indexed in the order of the entries in the date field. Things get strange, however, when you want a database indexed on a combination of fields and one of the fields is a date field. Since dBASE doesn't let you directly index on multiple fields of different types, you must use functions to convert the date into a character string. Assuming the database contains a date field named DIAGNOSED and a character field named PATIENT and you want it indexed by date and then by the name of the patient, it would seem feasible that you could get the desired results with commands that follow this syntax:

```
USE <database file>
INDEX ON DTOC(date field) + (character field) TO <index filename>
```

Unfortunately, this syntax doesn't give the correct results, as shown in this example:

```
USE PATIENT
INDEX ON DTOC(DIAGNOSED) + PATIENT TO COMBO
LIST PATIENT, DIAGNOSED

Record#  PATIENT           DIAGNOSED
     9   Smith, A.M.       02/03/86
     3   Jones, C.         02/08/85
     7   Keemis, M.        02/23/86
     4   Jones, J.L.       03/02/85
     2   Johnson, L.       03/06/85
     1   Smith, A.         03/17/85
     8   Artis, K.         04/19/86
     5   Allen, L.         05/12/86
     6   Walker, B.        05/16/86
    10   Williams, E.      06/01/86
    11   Jones, J.         06/13/86
```

The index is not in true chronological order because the DTOC( ) function converts the date into a character field, while maintaining the date format. Assuming you are using the American date format of MM/DD/YY, the conversion causes a date like 02/23/86 to appear in the index before 03/02/85, even though that is not chronologically correct.

You have at least two ways to get the dates in the index in the correct order. The first is to use functions to break down the date into its component parts of month, day, and year, and build an index based on that expression, as shown here:

```
INDEX ON STR(YEAR(<date field>),4)+;
         STR(MONTH(<date field>),2)+;
         STR(DAY(<date field>),2)+;
         <rest of character expression> TO <index filename>
```

Recall that any time an index expression is based on dissimilar types of fields, the expression must evaluate to a common data type. The preceding syntax lets dBASE convert a date into a character expression in the year/month/day format. This portion of the expression can be combined with other character-based expressions to build the desired index. Going back to our prior example, these commands provide the results shown here:

```
USE PATIENT
INDEX ON STR(YEAR(DIAGNOSED),4) + ;
         STR(MONTH(DIAGNOSED),2) + ;
         STR(DAY(DIAGNOSED),2) + PATIENT TO COMBO
```

If you need to find the record, you can do it easily by using memory variables and @...SAY...GET commands to create an expression that can be used with a FIND or SEEK command. For example, the following commands could be used to find a desired record in the index built with the steps just described.

```
*Finder.PRG*
Whatdate = DATE()
Whatname = SPACE(20)
CLEAR
@ 5, 5 SAY "Date? " GET Whatdate
@ 6, 5 SAY "Name? " GET Whatname
READ
Findit = STR(YEAR(Whatdate),4) + STR(MONTH(Whatdate),2)+;
         STR(DAY(Whatdate),2) + Whatname
SEEK Findit
IF FOUND()
    EDIT
ENDIF
<...other commands...>
```

A second way to index on a combination of field types when one field is a date field is to convert the date from American (or other country format) to a year/month/day format with SET DATE ANSI. This approach makes it easy to build the index, but can also make for trouble when updating records. The approach uses commands like these:

```
SET DATE ANSI
INDEX ON DTOC(<date field>) + (<rest of character
expression>) TO <index filename>
```

If, for example, you do this:

```
USE PATIENT
SET DATE ANSI
INDEX ON DTOC(DIAGNOSED) + PATIENT TO COMBO
SET DATE AMERICAN
LIST PATIENT, DIAGNOSED
```

```
Record#  PATIENT              DIAGNOSED
      3  Jones, C.            02/08/85
      4  Jones, J.L.          03/02/85
      2  Johnson, L.          03/06/85
      1  Smith, A.            03/17/85
      9  Smith, A.M.          02/03/86
      7  Keemis, M.           02/23/86
      8  Artis, K.            04/19/86
      5  Allen, L.            05/12/86
      6  Walker, B.           05/16/86
     10  Williams, E.         06/01/86
     11  Jones, J.            06/13/86
```

this time, the order is correct.

A disadvantage of this method is that for the index to be properly updated, any additions or edits of the data in the date field must be done with SET DATE ANSI in effect. This is no problem if you work in an environment where users prefer a year/month/day format, but most users prefer a different format. In a program, you can add and edit data to memory variables while using SET DATE AMERICAN or some other preferred format, then change the format to ANSI with a SET DATE ANSI command before updating the database record, but it is usually easier simply to build the index file using the string functions described earlier. The simplicity of the SET DATE ANSI variation comes in handy for chronological reports because the variation results in no editing of the database records.

Indexing on Dates in Descending Order

If you need a file indexed in reverse chronological order (latest date to earliest), you can use the index-on-negative-values technique to build an index file based on negative date values. Simply subtract the actual dates from any date that is larger (that is, later) than the latest date in the database. Some arbitrary date far in the future works well. The technique is shown in this example:

```
USE PATIENT
INDEX ON CTOD("12/31/1999")-DIAGNOSED TO REVERSE
LIST PATIENT, DIAGNOSED

Record#   PATIENT             DIAGNOSED
    11    Jones, J.           06/13/86
    10    Williams, E.        06/01/86
     6    Walker, B.          05/16/86
     5    Allen, L.           05/12/86
     8    Artis, K.           04/19/86
     7    Keemis, M.          02/23/86
     9    Smith, A.M.         02/03/86
     1    Smith, A.           03/17/85
     2    Johnson, L.         03/06/85
     4    Jones, J.L.         03/02/85
     3    Jones, C.           02/08/85
```

In the example, the index key is built on a number that represents the difference in number of days between 12/31/1999 and the date DIAGNOSED in the database. As the dates get earlier, this number increases, causing the position of the date to be farther down in the index file.

If you need to index on a combination of fields where one field is a date and the dates are to be in descending order, you can still use the STR( ) function. With STR( ), break the date into its component parts of year, month, and day; then use the VAL( ) function to combine the parts into one value; then subtract that value from an arbitrarily large number and use the STR( ) function to convert the result back into a character expression for use in the index expression. This method is less complicated than it sounds. To first break the date into a year, month, day format, you can use the same syntax described earlier, which is

```
STR(YEAR(<date field>),4)+;
STR(MONTH(<date field>),2)+;
STR(DAY(<date field>),2)+;
```

then use the VAL( ) function to convert the expression to a number. If the contents of the date field for a particular record were 9/14/87, the expression, converted with the VAL( ) function into a number, would become 19870914. You could subtract that number from an arbitrarily chosen large number (such as 99,999,999) to build a portion of the index. As an example, assuming that a combination of patient name (a character field) in ascending order and dates admitted (a date field) in descending order is what is wanted in the index, you could use a command like the following, with the results shown:

```
INDEX ON PATIENT + ;
STR(99999999-(YEAR(ADMITTED)*10000 ;
+ MONTH(ADMITTED)*100 + DAY(ADMITTED))) TO ADMITDAY

LIST PATIENT, ADMITTED

Record#  PATIENT              ADMITTED

    5  Allen, L.            05/20/86
    8  Artis, K.           05/20/86
    2  Johnson, L.         04/15/85
    3  Jones, C.           04/15/85
   11  Jones, J.           06/22/86
    4  Jones, J.L.         04/15/85
    7  Keemis, M.          05/20/86
    1  Smith, A.           04/05/85
    9  Smith, A.M.         05/20/86
    6  Walker, B.          05/20/86
   10  Williams, E.        06/14/86
```

MANAGING MULTIPLE INDEX FILES

Complex applications often need more than one index file open if you are going to hold search times down to a minimum, yet maintain the flexibility of looking for data in a variety of ways. Take a database of employees. The users want to search quickly by employee ID number, or by work location and employee name, or by job title and employee name. dBASE lets you open up to seven index files at once, and therefore building the indexes is no problem with commands like

```
USE PERSONNL
INDEX ON EMP_ID TO EMPLOYEE
INDEX ON JOBSITE + LASTNAME + FIRSTNAME TO LOCATION
INDEX ON TITLE + LASTNAME + FIRSTNAME TO POSITION
```

You use all three index files by including the names in the SET INDEX TO statement, as with

```
SET INDEX TO EMPLOYEE, LOCATION, POSITION
```

which keeps all the index files open, so any changes to the key fields in the database will also update the index files.

Of course, the first-named index is the active index, so if you want to search on something other than the employee ID, you must change the active index. Use the SET ORDER TO *n* command to make the desired index the active one. From the dot prompt, if you wanted to make the index file named LOCATION the active index, the command would be

```
SET ORDER TO 2
```

because LOCATION is the second-named index file in the original SET INDEX TO command. In a program, you can select the desired index file by prompting the user for an appropriate search key, and setting the active index to that key. The following code shows such an approach.

```
M_EMPID = 9999
M_LAST = SPACE(20)
M_FIRST = SPACE(20)
M_LOCATE = SPACE(15)
M_POSITION = SPACE(15)
CLEAR
ACCEPT "Search by (1) ID No., (2) Name and location, ;
or (3) Name and title? " TO ANS
CLEAR
USE PERSONNL INDEX EMPLOYEE, LOCATION, POSITION
DO CASE
     CASE ANS = "1"
     SET ORDER TO 1
     a 5, 5 SAY "Employee ID?" GET  M_EMPID
     READ
     SEEK M_EMPID

     CASE ANS = "2"
     SET ORDER TO 2
     a 5, 5 SAY "Last name?" GET M_LAST
     a 6, 5 SAY "First name?" GET M_FIRST
     a 7, 5 SAY "Location?" GET M_LOCATE
     READ
     Findit = M_LOCATE + M_LAST + M_FIRST
     SEEK Findit

     CASE ANS = "3"
     SET ORDER TO 3
     a 5, 5 SAY "Last name?" GET M_LAST
     a 6, 5 SAY "First name?" GET M_FIRST
     a 7, 5 SAY "Title?" GET M_POSITION
```

```
READ
Findit = M_POSITION + M_LAST + M_FIRST
SEEK Findit

OTHERWISE
WAIT "Invalid choice!  Press any key..."
CLOSE DATABASES
RETURN

ENDCASE
IF FOUND()
     <...commands to display or edit record follow...>
ENDIF
<...more commands...>
```

You can present a similar choice to users for generating reports based on the order of various indexes.

```
CLEAR
TEXT
     (1) Employees listed by ID number
     (2) Employees listed by job site
     (3) Employees listed by position
ENDTEXT
ACCEPT "Your choice?" TO ANS
DO CASE
     CASE ANS = "1"
     SET ORDER TO 1

     CASE ANS = "2"
     SET ORDER TO 2

     CASE ANS = "3"
     SET ORDER TO 3

     OTHERWISE
     WAIT "Invalid choice!  Press any key..."
     RETURN

ENDCASE
REPORT FORM WORKERS TO PRINT
<...other commands...>
```

THE MAINTENANCE OF REINDEXING

At times, index files will become corrupted, especially if power is lost or the computer is turned off without exiting dBASE. The best you can do is to make it easy to rebuild indexes. How to rebuild is probably obvious to dot prompt users, but not may be so obvious to users who may be running a program you've designed. The worst that can happen is that the program crashes with an error message like

```
Index damaged. REINDEX should be done before using data.
Cancel, Ignore, or Suspend?
```

and the frantic user, having never seen this message, tries to reach you by phone while you are vacationing in Maui. The best way to deal with this possibility in a program is to include a routine that reindexes files on demand. The program can be called as an option from a main menu or from a utilities menu, and might resemble the following:

```
*Indexer.PRG rebuilds indexes.
CLEAR
@ 5,5 SAY " Please wait...this will take a while..."
SET TALK ON
SET SAFETY OFF
USE PERSONNL
INDEX ON EMPID TO EMPLOYEE
INDEX ON JOBSITE + LASTNAME + FIRSTNAME TO LOCATION
INDEX ON JOBTITLE TO POSITION
SET TALK OFF
SET SAFETY ON
SET INDEX TO EMPLOYEE, LOCATION, POSITION
RETURN
```

This routine rebuilds the index from scratch rather than using the faster REINDEX command for an important reason: if the index files are badly damaged or missing, the REINDEX command will not work.

To avoid unpleasant interruptions while on the beach at Maui, you can use the error-trapping ability of dBASE to automatically recover from a program error caused by a corrupted or erased index file. At the start of your program, include a line that reads

```
ON ERROR DO RECOVER
```

and in a separate program file (in this example, named RECOVER. PRG) include a conditional statement that tells dBASE to run the indexing program if this type of error occurs. As an example, a few lines in the program named RECOVER.PRG might read as follows:

```
IF ERROR() = 114 .OR. ERROR() = 20
    DO INDEXER
        RETRY
ENDIF
```

and if dBASE crashes because of a "record not in index" error or an "index damaged" error, the resultant error codes that dBASE stores to the ERROR( ) function can be used as the trigger that causes the reindexing program to run.

POWER HINTS WHEN INDEXING

A few tips when you are using index files will help speed things along in dBASE.

Use short keys when you don't need long ones. Most indexes are directly based on a series of character fields. And in real life, most character fields become unique around the tenth character, if not sooner. If you can get by with indexing on fewer characters, do so. dBASE will manage the index in less time. Take a real-world example: you are building a customer file for a store in a medium-sized city (100,000 or so population), so you do not need to deal with the duplication of names that you would get in New York or Los Angeles. The customer base is manageable: you might see a maximum of 5000 to 10,000 records in the file over the next ten years. The store manager despises labels with names cut off for lack of field width, so you have specified a width of 30 characters each for the LASTNAME and FIRSTNAME fields. You are going to index on a key field of customer number as the primary index, but you also want an index based on a combination of last and first names so users can quickly find a record when a customer is on the phone and that customer does not have his or her customer number handy. In this situation, do you really need an index based on the LASTNAME and FIRSTNAME fields? Quite likely not, but we do this out of force of habit and make dBASE work harder for it. If instead you do something like

```
INDEX ON LEFT(LASTNAME,10) + LEFT(FIRSTNAME,10)
```

you will, in this case, build an index that contains 20 characters per entry as opposed to an index that contains 60 characters per entry. Given the customer base, having the first ten characters of the last and first names should be more than enough to keep the records in order and enable the user to find a given record. And the index file will use considerably less disk space.

Store numbers in character fields if you are never going to perform calculations on those numbers. If you use numbers as a unique identifier (for example, part numbers, employee numbers, invoice numbers) and you plan to use these fields as a part of the index, don't create a numeric field. Use a character field instead. dBASE does a better job of indexing on character fields than on numeric fields. Consider the following database structure:

```
Structure for database: C:test2.dbf
Number of data records:      10890
Date of last update   : 09/04/87

Field  Field Name  Type        Width    Dec
    1  CLIENTID    Character        6
    2  NAME        Character       50
    3  ADDRESS1    Character       30
    4  ADDRESS2    Character       15
    5  CITY        Character       15
    6  STATE       Character        2
    7  ZIP         Character       10
    8  CONTACT     Character       32
    9  TITLE       Character       15
   10  CTLNAME     Character       15
   11  PHONE       Character       12
   12  COMMENTS    Memo            10
** Total **                      213
```

Indexing this file on the CLIENTID field, which contained 10,890 records, took a total of 2 minutes and 7 seconds. By comparison, the following database contains an identical number of records and differs only in the type of field used for the CLIENTID field:

```
Structure for database: C:test1.dbf
Number of data records:     10890
Date of last update   : 09/04/87

Field  Field Name  Type        Width    Dec
    1  CLIENTID    Numeric          6
    2  NAME        Character       50
    3  ADDRESS1    Character       30
    4  ADDRESS2    Character       15
    5  CITY        Character       15
    6  STATE       Character        2
    7  ZIP         Character       10
    8  CONTACT     Character       32
```

```
    9   TITLE       Character    15
   10   CTLNAME     Character    15
   11   PHONE       Character    12
   12   COMMENTS    Memo         10
**  Total  **                   213
```

In this case, the field is a numeric field with six digits and no decimals. The data contained within the CLIENTID field is identical to the data in the same field in the first example. Same hardware, same number of records, and indexing the entire file on the CLIENTID field took 3 minutes, 1 second, or roughly 30% more time to do the equivalent job.

Once you try substituting character for numeric fields in other large files, it becomes apparent that dBASE takes considerably longer to index a numeric field than a character field of equivalent size. And assuming you are not going to calculate such fields, they don't need to be numeric. If you are using a numeric field only so you can let the computer assign the number by incrementing a value by 1 for each new entry, you can handle this task while using a character field for the numbers. You could use commands like these

```
*Assign new customer number.*
USE CUSTOMER INDEX CUSTID
GO BOTTOM
STORE VAL(CUSTIDNO) + 1 TO NEWCUST
APPEND BLANK
REPLACE CUSTIDNO WITH STR(NEWCUST)
  .
  .
  .
```

to accomplish the same result.

Perform routine maintenance often. When dBASE must perform sequential operations while your index files are open, it has to work harder. You can cut down processing times by regularly putting your database files back in their natural order. To do this, open the file along with the index most often used for sequential reporting or processing, and use the COPY TO *filename* command to copy the contents of the file to another file. Then delete the original database, rename the new database with the same name as the original database, and rebuild the necessary indexes. In applications using large files that are regularly updated, this simple step can make a dramatic difference to the users in terms of response time when performing any reporting or processing based on sequential operations in dBASE. Part of the speedup may also occur because the creation of a new database with the COPY command results in a new file under DOS that may have more contiguous sectors. Often when a file has been updated over months of time, it may be arranged in sectors that are broken up all over the hard disk. You can use this technique to reduce such fragmentation of files over a hard disk, or you can use one of the many "disk optimizer" software packages available to clean up your hard disk and make all of your files more accessible to your software.

6: Maximizing the Relational Power of dBASE

Above all, dBASE is a relational database manager. It is surprising how often this fact gets ignored and how often the full relational capabilities of dBASE aren't taken advantage of. Some simple applications, like the mailing list with less than a dozen fields, do not demand relational capabilities. (Such applications also make you wonder why dBASE was chosen in the first place, but that's a topic for another discussion.) It is the complex applications that present a relational challenge to the dBASE user.

RELATIONAL DATABASE MANAGEMENT

When you are working with a complex relational application, dBASE offers two different ways to accomplish the same results. Both ways have their advantages. You can jump between multiple work areas and use the "lookup" approach to find related data, or you can use the SET RELATION command to establish a link between multiple databases.

Take a classic textbook example: the "sales" versus "orders" database. If you are tracking the sales of a product, you are faced with two databases at the very least. One file contains a record of all sales, and might be structured like this:

```
Structure for database: D:sales.dbf
Number of data records:      5
Date of last update   : 09/21/87
Field  Field Name  Type        Width    Dec
    1  CUSTNO      Character      4
    2  CUSTNAME    Character     20
    3  ITEMNUMB    Character      4
    4  QUANTITY    Numeric        2
** Total **                     31
```

Another file, which contains a record for each item sold by the firm, might have a structure like this one:

```
Structure for database: D:stock.dbf
Number of data records:      4
Date of last update   : 09/21/87
Field  Field Name  Type        Width    Dec
    1  ITEMNUMB    Character      4
    2  ITEMNAME    Character     20
    3  ITEMCOST    Numeric        6      2
** Total **                     31
```

This structure is not an ideal one for such an application, but its simplicity makes it suitable for discussion. dBASE lets you select up to 10 work areas, or at least so say the specifications for dBASE III PLUS. This is true within the limits of DOS and open files, so if your system has room for 15 remaining files, you may have to juggle some work areas if your programs or dot prompt commands open multiple files in multiple work areas.

dBASE numbers its work areas from 1 to 10, and any database file (along with corresponding index files) can be opened in a work area. When you enter something like

```
SELECT 1
USE MyFile
```

the named file is opened in work area 1. The numbering scheme works well with as few as two databases, but open five or six and it gets hard to recall which database is open in what work area. To minimize such confusion, dBASE lets you refer to the work area by the alias, which is the filename unless specified otherwise. For example, after entering the commands shown above, you could later enter

```
SELECT MyFile
```

to return to work area 1. If you don't want to use the filename, you can assign a different name for the alias at the same time that you open a file within a work area. For example, entering

```
SELECT 1
USE MyFile INDEX Names ALIAS Mine
```

would assign the alias "Mine" to the work area, and you could access fields in the database from outside the work area by including the alias name along with the fieldname.

If none is specified, the default work area in which dBASE opens a database is work area 1. However, you do not necessarily have to open files in any particular sequence of work areas. You could, for example, open a file in work area 2, followed by another in work area 4, followed by a third in work area 7, although most users follow a normal sequence of 1,2,3, and so on. To select the desired work area, use the SELECT command, followed by the normal USE and INDEX or SET INDEX TO commands. For example, the SALES database could be opened in work area 1 and the STOCK database in work area 2 with these commands:

```
SELECT 1
USE SALES
SELECT 2
USE STOCK
```

Once the database files are open in the desired work areas, you can switch between them with the appropriate SELECT command. This is the basic method of the lookup approach to relational database management, which can be summarized in seven steps:

1. Select the first database.

2. Find the first desired record.

3. Display any needed data.

4. Select the second database.

5. Find the record that is related to the current record in the first database.

6. Display any needed data.

7. Repeat steps 1 through 6 for all additional records as necessary.

The term "lookup" fits this approach well because dBASE in effect links two files by first checking one record and then looking up the appropriate matching record in the related file. If you were to draw a chart of this process, it might look like this:

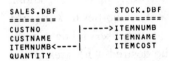

```
SALES.DBF           STOCK.DBF
=========           =========
CUSTNO       |----->ITEMNUMB
CUSTNAME     |      ITEMNAME
ITEMNUMB<----|      ITEMCOST
QUANTITY
```

If you wanted to show, for a given sale, the customer name, quantity, item name, and cost of the item, the following commands would work.

```
SELECT 1
LOCATE FOR CUSTNAME = "Allen"
? CUSTNAME, QUANTITY

Allen, L.                2

SELECT 2
LOCATE FOR ITEMNUMB = SALES->ITEMNUMB
? ITEMNAME, ITEMCOST

Enhanced keyboard    171.20
```

This tells you that a customer named L. Allen ordered two enhanced keyboards at $171.20 each. In most cases, the second database is indexed on the search field, so you can use the faster FIND or SEEK in place of the LOCATE command shown here. If the data needs to be displayed for a series of records, you can place the commands within a program, inside of a DO WHILE loop, as shown in this example:

```
*Sales1.PRG*
CLEAR
? " Name              Quantity          Item          Cost"
SELECT 1
USE SALES
SELECT 2
USE STOCK INDEX ITEMS
SELECT 1
DO WHILE .NOT. EOF()
    ? CUSTNAME, QUANTITY
    ?? "     "
    SELECT 2
    SEEK SALES->ITEMNUMB
    ?? ITEMNAME, ITEMCOST
    SELECT 1
    SKIP
ENDDO
*End of Sales1.PRG*
```

When the program runs, the result is something similar to this:

```
Name          Quantity       Item            Cost
Smith, A.        2      Enhanced keyboard    171.20
Jones, E.        1      AT power supply      209.90
Smith, A.        1      3.5 inch disk drive  148.50
Allen, L.        2      Enhanced keyboard    171.20
```

This method works, but there are better ways to relate files. The problem with the lookup method is that it requires extensive amounts of program coding. It is maddening to do anything of any complexity from the dot prompt, and even if you do all of your work from within a program, you can't make use of the REPORT FORM or LABEL FORM commands, nor can you enter and update data in either file simultaneously from an on-screen form. This method remains popular primarily because it was the principal method of relating files with dBASE II. dBASE II did not offer the SET RELATION and SET VIEW commands or the CATALOG facilities, and thus programmers carried over the dBASE II coding habits into many relational applications written in dBASE III PLUS.

Another disadvantage of this method of relating files is that it can grow into a collection of lookup routines that becomes difficult to manage when you are working with more than one file. Again, consider the problem of tracking sales. As it is currently structured, the SALES database file will require unneeded duplication of customer names. If the same customer places ten different orders, then that customer's name must be entered in identical fashion in ten different records in the SALES file, just the sort of trap one hopes to avoid when spending the money on a relational database manager like dBASE. The database design could be significantly improved if the customer name (CUST-NAME) field were deleted from the SALES database and another related file, called CUSTOMERS, was created to store customer numbers and corresponding customer names. Such a database might resemble this one:

```
Structure for database: D:customer.dbf
Number of data records:        4
Date of last update   : 09/21/87
Field   Field Name  Type        Width    Dec
    1   CUSTNO      Character       4
    2   CUSTNAME    Character      20
    3   ADDRESS     Character      20
    4   CITY        Character      20
    5   STATE       Character       2
    6   ZIP         Character       5
** Total **                       72
```

and it would then make sense to delete the CUSTNAME field from the SALES database or, better still, not design it into the structure in the first place. A map of the relations between the files now looks like this:

```
CUSTOMER.DBF        SALES.DBF            STOCK.DBF
============        =========            =========
CUSTNO<-----------CUSTNO      |----->ITEMNUMB
CUSTNAME          ITEMNUMB-----|      ITEMNAME
ADDRESS           QUANTITY            ITEMCOST
CITY
STATE
ZIP
PHONE
```

Now consider what has to be done inside the program to display the data in a columnar report similar to the prior program's display. For a given sale (or record contained in the SALES database), you must select the work area containing the CUSTOMER database, find the record with a matching customer number, display the desired data, select the work area containing the STOCK database, find the record with a matching item number, and display the desired data. The prior program, modified to handle this need, might resemble the following:

```
*Sales2.PRG*
CLEAR
? " Name              Quantity        Item        Cost"
SELECT 1
USE SALES
SELECT 2
USE STOCK INDEX ITEMS
SELECT 3
USE CUSTOMER INDEX CUSTOMER
SELECT 1
DO WHILE .NOT. EOF()
    SELECT 3
    SEEK SALES->CUSTNO
    ? CUSTNAME
    SELECT 1
    ?? QUANTITY
    ?? "     "
    SELECT 2
    SEEK SALES->ITEMNUMB
    ?? ITEMNAME, ITEMCOST
    SELECT 1
    SKIP
ENDDO
```

This program can become challenging as you open additional related files. The biggest challenge is to keep track of precisely where your program is at all times; the accidental omission of a SELECT command to switch back to a primary database before a SKIP command has been known to wreak havoc during the development process. Finally, as you work with more files, establishing such a relation from the dot prompt becomes virtually impossible purely because of the number of required commands. The result is that with the lookup approach, you are forced into programming whether you want to or not.

USING SET RELATION

With the SET RELATION command, you can establish a virtual link between two files that are open in different work areas. The link is made on a common key field or combination of fields. The syntax of the SET RELATION command is

```
SET RELATION TO <key expression> INTO <alias>
```

where *key expression* is the common expression used in the index of the related database, and *alias* is the name or alias of the other database that the active database is to be linked to. The SET RELATION command also comes with a few strings attached. Among them are

1. The target database, the database you are establishing the relationship *to,* must be indexed on the key expression.

2. The source database, the database you are establishing the relationship *from,* can establish only one relationship at a time. Note that some dBASE look-alikes, such as FoxBase, and some compilers, including Clipper, offer features for setting multiple relations out of the same work area.

Consider the need to display data from two databases at once. Instead of being forced to execute a series of SELECT and FIND or SEEK commands for every desired set of related records, you can use SET RELATION a single time in a manner similar to this:

```
SELECT 1
USE SALES
SELECT 2
USE STOCK INDEX ITEMS
SELECT 1
SET RELATION TO ITEMNUMB INTO STOCK
```

You can then retrieve data in the related file by including the alias name along with the fieldname, as demonstrated with the following command and its accompanying results:

```
LIST CUSTNO, QUANTITY, STOCK->ITEMNAME, STOCK->ITEMCOST

Record#  custno quantity stock->itemname      stock->itemcost
      1  1001        2 Enhanced keyboard    171.20
      2  1002        1 AT power supply      209.90
      3  1001        1 3.5 inch disk drive  148.50
      4  1003        2 Enhanced keyboard    171.20
```

Once such a relation has been established, dBASE will try to locate a matching record in the related database whenever you move the record pointer within the active database. dBASE behaves in a manner similar to that of the FIND and SEEK commands: if more than one record in the target database meets the condition for the relation, dBASE finds the first occurrence of that condition; if no record meets the condition, dBASE places the record pointer in the related file at the end of the file.

One advantage of the SET RELATION command is that it can be used for setting up a chain of related files. For example, suppose you are billing your customers. The relationship of the CUSTOMER file to the SALES file happens to be one-to-many (one customer, many orders for that customer), so an initial thought might be to discard the use of SET RELATION, and go back to the lookup method. However, with some forethought and planning, you can use SET RELATION effectively. If you index the SALES file on the CUSTNO field, the SET RELATION command can be used to find the first record in the SALES file having a given customer number; then you can display or print a list, from the SALES and related STOCK file, while that customer number is still valid. The following program and the accompanying results show how this method works.

```
*Sales3.PRG*
CLEAR
SET HEADING OFF
SELECT 1
USE CUSTOMER INDEX NAMES
*index here is in alpha order just for clarity.
SELECT 2
USE SALES INDEX CUSTNO
*index here is by customer number.
SELECT 3
USE STOCK INDEX ITEMS
*index here is by stock number.
SELECT 1
SET RELATION TO CUSTNO INTO SALES
SELECT 2
SET RELATION TO ITEMNUMB INTO STOCK
SELECT 1
DO WHILE .NOT. EOF()
    ? "    Name: " + CUSTNAME
    ? "Address: " + ADDRESS
```

```
    ? "          " + TRIM(CITY) + ", " + STATE + " " +
ZIP
    ? REPLICATE("=",50)
    SELECT 2
    LIST OFF QUANTITY, STOCK->ITEMNAME, STOCK->ITEMCOST;
    WHILE CUSTNO = CUSTOMER->CUSTNO
    ?
    SELECT 1
    SKIP
ENDDO
```

```
    Name: Allen, L.
 Address: 345 Pinetops Highway
          Pinetops, NC 27404
==================================================
    2 Enhanced keyboard                 171.20


    Name: Jones, E.
 Address: P.O. Box 1834
          Herndon, VA 22070
==================================================
    1 AT power supply                   209.90


    Name: Smith, A.
 Address: 1412 Wyldewood Way
          Phoenix, AZ 78009
==================================================
    2 Enhanced keyboard                 171.20
    1 3.5 inch disk drive               148.50
```

The SET RELATION command is also compatible with the LABEL
FORM and REPORT FORM commands. When creating a report or
label form, simply include the alias name, followed by → along with any
fields that are in related database files. Note that you will need to open
the necessary files before using the REPORT FORM or LABEL FORM
commands; otherwise, the stored report or label form won't be able to
access the desired fields, and you will get an "error in contents expression" when trying to run the report or generate the labels.

Set Relation Versus Lookup

If the SET RELATION command is such an improvement over the
lookup method, why were the first few pages of this chapter devoted
entirely to the lookup method? It turns out that SET RELATION can't
be used in every case. It works best either when you are working with

one-to-one relationships, where one record in a database can be systematically related to one (and only one) record in another database, or in many-to-one relationships, where many records in one database can be related to only one record in a linked database.

Before you can design the code to deal with the relationships, you may find it necessary to do some system analysis and determine the relationships that need to be drawn between the fields. For example, when one field in one record of a database relates in a unique manner to a field in another record in a different database, you have a one-to-one relationship. Suppose you are managing a personnel system that contains employees' medical benefits information in one file and salary information in another file. Each database contains one record per employee, meaning that for every record in the medical file, there is a corresponding record for that same employee in the salary file. The relationship between the files is one-to-one.

By comparison, if one field of one record in the first file relates to a field in one or more records in the second file, you have a one-to-many relationship. An example is a billing database for customers that tracks sales; for every customer, there are a number of records in the sales database corresponding to each actual sale item to that customer.

Last is a type of relationship not as common as the first two: the many-to-many relationship, which occurs when a field in several records in one database will relate to a field in several records in another database. An example might comprise a database of software sold by a software store and a database of suppliers for that software. In a file of available products, the software store might have several products manufactured by Ashton-Tate. And in a related file of suppliers, the software store might have several suppliers, any one of which can be called to ship any one of the Ashton-Tate products listed in the products database. The relationship between these files is a many-to-many relationship.

As the last example of program code demonstrated, using SET RELATION with one-to-many relationships calls for some planning and some programming. If you are going to stick to the dot prompt, building entry and edit forms and reports entirely from the dot prompt mode, you become pretty much limited to the one-to-one relationships.

A more serious limitation of SET RELATION is its inability to draw a relationship to more than one file from the same source database. While some dBASE compilers and look-alike programs like FoxBase neatly step around this limitation, dBASE III PLUS restricts you to the one-relation-per-source rule. This restriction would cause a problem in our sales application if you wanted to add a file of suppliers and draw a relation out of the STOCK database by the ITEMNUMB field to the supplier's file. Logically, you might decide to design the relationship as illustrated in the following diagram:

```
CUSTOMER.DBF        SALES.DBF           STOCK.DBF
============        =========           =========
CUSTNO<-----------CUSTNO      |------ITEMNUMB---|
CUSTNAME          ITEMNUMB<----|       ITEMNAME  |
ADDRESS           QUANTITY             ITEMCOST  |
CITY                                             |
STATE                                            |
ZIP                           SUPPLIER.DBF       |
PHONE                         ============       |
                              ITEMNUMB<-------------|
                              SUPPNAME
                              SUPPADDR
                              SUPPCITY
                              SUPPSTATE
                              SUPPZIP
```

In theory this may look reasonable, but in practice you cannot do it with SET RELATION because you can establish a relationship out of the STOCK database to only one other database. Try to enter two different SET RELATION commands from the same work area, and the second one will simply override the first. One way around this limitation is to make partial use of the lookup method, but this means that you are back to using program code for drawing the relationships. Another way that permits the use of SET RELATION from the dot prompt is to restructure the databases so that the relationship can be drawn from the other database in question. In this case, you could add a field for a unique supplier ID code to both the STOCK and the SUPPLIER databases. The new relationship could then be drawn from the SUPPLIER database to the STOCK database, as illustrated in the following diagram:

```
CUSTOMER.DBF        SALES.DBF            STOCK.DBF
============        =========            =========
CUSTNO<------------CUSTNO       |------ITEMNUMB
CUSTNAME           ITEMNUMB<----|        ITEMNAME
ADDRESS            QUANTITY               ITEMCOST
CITY                                      SUPPLIERID<--|
STATE                                                  |
ZIP                          SUPPLIER.DBF              |
PHONE                        ============              |
                             SUPPLIERID-------------|
                             SUPPNAME
                             SUPPADDR
                             SUPPCITY
                             SUPPSTATE
                             SUPPZIP
```

Such an approach adds the work of maintaining an additional field
in two databases, but nevertheless, if you work primarily from the dot
prompt, this is probably the way you would want to go. If you write
applications for others, it may be less work to give up SET RELATION
(as long as you don't need the capability for a dBASE REPORT FORM or
LABEL FORM command) and go back to the lookup approach for a
portion of the job.

VIRTUAL FILES

Two additional commands, new to dBASE III PLUS, let you manage
multiple fields with minimal amounts of hassle; these are the SET
FIELDS and SET VIEW commands.

With SET FIELDS you can specify a list of fields from any number of
available related files. Those fields become a virtual database, and you
can then refer to fields in other database operations, including LIST,
BROWSE, REPORT FORM, or COPY TO. As an example, consider our
original relationship between the SALES and STOCK databases. That
relationship was created with the following commands:

```
SELECT 1
USE SALES
SELECT 2
USE STOCK INDEX ITEMS
SELECT 1
SET RELATION TO ITEMNUMB INTO STOCK
```

If you knew that the fields you would want to access are the CUSTNO and QUANTITY fields from the SALES file, along with the ITEMNAME and ITEMCOST fields from the related STOCK file, you could use the SET FIELDS command to build a virtual database containing those fields. The syntax for the SET FIELDS command is

```
SET FIELDS TO [<fields list>] [<ALL>]
```

In the case of the example described above, you could enter

```
SET FIELDS TO CUSTNO, QUANTITY, STOCK->ITEMCOST, ;
STOCK->ITEMNAME
```

to create a pool of selected fields that becomes the virtual database. You can refer to the fields by name only, omitting the alias. The mere prospect of omitting all of those greater-than and hyphen signs makes the use of SET FIELDS worth the added effort, as shown in this example:

```
SELECT 1
USE SALES
SELECT 2
USE STOCK INDEX ITEMS
SELECT 1
SET RELATION TO ITEMNUMB INTO STOCK
SET FIELDS TO CUSTNO, QUANTITY, STOCK->ITEMCOST, ;
STOCK->ITEMNAME

LIST CUSTNO, QUANTITY, ITEMCOST, ITEMNAME
Record#  CUSTNO QUANTITY ITEMCOST ITEMNAME
      1  1001        2   171.20 Enhanced keyboard
      2  1002        1   209.90 AT power supply
      3  1001        1   148.50 3.5 inch disk drive
      4  1003        2   171.20 Enhanced keyboard
```

Note that you must still specify an alias if you use the same fieldnames in multiple open databases. If you want to cancel the effects of the SET FIELDS command, use the CLEAR FIELDS command. The SET FIELDS command is an additive command, so be warned that entering a SET FIELDS command after you have entered an earlier SET FIELDS command will not clear the effects of the earlier command. You will simply add new fields to the virtual database.

You can also temporarily turn the effects of the fields list on and off with the SET FIELDS ON and SET FIELDS OFF commands. The first time you specify a list of fields with a SET FIELDS command, those fields are turned on by default, just as if you had entered a SET FIELDS ON command.

For dot prompt users, the use of SET FIELDS along with SET RELATION is an invaluable aid when working with multiple files. You can use Screen Painter to build screens based on the virtual file for inquiry purposes, and the dBASE Report Generator and Label Form Generator will see the fields in the virtual file as available fields for inclusion in any reports or labels.

A VIEW TO A FILE

With the CREATE VIEW FROM ENVIRONMENT command, you can take a "snapshot" of all relations, databases and related index files, one format file, and one filter condition. Once you have opened your databases and indexes in the desired work areas, used SET RELATION to establish any desired links, and used SET FIELDS to define a list of fields, you can enter the command

```
CREATE VIEW <filename> FROM ENVIRONMENT
```

where *filename* is the name for the view file. Once you have done this, you no longer need to repeat the same string of commands to duplicate the opening of files and the setting of relationships. You can simply enter

```
SET VIEW TO <filename>
```

where *filename* is the name of the view saved earlier, and dBASE will open the same files in the same work areas, set the same relations, and establish the same pool of fields for the virtual file. If a filter was in effect when you used the CREATE VIEW FROM ENVIRONMENT command, it will be in effect when you open the view with the SET VIEW command.

Why JOIN?

Seasoned dBASE hands will note similarities between the use of the CREATE VIEW and SET VIEW commands and the use of the JOIN command, but the more significant difference is one of truth versus imagination. The JOIN command combines select fields in two database files to create a third database file. The combined use of SET RELATION, SET FIELDS, and CREATE VIEW FROM ENVIRONMENT results in a selective combination of records and fields from multiple files that create an imaginary database. Clearly, the latter has its advantages over the use of JOIN. The JOIN command uses large amounts of disk space and requires a relatively large amount of time to create that new file. By comparison, when you enter a SET VIEW command, the results are immediate, and no additional disk space is used. The use of JOIN was advised sparingly in the days of dBASE III, and given the new commands available in dBASE III PLUS, the JOIN command should probably be used even less, if ever.

Two rare possibilities come to mind for the use of JOIN. First, if you let long reports based on relational combinations of data print in an unattended mode (like at 3 A.M.), the JOIN command may actually be preferable. Response times become less of an issue when you select a report and walk out the door at 5 P.M., leaving the PC to fend for itself. In such instances, it may not be a wise idea to leave your primary data files open (and susceptible to damage caused by a hardware malfunction) when you can create a temporary database with JOIN, leave that file open for the reporting, and erase the file when the reports are done.

The other instance when JOIN can be useful is in creating a dBASE file that can be used by a nonrelational program, like Ashton-Tate's RapidFile, or Lotus 1-2-3.

CAVEATS: THE NATURE
OF A VIRTUAL DATABASE

Some commands operate the same with a virtual file as with an actual file and some don't. For example, virtual databases created through views work well for inquiries and reporting, but can be dangerous if used for data entry or updating. The APPEND, INSERT, and APPEND BLANK commands will add records to the active file only and not to every database used by the view. If you build a format file containing fields that are outside of the active file, and you use the APPEND command along with the format file, you may see fields for the fields in the related files. But the data entered won't get added to any records in the related files. One way around this problem is to use the APPEND BLANK command in each of the work areas, and then open the format file that contains fields for each of the databases. This approach works if it is done carefully; however, massive additions and edits performed through a view can foul up the relational integrity of the files, particularly if key fields or fields that are parts of key expressions are changed in one file while the corresponding entry is left unchanged in another. The preferred method of data entry and updates is to add or change records in one database at a time, instead of trying to make global updates through a view.

Another occurrence to watch out for when dealing in a relational area is the occasional tendency of dBASE to be somewhere other than where you would like it to be. Although it is easy to blame dBASE and say that the program doesn't know where it should be, it is more often the fault of either the program directing dBASE or the dBASE user. If the program causes dBASE to move the record pointer in one database independently of the others, things may be temporarily out of sync. Once you move back to the database that is setting the relations and move the record pointer, dBASE will reestablish the correct relations.

UNCOMMON RELATIVES

One less used option of the SET RELATION command lets you link files on the basis of record numbers. The syntax of the SET RELATION command when used in this manner is

```
SET RELATION TO RECNO() INTO alias
```

When the RECNO( ) function is used to establish the relation, the target file does not have to be indexed, as it does with more conventional uses of the SET RELATION command. As an example, you could link two databases by record number with these commands:

```
SELECT 1
USE PATIENTS
SELECT 2
USE LABTESTS
SELECT 1
SET RELATION TO RECNO() INTO LABTESTS
```

This technique can be quite useful for relating records in two or more databases with a parallel relationship, that is for every record in database A, there is a matching record at same position in database B. It may also be needed in unusual applications, such as a database containing more fields than dBASE can handle. If you run into an application that would require 150 fields, you could create one database containing 100 fields, and a second database containing 50 fields. You could then relate the two files using the record number. This works well as long as that parallel relationship is maintained: each time a record is added to one file, a corresponding record must be added to another. Any deletions and any sorts must also be performed in tandem, or the relationship will no longer be parallel, rendering the scheme useless. Be warned that this type of design should be necessary only in the rarest of circumstances. Very few applications require a database to contain more than 128 fields. Databases with an abnormally large number of fields are usually the result of poor system design. If a database seems to require over 100 fields, it is possible that all those fields are really needed, but it is more likely that some inherent data relationships are being ignored and an inefficient system has been designed.

GETTING EFFICIENT WITH CATALOGS

Catalogs are a feature of dBASE III PLUS that can make things easier for other users, particularly novices. The primary objective of a catalog is to group the files you use for a particular purpose into a cohesive unit. Having your database, associated index, view, query, screen, and report files grouped into catalogs helps minimize confusion about which files are used for which purpose, particularly when you are using a hard disk.

Catalogs can also be a significant help to the power user who works primarily from the dot prompt. If you write applications entirely in the dBASE programming language, catalogs will be of little use. Catalogs help minimize user confusion because the end user does not see a large number of files when selecting a file option from the Assistant menus; only files in the catalog will appear. On the other hand, if you are controlling the availability of files, reports, views, and so forth through the code of a dBASE program, then the end users are already restricted by the options presented through your program. Using a catalog within a program won't buy you anything that a well-written program does not already provide.

Catalogs are created with the SET CATALOG TO *filename* command, where *filename* is the name of either an existing or a new catalog. If the catalog exists, this command will select the catalog, and all files opened from then on will be added to the catalog. If the catalog does not exist, a new one will be created, and you will be prompted to supply a title for the catalog. A catalog is simply a special database that is assigned a .CAT extension. In this database are stored the names of all database files, views, index files, format files, reports, and queries that are to be included in the catalog. Each time you open another file, it is added to the active catalog. To stop adding files to a catalog, you close the catalog with the SET CATALOG TO command, without specifying any filename.

When you open an existing catalog (either from the Assistant, using the Catalog option of the Set Up menu, or with the SET CATALOG TO *filename* command), dBASE reads all entries from the catalog file and makes these files available from the Assistant menus. For example, open a combination of database and index files, format files, and a view file with commands similar to these:

```
SET CATALOG TO SALES
SELECT 1
USE SALES INDEX SALES
SET FORMAT TO SALES
SELECT 2
USE CUSTOMER INDEX CUSTOMER
SET FORMAT TO CUSTOMER
SELECT 1
SET RELATION TO CUSTNO INTO CUSTOMER
CREATE VIEW SALES FROM ENVIRONMENT
CLEAR ALL
```

As the new catalog and each new file (with the exception of index files) are opened, dBASE will prompt for a descriptive title for the file; this title will be added to the catalog and can serve as an aid to keeping up a file's purpose. After the entry of commands like these, you could exit from dBASE, and the catalog could be used later on a repeated basis to limit the files other users will see when they get into dBASE through the Assistant. As an example, you might get back into dBASE after using the command described above and exiting the program. From the Assistant menus you could choose the Catalog option of the Setup menu and highlight the name SALES to use that catalog. Then, when you are using the Assistant to choose among the available files, only the files contained in the catalog would be visible within the Assistant. If the machine is customarily used for a particular purpose, you could place a command like

```
CATALOG = SALES.CAT
```

in the CONFIG.DB file to tell dBASE to default to a particular catalog upon startup so that others using the system will see the preferred files when using the Assistant menus.

As mentioned earlier, a catalog is a database with a .CAT extension. The database contains the following structure:

```
Structure for database: D:SALES.CAT
Number of data records:       8
Date of last update    : 01/03/80
Field  Field Name  Type        Width    Dec
    1   PATH        Character      70
    2   FILE_NAME   Character      12
    3   ALIAS       Character       8
    4   TYPE        Character       3
    5   TITLE       Character      80
    6   CODE        Numeric         3
    7   TAG         Character       4
** Total **                      181
```

The PATH and FILE__NAME fields contain the path and filenames, the ALIAS contains an alias name, if any has been defined, the TYPE field contains the type of disk file, the TITLE field contains the optional description you gave the file when it was opened for the first time within the catalog, and the CODE field contains data used internally by dBASE. (The TAG field is not used.) As you can with all databases, you can manually add and change entries in the catalog. This capability may come in handy if you want to design an application that gives the users the option to drop into the Assistant menus, and you want to activate and change the contents of the catalogs through menu options in your application.

WARNING: If you use catalogs, keep in mind that dBASE opens the active catalog in work area 10. If you later use work area 10 for another database, you may inadvertently close the active catalog.

7: Handling
Screen Display

A widely published advertisement for one of dBASE's many competitors shows a brightly painted display with colors, highlighting, and reverse video on one side of the printed page. On the opposite side is a plain boxed menu, created for a dBASE application. In comparing the two, the ad makes the remark, "Maybe the d stands for dull." What the ad fails to mention is that the visual effects possible in the competitor's products can also be done with dBASE. But the standard, unimaginative display is generally the fastest, so it finds its way onto a lot of dBASE screens. Despite what this ad implies, however, your dBASE displays need not be dull. After some coverage of not-so-basic display challenges, this chapter will provide tips to add sparkle to your dBASE screens.

THE CHALLENGE OF MULTIPLE-PAGE SCREENS

It is wonderful but rare to design a screen in which all of the fields fit on a single screen with room to spare. What usually happens is that you have more fields than you can possibly (or reasonably) fit on a single screen: you are faced with deciding how to handle multiple screens, where the information covers several pages of screen display.

Screen Painter and the use of format files can provide assistance with this problem. (If you use format files with full-screen commands, however, the problems of effective data validation mentioned in Chapter 3 may come back to haunt you.) Screen Painter builds multiple screens with ease. To build a multiple-screen format file, enter the CREATE SCREEN *filename* command to get into Screen Painter, and lay out the fields, text, and borders that are to fit on the first screen in the usual manner. Figure 7-1 shows a complete screen created with Screen Painter. (The function key designations shown in this screen have been programmed elsewhere in the program with SET FUNCTION TO statements; it is not possible to program function keys as a part of the format file.) Note the cursor position (page number, row, and column) indicated in the status bar at the bottom of the screen.

Too often ignored, the status bar helps you keep track of where you are when using Screen Painter to design a multiple-page form. Once your first screen of fields is designed and laid out, use the PGDN key or the cursor keys to move the cursor until the status bar indicates you are at Page 02, Row 01, Column 00. The "Page 02" designation within the status bar indicates that you are now on the second page of a multiple-page screen. To build the second page of the form, you select and load additional fields, add more text, and lay out any desired borders. Repeat the entire process for as many pages as are needed. Once you save the screen, the resultant format file will be divided into screen pages, with the end of each page marked by the presence of a READ command. In the preceding example, the second and third screens were filled in as shown in Figure 7-2 and Figure 7-3.

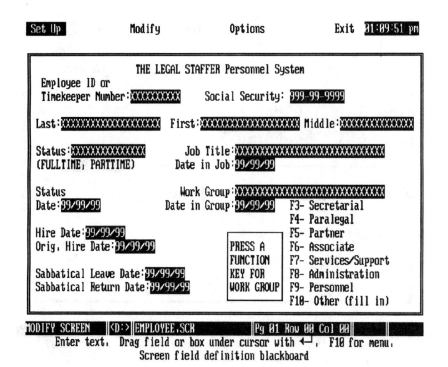

Figure 7-1.

First page of screen created with
Screen Painter

The resulting format (.FMT) file, created by Screen Painter, is
shown here:

```
@  2, 22   SAY  "THE LEGAL STAFFER Personnel System"
@  3,  3   SAY  "Employee ID or"
@  4,  3   SAY  "Timekeeper Number:"
@  4, 21   GET   EMPLOYEE->EMPNUMB
@  4, 36   SAY  "Social Security:"
@  4, 53   GET   EMPLOYEE->SOCIALSEC   PICTURE "999-99-9999"
```

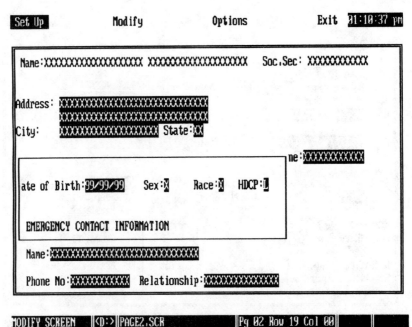

Figure 7-2.

Second page of multiple-page screen

```
a  6,  2  SAY "Last:"
a  6,  7  GET   EMPLOYEE->LASTNAME
a  6, 29  SAY "First:"
a  6, 35  GET   EMPLOYEE->FIRSTNAME
a  6, 56  SAY "Middle:"
a  6, 63  GET   EMPLOYEE->MIDDLE
a  8,  2  SAY "Status:"
a  8,  9  GET   EMPLOYEE->STATUS
a  8, 32  SAY "Job Title:"
a  8, 42  GET   EMPLOYEE->JOBTITLE
a  9,  2  SAY "(FULLTIME, PARTTIME)        Date in Job:"
a  9, 42  GET   EMPLOYEE->DATEINJOB
a 11,  2  SAY "Status                      Work Group:"
```

```
@ 11, 42    GET   EMPLOYEE->WORKGROUP
@ 12,  2    SAY  "Date:"
@ 12,  7    GET   EMPLOYEE->STATUSDATE
@ 12, 28    SAY  "Date in Group:"
@ 12, 42    GET   EMPLOYEE->DATEWORKGR
@ 12, 53    SAY  "F3- Secretarial"
@ 13, 53    SAY  "F4- Paralegal"
@ 14,  2    SAY  "Hire Date:"
@ 14, 12    GET   EMPLOYEE->HIREDATE
@ 14, 53    SAY  "F5- Partner"
@ 15,  2    SAY  "Orig. Hire Date:"
@ 15, 18    GET   EMPLOYEE->ORIGHIRED
@ 15, 41    SAY  "PRESS A      F6- Associate"
@ 16, 41    SAY  "FUNCTION     F7- Services/Support"
@ 17,  2    SAY  "Sabbatical Leave Date:"
@ 17, 24    GET   EMPLOYEE->LEAVEDATE
@ 17, 41    SAY  "KEY FOR      F8- Administration"
@ 18,  2    SAY  "Sabbatical Return Date:"
@ 18, 25    GET   EMPLOYEE->RETURNDATE
@ 18, 41    SAY  "WORK GROUP   F9- Personnel"
@ 19, 53    SAY  "F10- Other (fill in)"
@ 20, 22    SAY  "PP"
@ 14, 40    TO 19, 51
@  1,  0    TO 20, 79     DOUBLE
READ
@  2,  2    SAY  "Name:"
@  2,  7    SAY   EMPLOYEE->LASTNAME
@  2, 28    SAY   EMPLOYEE->FIRSTNAME
@  2, 51    SAY  "Soc.Sec:"
@  2, 60    SAY   EMPLOYEE->SOCIALSEC
@  5,  1    SAY  "Address:"
@  5, 10    GET   EMPLOYEE->ADDRESS1
@  6, 10    GET   EMPLOYEE->ADDRESS2
@  7,  1    SAY  "City:"
@  7, 10    GET   EMPLOYEE->CITY
@  7, 31    SAY  "State:"
@  7, 37    GET   EMPLOYEE->STATE
@  9,  1    SAY  "ZIP Code:"
@  9, 11    GET   EMPLOYEE->ZIP
@  9, 23    SAY  "Home Phone:"
@  9, 34    GET   EMPLOYEE->HOMEPHONE
@  9, 48    SAY  "Work Phone:"
@  9, 59    GET   EMPLOYEE->WORKPHONE
@ 11,  1    SAY  "Date of Birth:"
@ 11, 15    GET   EMPLOYEE->BIRTHDATE
@ 11, 27    SAY  "Sex:"
@ 11, 31    GET   EMPLOYEE->SEX
@ 11, 37    SAY  "Race:"
@ 11, 42    GET   EMPLOYEE->RACE
@ 11, 46    SAY  "HDCP:"
@ 11, 51    GET   EMPLOYEE->HANDICAP
@ 14,  3    SAY  "EMERGENCY CONTACT INFORMATION"
@ 16,  3    SAY  "Name:"
@ 16,  8    GET   EMPLOYEE->EMERNAME
@ 18,  3    SAY  "Phone No:"
@ 18, 12    GET   EMPLOYEE->EMERPHONE
```

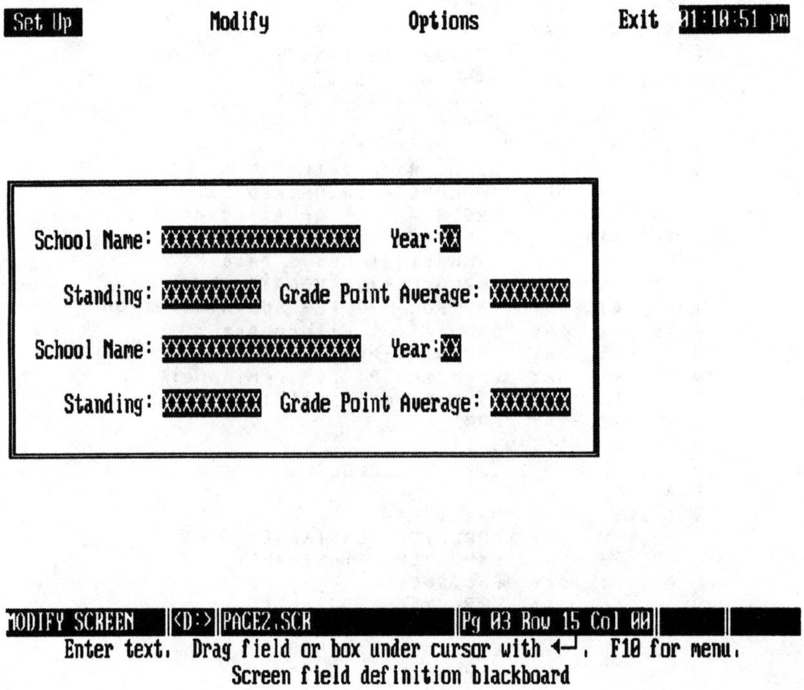

Set Up   Modify   Options   Exit 01:10:51 pm

```
School Name: XXXXXXXXXXXXXXXXXX    Year: XX

   Standing: XXXXXXXXX  Grade Point Average: XXXXXXX

School Name: XXXXXXXXXXXXXXXXXX    Year: XX

   Standing: XXXXXXXXX  Grade Point Average: XXXXXXX
```

MODIFY SCREEN   <D:> PAGE2.SCR   Pg 03 Row 15 Col 00
        Enter text. Drag field or box under cursor with ←┘. F10 for menu.
                     Screen field definition blackboard

Figure 7-3.

Third page of multiple-page screen

```
@ 18, 26  SAY "Relationship:"
@ 18, 39  GET   EMPLOYEE->ERELATION
@  9,  1  TO 15, 55
@  1,  0  TO 19, 78   DOUBLE
READ
@  3,  3  SAY "School Name:"
@  3, 16  GET   EMPLOYEE->JDNAME
@  3, 39  SAY "Year:"
@  3, 44  GET   EMPLOYEE->JDYEAR
@  5,  6  SAY "Standing:"
@  5, 16  GET   EMPLOYEE->JDSTANDING
@  5, 28  SAY "Grade Point Average:"
@  5, 49  GET   EMPLOYEE->JDGPA
```

```
@  7,  3   SAY  "School Name:"
@  7, 16   GET   EMPLOYEE->GRADNAME
@  7, 39   SAY  "Year:"
@  7, 44   GET   EMPLOYEE->GRADYEAR
@  9,  6   SAY  "Standing:"
@  9, 16   GET   EMPLOYEE->GRADSTAND
@  9, 28   SAY  "Grade Point Average:"
@  9, 49   GET   EMPLOYEE->GRADGPA
@  1,  0   TO 11, 59    DOUBLE
```

If you are going to use the commands within the format file as a part of a program, you could use commands like

```
USE EMPLOYEE INDEX NAMES
<...commands to locate record pointer here...>
SET FORMAT TO EMPLOYEE
READ
```

Assuming you have positioned the record pointer, you can edit the desired record. A great advantage here is the ability to move between screens in *either direction.* When the READ command (or other full-screen command) is executed, the first page appears. Once all fields have been filled or the PGDN key is pressed, the second screen appears. Fill these fields or press PGDN again, and the third screen appears. If the user gets to the third screen and decides that an error was made on the first screen, pressing the PGUP key twice will get back to the first screen.

Unfortunately, this back-and-forth ability exists only when using the multiple-page format files along with a full screen command. If you copy the contents of the format file into an "adder" or "editor" program so you can have greater control through data validation or the use of memory variables, you lose the ability to move in reverse with the PGUP key, although the PGDN key will continue to move you forward through the screens. One way around this limitation is to place all of the editing commands inside a DO WHILE loop, as shown in the following example:

```
*TestEdit.PRG*
USE EMPLOYEE
GO TOP
DO WHILE .T.
    STORE .F. TO NEXT
    STORE .F. TO DONE
    DO WHILE .NOT. DONE
        CLEAR
        a 5, 5 SAY "Last Name: " GET LASTNAME
        a 6, 5 SAY "First name: " GET FIRSTNAME
        * <...rest of a...SAY...GETs for this screen...>
        READ
        CLEAR
        a 5, 5 SAY "Address: " GET ADDRESS
        a 6, 5 SAY "City: " GET CITY
        * <...rest of a...SAY...GETs for this screen...>
        READ
        CLEAR
        a 5, 5 SAY "Grad School Name: " GET GRADNAME
        a 6, 5 SAY "Grad School Year: " GET GRADYEAR
        * <...rest of a...SAY...GETs for this screen...>
        a 18, 5 SAY "Done editing? Y/N:" GET DONE;
        PICTURE 'Y'
        READ
        CLEAR
    ENDDO the do-while not done
    a 5, 5 SAY "Edit next record? Y/N:" GET NEXT;
    PICTURE 'Y'
    READ
    IF .NOT. NEXT
        EXIT
    ENDIF
    SKIP
ENDDO
RETURN
```

Use of the DO WHILE loop works, but certainly not with the finesse of the format-file approach. The user still cannot go in reverse through the screens, but he or she can page repeatedly through the screens, viewing the same record, until ready to move on to another record. Once the user answers "Yes" to the "Done editing?" prompt, program control leaves the loop that allows editing of a single record, and the user can go on to edit a different record. (The foregoing simplified example uses the SKIP command to proceed to the next record in sequence; you may want to use a different approach, such as querying the user for information to execute a search.) A disadvantage of this approach is that the user is forced to enter additional keystrokes to get out of the editing mode. Still, if the user wants to validate his or her data precisely or use the memory-variables method of data entry and updating, this approach is one reasonable way to backtrack while editing through multiple screens.

It is possible to page back and forth through multiple screens using the READKEY( ) function of dBASE to test for certain keys, such as the UP-ARROW, DOWN-ARROW, PGUP, and PGDN keys. In design, this approach is similar to the previous example, but the addition of the READKEY( ) function provides the editing power of the format-file method. The code to perform such editing might resemble the following:

```
USE EMPLOYEE
GO TOP
DO WHILE .T.
     STORE .F. TO NEXT
     STORE 1 TO SCREEN
     DO WHILE SCREEN < 5
          CLEAR
          DO CASE
               CASE SCREEN = 1
               <...a...SAY...GETS for first page...>
               *no READs necessary*

               CASE SCREEN = 2
               <...a...SAY...GETS for second page...>
               *no READs necessary*

               CASE SCREEN = 3
               <...a...SAY...GETS for third page...>
               *no READs necessary*

               CASE SCREEN = 4
               <...a...SAY...GETS for fourth page...>
               *no READs necessary*
          ENDCASE
          READ
          IF(MOD(READKEY(),256)=6 .OR.;
          (MOD(READKEY(),256=4);
          .AND. SCREEN > 1
               SCREEN = SCREEN - 1
          ELSE
               SCREEN = SCREEN + 1
          ENDIF
     ENDDO
     CLEAR
     a 5, 5 SAY "Edit next record? Y/N: " GET NEXT;
     PICTURE 'Y'
     READ
     IF .NOT. NEXT
          EXIT
     ENDIF
     SKIP
ENDDO
RETURN
```

The line of code that makes most of this possible is the line that reads, in part,

IF(MOD(READKEY( ),256)=6 .OR. (MOD(READKEY( ),256=4);

The MOD and READKEY functions are used to test whether the UP-ARROW, DOWN-ARROW, PGUP, or PGDN key was pressed. Depending on which key was pressed, the CASE statements cause the next or the prior screen to be displayed. If the user is at the final screen and pressed PGDN or the DOWN-ARROW key, the value of SCREEN becomes greater than 5, and the "Edit next record?" prompt appears.

BUILDING COMBINED SCREENS FOR RELATIONAL APPLICATIONS

Screen Painter also proves useful in the rapid design of screens that access data from more than one file at a time. Because the format files built by Screen Painter contain the default alias along with the field-names, you can change the database in use as you build forms with Screen Painter. And as long as you use the proper commands to set the relations, you can use the resulting format files either from the dot prompt or within your programs. Take the sales application described in Chapter 6. In this case, you are interested in two database files: SALES.DBF and STOCK.DBF, with the structures shown:

```
Structure for database: D:sales.dbf
Number of data records:      4
Date of last update   : 09/24/87
Field  Field Name  Type      Width    Dec
    1  CUSTNO      Character     4
    2  ITEMNUMB    Character     4
    3  QUANTITY    Numeric       2
** Total **                    11
```

```
Structure for database: D:stock.dbf
Number of data records:        4
Date of last update    : 09/21/87
Field  Field Name  Type       Width    Dec
    1  ITEMNUMB    Character      4
    2  ITEMNAME    Character     20
    3  ITEMCOST    Numeric        6      2
** Total **                     31
```

You would like to create a data-entry/data-update form that allows editing of the customer number (CUSTNO), item number (ITEM-NUMB) and quantity fields, while displaying the cost (ITEMCOST) and description (ITEMNAME) fields for informational purposes. These fields are spread across two different databases, but this is no problem for Screen Painter. Here is one way this task could be approached: you start to build a new format file with CREATE SCREEN *newfile*. From the Setup menu of Screen Painter, choose Select Database File, and then choose the first database (in this case, SALES.DBF). Use the Load Fields option to load the desired fields on the Screen Painter blackboard; in this case, the fields are CUSTNO, ITEMNUMB, and QUANTITY. Then, arrange the fields and enter the desired headings on the blackboard. Figure 7-4 shows an example with these steps completed.

Once the fields for the first database are positioned on the screen, get back to the Screen Painter menu with F10, choose Select Database File from the Setup menu, and choose the other database from the list that appears (in this example, STOCK.DBF). Use the Load Fields option of the Setup menu to choose the desired related fields from the other database (in this case, ITEMNAME and ITEMCOST). You should prevent users from editing these fields by changing the display characteristics from edit (which allows data entry) to display (which allows viewing only). To do this, place the cursor in the field, select Action from the Modify menu, and change the action from Edit/GET to Display/

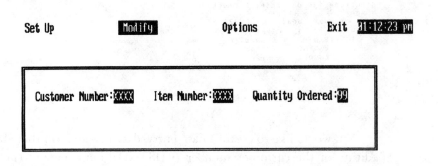

Figure 7-4.

Screen with fields from first database

SAY. Do this for each field that is to be a view-only field. Add any desired titles and borders and arrange the location of the fields as desired with the usual Screen Painter editing keys. Figure 7-5 shows the example described at this stage.

Once you save the screen file, the resultant format file contains the necessary alias names to access the related files, as shown in the listing of the format file that follows:

```
@  4,  3  SAY "Customer Number:"
@  4, 19  GET  SALES->CUSTNO
@  4, 27  SAY "Item Number:"
@  4, 39  GET  SALES->ITEMNUMB
@  4, 47  SAY "Quantity Ordered:"
@  4, 64  GET  SALES->QUANTITY
@  6,  4  SAY "Cost of Item:"
@  6, 17  SAY  STOCK->ITEMCOST
@  6, 29  SAY "Item Name:"
@  6, 39  SAY  STOCK->ITEMNAME  PICTURE
"XXXXXXXXXXXXXXXXXXX"
```

| Set Up | Modify | Options | Exit | 01:13:01 pm |

```
┌──────────────────────────────────────────────────────────┐
│                                                            │
│  Customer Number:XXXX   Item Number:XXXX   Quantity Ordered:99 │
│                                                            │
│  Cost of Item:999.99   Item Name:XXXXXXXXXXXXXXXXXX        │
│                                                            │
└──────────────────────────────────────────────────────────┘
```

| MODIFY SCREEN | <D:> NEWFILE.SCR | Pg 01 Row 06 Col 28 | | |

Enter text. Drag field or box under cursor with ↵, F10 for menu.
Screen field definition blackboard

Figure 7-5.

Screen with fields from both databases

Assuming you have established the relations beforehand through the use of the SET RELATION command or with a view file, you can use the format file to update records in the active database while viewing the data in the related databases. In this example, it is a simple enough job to do so with commands like

```
SELECT 1
USE SALES
SELECT 2
USE STOCK
INDEX ON ITEMNUMB TO STOCK
SELECT 1
SET RELATION TO ITEMNUMB INTO STOCK
SET FORMAT TO NEWFILE
CREATE VIEW NEWFILE FROM ENVIRONMENT
```

Then, every time you want to use the format file along with a full-screen EDIT or similar command, you simply use commands like

```
SET VIEW TO NEWFILE
EDIT
```

The display will be similar to that shown in Figure 7-5. As different records are accessed, fields in the active database are available for full-screen editing, while fields in the related databases are shown in a display-only mode. A drawback is that the records viewed correspond only as long as the field making the link (in this case, the ITEMNUMB field) is not edited. If the field is edited, the fields in the related records (in this case, ITEMNAME and ITEMCOST) will not change until the record is redisplayed. If you use this approach, you may want to include screen messages that warn users of this aspect of editing in such a screen.

One trap to watch out for when building format files or portions of programs using Screen Painter is that the @...SAY...GET commands are stored in a file following the natural order of data entry in the English language, which is left to right, then top to bottom. The cursor will move in the resultant format file created with Screen Painter in this order, which may not be what you had in mind. Consider a screen like the one in Figure 7-6, taken from a personnel tracking system.

When originally created with Screen Painter, the format file caused the cursor to move from the first ADDRESS field to the SEX field, to the second ADDRESS field, to the RACE field, to the HANDICAP field, to the CITY field. Obviously, this is not a natural order for data entry. Certainly the problem could be avoided in the design stage by placing the EEO data underneath the address data, but changes in placement are not always desirable. In this case, the design had to mimic a paper-based

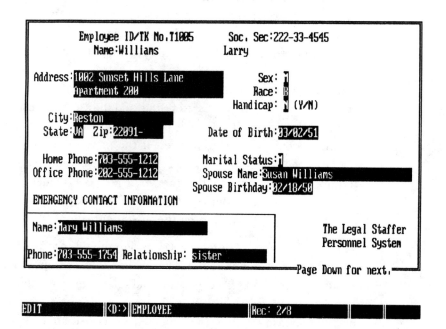

Figure 7-6.

Sample screen in personnel system

system that was already laid out in this manner. The solution is to use your word processor (or dBASE's own MODIFY COMMAND) to re-arrange the lines in the format file so that the cursor follows the desired order of data entry.

SCREEN APPEARANCE

You can enliven the appearance of your screens in three ways: in layout, in graphics, and in the use of color (if you have a color monitor). Good screen layout should be considered before any flashy graphics or sophis-ticated borders and colors come into the picture. If you are designing screens that you and only you will use, then whatever makes you happy is appropriate. However, if other people must use your screens on a day-in and day-out basis, the screens should be pleasing and effective, not busy or confusing. Here are some general tips you should follow:

- *Imitate reality whenever possible* If an application has been done for years using a manual, paper-based system and the users are comforta-ble with it, then your dBASE equivalent probably should not deviate from the system to any large degree. If the paper-based forms are badly designed to begin with, then you may have valid reason for trying to do things differently. But when possible, modeling your screens after existing manual applications will make things easier on the users, who may be terrified at the thought of computers anyway.

- *Avoid visual overload* The viewer's attention should be focused on an area of the screen by the liberal use of blank lines and open spaces. Use indentations and blank lines to hold crowding to a minimum. When building menus within a program, avoid too many menu choices; in no case should a single menu have more than ten options. If necessary, break the menu down into more than one menu by grouping common tasks (such as printing or updates) under individ-ual menus.

- *Be consistent* If names and addresses appear in the upper half of the screen when the user is adding records, then those fields should appear in the same location when the user is editing records. Likewise, menu titles and choices and alerts or error messages should appear in the same general area, no matter where a user may be in your system.

- *Always leave a way out* Escape may fall into the realm of general system implementation, but it deserves mention since we are talking about design. Few things infuriate a user as much as being backed into a corner by a computer screen that does not provide a clearly labeled option for getting out of somewhere that the user does not want to be.

CENTERING HEADINGS

On occasion you may need to center a string of text precisely relative to the left and right margins. You could count the number of characters, divide by 2, calculate the length of the text string, divide that by 2, and base the starting position on the difference between the two measurements. But, if you center material often, it is a lot less trouble to let dBASE handle the work for you. Assuming the heading text is stored to a variable named *heading* and the right margin is stored to a numeric variable named *margin,* the following command will do the trick:

```
FILL = ((MARGIN/2)-(LEN(TRIM(HEADING))/2))
@ 5, FILL SAY HEADING
```

Roughly half the time an instruction like this is used, the value of FILL will be a fractional value ending in .5, but dBASE will simply ignore the fractional value and display the heading at the closest position (for example, if the value of FILL is 30.5, the heading gets displayed at position 30). If you do this sort of centering often, it makes sense to store a routine like this as a user-defined procedure and pass the margin and heading values to the procedure as parameters. You could use something like the following within your procedure file:

```
PROCEDURE Centers
PARAMETERS ROW, MARGIN, HEADING
FILL = ((MARGIN/2)-(LEN(TRIM(HEADING))/2))
@ ROW, FILL SAY HEADING
RETURN
```

You can then call the routine from anywhere in the program with commands like the following:

```
DO CENTERS WITH 5, 80, "Dens of Iniquity / Home
Improvements"
DO CENTERS WITH 6, 20, "Job Estimating System"
DO CENTERS WITH 8, 80, "(C) 1987, Apple Blossom Software
Co."
```

VISUAL PIZAZZ

Once you have effectively laid out screens, you can emphasize various aspects of the layout through the use of graphic symbols and color. As for graphics symbols, it is a given that you can draw lines and boxes to your heart's content. The commands

```
@ <row,col> to <row,col>
```

and

```
@ <row,col> to <row,col> DOUBLE
```

result in single or double lines between the coordinates specified. If the coordinates lie on different rows and columns, dBASE draws a box from an upper left corner to a lower right corner. If you use Screen Painter to design your screens, you can obtain the same borders by choosing the Single Bar and Double Bar choices from the Options menu. However, you can also use any of the IBM extended character graphics in your screens, although not with the speed and ease of drawing lines and boxes.

To draw lines and boxes, you can use the ALT key in combination with the numeric keypad on the IBM PC (or compatible) keyboard. All ASCII characters between 176 and 223 translate to various characters for drawing lines and for filling in areas with checkered or solid patterns. The ASCII characters are shown in Figure 7-7.

Extended ASCII Characters- Graphic Set

176 ░	177 ▒	178 ▓	179 │	180 ┤
181 ╡	182 ╢	183 ╖	184 ╕	185 ╣
186 ║	187 ╗	188 ╝	189 ╜	190 ╛
191 ┐	192 └	193 ┴	194 ┬	195 ├
196 ─	197 ┼	198 ╞	199 ╟	200 ╚
201 ╔	202 ╩	203 ╦	204 ╠	205 ═
206 ╬	207 ╧	208 ╨	209 ╤	210 ╥
211 ╙	212 ╘	213 ╒	214 ╓	215 ╫
216 ╪	217 ┘	218 ┌	219 █	220 ▄
221 ▌	222 ▐	223 ▀		

Figure 7-7.

Graphic characters

You can use these characters in Screen Painter simply by holding down the ALT key and entering the three-digit number for the desired symbol and then letting up on the key. When you save the screen file, the graphic symbols will be included in the resultant format file. This is, however, an admittedly slow way to draw graphic characters. You can manually create a series of any character with the REPLICATE function, which repeats a character expression by a given number of times. For example, the command

```
@ 5, 5 SAY REPLICATE(CHR(176),60)
```

will cause the character represented by ASCII 176 (a checkered box) to be repeated 60 times across the screen beginning at row 5, column 5. This particular character is helpful in building screens that resemble the desktop in Framework, another well-known Ashton-Tate product. If you like this kind of look, you can readily fill large areas of the screen by using the REPLICATE command along with the ASCII 176 character. For example, the following portion of a program:

```
STORE 4 TO X
DO WHILE X < 12
   @ X, 10 SAY REPLICATE(CHR(176),50)
   STORE X+1 TO X
ENDDO
```

will build a shaded area using the character described from row 4, column 10 to row 11, column 60. If you don't care for shaded desktops, you can substitute another character of your choice. Even under the interpreted speed of dBASE, this kind of shading gets drawn very quickly; once drawn, you can use @...SAY statements to position text and entry fields over the shaded area as desired.

If you use the ALT key and numeric keypad method to enter graphic characters in a program file you are building with a word processor, the word processor should handle the characters without a problem. Be aware of one possible trap: if you use dBASE's own editor to build a program file with graphic characters entered in this manner, you can create the characters and save the file. However, the first time you try to edit the file, the dBASE word processor will convert the graphics characters to text characters, which are the equivalents of the ASCII value minus 128. The dBASE word processor strips the 8 bit of any ASCII value as it reads in a stored file, in the process eliminating the graphics.

Color is one of the strongest tools available at your disposal, assuming the system is running a color monitor. Even many monochrome monitors, when connected to graphic display adapters, will display a range of shading when you use the SET COLOR command to change colors. The syntax for the command is

```
SET COLOR TO <foreground/background>, <enhanced
foreground/enhanced background>, <border>
```

and the parameters are indicated by different combinations of single and double letters, as indicated in Table 7-1. The first combination controls the normal foreground and background colors. The second combination controls the foreground and background for items that normally appear in reverse video, such as the full-screen fields provided by the GET command. The final parameter controls the border color.

In addition to the indicated letters, you can also include the asterisk (*) or plus sign (+) along with the letters. The asterisk indicates blinking, while the plus sign indicates high intensity. As an example of the use of SET COLOR, the statement

```
SET COLOR TO W/B, B+/W+, BG
```

puts white letters on a blue background for normal display, bright blue on a bright white background for enhanced display, and a cyan border. dBASE also offers a useful ISCOLOR( ) function that lets you test for the

Table 7-1.

Color Codes Used by SET COLOR

Code	Resultant Color
Space	Black
B	Blue
G	Green
BG	Cyan
R	Red
BR	Magenta
GR	Brown
W	White
U	Underlined (on monochrome monitors *only*)

presence of color hardware. You can include commands like

```
IF ISCOLOR()
    SET COLOR TO W/B, I+/L+, BG
ENDIF
```

within a program to take advantage of color hardware that may be present. You can use the SET COLOR statement at numerous places in a program, either for effectiveness or just to call attention to a screen. (The latter tactic may be best reserved for title screens and menus.) As an example of plentiful use of color, consider the following program:

```
* Program..: MAINMENU.PRC
SET TALK OFF
SET STATUS OFF
DO WHILE .T.
    STORE C TO ANS
    SET COLOR TO B/W
    CLEAR
    STORE 2 TO X
```

```
DO WHILE X < 17
    @ X,9 SAY REPLICATE(chr(176),50)
    STORE X+1 TO X
ENDDO
@ 1,7 TO 16,60 DOUBLE
@ 2,20 SAY [SHADY MUFFLER REPAIR]
@ 3,20 SAY [JOBS TRACKING SYSTEM]
@ 13,10 SAY "Enter a choice, then press Return."
SET COLOR TO W/B
@  6, 20 SAY " 1. Add Records      "
@  7, 20 SAY " 2. Edit Records     "
@  8, 20 SAY " 3. Delete Records   "
@  9, 20 SAY " 4. Print Reports    "
@ 10, 20 SAY " 5. FRAMEWORK Export "
@ 11, 20 SAY " 0. EXIT This System "
SET COLOR TO * /GR, * /GR
@ 15, 10 SAY "Your option?"
@ 15, 24 GET ANS PICTURE '9' RANGE 0,5
READ
SET COLOR TO B/W
DO CASE
    CASE ANS = 1
    *<...more commands...>
```

The result is shown in Figure 7-8.

Unfortunately, the limitations of book printing make it impossible to show this screen in all of its glory — or gaudiness, depending on your taste. In this example, the multiple use of the SET COLOR statements results in a menu that mostly uses blue characters on a white background. The menu headings, however, are displayed in white characters on a blue background, and the heading "Your option" and the number entered as a menu choice are displayed in flashing black letters on a brown background.

An overall SET COLOR statement can be pleasing to most viewers who have to live with your screens day in and day out, and the above example shows that you can be creative in programming by changing colors for a specific reason. This is not to suggest a garish display of colors for no good reason. Without being outlandish, you can use different colors to highlight fields for data entry or to emphasize an error condition or an important message. If you like to use one color combination for menus, another for data entry and update fields, and still another for user messages, you can store the parameters to memory variables at the start of the program with commands like

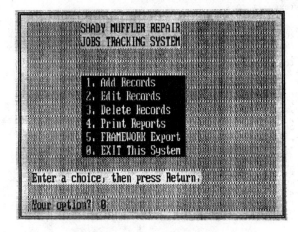

Figure 7-8.

Resultant menu display

```
MAINMENU.PRG
*main menu for sales tracking system.*
SET TALK OFF
NORMAL = "W/B, B/W"
GETTER = "W/B, GR*/BG"
ALERT = "R+*/G"
*<...more main menu commands...>
```

In your adding and editing routines, you might have code including statements like the following:

```
CLEAR
SET COLOR TO &GETTER
@ 3, 1 TO 8, 60 DOUBLE
@ 3, 10 SAY "Sales Transaction Data Entry Screen"
@ 4, 3 SAY "Customer Number:"
@ 4, 19 GET  SALES->CUSTNO
@ 4, 27 SAY "Item Number:"
@ 4, 39 GET  SALES->ITEMNUMB
```

```
ə  4, 47  SAY "Quantity Ordered:"
ə  4, 64  GET  SALES->QUANTITY
ə  6,  4  SAY "Cost of Item:"
ə  6, 17  SAY  STOCK->ITEMCOST
ə  6, 29  SAY "Item Name:"
ə  6, 39  SAY  STOCK->ITEMNAME  PICTURE
"XXXXXXXXXXXXXXXXXX"
READ
IF SALES->QUANTITY > 50
     SET COLOR TO &ALERT
     ə 9, 5 SAY "OBTAIN APPROVAL BEFORE SHIPPING THIS
ORDER!"
     WAIT
ENDIF
SET COLOR TO &NORMAL
* <...more commands...>
```

The question of the best colors to use is highly subjective. The combination of white characters on a blue background is generally accepted as pleasing to the eyes, although an increasing number of computer users prefer the "imitation paper" look of black letters on a bright white background. If you are having a hard time deciding, you can enter and run the following program, which will display every possible foreground and background color choice. Note the intentional placement of three leading spaces in the character string stored as a memory variable in the third line of the program.

```
*shows all colors*
STORE 1 TO Y
STORE "   B GBG RBRGR W" TO Lookup
BACKGROUND = 0
DO WHILE BACKGROUND < 8
   STORE 1 TO X
   FOREGROUND = 0
   DO WHILE FOREGROUND < 8
      IF FOREGROUND # BACKGROUND
         STORE (SUBSTR(Lookup,X,2)) to VAR1
         STORE (SUBSTR(Lookup,Y,2)) TO VAR2
         CLEAR
         SET COLOR TO &VAR1/&VAR2
         ə 5,5 SAY "The colors are set to " + VAR1 +;
         "/" + VAR2
         TEXT
         This is a test of the available colors which
         can be generated with the different SET COLOR
         settings.
         ENDTEXT
      ENDIF
      WAIT
      STORE 1+FOREGROUND TO FOREGROUND
      STORE X + 2 TO X
```

```
   ENDDO
   STORE 1 + BACKGROUND TO BACKGROUND
   STORE Y + 2 TO Y
ENDDO
SET COLOR TO
*end of show.prg.*
```

8: Power Printing
for
Nonprogrammers

This chapter shows how the Report Generator can be used to its maximum potential to generate reports with little or no programming. The discussion is relevant for programmers as well, however. It turns out that a surprisingly large number of programmers are not familiar with the dBASE Report Generator because they implement all their reports by writing lines of code. A random sampling of dBASE consultant/programmers revealed that about 30% of them did not use the Report Generator in their applications. They preferred instead to code entire reports, even the simple columnar ones, from the ground up. (Chapter 9 will discuss getting the most from reports generated mostly or entirely with program code.)

Granted, it is the final results that count, and reports produced from program code achieve the same results as identical reports produced with the Report Generator. And the Report Generator clearly has its limits; it is designed to do columnar reports, with one or two optional levels of breakpoints, or grouping. The page headings are pretty fixed — either you have them or you don't — and you cannot center or move the date and page number or change the design of the page number and date headings. Numeric amounts can also cause a problem because most numbers in reports are currency, and you cannot show commas with dollar signs, which irritates accounting personnel. If you use the TRANSFORM function (covered shortly) to add commas and dollar signs, you can no longer total the numbers, which irritates the accounting personnel still further.

Nevertheless, the Report Generator has its advantages. If your report clearly falls into a category that the Report Generator can handle, there is no faster way to create a report. A person who is fluent with the Report Generator menus can create a columnar report, with a half-dozen fields and two levels of grouping, within about two minutes. When writing a program, it takes about that long just to get the word processor started and enter the program headings and environmental variables. The speed advantage also appears when generating the report. The Report Generator uses compiled code, as opposed to the interpreted nature of a dBASE program. A report constructed with the Report Generator does not have to stop and interpret every line of code in a program to build a single report. The Report Generator offers the only painless way to display the contents of memo fields.

Finally, the report form (.FRM) files created by the Report Generator are compatible with most compilers. If you compile your applications, chances are you can use the reports in the compiled application with no changes. In summary, if you are among the dBASE users who have sworn off the Report Generator, take another look at using it for at least some of your applications. With a little bit of creativity, you can find ways around some of the Report Generator's limitations, either by using complex expressions within the Report Generator CONTENTS field or by using combinations of the REPORT FORM command and program code.

CREATING A REPORT

To build a report with the Report Generator, you enter either the command CREATE REPORT *filename* or the command MODIFY REPORT *filename*, where *filename* is the name for the report. Both versions of the command operate identically, causing the Report Generator menus to appear, along with the report specifications, if the report previously existed. Five menus are available within the Report Generator: Options, Groups, Columns, Locate, and Exit. You can select menu options in the usual manner by using the cursor keys to highlight a choice and pressing RETURN to select the choice.

Options Menu

The Options menu (Figure 8-1) contains entries for a page title, page width and left and right margin settings, lines per page, double spacing, and whether you want page ejects before and after printing. The plain page option is a toggle to hide or display the page headings at the top of the report; they are normally displayed by default. If you enter a page title, it can be up to four lines in length and will be centered between the left and right margins.

Groups Menu

The Groups menu (Figure 8-2) offers optional control over the two levels of grouping (also known as breakpoints) that can be present in a report. If you group on an expression, such as a fieldname or an index key, the Report Generator will place a blank line, followed by a change in heading, each time that key expression changes. By choosing Summary report only, you can print just the totals and breakpoint information for a group instead of all of the actual data. The Page eject after group

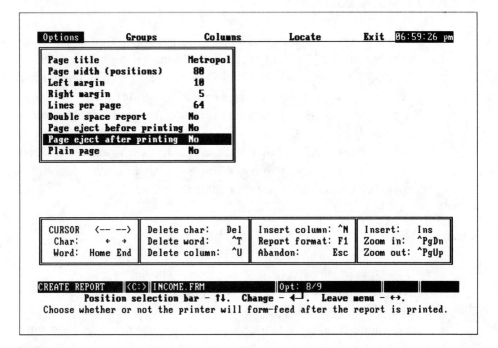

| Options | Groups | Columns | Locate | Exit | 06:59:26 pm |

Page title	Metropol
Page width (positions)	80
Left margin	10
Right margin	5
Lines per page	64
Double space report	No
Page eject before printing	No
Page eject after printing	**No**
Plain page	No

CURSOR	<-- -->	Delete char:	Del	Insert column:	^N	Insert:	Ins
Char:	← →	Delete word:	^T	Report format:	F1	Zoom in:	^PgDn
Word:	Home End	Delete column:	^U	Abandon:	Esc	Zoom out:	^PgUp

| CREATE REPORT | <C:> | INCOME.FRM | Opt: 8/9 | | |

Position selection bar - ↑↓. Change - ◄┘. Leave menu - ←→.
Choose whether or not the printer will form-feed after the report is printed.

Figure 8-1.

Options menu

option, if set to "Yes," will cause a new page to appear each time the group changes. The Sub-group on expression and Sub-group heading options are used in a manner identical to that of the Group on expression and Group heading options, except that they are used to indicate the expression that should be used for the second level of grouping. As an example, if you wanted a report grouped by states, then by cities within each state, you might enter STATE in the Group on expression option, and CITY in the Sub-group on expression option.

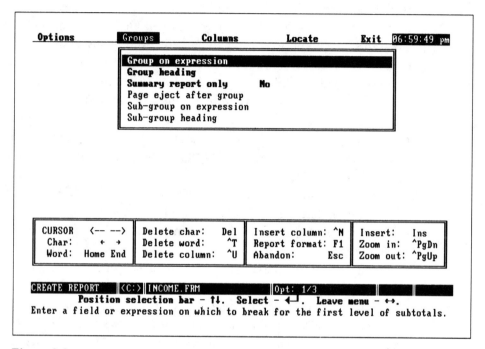

Figure 8-2.

Groups menu

Columns Menu

The Columns menu does all of the work in creating a report. Use the
Columns menu to define the data that should appear in each column of
the report. After you have pressed RETURN with the Contents option
highlighted, a cursor appears, and you can either enter an expression or
press F10 to get a list of fields from a file or view that is in use. The
Heading option lets you enter the heading that appears at the top of the
column. The Width option lets you specify a width. If you do not choose

one, the value will default to either the width of the field or expression or the width of the heading, whichever is wider. The Decimal places and Total this column options apply to numeric expressions or fields; you can choose to display a total of the values at the end of the report. In a report with multiple columns (meaning nearly all of them), you can use the PGUP or PGDN key to move from column to column. When building the report, press PGDN after entering the information for each column to display the next blank column. Existing columns that are no longer wanted can be removed by using PGUP or PGDN to get to the desired column and then pressing CTRL-U.

The Locate and Exit menus of the Report Generator are fairly simple. The Locate menu simply shows a list of existing columns in a report; by selecting any column shown in the list, you can immediately move to that column for further edits of the settings. The Exit menu, like all dBASE III PLUS Exit menus, gives you Save or Abandon choices for either saving the file or escaping without saving any changes.

You do not have to save the report and run it to get an idea of what it will look like. A visual representation appears at the bottom of the screen when the Locate or Columns menus are open. This representation (Figure 8-3) contains the headings and fields of the report, designated by X's for character fields, 9's for numeric, #'s for totaled numeric, .L. for logical, and mm/dd/yy for date. To the immediate right of the last field heading will appear dashes indicating the amount of space remaining for additional columns before the right margin is reached.

Once you have designed the report using the menu options and saved it with the Save option of the Exit menu, a file with an .FRM extension is created. To run the report, use the REPORT FORM command, which has the following syntax:

```
REPORT FORM <filename> [<scope>][WHILE<condition>][FOR <condition>]
[PLAIN][NOEJECT][HEADING<character expression>][TO PRINT][TO
FILE<filename>][SUMMARY]
```

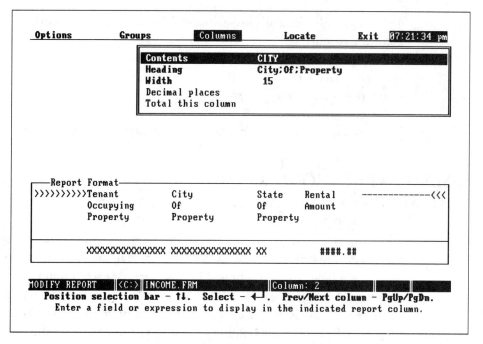

Figure 8-3.

Columns menu

Some of the options in the REPORT FORM command can also be controlled from the Options menu when you are building the report. For example, the PLAIN and NO EJECT options have the same effect as choosing the Plain page option and setting both Page eject options to off from within the Options menu of the Report Generator. Likewise, the SUMMARY option has the same effect as choosing the Summary report only option from the Groups menu. The TO FILE *filename* option routes the report to a text file, while the TO PRINT option routes the report to the printer and screen simultaneously. You can be selective by using the WHILE or FOR conditions, as detailed in Chapter

4. For example, in a database indexed by state, you can enter the following command:

```
USE MAILER INDEX STATE
FIND "CA"
REPORT FORM MAILING WHILE STATE = "CA" TO PRINT
```

The result will be a printing of all records with CA in the state field.

USING EXPRESSIONS WITHIN THE REPORT GENERATOR

Much flexibility can be coaxed out of the Report Generator by using various expressions within the CONTENTS field in the Columns menu. Typically, a field is what is entered in this entry for each column of the report, as shown in Figure 8-3. dBASE provides a hint of the flexibility possible with the Report Generator when you place the cursor in the CONTENTS field of the Columns menu and press RETURN: the message at the bottom of the screen asks for an expression to form the basis of the column's contents. You can use any valid dBASE expression here including memory variables, fieldnames, fields with alias names for related database files, and combinations of fields with or without string conversions. Combinations of character fields are routinely used. For example, the expression

```
TRIM(FIRSTNAHE)+" "+LEFT(MIDNAME,1)+". "+TRIM(LASTNAME)
```

will cause a name—say, "Thomas A. Harris"—to appear in a single column. If there is no entry in the middle initial field, you will get an unwanted space and a period. However, this problem can be avoided by including the IIF( ) function in the report contents field, a topic covered later in this chapter. Combine names like this to save space in the report; if you can safely assume that 25 characters is enough for any reasonable combination, you can set the column width within the Report Generator to 25, regardless of the actual field width. If 25 characters turn out to be too small for a given name, the Report Generator will neatly wrap part of the name onto the next line.

You can also combine various expressions of different types by converting the noncharacter portions of the expressions to characters, using string functions. As an example, you could enter an expression like

```
STR(AMOUNT) + " " + DTOC(DATESOLD)
```

to combine a numeric amount and a date field into the contents of a single column. Now normally such combinations are not necessary because you can just put the fields into separate columns of the report. But what if you want to put one data category underneath another? For example, a report laid out like the following one may be what is desired:

```
NAME: FIRSTNAME LASTNAME          HOURLY SALARY: $99.99
ADDRESS:XXXXXXXXXXXXXXXX          DATE OF BIRTH: MM/DD/YY
CITY:XXXXXXXXXXXXXX
STATE:XX   ZIP:99999

NAME: FIRSTNAME LASTNAME          HOURLY SALARY: $99.99
ADDRESS:XXXXXXXXXXXXXXX           DATE OF BIRTH: MM/DD/YY
CITY:XXXXXXXXXXXXXX
STATE:XX   ZIP:99999

NAME: FIRSTNAME LASTNAME          HOURLY SALARY: $99.99
ADDRESS:XXXXXXXXXXXXXXX           DATE OF BIRTH: MM/DD/YY
CITY:XXXXXXXXXXXXXX
STATE:XX   ZIP:99999
```

In effect, this is a *line-oriented report*. Although it uses two columns, it also puts different data fields underneath one another. While the Report Generator is designed mainly for columnar reports, it can be coaxed into handling a report like this one by the use of a semicolon between quotes to force a line feed between fields or expressions. In the above example, assuming the database contains fields titled FIRSTNAME, LAST-NAME, ADDRESS, CITY, STATE, ZIP, HOURLY__SAL, and HIRE__DATE, you could enter the following expression in the contents option for the first column:

```
"NAME: "+TRIM(FIRSTNAME)+" "+TRIM(LASTNAME)+";"+
"ADDRESS: "+TRIM(ADDRESS)+";"+TRIM(CITY)+" ";
+ "STATE:" +STATE+" "+ "ZIP:" +ZIP
```

In the CONTENTS field for the second column, you could enter an expression like this one:

```
"HOURLY SALARY: $"+LTRIM(STR(HOURLY_SAL,4,2))+";"+
"DATE OF BIRTH: "+DTOC(BIRTH_DATE)
```

In these examples, the end of each line is continued on the next line because of the limitations in printing computer books, but when you are entering expressions like these into the Report Generator, you would enter the expression in one single line. The report using such expressions looks like this:

```
Name and                                Hourly Salary and
Address                                 Date of Birth


NAME: Jerry Sampson                     HOURLY SALARY: 7.50
ADDRESS: 1412 Wyldewood Way             DATE OF BIRTH: 04/23/52
Pheonix AZ 78009

NAME: Peter Williamson                  HOURLY SALARY: 6.50
ADDRESS: P.O. Box 1834                  DATE OF BIRTH: 03/18/70
Herndon VA 22070

NAME: Mary Smith                        HOURLY SALARY: 8.90
ADDRESS: 37 Mill Way                    DATE OF BIRTH: 06/17/55
Great Neck NY 12134

NAME: Nancy McNiell                     HOURLY SALARY: 7.75
ADDRESS: 345 Pinetops Highway           DATE OF BIRTH: 03/08/67
Pinetops NC 27404
```

Using the Double space report selection in the Options menu of the Report Generator adds the extra space only between records and not between lines within a record. This feature is useful when designing reports like the one above. When entering a complex expression into the CONTENTS field of the Columns menu, keep in mind that the expression is limited to a maximum of 254 characters. The spaces used around the plus signs are optional and can be deleted to trim the length of a long expression.

Using TRANSFORM( )

The TRANSFORM( ) function lets you change the format of the data displayed in your reports, which is often useful when fiscal amounts are expected to be displayed with commas. The syntax for the TRANS-FORM() function is

```
TRANSFORM(<expression>,<character expression with
picture clause>)
```

and you can use the same picture clauses used with @...SAY commands to change the format of the desired data. For example, if you include a numeric field named BALANCE in a report, you get the numbers formatted without commas when you run the report. You can resolve this problem by changing the contents of the report column to something like

```
TRANSFORM(BALANCE,"9,999.99")
```

and the result will be the same numeric value, but with commas in the appropriate places. One annoying result of the TRANSFORM() function is that the values get converted to character values, so you cannot get totals at the bottom of the columns. If you want both totals and commas, you will have to calculate the totals separately, using some variation of the SUM command outside of the report form. Like all functions, TRANSFORM() can be used in other applications besides reports; you may find it useful for writing data to the screen or for custom printing tasks within your programs.

Using the IIF() Function in Expressions

The Immediate IF function (IIF()) is also useful as a part of an expression in the Report Generator when you want to display one set of data if a condition is true and another set if a condition is false. For example, in a personnel report you may want to indicate the number of weeks' vacation that an employee gets; the company gives two weeks for employees who have fewer than five years' experience and three weeks for all others. Assuming five years is equivalent to 365 days multiplied by 5, this means that any employee who has over 1825 days with the firm

from hire date to the date on the computer's clock gets three weeks'
vacation. This is simple enough to calculate: for a given record, the
expression

```
IIF((DATE()-HIRE_DATE) < 1825, "two weeks", "three
weeks")
```

would return the character string "two weeks" if less than 1825 days
have passed since the date of hire, and "three weeks" if 1825 or more
days have passed since the date of hire. You could place the entire
expression shown above into the CONTENTS field for a column of the
report, and the report would display the appropriate number of weeks
of vacation for that employee. As another example of the use of the IIF( )
function, recall that a combination of fields in a report expression had
the problem of an unwanted period if no name was entered in the
middle name field. To avoid the problem, you could use an expression
like the following:

```
TRIM(FIRSTNAME) +" " + IIF(LEN(TRIM(MIDNAME)) > 0,
(LEFT(MIDNAME,1))+". ","") + TRIM(LASTNAME)
```

If the trimmed length of the MIDNAME field is zero (indicating no
middle name), a space appears rather than the middle initial and a
period.

Yet another common use for the IIF( ) function within a report is to
blank out numeric amounts that are equivalent to zero. For example, to
display hyphens in place of a zero if a numeric field called BALANCE
contains a zero, you could use the following expression in the CON-
TENTS field of the Report Generator:

```
IIF(BALANCE=0," ---",STR(BALANCE,7,2))
```

The results are shown in the sample report below.

```
Page No.     1
09/26/87
                    Credit Sales
                  Account Report
```

```
Customer Name    Cust.      High Account
                 Number   Credit Balance

Smith, A.        1001     2000.00  788.50
Johnson, L.      1002     1200.00  675.00
Jones, C.        1003      900.00  350.00
Jones, J.L.      1004     2000.00 1850.00
Allen, L.        1005     2000.00  312.00
Walker, D.       1006     1300.00 1167.00
Keemis, M.       1007     2000.00    ---
Artis, K.        1008     1200.00    ---
Smith, A.M.      1009     2000.00  220.00
Williams, E.     1010     2000.00    ---
Jones, J.        1011     2000.00  875.00
```

MULTIPLE GROUPING LEVELS
WITH REPORT FORM

Although it is true that the REPORT FORM command alone will not support more than two levels of grouping, it is a shame that many programmers consider this limitation serious enough to avoid the use of the Report Generator entirely and proceed to write dozens of lines of code to create the needed report manually. Sometimes all of this programming is necessary, but sometimes it isn't. You can avoid all of the programming and still obtain grouping past two levels by getting into the habit of combining the REPORT FORM command within code that defines additional groups. The advantages of such an approach are twofold: in addition to requiring considerably less writing of program code, the report execution time is decreased because of the faster execution of the REPORT FORM command.

First, consider the theory behind the problem of grouping beyond two levels. When you create a grouped report, you base the report output on a series of subgroups. As an example, take a listing of employees for a national manufacturing concern. The employees are in 11 manufacturing plants in 3 regions. In each plant, the employees are divided into departmental groups. The company headquarters wants to see a report divided into three groups: Central, Western, and Eastern regions. In each group, it wants a listing by plant. And within each plant, it wants to see the employees grouped by department.

In this example, the first level of grouping is by region; the second level is by plant; and the third level is by department. Groups may be visually defined by your choices of page breaks and headings, depending on how you design a program that provides a report based on multiple groups. For example, the manufacturing concern may want to see each region start on a new page, with each plant and each department within a plant identified by headings and blank spaces.

The secret of using the Report Generator as a part of the solution to this problem is to create a report that will handle the final two levels of grouping. In the example, the report is to be grouped by regional division, then by plant, then by department. The report form created with the Report Generator should group records by plant, then by department. Once the report has been created, a small amount of program code can be written to use the same report form for each higher level of grouping. In this example, a program that would use the report form once for each region would provide the three necessary levels of grouping, despite the fact that the Report Generator can technically handle only two levels of grouping.

For the example, the database structure is as follows:

```
Structure for database: D:employee.dbf
Number of data records:    318
Date of last update    : 09/25/87
Field  Field Name  Type        Width    Dec
    1   LASTNAME    Character      20
    2   FIRSTNAME   Character      20
    3   SOC_SEC     Character      11
    4   BIRTH_DATE  Date            8
    5   HOURLY_SAL  Numeric         5      2
    6   INSURED     Logical         1
    7   DIVISION    Character      10
    8   PLANT       Character      10
    9   DEPARTMENT  Character      10
** Total **                       96
```

The fields that will provide the grouping are the DIVISION, PLANT, and DEPARTMENT fields. To obtain the proper results in grouping, whether you are using a stored report form or are writing program code to do the entire job, you must have the records in the order needed for the groups. In this case, you can create an index file that will support the desired grouping levels with the command

```
INDEX ON DIVISION + PLANT + DEPARTMENT TO EMPLOYEE
```

and the resultant index file will cause the database to be ordered by division name, then by plant, and within each plant by department.

Next, use the command CREATE REPORT STAFF to create a report form, called STAFF.FRM in this example. In the Options menu (Figure 8-4), some notable options are chosen. First, both Page eject options are set to "No" because any page ejects will be under the command of the program written around the use of the report form. Second, no page title is indicated, and the Plain page option is set to "Yes." These options, too, will be under the control of the program. (You could accomplish the same result by using the PLAIN and NO EJECT options along with the REPORT FORM command when it is used within the program.)

Next, the Groups menu of the Report Generator is used to indicate the final two levels of grouping. In the Sub-group on expression option, enter the lowest level group for your report, and in the Group on expression option, enter the next higher level of grouping for your report. Figure 8-5 shows the Groups menu with the choices needed for the example filled in. If you want to see this level of group defined by page breaks, you can set the Page eject after group expression to "Yes."

Finally, choose the desired columns from the Columns menu in the normal manner. The example uses choices displayed in Figure 8-6, which will provide a listing of names, social security numbers, and hourly salaries.

Save the report with the Save option of the Exit menu, and you are ready to build the program that will use the report form and provide the additional levels of grouping. Even if programming is not your forte, this approach will require such a small amount of it that it is worth the design. The basic design behind such a program is relatively simple. You

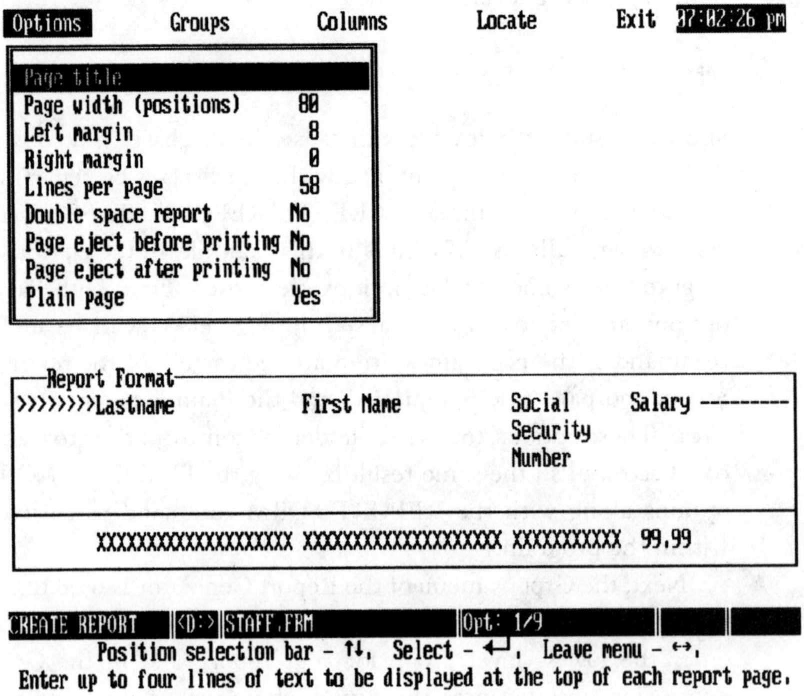

Options	Groups	Columns	Locate	Exit	07:02:26 pm

```
Page title
Page width (positions)     80
Left margin                 8
Right margin                0
Lines per page             58
Double space report        No
Page eject before printing No
Page eject after printing  No
Plain page                 Yes
```

Report Format
>>>>>>>Lastname   First Name   Social   Salary ----------
                                        Security
                                        Number

XXXXXXXXXXXXXXXXXXXX XXXXXXXXXXXXXXXXXXXX XXXXXXXXXX 99.99

CREATE REPORT	<D:> STAFF.FRM	Opt: 1/9		

Position selection bar - ↑↓, Select - ←┘, Leave menu - ↔,
Enter up to four lines of text to be displayed at the top of each report page.

Figure 8-4.

Options menu for staff report

must isolate a subset of records for the next group above the group handled by the report form. For this next higher group, you must execute a REPORT FORM command once each time that this group changes. Your program must provide any page breaks and headings for this next higher group. If there exists another group above this group, the program must handle changes in that group in a similar fashion.

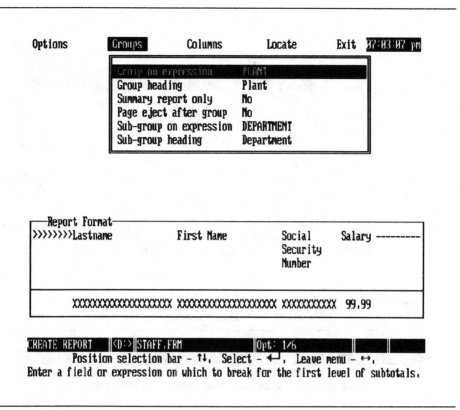

Figure 8-5.

Groups menu for staff report

The example requires a program that will execute the command REPORT FORM STAFF for each group of records comprising a regional division. For the first division, you need to print headings that include the division name and execute a REPORT FORM STAFF command that applies only to all of the records in that *division*. Once the division changes, you need to eject the page, print headings at the top of

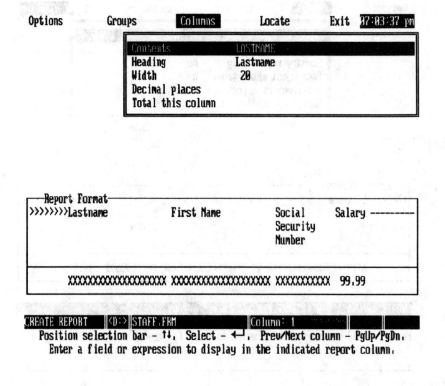

Figure 8-6.

Columns choices for staff report

a new page for the next division, and then execute another REPORT FORM STAFF command for all of the records in that division. Repeat this process for each division to accomplish the desired result. An example of a program to handle this task is shown below; from within dBASE, you can use MODIFY COMMAND to create the program.

```
*STAFF.PRG is grouped report for employees*
SET TALK OFF
USE EMPLOYEE INDEX EMPLOYEE
DO WHILE .NOT. EOF()
    STORE DIVISION TO MVAR
    SET PRINT ON
    ? "***DIVISION: " + MVAR + "***"
    SET PRINT OFF
    REPORT FORM STAFF WHILE MVAR = DIVISION PLAIN TO;
    PRINT
    EJECT
ENDDO
*end of Staff.PRG*
```

The program is a relatively simple one, considerably less complex than a program that must handle all of the reporting without the use of the REPORT FORM command. After opening the database and index file, the program stores the contents of the first grouping field (in this case, DIVISION) to a memory variable. Since the database is indexed on a combination of division, plant, and department, the first record in index order sequence will by default contain the first division. At the start of the repetitive DO WHILE loop, the division name is printed as a page heading.

The command REPORT FORM STAFF WHILE MVAR = DIVISION PLAIN TO PRINT is used to print the report for the group of records for one specific division. At the end of the execution of the REPORT FORM WHILE command, the database is positioned at the start of the next division. At that point, the new division name is stored to the variable, and the process starts over again for the next division. (Note that the PLAIN option is not necessary if you set the Plain Headings option in the Report Generator to "Yes" while you are designing the report.) When run with the example database, the program provides a result similar to that shown:

```
***DIVISION: CENTRAL   ***


        Lastname            First Name        Social       Salary
                                              Security
                                              Number

    ** Plant COLUMBUS

    * Department FINANCE
    Atkins                  Wendy             829-58-6881   7.50
```

```
* Department RECEIVING
Smith            Stephen           324-57-6371    7.75
Roberts          Cindy             425-58-6481    7.75


* Department SHIPPING
Atkins           Carol             324-53-6331    7.75
Curtis           Lynn              324-55-6351    7.75
Atkinson         Fred              324-59-6391    7.75
McNiell          Phyllis           829-52-6821    7.75
Jackson          Nancy             829-54-6841    7.75


** Plant DETROIT

* Department FINANCE
Ford             Wendy             324-59-6391    9.20

<...more records followed by page break...>


***DIVISION: EASTERN   ***


    Lastname          First Name        Social       Salary
                                        Security
                                        Number


** Plant NASHVILLE

* Department ADMIN.
Hayes            Christine         324-53-6331    6.75
Hart             Richard           324-57-6371    6.75

* Department PACKAGING
Baker            Richard           728-59-6791    6.75
Smith            Wendy             829-54-6841    6.75

* Department PRODUCTION
Williamson       Louise            829-56-6861    6.75
Clay             Frank             829-56-6861    6.75
Atkins           Gloria            829-58-6881    6.75

* Department SERVICE
Roberts          Monica            324-55-6351    6.75
Smith            Frank             324-57-6371    6.75
Roberts          Cynthia           728-57-6771    6.75

** Plant RALEIGH

* Department ADMIN.
Shaw             Michael           304-90-8845    7.50
Hayes            Cynthia           565-30-2928    7.50
Parker           Edward            747-35-7752    7.50

* Department PACKAGING
Atkins           Lonnie            023-11-9887    8.50
Curtis           Gloria            121-45-6754    8.50
Smith            Mary              133-44-5352    8.90
Williamson       Carol             545-33-7532    8.50

* Department PERSONNEL
Williamson       Peter             121-33-1221    6.50
Clay             Henry             208-33-4056    6.75

* Department PRODUCTION
Jones            Renee             120-34-5686    9.50
Robertson        Jean              343-37-7372    5.50
Adamson          Sharon            343-38-7382    5.50
Ford             Cynthia           444-38-7482    5.50
Duran            Bruce             444-39-7492    5.50
```

```
* Department RECEIVING
  Jackson            Jennifer              210-44-5402    7.75
  McNiell            Nancy                 312-99-9002    7.75
  Johnston           Jeanette              565-02-3044    8.00
  Smith              Mary Jo               646-34-7642    7.75

* Department SHIPPING
  Sampson            Jerry                 111-11-1111    7.50

** Plant RICHMOND

* Department ADMIN.
  Williamson         Morris                324-55-6351    7.50

* Department PACKAGING
  Ford               Douglas               324-59-6391    8.50
  Goodwin            Wendy                 425-52-6421    8.50

  <...more records followed by page break...>


***DIVISION: WESTERN    ***


  Lastname           First Name            Social         Salary
                                           Security
                                           Number


** Plant OAKLAND

* Department PACKAGING
  Robertson          Richard               324-55-6351    8.50
  Shaw               Albert                324-57-6371    8.50

* Department RECEIVING
  Atkins             Cynthia               324-53-6231    7.75
  Curtis             Renee                 324-55-6351    7.75
  Atkinson           Edward                324-59-6391    7.75
  Williamson         Carl                  425-52-6421    7.75

  <...more records followed by page break...>
```

Before you submit to writing dozens of lines of code to create grouped reports, examine your needs to see if the Report Generator can't be coaxed into doing some or most of the work for you.

REPORTING ON RELATED DATABASES

The Report Generator can also be used to provide reports based on multiple databases. Once you use the SET RELATION command or open a view file containing a relationship with a SET VIEW command, a report form containing fields from the active and the related files can be used. When designing the report form, simply include the alias name along with the fieldname when accessing related files. You should establish the relationship before creating the desired report so that the Report Generator will be able to access those fields during the design phase.

As an example, consider the SALES and STOCK databases used in Chapter 6. Those databases have the following structures:

```
Structure for database: D:SALES.DBF
Number of data records:        4
Date of last update   : 09/24/87
Field  Field Name  Type        Width      Dec
    1   CUSTNO      Character       4
    2   ITEMNUMB    Character       4
    3   QUANTITY    Numeric         2
** Total **                        11


Structure for database: D:STOCK.DBF
Number of data records:        4
Date of last update   : 09/21/87
Field  Field Name  Type        Width      Dec
    1   ITEMNUMB    Character       4
    2   ITEMNAME    Character      20
    3   ITEMCOST    Numeric         6        2
** Total **                        31
```

If you index the STOCK database on the ITEMNUMB field, use the SALES database in work area 1, and set a relation into the STOCK database in work area 2 into the indexed field, you can include the alias names and pointers along with the fieldnames in the STOCK database. Figure 8-7 shows the Locate menu, which displays the contents of each column in a sample report that uses fields from both database files.

The first and second columns of the report contain the Customer Number (CUSTNO) and Item Number (ITEMNUMB) fields from the SALES file open in work area 1. The third column uses an alias and pointer (STOCK->) to reference the ITEMNAME field in the STOCK database, open in work area 2. The fourth column contains the QUAN-TITY field from the SALES file, while the fifth column contains the ITEMCOST field, referenced from the STOCK database. Finally, the last column contains a calculated field, derived by multiplying the contents of the QUANTITY field by the ITEMCOST field in the STOCK data-

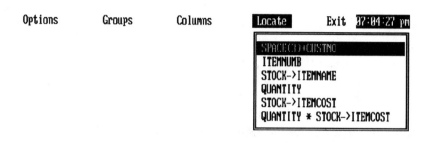

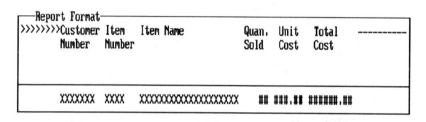

Figure 8-7.

Locate menu for relational report

base. The report will resemble the one shown below:

```
Page No.      1
09/26/87
                        Relational Report
                        for Sales & Stock
                         Database Files
```

Customer Item Number Number		Item Name	Quan. Sold	Unit Cost	Total Cost
1001	8001	Enhanced keyboard	2	171.20	342.40
1002	8004	AT power supply	55	209.90	11544.50
1001	8002	3.5 inch disk drive	57	148.50	8464.50
1003	8001	Enhanced keyboard	2	171.20	342.40
*** Total ***					
			116		20693.80

Using the SET RELATION command works well with the Report Generator for some applications — indeed, it is the only way you can obtain from the Report Generator reports that are based on more than one database. The command is ideal for one-to-one relationships such as the one illustrated here: for every record in the SALES database, there is one appropriate record in the STOCK database. If you have a one-to-many relationship, that is, one customer number and many sales against that customer number, you may or may not be able to use SET RELA-TION and a stored report. You can use the SET RELATION command only if the active database is the "many" database in the one-to-many relationship. If the active database is the "one" in the one-to-many relationship, setting up a relation with a SET RELATION command will provide a link only to the first record in the "many" database file that corresponds the record in the "one" file. Normally, you want to see all the records in the "many" file, and the only way to do that is to set up a DO WHILE loop to display the records, which gets you back to programming.

One other possible problem with programming that must be resolved arises when you need to set a relationship to more than one file out of the same active file. In the above sales example, it would be desirable to display the customer's name in the same report by relating the customer number field in the SALES file back to the same customer number in the CUSTOMERS file. But doing so would require setting a relation out of the SALES file into both the CUSTOMERS file and the STOCK file, something that dBASE does not support (at least not in this incarnation). If you must build such reports, you have two choices: you can resort to programming, in which case the topics in Chapter 9 will be of help; or you can use an external report generator designed to create complex reports from your dBASE files. A number of products on the market try to fill the gap left by the Report Generator's limitations. Some of these products are discussed in Chapter 12.

9: Power Printing
for Programmers

If you are reading this chapter, you probably both write programs in dBASE and know that the Report Generator cannot meet all of your reporting needs. Complex reporting needs often require programming. Among the more common examples of such reports are line-oriented reports with far too many fields to use the Report Generator; relational reports based on complex relationships or on one-to-many relationships; reports with unusual headers or footers; or reports that support statistical analysis.

PROGRAM DESIGNS FOR REPORTS

There are about as many ways to design a reporting program as there are ways to build data-entry screens. All of these programs will have one or more repetitive (DO WHILE) loops that print selected contents of a record for each record within a group of records. Beyond this, the commands you will need will vary, depending on the complexity of the reports, the levels of grouping, whether or not the report is relational, and numerous other factors. Many reports share a common design framework, however, which is something like this:

```
OPEN Database and Index files
FIND first record in desired group, or SET FILTER and go top
Initialize any variables for breakpoints, page and line counters
Route output to the printer
Print report headings
DO WHILE not at the end of the file or the desired group
    Print the desired fields or expressions for one record
    Update counter for page position
    IF form feed counter exceeds max lines per page
        Print footers, if any
        EJECT the paper
        Print headers, if any
    ENDIF
    SKIP to the next record in logical sequence
ENDDO
```

And there are two ways to route the data to the printer: by using SET PRINT ON and a series of ? statements, or by using SET DEVICE TO PRINT followed by a series of @...SAY statements. The first of the two following simple programs uses the first method, within the preceding design framework:

```
*LIST.PRG prints employee roster.*
CLEAR
STORE 1 TO LINES
STORE 1 TO PAGES
USE EMPLOYEE INDEX NAMES
SET PRINT ON
? REPLICATE("=",50)
? "Employee Address Roster" + SPACE(30) + DTOC(DATE())
? REPLICATE("=",50)
DO WHILE .NOT. EOF()
    ? "Name: " + TRIM(FIRSTNAME) + " " + LASTNAME
    ? "Work location: " + LOCATION
    ?? "Date hired: " + DTOC(DATEHIRED)
    ? "Home address: " + ADDRESS
    ? SPACE(15) + TRIM(CITY) + " " + STATE + " " + ZIP
    ? REPLICATE("=",30)
    STORE LINES+ 5 TO LINES
    IF LINES > 55
        ?
        ? SPACE(40) + "Page" + LTRIM(STR(PAGE))
        EJECT
        STORE 1 + PAGES TO PAGES
        STORE 1 TO LINES
        ? REPLICATE("=",50)
        ? "Employee Address Roster" + SPACE(30) + DTOC(DATE())
        ? REPLICATE("=",50)
    ENDIF
    SKIP
ENDDO
IF LINES > 1
    EJECT
ENDIF
SET PRINT OFF
RETURN
```

The use of SET PRINT ON and the ? statements get the job done, but do not offer precise control over where the data appears in the report. For more precision, you can use the second method of printing in a program, which is to use SET DEVICE TO PRINT to reroute output to the printer, combined with @ . . . SAY commands to position the data on the printed page. The following code creates a simple tabular report with custom headers and footers:

```
CLEAR
STORE 5 TO LINES
STORE 1 TO PAGES
USE EMPLOYEE INDEX NAMES
SET DEVICE TO PRINT
@ 2, 30 SAY "SALARY REPORT"
@ 3, 10 SAY REPLICATE("=",50)
@ 4, 10 SAY "Name                    Plant"
@ 4, 50 SAY "Group      Salary"
DO WHILE .NOT. EOF()
    @ LINES, 5 SAY TRIM(FIRSTNAME) + " " + LASTNAME
    @ LINES, 30 SAY LOCATION
    @ LINES, 50 SAY GROUP
    @ LINES, 60 SAY SALARY
    STORE LINES + 1 TO LINES
    IF LINES > 50
        @ LINES + 2, 40 SAY "PAGE " + TRIM(STR(PAGES))
        EJECT
        STORE PAGES + 1 TO PAGES
        STORE 5 TO LINES
        @ 2, 30 SAY "SALARY REPORT"
        @ 3, 10 SAY REPLICATE("=",50)
        @ 4, 10 SAY "Name                    Plant"
        @ 4, 50 SAY "Group      Salary"
    ENDIF
    SKIP
ENDDO
IF LINES > 5
    EJECT
ENDIF
SET DEVICE TO SCREEN
RETURN
```

Both methods can be modified to handle any complex reporting need. Multiple-file reporting, for example, is simple to implement by selecting appropriate work areas and performing a lookup to find the related data. To create a report based on a one-to-many relationship, index the "many" file on the basis of the "many" item, do a FIND or SEEK to find the first record that matches the related information in the "one" file, and then use a DO WHILE loop to display additional records while the item used for the FIND or SEEK matches the index key in the related file. The code below, taken from a system that monitors stock trades, draws such a relationship to list relatives of the person who traded the stock.

```
*RDETAIL.PRG includes relatives.*
CLEAR
STORE 0 TO X
SELECT 1
USE STOCKS INDEX STOCKS
SELECT 2
USE RELATIVE INDEX RELATIVE
SELECT 1
GO TOP
? "  Printing report... please wait..."
SET MESSAGE TO "DO NOT DISTURB... PRINTING..."
SET DEVICE TO PRINT
@ X, 5 SAY DTOC(DATE())
@ X+2, 5 SAY "DETAIL REPORT OF STOCK TRADES"
DO WHILE .NOT. EOF()
    @ X+3, 5 SAY REPLICATE("=", 40)
    @ X+4, 5 SAY "NAME: " + TRIM(FIRSTNAME)+ "     " + LASTNAME
    @ X+5, 5 SAY "Attn. of:" + TRIM(ATTNOF)
    @ X+6, 5 SAY "ADDRESS: " + TRIM(ADDR1)+ " " + ADDR2
    @ X+7, 14 SAY TRIM(CITY) + " " + STATE + " " + ZIP
    @ X+8, 5 SAY " H.PHONE: " + HOMEPHONE + " W.PHONE: " + WORKPHONE
    @ X+9, 5 SAY "EMPLOYER: "+ TRIM(EMPLOYER)+ " " ;
    + TRIM(EMPCITY) + " "+ EMPSTATE
    @ X+10, 5 SAY "TRADED: "+TRIM(DTOC(TRADED))
    @ X+10, 25 SAY "SHARES: " + TRIM(STR(SHARES))
    @ X+10, 45 SAY "BUY OR SELL:" + ACTION
    @ X+11, 5 SAY "PRICE: " + TRIM(STR(PRICE))
    @ X+12, 5 SAY "BROKER: "+ TRIM(BROKFIRM)+    "PHONE: " + BROKPHONE
    *now check for relatives.
    STORE RELCODE TO FINDER
    SELE 2
    SEEK FINDER
    IF EOF()
        @ X+14, 5 SAY "=====No relatives for this record.===="
    ELSE
        @ X+14, 15 SAY "==========Relatives=========="
        @ X+15, 2 SAY " -Relative Name-"
        @ X+15, 42 SAY "City, State, Zip"
        DO WHILE RELCODE = FINDER
            @ X + 17, 3 SAY TRIM(RELLAST) + ";    " + TRIM(RELFIRST)
            @ X + 17, 40 SAY TRIM(RELCITY)
            @ X + 17, 60 SAY TRIM(RELSTATE)
            @ X + 17, 70 SAY TRIM(RELZIP)
            STORE X + 1 to X
            SKIP
        ENDDO the relcode is finder...
    ENDIF the if not eof...
    STORE 1 TO X
    EJECT
    @ X, 5 SAY DTOC(DATE())
    @ X+2, 5 SAY "DETAIL REPORT OF STOCK TRADES"
    SELECT 1
    SKIP
ENDDO
EJECT
SET MESSAGE TO DTOC(DATE())
SET DEVICE TO SCREEN
RETURN
```

In this particular example, the program prints the report of one person's stock trade along with a list of that person's immediate relatives. The relatives' names are stored in a separate database that lists relatives, indexed by a code that matches a field in the primary database of stock trades. After a SEEK command in work area 2 finds the first record for a relative that matches the record for a stock trade in work area 1, a DO WHILE loop (in this case, DO WHILE RELCODE = FINDER) causes a listing of all relatives to be printed. In this case, handling page counts was a simple matter, because the end users wanted to see one stock trade per printed page, and no one person had so many immediate relatives that a list of them would not fit on a single page. In one-to-many relationships where one record in the controlling database may have dozens or even hundreds of records in a related file, you must add program code to monitor the page count and line count and eject pages and print new headings when appropriate.

TWO FOR THE PRICE OF ONE

Often a report is needed for both screen and printer. A program may need to display a report on the screen or optionally send the output to the printer. Anyone who has tried to design a single report to meet the two different needs of screen and printer has discovered that the tasks of designing for display and designing for print are similar, but not identical. The screen limitation of 24 lines puts a severe constraint on the amount of information that can be displayed at once; the program must prompt for each display or the data scrolls by so fast as to be useless. There is no need to stop every 24 lines when driving a printer, but page ejects must be considered. A lot of programs handle these needs with different reports for the different tasks, using menu code like this:

```
PRINANS = "S"
a 5, 5 SAY "Screen (S) or Printer (P)?" GET PRINANS
READ
IF UPPER(PRINANS) = "P"
      DO PREPORT
ELSE
      DO SREPORT
ENDIF
```

The two programs handle the appropriate reports for the screen

display or for printing. With a little planning, however, you can make
the same report work for both screen and printer by making parts of the
report program change in response to whether the report is being sent
to the screen or to the printer. You can use a variable stored in response
to a prompt to indicate whether the report is to be printed or displayed
and control the number of lines before a screen clear or a page eject
based on that variable. Another key to this trick is to use a variable for
the row in question within the @ . . . SAY statements to control the row
locations. The following program demonstrates this technique:

```
*DETAIL.PRG
CLEAR
STORE 0 TO X
STORE 1 TO PCOUNT
GO TOP
IF UPPER(PRINANS) = "P"
     ? "  Printing report... please wait..."
     SET DEVICE TO PRINT
ENDIF
@ X, 5 SAY DTOC(DATE())
@ X+2, 5 SAY "DETAIL REPORT OF STOCK TRADES"
DO WHILE .NOT. EOF()
     @ X+3, 5 SAY REPLICATE("=", 40)
     @ X+4, 5 SAY "NAME: " + TRIM(FIRSTNAME)+ "      " + LASTNAME
     @ X+5, 5 SAY "Attn. of:" + TRIM(ATTNOF)
     @ X+6, 5 SAY "ADDRESS: " + TRIM(ADDR1)+ " " + ADDR2
     @ X+7, 14 SAY TRIM(CITY) + " " + STATE + " " + ZIP
     @ X+8, 5 SAY " H.PHONE:" + HOMEPHONE + "W.PHONE:" + WORKPHONE
     @ X+9, 5 SAY "EMPLOYER: "+ TRIM(EMPLOYER)+ " " + ;
     TRIM(EMPCITY) + " "+ EMPSTATE
     @ X+10, 5 SAY "TRADED: "+TRIM(DTOC(TRADED))
     @ X+10, 25 SAY "SHARES: " + TRIM(STR(SHARES))
     @ X+10, 45 SAY "BUY OR SELL:" + ACTION
     @ X+11, 5 SAY "PRICE: " + TRIM(STR(PRICE))
     @ X+13, 10 SAY "NAME"
     @ X+13, 30 SAY "NUMBER"
     @ X+13, 50 SAY "PHONE"
     @ X+14, 5 SAY "AE:"
     @ X+14, 10 SAY AENAME
     @ X+14, 30 SAY AENUMBER
     @ X+14, 50 SAY AEPHONE
     @ X+15, 5 SAY "RR:"
     @ X+15, 10 SAY RRNAME
     @ X+15, 30 SAY RRNUMBER
     @ X+15, 50 SAY RRPHONE
     @ X+16, 5 SAY "BROKER: "+ TRIM(BROKFIRM)+    "PHONE: " + BROKPHONE
     @ X+17, 5 SAY "ADDRESS: "+TRIM(BROKADDR)+ " " + ;
     TRIM(BROKCITY)+ " " +BROKSTATE
     @ X+18, 5 SAY "BRANCH: " + TRIM(BRANCH)+    "PHONE : " + BRANPHONE
     @ X+19, 5 SAY "ADDRESS: "+TRIM(BRANADDR)+ " " + ;
     TRIM(BRANCITY)+ " " + BRANSTATE
     IF UPPER(PRINANS)= "P"
        STORE 1 + PCOUNT TO PCOUNT
        STORE X + 18 TO X
     ELSE
        STORE 1 TO X
        WAIT "PRESS A KEY FOR NEXT RECORD, ESC TO CANCEL."
        CLEAR
     ENDIF
     IF PCOUNT > 3
         STORE 1 TO X
         STORE 1 TO PCOUNT
```

```
            EJECT
            @ X, 5 SAY DTOC(DATE())
            @ X+2, 5 SAY "DETAIL REPORT OF STOCK TRADES"
        ENDIF
        SKIP
ENDDO
IF UPPER(PRINANS)= "P"
    EJECT
    SET DEVICE TO SCREEN
ENDIF
SET FILTER TO
RETURN
```

At the start of the program, a numeric variable called X is initialized with a value of zero; this variable serves as a base for positioning the rows. If the printed report was chosen, an IF...ENDIF statement causes a SET DEVICE TO PRINT command to be executed, routing output to the printer. The actual report generating code falls within a DO WHILE loop; the @...SAY lines use values based on X to display the information, which in this case occupies roughly 20 lines.

Next, an IF...ENDIF group of statements increments the value of X by 18, which lets the next repetition of the @...SAY commands begin after line 20. If the report is not being printed, the ELSE clause within the IF...ENDIF group of commands causes the screen to be cleared, and the row position variable (X) to be reset to 1. This type of decision making combined with the flexible addressing lets the program put more than 20 lines of data on a printed page while restricting itself to fewer than 20 lines of data per screen. In this example, a variable called $PCOUNT$ is used to force a page eject when necessary. $PCOUNT$ is incremented only when the report is sent to the printer; in such cases, after three repetitions of the loop (and 60 lines of data on a single page), the variable is reset to 1 and a page eject is sent to the printer.

HYBRID REPORTS

Often you can produce the report you want by combining program code and a stored report form to create a *hybrid report*. In Chapter 8 the report that used a stored report format to generate three levels of grouping was a hybrid report. If you are avoiding the Report Generator because you need more control over headers and footers, line orientation, or the display of relational data, you may save some programming time by using the REPORT FORM command along with a scope of NEXT 1 and the PLAIN and NOEJECT options. You can use a stored report with these options to generate a separate report for each record and combine the report form with your programming code. As an example, perhaps what is desired is a report like the following:

```
Ward 5 Patient Update          09/29/87
                               21:41:53

Patient Name: Keemis, M.       Diagnosed: 02/23/86
Room: 2102                     Admitted:  05/20/86


Cancer appears to be in remission; scan of 05/29/86
was negative.
```

Besides having unusual headings, the body of the report is line-oriented; the report is not an ideal candidate for the Report Generator. However, the comments field is a memo field, which the Report Generator handles well. Perhaps a hybrid report is called for, using code like the following:

```
*Doctor1.PRG*
SET TALK OFF
USE PATIENT INDEX NAMES
WAIT "Ready printer, press any key..."
SET DEVICE TO PRINT
DO WHILE .NOT. EOF()
     a 2,  5 SAY "Ward 5 Patient Update"
     a 2, 50 SAY DATE()
     a 3, 50 SAY TIME()
     a 5,  5 SAY "Patient name: " + PATIENT
     a 5, 40 SAY "Diagnosed: " + DTOC(DIAGNOSED)
     a 6,  5 SAY "Room: " + ROOM
     a 6, 40 SAY "Admitted: " + DTOC(ADMITTED)
     REPORT FORM COMMENTS NEXT 1 PLAIN TO PRINT
     EJECT
     SKIP
ENDDO
SET DEVICE TO SCREEN
RETURN
```

A hybrid can also be useful when you are doing relational reporting based on a one-to-many relationship and the active file is the "one" file. You can use the program code to display the record in the active file and use the stored report form along with a WHILE qualifier to display the "many" records in the related file. As an example, perhaps a hospital ward has a staff of three resident physicians; each physician attends to a group of patients. The hospital might want a report styled like this:

```
Physician: Roberts        Phone: 213-555-9001

    Carter, A.            03/17/85 04/05/85
    Walker, B.            05/16/86 05/20/86
    Keemis, M.            02/23/86 05/20/86
    Andrews, J.           06/13/86 06/22/86


Physician: Willi          Phone: 213-555-1232

    Jones, L.             03/02/85
    Artis, K.             04/19/86
    Mathews, A.M.         02/03/86


Physician: Smith          Phone: 213-435-9002

    Johnson, L.           03/06/85
    Bentley, C.           02/08/85
    Allen, L.             05/12/86
    Williams, E.          06/01/86
```

You could meet this design requirement with a report program like the following:

```
WAIT "Press a key to start printing..."
SET DEVICE TO PRINT
@ 2, 0
SELECT 1
USE DOCTORS
SELECT 2
USE PATIENT INDEX DRNAMES
SELECT 1
DO WHILE .NOT. EOF()
    @ ROW()+1,  5 SAY "Physician:"
    @ ROW()+1, 17 SAY DOCTOR
    @ ROW()+1, 40 SAY "Phone:"
    @ ROW()+1, 46 SAY PHONE
    PHYSNAME = DOCTOR
    SELECT 2
    SEEK PHYSNAME
    REPORT FORM PATIENTS PLAIN NOEJECT TO PRINT WHILE ;
    PHYSNAME = DOCTOR
    @ ROW()+1, 5 SAY REPLICATE("=",40)
    @ ROW()+3,0
    SELECT 1
    IF ROW() > 40
        EJECT
        @ 2, 0
    ENDIF
    SKIP
ENDDO
SET DEVICE TO SCREEN
EJECT
RETURN
```

The report gets data from multiple files with the lookup approach. After @ . . . SAY commands are used to display the appropriate doctor's name, a SEEK finds the first occurrence of that physician among the patient records. Then a REPORT FORM command with a WHILE qualifier displays the names of all patients assigned to that physician. Relative cursor addressing is used to reposition the successive printing of new physician names. When the ROW( ) function indicates that the printer is getting close to the bottom of the page (IF ROW( ) > 40), an EJECT command performs a form feed, and the printing row is repositioned at row 2.

USING SCREEN PAINTER
TO CREATE REPORTS

No, this heading is not a typographical error. You *can* use Screen Painter to create reports, although it was never designed for such a purpose. The secret of doing so lies in converting the resultant format file that Screen Painter produces into a file that directs all output to the printer instead of to the screen. A little help from a word processor (preferably an external one that supports automated search-and-replace) will make this task a quick affair.

To create such a report, first create the screen, if necessary, using Screen Painter in the usual manner. Lay out the fields as you would want to see them appear on the report. Since you are using Screen Painter, you will be limited to 24 lines of information per page during the initial design, but once the design has been finished, you can modify the code to print as many lines on a page as will fit. By all means, use multiple-page forms if they are needed to handle all the fields.

Once the screen exists, copy the resulting format (.FMT) file to a program file. From within dBASE, you can use the RUN command along with the DOS COPY command to do this, with a command like the following:

```
RUN COPY MYFILE.FMT MYFILE.PRG
```

or, using dBASE syntax, the command:

```
COPY FILE MYFILE.FMT TO MYFILE.PRG
```

Next, use a word processor to load the new file with the .PRG extension. Like all format files created with Screen Painter, this file will contain a series of @ . . .SAY statements and corresponding @ . . .GET statements for displaying headings and placing data-entry fields on the screen. The major problem with this program as it now exists is that the data is being sent to the wrong place. First, dBASE will have a hard time interpreting a GET command sent to a printer, so all GET commands will have to be replaced with SAY commands. Replace each occurrence of GET in the file with SAY. (You can save yourself this step if, during the creation of the screen, you use the Options menu in Screen Painter to change the GETs to SAYs.) And while you are in a search mode, find all occurrences of the READ command and delete these lines entirely. Finally, if there are any statements present that draw lines or borders on the screen, such as

```
@ 1, 5 TO 19, 70
@ 2, 8 TO  4, 67 DOUBLE
```

they should be deleted from the file.

If your file contains more than one occurrence of a READ command, then you are working with what was a multiple-page format file, and you have two choices. You can leave the row and column coordinate numbers for the @ . . .SAY commands as is, and the resultant report will have a page for every page that your original screen form contained. Alternatively, you can choose to renumber the coordinates starting after

the first deletion of the READ command. For example, what might
have been lines like

```
@ 19,  5 SAY "Salary:"
@ 19, 13 SAY SALARY
@ 20,  5 SAY "Date of status:"
@ 20, 21 SAY STATDATE

@  2,  5 SAY "Work location:"
@  2, 19 SAY LOCATE
@  3,  5 SAY "Supervisor name:"
@  3, 22 SAY SUPER
@  5,  5 SAY "Union Code:"
@  5, 17 SAY UNION
*<...more commands...>
```

will, with renumbering, begin to look like this:

```
@ 19,  5 SAY "Salary:"
@ 19, 13 SAY SALARY
@ 20,  5 SAY "Date of status:"
@ 20, 21 SAY STATDATE
@ 21,  5 SAY "Work location:"
@ 22, 19 SAY LOCATE
@ 23,  5 SAY "Supervisor name:"
@ 23, 22 SAY SUPER
@ 25,  5 SAY "Union Code:"
@ 25, 17 SAY UNION
*<...more commands...>
```

If you renumber, you can fit more information on each page of the
report, depending on the size of the paper. Assuming you are using
standard length paper with 66 lines, you would want to have the last line
occur at or before line 60 to leave some blank space at the bottom of the
page and to avoid any margin conflicts with laser printers, which may
not print past line 60 without ejecting the page. If you choose not to
renumber any lines, dBASE will automatically eject the page after the
24th line because the row numbers will suddenly be fewer than the
previous row numbers.

Once you have made these changes, there is the small matter of
redirecting dBASE output to the printer instead of to the screen and
building a program that will perform this redirection for every desired
record. All that is required is a few lines of additional code at the start
and end of the program. At the top of the file, insert the following lines:

```
*MyFile is description of report program.
USE <database>
SET INDEX TO <index file>
CLEAR
```

```
WAIT "Ready printer, then press a key..."
SET DEVICE TO PRINT
DO WHILE .NOT. EOF()
```

Insert the names of your database and index file where indicated in the second and third lines of the program. Then move to the bottom of the program and add the following lines:

```
SKIP
ENDDO
SET DEVICE TO SCREEN
EJECT
RETURN
```

Save the file, and you have a complete program that will print reports for each record in the database, following the general layout of the original screen form. If you want to make a "quick and dirty" conditional report, add the lines

```
SET FILTER TO <condition>
GO TOP
```

just before the SET DEVICE TO PRINT statement, and define *condition* as the condition to qualify the records for the report. This is certainly the route of least effort on the part of the programmer, but it is not usually the fastest or most efficient way to isolate a subset of records, for reasons detailed in Chapter 4.

CREATING COLUMNAR LISTINGS WITH LABEL FORM

Sometimes you need a report with data grouped across the page. You can spend an inordinate amount of time writing a program to handle this need, or you can use the LABEL FORM command as a part of your report. This command works well when the data can be put in a format like this one:

```
                                        Page 1
                                        10/06/87

              Employee Address Roster
                ABC Company


   Marcia Morse        Carol Levy          David Jackson
   4260 Park Avenue    1207 5th Street     4102 Valley Lane
   Chevy Chase, MD     Washington, DC      Falls Church, VA
```

Using the LABEL FORM command is similar to using the REPORT FORM command within a program. The trick is to create a label form using the CREATE LABEL command, and choose 3-across or 2-across as desired from the Label menu, then decide how many records you wish to have appear on each page and use the command

```
LABEL FORM <filename> NEXT <no. of recs per page> TO PRINT
```

within your program. The following program shows how this can be handled:

```
SET TALK OFF
USE ABC1
STORE 1 TO PAGES
SET DEVICE TO PRINT
DO WHILE .NOT. EOF()
      @ 3, 50 SAY "Page: " + LTRIM(STR(PAGES))
      @ 4, 50 SAY DATE()
      @ 5, 20 SAY "ABC Company Employee Address Roster"
      @ 7, 0
      LABEL FORM ABC1 NEXT 20 TO PRINT
      STORE PAGES + 1 TO PAGES
      EJECT
ENDDO
SET DEVICE TO SCREEN
```

This program will give you a report fashioned after the employee address roster shown above, with a minimum amount of programming. You will need to decide how many records can appear on each page given the size of the paper and the position of headers and footers and then adjust accordingly the number that you use along with the NEXT scope in the LABEL FORM command.

DEALING WITH LARGE TEXT FIELDS

Large fields containing text occasionally present a problem. Because you can't use the Report Generator for one reason or another, you may be writing code to display a report. Perhaps you are not using memo fields because you need to be able to search the fields; at the same time, you can't place the character field in a column in a report generated with the Report Generator because you need customized or relational reporting, which the Report Generator can't provide. In such cases, you are stuck with writing a word-wrap routine, which will look for spaces between words and break sentences at the appropriate spaces between words when they fall into an established "hot zone" at the right margin. The following example of program code may be used to handle this common task:

```
*Wrapper.PRG wraps words.*
SET TALK OFF
CLEAR
STORE 20 TO Width
STORE 12 TO PageBreak
STORE 80 TO StartPos

****************************************************************
*width is maximum width of a word.                            *
*page break indicates line count after which screen clears.*
*StartPos will affect starting position of column.           *
*Change any of these if desired. Width MUST be greater        *
*than the length of the longest word in your field.           *
*To make it print, add 'Set Device To Print', at start of     *
*program, and change the 'WAIT' statement to 'EJECT'.         *
****************************************************************
USE ILLNESS
*substitute your database with the long text fields.
DO WHILE .NOT. EOF()
    TSTRING = COMMENT
    *'comment' is a 254-char wide text field.
    *substitute your field name for 'comment.'
    LENGTH = LEN(TRIM(TSTRING))
    MIDSTRING = (StartPos-Width)/2
    DO WHILE LEN(TSTRING) > Width
        HOTZONE = Width
        *find blank closest to hot zone
        DO WHILE SUBSTR(TSTRING,HOTZONE,1) # " "
            HOTZONE = HOTZONE - 1
        ENDDO
        @ ROW()+1, MIDSTRING SAY SUBSTR(TSTRING, 1, HOTZONE - 1)
        TSTRING = SUBSTR(TSTRING, HOTZONE + 1, LENGTH - HOTZONE)
        LENGTH = LEN(TSTRING)
    ENDDO
ENDDO
```

```
        @ ROW() + 1, MIDSTRING SAY TSTRING
        @ ROW() + 1, 0 SAY " "
        SKIP
        IF ROW() > PageBreak
            WAIT "Press a key for next screen of data..."
            CLEAR
        ENDIF
ENDDO
*end of Wrapper.PRG*
```

As written, the program displays a long character field in a column on the screen. If you redirect the output with a SET DEVICE TO PRINT command at the start of the program, you can get a printed report. (Be sure to use a SET DEVICE TO SCREEN command at the end to change the output back to the screen.) The program performs a substring search, looking for a space (assumed to be a break between two words) and word wraps based on spaces that fall close to the right margin. Depending on your application, you can modify the *Width*, *PageBreak*, and *StartPos* variables to change the appearance of the column and to control how many records will appear on a single screen or page.

CONTROLLING YOUR PRINTER

dBASE differs from many software packages in that it requires no complex installation or configuration routines to work with your particular model of printer. dBASE treats the printer as a simple device capable of receiving ASCII and sends it that information. Thus, although you do not have to worry about getting a particular printer to match the output of dBASE, dBASE can't take advantage of any special effects that your printer has to offer. However, *you* can take advantage of the printer's special effects by sending escape codes to your printer, using the CHR( ) function to send the applicable code. As an example, the code for compressed print from Epson-compatible printers is the ASCII value of 27, followed by the ASCII value of 15. You can therefore switch an Epson-compatible printer into compressed mode with commands like

```
SET PRINT ON
? CHR(27) + CHR(15)
SET PRINT OFF
```

The printer will remain in this mode until you send another escape code that either clears the prior one or selects a different font or until you manually reset the printer. Consult your printer manual for a listing of your escape codes; the popular escape codes for Epson-compatible printers are listed in Table 9-1.

If you often use the escape codes to select different print styles, consider storing them as memory variables and saving those variables as a part of a configuration file. By having the escape codes stored as variables, you can use them where appropriate in your various printer routines by using a SET PRINT ON statement, followed by a ? *varname,* where "varname" is the memory variable that contains the escape code.

Table 9-1.

Epson Printer Codes

CHR(27) + CHR(4)	Italics On
CHR(27) + CHR(5)	Italics Off
CHR(27) + CHR(15)	Compressed On
CHR(27) + CHR(18)	Compressed Off
CHR(27) + CHR(45)	Emphasized On
CHR(27) + CHR(46)	Emphasized Off
CHR(27) + CHR(47)	Bold On
CHR(27) + CHR(48)	Bold Off

As an example, you can store an escape code to a variable with a command like

```
BOLD = CHR(27) + CHR(47)
```

and within your printer routines you can start printing with commands like

```
WAIT "Press a key to begin printing report..."
SET PRINT ON
? BOLD
<...more commands to print report...>
```

If you are using the Hewlett-Packard LaserJet printer or another laser compatible with the HP description language, you can use similar escape codes to select fonts, assuming they are available with your printer. The following simple menu program stores the escape codes for the HP LaserJet to a series of memory variables; then, depending on the selection, the escape codes are routed to the printer to select the desired fonts.

```
*Fonts.PRG for HP Laserjet and compatibles.*
STORE CHR(27)+"(OU"+CHR(27)+"(s 1p 10v 1s 0b 5T" to TmsRoman
STORE CHR(27)+"(OU"+CHR(27)+"(s 1p 10v Cs 3b 5T" to TmsRomanB
STORE CHR(27)+"(OU"+CHR(27)+"(s -1p 10v Os 0b 5T" to TmsRomanC
STORE CHR(27)+"(OU"+CHR(27)+"(s 1p 10v 1s 0b 5T" to TmsRomanI
STORE CHR(27)+"(8U"+CHR(27)+"(s 0p 10h 12v 1s 0b 3T" to CourierI
STORE CHR(27)+"(8U"+CHR(27)+"(s 0p 10h 12v 1s 3b 3T" to CourierB
STORE CHR(27)+"(OU"+CHR(27)+"(s 1p 10h 14.4v Os 3b 4T" to HelvBold
CLEAR
@ 3, 25 SAY [SELECT A PRINTER FONT]
@ 5, 15 SAY [ 1. Times Roman]
@ 7, 15 SAY [ 2. Times Roman Italic]
@ 9, 15 SAY [ 3. Times Roman Bold]
@ 11, 15 SAY [ 4. Times Roman Compressed]
@ 13, 15 SAY [ 5. Courier Italic]
@ 14, 15 SAY [ 6. Courier Bold]
@ 15, 15 SAY [ 7. Helvetica Bold]
@ 17, 28 SAY [0. EXIT]
STORE 0 TO SELECTNUM
@ 19, 10 SAY " YOUR CHOICE?" GET SELECTNUM PICTURE '9'
READ
SET PRINT ON
```

```
DO CASE
     CASE SELECTNUM = 1
     ? TmsRoman
     CASE SELECTNUM = 2
     ? TmsRomanI
     CASE SELECTNUM = 3
     ? TmsRomanB
     CASE SELECTNUM = 4
     ? TmsRomanC
     CASE SELECTNUM = 5
     ? CourierI
     CASE SELECTNUM = 6
     ? CourierB
     CASE SELECTNUM = 7
     ? HelvBold
ENDCASE
SET PRINT OFF
RETURN
```

If you are using an HP-compatible laser printer, you may want to
experiment with the various fonts before using them in an application.
Because dBASE assumes a standard character width for each printed
character, the proportionally spaced fonts generated by a laser printer
may or may not appear where you would like to see them. Figure 9-1

J.E. Jones Associates	Reston	VA	22094
The Software Bar, Inc.	Herndon	VA	22070
Computers R Us	Pasadena	CA	90556
Chapel Hill Life & Casualty	Carrboro	NC	27805
Sun City Transit Corporation	El Paso	TX	78809
Osborne-McGraw Hill	Berkeley	CA	94710

Figure 9-1.

Results of list with Courier Italic font

J.E. Jones Associates	Reston	VA	22094
The Software Bar, Inc.	Herndon	VA	22070
Computers R Us	Pasadena	CA	90556
Chapel Hill Life & Casualty	Carrboro	NC	27805
Sun City Transit Corporation	El Paso	TX	78809
Osborne-McGraw Hill	Berkeley	CA	94710

Figure 9-2.

Results of list with Helvetica bold
font

shows the results of a list command using the Courier Italic font of the
HP LaserJet, while Figure 9-2 shows the results of the same list
command, with the HP LaserJet set to the Helvetica Bold font. Without
the ability to incrementally space characters on the printed page, it
becomes impossible to maintain proper character spacing with the
laser's proportional fonts. The use of the proportional fonts is limited to
items like headings and cover pages.

10: Protection

Protecting your data and your application, when done effectively, is a three-part process: security, backup, and recovery are the pieces of the whole that must be taken in tandem.

IMPLEMENTING SECURITY

Security is the process of protecting the integrity of your data, of keeping out those who are not authorized to enter your system. Most data loss occurs either because of hardware malfunctions or the carelessness of someone in your work organization, and therefore care should be taken to avoid paranoia: "The high-school pirates are out to get my data," is almost certain to be a misguided belief.

The security of a dBASE application can be implemented in a number of ways, most of them requiring either a user name and password or an access level scheme or a combination of both. A user logon with a password access provides a simple yet effective way to guard against unwanted intrusions. You can store a combination of valid user IDs and passwords in a database or in memory variables that are written to disk. The structure for a security database might be similar to the following:

```
SECURE.DBF

Name      Type     Width
LOGIN     Char      20
PASSWORD  Char       8
GROUP     Char      10
ACCESS    Numeric    1
DATE      Date       8
```

In this particular case, the LOGIN field contains the name that will be used by the user to log into the system, and the PASSWORD field contains the matching password. The GROUP field is the name of a group to which the user may belong (such as ACCOUNTING or PERSONNEL) and is included as an alternative way to determine whether database access will be allowed in some cases. The ACCESS field contains a number from 1 to 9 and is used to control levels of access for various users to certain files. For example, an access level of 1 may be used to denote that a person has read-only capabilities, while an access level of 2 denotes that a person can read and write to a file. For later use in the design of the available menu options, you may find it helpful to draw a simple chart, like that shown in Figure 10-1, showing what the access levels mean.

The DATE field is used solely for record-keeping purposes to indicate when a user's security status was last changed in the database. A call to a procedure that checks the security database can be implemented early in the application, as shown in this portion of code from a main menu:

```
*MainMenu.PRG
SET TALK OFF
SET DELETED ON
SET COLOR TO W/B
CLEAR
ACCEPT "User name?" TO UNAME
? "Password? (will NOT be displayed on screen):"
SET CONSOLE OFF
ACCEPT TO UPASS
SET CONSOLE ON
SELECT 10
```

```
USE SECURE
LOCATE FOR UPPER(LOGIN) = UPPER(UNAME)
IF .NOT. FOUND()
   CLEAR
   @ 5, 5 SAY "INVALID USER!  Press any key."
   WAIT
   QUIT
ENDIF
IF UPPER(PASSWORD) <> UPPER(UPASS)
   CLEAR
   @ 5, 5 SAY "INVALID PASSWORD!  Press any key."
   WAIT
   QUIT
ENDIF
PUBLIC ACESSLEV, GROUPS, USER
STORE ACCESS TO ACCESSLEV
STORE GROUP TO GROUPS
STORE LOGIN TO USER
RETURN
*End of Secure.PGR*
```

The use of the SET CONSOLE OFF command prior to the entry of the password disables screen display so that the password is not displayed during entry.

Another way to accomplish the same result is to set the foreground and background colors of the enhanced display to the same color, as

	add?	edit?	del?	pack?
data entry personnel	yes	X	X	X
proof readers	yes	yes	X	X
supervisors	yes	yes	yes	X
dept. heads	yes	yes	yes	yes

Figure 10-1.

Access levels

shown in the following portion of code:

```
a 5, 5 SAY "ENTER PASSWORD: "
SET COLOR TO W, N/N
a 5, 21 GET UPASS
READ
SET COLOR TO W, N/W
<...more commands...>
```

The access level and group names are stored to public memory variables for later use by the system. You may also want to store the login date and time and the name of the user to some sort of audit file that tracks who logged on the sytem and when. Assuming a database file with the following structure, where LOGIN is the user ID name, USEDATE and USETIME will be the date and time the user logs on or off the system and TYPE will be a field indicating whether a user has logged on the system or off the system:

```
Audits.DBF

Name       Type        Width
LOGIN      Character    20
USEDATE    Date          8
USETIME    Character      8
TYPE       Character      3
```

You could add commands to the code that check for the valid user ID and password prior to allowing any menu selections:

```
USE AUDITS
APPEND BLANK
REPLACE LOGIN WITH USER
REPLACE USEDATE WITH DATE()
REPLACE USETIME WITH TIME()
REPLACE TYPE WITH "ON"
USE
SELECT 1
```

In the menu choice to exit the system, you could use a similar set of commands to open the audit trail database and store the same data to another record, placing an OFF entry in the TYPE field to signify that the user has logged off the system at the specified time. If a question of improper system use or security practices later arises, you can use the audit trail stored in the database to determine who was using the system at a particular time.

The number representing the user's access level, stored in a public variable called ACCESSLEV, can be used throughout the program to determine which functions are available to a given user and which are not. You have two options. The first is to display standard menus with all available choices and in the CASE statements that interpret the menu options test for the proper access levels with IF...ENDIF conditionals, as in the following example:

```
.
.
.
ACCEPT "Enter selection:" TO ANS
DO CASE
   CASE ANS = 1
   DO ADDER

   CASE ANS = 2
   IF ACCESSLEV >= 2
      DO EDITOR
   ELSE
      WAIT "IMPROPER ACCESS LEVEL!  Press any key."
   ENDIF

   CASE ANS = 3
   IF ACCESSLEV >= 3
      DO ERASER
   ELSE
      WAIT "IMPROPER ACCESS LEVEL!  Press any key."
   ENDIF
   .
   .
   .
ENDCASE
```

Although this approach is easier to implement in program code, it has the disadvantage of making it evident to users that there are options that they may not be authorized to perform. The more adventurous users will be curious about these options and are likely to try to find out how they can perform them (for example, try to find out their supervisor's access code).

You can take the second approach, which is more complex to implement in program code but less tempting to the users. This approach displays different menus for different users. At the start of your menu code, use the conditional statements to control the menu options that are displayed. As an example, if data-entry personnel are given "Add" and "Edit" capability, supervisors are given "Delete" capability, and the department head has "Pack" capability, you can create three menus offering some or all of these options, depending on whether the person who has logged on the system is a data-entry person, a supervisor, or a department head. If you take this approach, be sure to also include conditional statements in your CASE routines; just because a menu option number does not appear on a menu does not mean that some enterprising soul will not try that response just for the fun of it.

CHANGE THE NAMES TO PROTECT THE INNOCENT

With any security system, you want to do what you can to minimize the danger of unauthorized changes by the staff. One very real danger in a dBASE application that is written and runs under dBASE is that the files consist of ordinary databases, format files and reports, and a series of programs that are nothing more than text files. If a user who happens to be taking a community college course on dBASE programming gets curious, that user could wreak havoc by getting in some programming practice on your application files. One way to minimize this threat is to use unrecognizable names. Change your filenames and extensions from the usual .DBF, .NDX, and .PRG names to names like GFSP__1.XL6 and PLCL.DN8, and your commands can then access the appropriate files as long as you include the full names and extensions. dBASE doesn't really care what you call the files as long as you include extensions when you don't use the default variety. Using such names will make it hard for someone who is not familiar with your file structure to determine which files are what, but the technique is by no means foolproof. A determined person will easily get past such a safeguard. If security is a real problem in your application, you should use dBCODE, included with dBASE III PLUS, to encode your application so that the program files can't be changed.

Using dBCODE

dBCODE is a part of RunTime +, a utility included with every dBASE III PLUS license. The dBCODE program, called DBC.COM, is on the Sample Programs and Utilities Disk. To use dBCODE, first create a subdirectory and copy all of your program files for the application into that subdirectory, which will serve as the source subdirectory for dBCODE. Rename all of the .PRG files in this source subdirectory so that they have .SRC extensions.

In the same directory that contains the dBCODE program, you must also create a text file with the names of all of your programs (minus the extensions) that currently reside in the source directory. This file can be created with any word processor that will write ASCII files, or you can get into dBASE and use MODIFY COMMAND to create the file. Place the name of one program on each line of the file and end each line with ENTER. The first program (usually the main menu) should be on the first line of this file; beyond that, the order of the remaining names does not matter.

Create another subdirectory to serve as the output subdirectory; the completed, encrypted application will be stored in this subdirectory. Finally, get back to the directory that contains the dBCODE program, and enter the command

```
DBC -TEXTFILE.EXT -S\SOURCE\ -O\OUTPUT\
```

where TEXTFILE.EXT is the name of the file containing the names of the programs to be encoded, SOURCE is the name of the source subdirectory, and OUTPUT is the name of the output subdirectory.

The result will be a series of files in the output directory that are dBASE programs encoded in a way that makes them unreadable with any text editor. dBASE can still run such programs, but they cannot be modified in the normal manner. You can then copy these files into the directory containing your application and delete the old program files. (Be sure to keep a copy on disk somewhere for later updates because there is no way to reverse the effects of a dBCODE file encryption.)

If you are going to go through this much trouble to safeguard your application files, you should also seriously consider compiling the entire application, which will have the same net result of encryption; in addition, your application will run faster as a result of the compilation process. Compilers are discussed at length in Chapter 12. If you decide in favor of dBCODE instead of a compiler, you should consider using dBLINK along with dBCODE to combine the files into a single, compact, encoded program. dBCODE alone will provide security; dBLINK along with dBCODE will provide the added benefits of less disk space consumed by the program and faster program operation. The use of dBLINK is described in the Ashton-Tate documentation.

ABOUT PROTECT

PROTECT is a stand-alone program, run outside of dBASE III PLUS, that lets you control access to databases. PROTECT is designed to be used in a multi-user environment (specifically, that used on a local-area network). However, the presence of a local-area network is not required for the use of the PROTECT utility. You do need to have the network version of dBASE III PLUS installed; if you are using a single-user machine for your application and you want the benefits of the PROTECT program, simply install the dBASE Administrator (the version of dBASE normally used on networks) along with a copy of the ACCESS program on the single-user machine. Instructions regarding the installation of the dBASE Administrator and the ACCESS program can be found in the dBASE III PLUS documentation.

You can use the PROTECT program to specify authorized users, passwords, whether databases will be encrypted, and whether users can make changes to databases or only view (read) them. Of course, if you are writing program code you can choose to establish similar levels of security through your own program. But it may make little sense to reinvent the wheel; if the PROTECT program will accomplish all of the security you need, the use of the utility may save considerable coding time. Three kinds of security are provided by PROTECT: Login Access, File Access and Field Access Levels, and Database Encryption.

Login access requires users to enter names and passwords before the system can be used. The names and passwords for each user are stored in a file that is read by dBASE Administrator when a user attempts to load dBASE. Login access will require three items from the users: a group name, a user name, and a password. Each item is entered on a separate line of a login screen presented by the dBASE Administrator. If valid names and passwords are provided by the user, access to the dBASE Administrator is granted.

File access and field access levels are used to assign privilege access levels to each user, restricting changes that can be made to a database in varying degrees. (Privilege access levels are also referred to as the file privilege scheme.) Such privilege access levels are optional; if you wish, you can allow all users unrestricted access to all fields in all databases. Access to databases and the fields present in the databases are controlled by the matching of file and field access levels with user access levels. User access levels are varying levels granted to users on a sliding scale of 1 (the least restrictive) to 8 (the most restrictive). The Network Administrator controls what privileges are available at the varying user access levels.

At the database file level, privileges can control a user's ability to read (read privilege), edit (update privilege), append (extend privilege), and delete (delete privilege) records within a database. At the field level, privileges can control whether users have full access (FULL), read-only access (R/O), or no access (NONE) to particular fields within a database. When you specify the most restrictive access level for each type of privilege (read, update, extend, and delete), all levels less restrictive than the specified level will be given the privilege; all levels more restrictive than the specified level will be denied the privilege. For example, if you choose level 5 as a level to grant delete privileges, then all users with access levels of 1 through 5 will have the ability to delete records while users with access levels of 6 through 8 will not be able to delete records.

USING PROTECT

Database encryption causes each database identified by PROTECT to be encrypted. Encrypted databases cannot be read unless proper user names, group names, and passwords are supplied. PROTECT automatically creates encrypted versions of database files. Whenever you specify privileges while using the PROTECT program, the database file will be encrypted. Once a database has been encrypted, it cannot be used without proper entry of the user name, group name, and password when the dBASE Administrator is started. The PROTECT program creates a copy of the original database file; the copy is encrypted, but the original file remains in its original condition. Database files that have been encrypted with PROTECT have an extension of .CRP. To implement complete security following the use of PROTECT, delete the database file with the .DBF extension and rename the database file with the .CRP extension to a .DBF extension.

When you add a user name to the file of user names and passwords that are valid for the PROTECT program, the new user is assigned a security profile. In addition to user name and password, the security profile will also contain the name of a group to which the user is assigned. Each group will be associated with a set of database files. Once the files have been encrypted by PROTECT, a user must belong to a qualified group to access a database. Groups can access various database files through a menu selection within the PROTECT program.

Although users can belong to more than one group, to gain access to a database that belongs to a different group, a user must log out with the QUIT command and log back in as a member of the other group.

The PROTECT program stores the security profile information in a special file named DBSYSTEM.DB. The file is a modified database containing a record for each user: user name, group name, password, and assigned access level. The file is encrypted; you cannot use dBASE III PLUS to read the DBSYSTEM.DB file directly. User names, group names, passwords, and access levels should be written down and stored in a safe place so that if the DBSYSTEM.DB file is accidentally erased, someone in authority will have a copy of the information. It is also a good idea to copy the DBSYSTEM.DB file created by PROTECT to a backup disk for safekeeping.

When a user attempts to gain access to the dBASE Administrator by using the ACCESS program, the dBASE Administrator will first attempt to read a file called DBSYSTEM.DB. If no such file is present, no login sequence will be required by dBASE Administrator. However, the database encryption codes are stored within the database files, and if the DBSYSTEM.DB file is missing, users will not be able to open encrypted databases until the missing file has been restored.

Running the PROTECT Program

The PROTECT program is located on the dBASE III PLUS Administrator Disk #1. Assuming the program (PROTECT.EXE) has been copied to the appropriate hard disk directory, you can enter PROTECT from the DOS prompt to run the program. When the program starts, a Network Administrator Login Screen appears (Figure 10-2).

You must enter a password of eight characters or fewer for use by the Network Administrator. The first time you use PROTECT, it will ask that the password be entered twice to verify spelling. Thereafter, the password will be asked for just once when you start the program. An incorrect password entry will result in the program displaying an

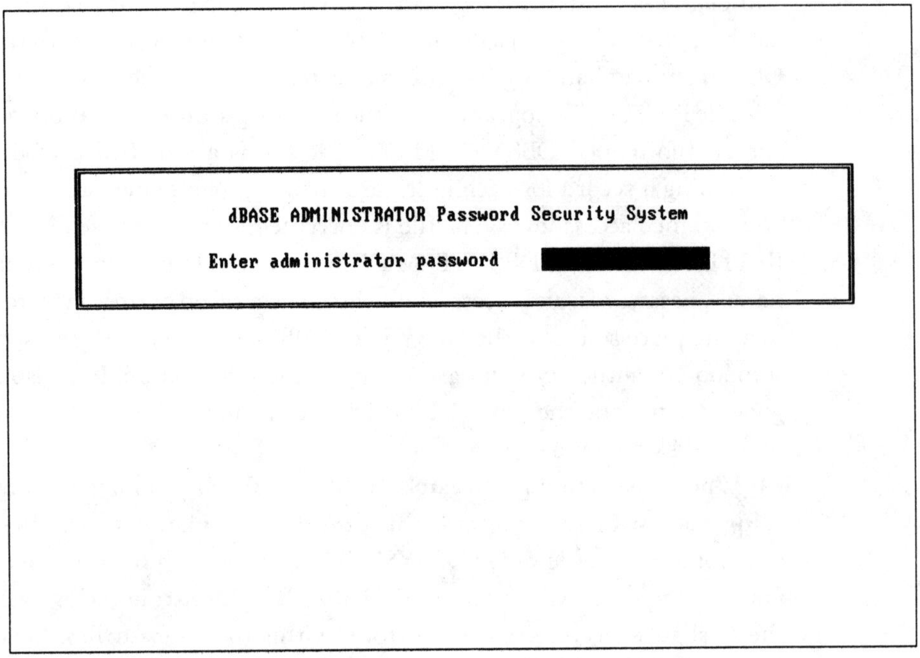

```
      dBASE ADMINISTRATOR Password Security System

   Enter administrator password        ███████████
```

Figure 10-2.

Network administrator login screen

"unauthorized login" message, and the user will be returned to the DOS
prompt.

Once the password has been entered correctly, the Protect menu
appears (Figure 10-3). The Protect menu is similar in design to other
menus used throughout dBASE III PLUS. The Menu bar offers three
choices: Users, Files, and Exit. The Users menu is used to specify user
names, passwords, group names, account names, and access levels of
network users. You can also delete existing users from a group of dBASE
III PLUS users through the Users menu.

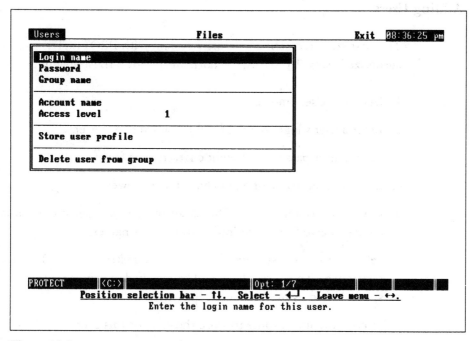

Figure 10-3.

Protect menu

The Files menu lets you identify file and field access privileges for a specific database file. Varying levels of privileges let you identify whether groups of users can read, edit (update), append to (extend), or delete records in the specified database.

The Exit menu lets you save changes made while in the User or Files menus. You can also abandon any changes made without saving the changes.

Adding Users

The first step in creating a security system with PROTECT is to add authorized users. To do this, you normally perform the following steps:

1. Open the Users menu.

2. Enter a user's login name of eight characters or fewer.

3. Enter a user password of eight characters or fewer.

4. Enter a group name of eight characters or fewer.

5. Enter an account name. (This is an option; you can use account names to give further definition to the user names.)

6. Select a user access level from 1 (least restrictive) to 8 (most restrictive). This access level will be matched to privileges that you specify when using the Files menu.

7. Select Store user profile to store the data for this user.

8. Repeat steps 1 through 7 for each additional user.

Changing and Deleting Users

To change the information on an existing user, simply enter the login name, password, and group name already established for that user. The remaining fields within the Users menu will be filled in with the existing data for that user. You can then make any desired changes and save the updated user information with the Save option of the Exit menu.

To delete a user from a specified group of users, select the Delete user from group option of the Users menu, and then save the selection with the Save option of the Exit menu.

Creating File Privileges

The Files menu of the PROTECT utility is used to assign file and field access privileges to a database file. You can assign any combination of read, update (or edit), extend (or append), and delete privileges to a specific group of users. Up to eight access levels can be specified, and you control precisely what privileges are available at each of these access levels. You may choose to use one, or two, or all of the available access levels. If you do not use the Files menu to specify privileges, all users of the dBASE Administrator can read and write to all database files.

By using the Field access privileges section of the Files menu, you can specify access to individual fields. Such access can be FULL (read/write), R/O (read-only), or NONE (no access) to a particular field. The default value is Full access; if you do not specify field privileges, all users of the network can access all database fields.

To identify file privileges by using the Files menu, perform the following steps:

1. Open the Files menu.

2. Choose the Select new file option. A menu of files will appear.

3. Highlight the desired database and press RETURN.

4. Select Group name, and enter the name of a group that will have access to the file.

5. Using a number of your choice from 1 (least restrictive) to 8 (most restrictive), specify the access level for the read, update, extend, and delete privilege levels.

6. If field privileges are also desired, select an access level and enter the desired field privileges for that access level. When you enter a number (from 1 to 8) for the access level and then select the Establish field privileges option, a list of fields will appear. Choose

the desired field privilege for each field by highlighting the field and pressing RETURN to display the available options. After all desired privileges have been set, press the LEFT- or RIGHT-ARROW key to leave the list of fields.

You can repeat step 6 for each access level desired. Doing so lets you set individual field privileges for all access levels that you have specified for groups of users. Note that when you specify field privileges as any choice other than the default value (FULL), all field privileges for more restrictive user-access levels are changed to NONE unless you specify otherwise.

7. Select the Store file privileges option from the Files menu. The privileges will be stored in memory and the Select new file option will be highlighted at the top of the menu.

8. Repeat steps 1 through 7 for each additional database for which you wish to assign privileges. You can also choose to assign different privileges for the same database to different groups. To do so, simply specify a different group name while giving the same file name when in the Files menu. Note that you can only enter privileges for up to ten databases at a time. You must save all changes with the Save option of the Exit menu if you wish to select privileges for more than ten database files.

To change the file and field privileges for an existing group, simply open the Files menu and enter the name of the database file and the name of the group. The rest of the information previously entered will then be accessible through the menu selections. Make the required changes, and choose the Store file privileges option to save any changes.

Exiting from the PROTECT Program

To save any entries while within PROTECT and continue using the PROTECT program, choose the Save option on the Exit menu. To cancel any entries and continue using PROTECT, choose the Abandon option of the Exit menu. To save your entries and exit the PROTECT program, choose the Exit option of the menu. Once you select Exit, appropriate databases will be encrypted, and user, password, and access level information will be stored in the DBSYSTEM.DB file. With large databases, the encryption process may take a few moments. When the process is complete, the DOS prompt will reappear.

Once the dBASE Administrator has been protected with the PRO-TECT program, any attempt to load dBASE with a copy of ACCESS will result in the login screen being presented to the workstation user. The user must enter a valid user name, group name, and password before the dBASE Administrator will display a dot prompt or run a program. The user name and group name are displayed during the entry process, but the password remains hidden as it is entered. If the entries match valid entries specified during the use of PROTECT, the user will be allowed access to the system. If the entries are invalid, the user will be given a maximum of three chances to enter valid information. If valid information is not entered, an error message will appear, and the user will be returned to the DOS prompt.

GENERAL SECURITY HINTS

Keep some general hints in mind when implementing security for dBASE applications, whether they are in a multi-user or network environment, or in a single-user application, and whether you use the resources of the PROTECT utility or your own security routines. A record of user names and passwords should be kept in a safe place. Users should be encouraged to memorize passwords and avoid using easily decipherable passwords like the name of a spouse. Only the system administrator and a responsible backup administrator should have the ability to add and change passwords at will. Any security system is only as strong as its weakest link. And in most large organizations, the person in charge is usually held responsible for any breach of security due to carelessness, whether the breach was the fault of that person or the fault of the programmer. dBASE III PLUS has effective tools to increase security, but it is up to you to put those tools to proper use.

BACK UP YOUR DATA

Probably the most important point that can be made about backup is that it must be done often enough to protect your users. How often is often enough? Daily is probably not too often with transaction-based systems that are disk-intensive. In addition to the regular backup, an occasional, perhaps weekly, backup should be performed, with the backup media stored off-site. You may be running that application on a micro, but with 80386 processors storing data to hard disks of over 100 megabytes in size, micros are handling tasks that would have strained the powers of the minicomputers of the 1970s. And minicomputer users have historically performed far more reliable backup routines than micro users. Two common practices of the mainframe/minicomputer environment you would do well to imitate are *rotating backups* and *hard-copy backups*. With rotating backups, you make your backups onto three sets of disks (or tapes), using different sets of backup media on different days. Making backups can be important because damaged or corrupted databases are not always immediately recognized as bad. If only one set of backup disks or tapes exists, a corrupted database may be backed up onto the backup media before anyone realizes the extent of the damage. And if the worst occurs, hard-copy backups can be invaluable for recreating lost information.

An excellent rule for determining how often backup should be performed is that if an application has accumulated more data than anyone wants to recreate, it is time to perform another backup. Remember that a given application consists of more than just database files. Index files can be easily recreated, but program files, format files, and report and label forms, cannot be so quickly recreated. It may not be necessary to back up the associated files on a regular basis, but keep a copy of these files somewhere. It sounds obvious, but it is surprising how often an omission of such a step leads to the recreation of substantial work.

Thanks to the RUN command, it isn't necessary to leave dBASE to execute an external program for backing up or restoring files. Assuming the use of the DOS BACKUP or RESTORE, you can add choices for backup or for restoring files from the menu of your choice with statements like these:

```
    .
    .
    .
CASE CHOICE = 2
CLOSE DATABASES
RUN BACKUP C:\DBFILES\*.DBF A:
RUN BACKUP C:\DBFILES\*.NDX A:/A

CASE CHOICE = 3
CLOSE DATABASES
RUN RESTORE A:\*.* C:
    .
    .
    .
```

The /A switch is a useful one because it makes the DOS BACKUP command an additive one and hence the second use of the BACKUP command does not overwrite the first files backed up onto the same disks. Such use of the BACKUP or RESTORE commands assumes that the executable files (BACKUP and RESTORE) are either available in the current directory or can be reached through a current path. If no valid path exists, you can precede the RUN BACKUP or RUN RESTORE command with the necessary DOS PATH command.

If you have disk space to spare, as an added precaution use the RUN command during the execution of a Quit option of the menu to copy the important databases to backup files on the hard disk. This step may seem redundant, but it has been known to provide a valuable safeguard if the backup process itself should fail. In one case where this approach was used, a database file was accidentally erased by the operator. The same operator had been reliably performing backups, but had been ignoring a "sector write" error on one of the backup disks. The error rendered the entire set of disks unusable for restoring the file. In this case, having the duplicate file on the hard disk was the only precaution that saved six weeks of work.

RESTORING DAMAGED FILES

Despite all the best intentions, you may see the day when you have a damaged dBASE database, no backup (or backup so old as to be nearly useless), and the less than thrilling prospect of dozens or hundreds of hours of data reentry. In the face of such prospects, it often makes sense to spend at least some time trying to recover the damaged file. You have little to lose at this point and possibly a great deal to gain.

There are two basic ways to repair a damaged database file: manually, using some type of editor to make changes that you hope will make the file useable again, and in an automated mode by using a file recovery package designed to analyze and restore damaged dBASE files. Both methods have their advantages and disadvantages. The manual method requires a knowledge of how dBASE structures a database, what types of damage occur, and what techniques can best be used to get around the damage. The automated methods of recovery are considerably less trouble but are designed for general problems and may not help with your particular type of file damage.

If you are going to take the manual approach, you should be familiar with the structure of a dBASE database. Every database consists of a file header, followed by data, followed by an end-of-file marker denoting the end of the database. The file header contains the information described in Table 10-1.

The header, although it contains significant information, makes up a small part of the file. The large part of the file is the data, which lies between the header and the end-of-file marker. The header can be thought of as a kind of map for dBASE to use in locating data precisely within a database. If the header is damaged or destroyed, dBASE will display the dreaded "Not a dBASE database" message when you attempt to open the file. And the only possible solutions are to recreate the entire database, to restore from backups, or to try to repair the damaged file. The second option is by far the most recommended one; file recovery makes sense only when the second option isn't valid because backup hasn't been done. If you are going to attempt to perform a

Table 10-1.

dBASE File Structure

Byte	Contains
01	03 hex if no memo fields; 83 hex if memo fields
02-04	Date of the last file update (byte 02 is year, byte 03 is month, byte 04 is day)
05-08	Number of records in database (byte 08 is most significant digit, byte 05 is least significant digit)
09-10	Number of bytes in header (byte 10 is most significant digit, byte 09 is least significant digit)
11-12	Length of each record (byte 12 is most significant digit, byte 11 is least significant digit)
13-32	Reserved by dBASE
33 to end of header	File specifications (fieldnames, types, widths, header and number of decimals)
DATA	Contains the data
HEX 1A (or ASCII-026)	End-of-file marker notes the end of the database file

manual file recovery, be sure to make a copy of the damaged database before proceeding. This way, if something goes wrong or you would like to try some step differently, you will at least have a file that is no worse than what you started with.

Most file damage is one of three general types: header damage, data damage, and misplaced end-of-file markers. Some damaged files contain a combination of more than one type. For example, a disk with a bad sector that happens to fall at the start of a database probably has a corrupted header and either corrupted or missing data at the beginning of the database. If you are familiar with the use of DOS DEBUG or a commercial program editor like the one found in the Norton Utilities, you can use such a program to attempt to reconstruct a damaged header. Any invalid data can be deleted; you may lose a few records, but that is better than losing the entire file. Use the same editor to search for and remove any end-of-file markers (HEX 1A or ASCII 26) that appear between records.

If file damage occurs often around your work environment (or if backups never seem to get done often enough), you may want to consider strongly having a file recovery program handy. File recovery programs are designed to perform automatically the repair process that you would manually undertake using DEBUG or a program editor. A good file recovery program will analyze the damage and make repairs based on its best guess of how to proceed. Assuming you have made a backup copy of the damaged file, you have nothing to lose by trying a file recovery program. One such offering is dSALVAGE from Comtech Publishing (Box 456, Pittsford, NY 14534). dSALVAGE is a $99 menu-driven program that analyzes the file for signs of damage in different classes and performs a file rebuild based on the type of damage. A similar package is Quickfix from Hilco Software (11266 Barnett Valley Road, Sebastopol, CA 95472). Quickfix, priced at $29, is not as complex as dSALVAGE, but it will adequately recover many damaged dBASE files. Quickfix writes a new header, resets the record counter, and resets the end-of-file marker. Programs like these, advertised in magazines like *Data Based Advisor*, are worth having around if the worst ever happens to one of your dBASE files.

11: Foreign Files

When it comes to sharing data with other programs, dBASE is multilingual. You can transfer files between dBASE III PLUS and most other popular software that is available for the PC. There are some limitations: the other programs must be able to transfer information in a format acceptable to dBASE III PLUS.

FILE FORMATS

You can transfer information between dBASE III PLUS and another program in one of seven formats: ASCII, Delimited, System Data Format (SDF), Document Interchange Format (DIF), Symbolic Link Format (SYLK), Lotus 1-2-3 worksheet format (WKS), and PFS:File format. ASCII files usually work best if you need to merge the contents of a database with a document created by a word processor. If your database contained a list of names, for example, you could save those names to a text file in ASCII format. You could then use your word processor to call up that text file and use it as part of a document.

Delimited files are files composed of records in which the fields are delimited, or separated, by some type of marker. The quotation mark is commonly used to separate the fields in a delimited file. Each record occupies an individual line, so all of the records are separated with a carriage return and line feed. Delimited files can look like this:

```
"Neuhoff","8653 Rita Drive","Bloomington","IN","47401"
"Lock","5788 Certified Way","Carson City","NV","89701"
"Cooke","568 East Welbourne","Mission","SD","57557"
```

SDF files are files created and stored on disk with a preset width for the individual fields. Most spreadsheets have the ability to "print to disk" in SDF format. dBASE can then read those files, using an SDF option of the APPEND command. The SDF files format looks like this:

```
Roarke      Roanoke       500.00
Butler      Raleigh       300.00
Randolph    Knoxville     850.00
Campbell    LaFayette     250.00
Neuhoff     Bloomington   275.00
Lakeland    Muskegon      800.00
```

The SDF format, like dBASE III, uses a fixed number of spaces for each category of information, regardless of the actual size of the particular record.

In addition to using ASCII text, many programs can transfer data using one of three common foreign file formats: SYLK, DIF, and WKS. The SYLK format, developed by Microsoft Corporation, is commonly used by Microsoft products as a means of exchanging files. Microsoft's Chart (graphics), Multiplan (spreadsheet), and File (database manager) can all work with files written in the SYLK format.

The DIF format can be used by a wide assortment of programs, including VisiCalc (spreadsheet), R:BASE 5000, and PC-File III (database managers). Internally, the DIF format resembles Delimited format files.

The WKS file format is used by Lotus 1-2-3 and by most other products that can directly read and write Lotus 1-2-3 files. The WKS files created by dBASE III PLUS can be used by current versions of Lotus 1-2-3 (version 1.1A and the newer Release 2 and Release 3) and by Symphony. Files with a .WR1 extension created by Symphony and files with a .WK1 extension created by Lotus 1-2-3 Release 2 can be read by dBASE III PLUS.

Finally, the IMPORT and EXPORT commands in dBASE III PLUS allow you to transfer databases and associated screen formats and views to and from PFS:File, PFS:Professional File, and PFS:First Choice.

Before attempting to transfer information between dBASE III and other programs, find out what format the other program can use. A list of some of the better-known programs and the types of data they can provide is listed in Table 11-1.

Table 11-1.

Software Interchange Formats

Brand	Type of Package	File Type
WordStar	Word processor	ASCII, Delimited, or SDF
MailMerge	Option of WordStar	Delimited
Microsoft Word	Word processor	ASCII, Delimited, or SDF
MultiMate	Word processor	ASCII, Delimited, or SDF
Lotus 1-2-3	Spreadsheet	WKS
PC-File III	Database manager	Delimited
R:BASE 4000	Database manager	Delimited
R:BASE 5000	Database manager	DIF or Delimited
Microsoft Multiplan	Spreadsheet	SYLK
Microsoft Chart	Graphics	SYLK

If you choose ASCII, you can use the SET ALTERNATE commands to open a text file and then perform the operations that will display the desired information on your screen. Once you turn off the SET ALTERNATE option, you can exit dBASE III and use the text file with your word processing software.

FOREIGN FILE OPTIONS
OF THE APPEND AND
COPY COMMANDS

Exchanges of data between dBASE III PLUS and other programs are accomplished using various TYPE options for the COPY and APPEND commands. Use COPY to copy data from a dBASE file to a foreign file, and use APPEND to append or transfer data from a foreign file into a dBASE database. The normal format for these commands when used with a TYPE option is

```
COPY TO (filename) (SCOPE) (FIELDS field list) TYPE (TYPE)
APPEND FROM (filename) (SCOPE) (FIELDS field list) TYPE (TYPE)
```

where (TYPE) is one of the six acceptable types: SYLK, DIF, WKS, ASCII, Delimited, and SDF. As a brief example, to copy a database named PATIENTS into a Lotus-compatible file, you could use the command

```
COPY TO 123FILE TYPE WKS
```

If you use Microsoft Multiplan's Save SYLK option to save a spreadsheet file in symbolic link format, you could enter

```
APPEND FROM MPFILE TYPE SYLK
```

When copying to and from foreign files, the COPY TO and APPEND commands can use options such as a scope (ALL, NEXT, or a record number) or a list of fields. You may want to use the FOR or WHILE condition to specify the records that will be transferred. Specifying records is necessary if the program receiving the data cannot handle the number of records in the entire database. As an example, early releases of Lotus 1-2-3 were limited to 2048 records in a database, and therefore you might not want to create a Lotus file with over 2000 records.

FORM LETTER TOOLS USING
dBASE AND ASCII TEXT

dBASE is frequently used to generate form letters: you print dozens of letters using different names and addresses, but the body of the letter either does not change at all or changes very little. Form letters can be created by exporting the data from dBASE to a word processor and using the word processor's mail merge option to generate the form letters. However, before you spend time learning to deal with yet another software package, consider doing the job entirely from within dBASE. You can use the TYPE command to display or print the text of a letter after you print the contents of various fields in desired places; and the dBASE word processor (or an external word processor accessed with the RUN command) can be used to create and edit the body text that becomes the form letter. As an example, consider the following program:

```
* Program..: APLETTER.PRG
*
SELECT 1
USE MAILER INDEX NAMES
CLEAR
STORE "Y" TO ANS
STORE SPACE(20) TO LN
```

```
STORE SPACE(20) TO FN
STORE 8 TO MARS
@ 5, 5 SAY "Last name of applicant? " GET LN
@ 6, 5 SAY "First name of applicant? " GET FN
@ 8, 5 SAY "Left Margin Setting To Print? " GET MARS
STORE LN + FN TO FINDIT
SEEK FINDIT
DO WHILE LAST + FIRST = FINDIT
      CLEAR
      @ 5, 5 SAY [Last name]
      @ 5,18 SAY LASTNAME
      @ 6, 5 SAY [First name]
      @ 6,18 SAY FIRSTNAME
      @ 7, 5 SAY [Mid. Name]
      @ 7,18 SAY MIDNAME
      @ 8,5  SAY [Address]
      @ 8,18 SAY ADDRESS1
      @ 9,18 SAY ADDRESS2
      @ 10,18 SAY CITY
      @ 10,35 SAY STATE
      @ 4,2 TO 14,50
      @ 16,0
      ACCEPT "Print form letter for this record? ;
      Y/N or C to CANCEL: " TO ANS
      IF UPPER(ANS)="C"
            RETURN
      ENDIF
      IF UPPER(ANS)="Y"
       ***Pick a letter to print.
         CLEAR
         @ 2,25 SAY [ CHOOSE A FORM LETTER ]
         RUN DIR *.TXT /W/P
         ?
         ACCEPT "     Enter name of letter: " TO FNAME
         CLEAR
         IF LEN(FNAME) > 8
               CLEAR
               @ 5,5 SAY "Filenames MUST be 8 characters or less!"
               @ 6,5 SAY "Do NOT include the TXT extension!"
               WAIT
               RETURN
         ENDIF
         STORE FNAME + ".TXT" TO FNAME
         IF .NOT. FILE('&FNAME')
               CLEAR
               WAIT "No such file exists!  Press a key to continue..."
               RETURN
         ENDIF
         ***Print the form letter
         CLEAR
         SET PRINT ON
         ***print the heading, including date, first.
         ?
         ?
         ?
         ? "                          " + SPACE(MARS)
         ?? CMONTH(DATE())+" "+LTRIM(STR(DAY(DATE())))+", "+ ;
         LTRIM(STR(YEAR(DATE())))
         ?
         ?
         ? SPACE(MARS)
```

```
            *test for gender.*
            IF UPPER(SEX) = "M"
                    ?? "Mr. " + TRIM(FIRSTNAME)
            ELSE
                    ?? "Ms. " + TRIM(FIRSTNAME)
            ENDIF
            IF LEN(TRIM(MIDNAME)) > 0
                    ?? " " + TRIM(MIDNAME)
            ENDIF
            ?? " " + TRIM(LASTNAME)

            ? SPACE(MARS)
            ?? ADDRESS1
            IF LEN(TRIM(ADDRESS2)) > 0
                    ? SPACE(MARS) + ADDRESS2
            ENDIF
            ? SPACE(MARS)
            ?? TRIM(CITY) + ", " + STATE + " "
            IF LEN(RTRIM(ZIP)) < 7
                ?? SUBSTR(ZIP,1,5)
            ELSE
                ?? ZIP
            ENDIF
            ?
            IF UPPER(SEX) = "M"
                    ? SPACE(MARS) + "Dear Mr. " + TRIM(LASTNAME) + ":"
            ELSE
                    ? SPACE(MARS) + "Dear Ms. " + TRIM(LASTNAME) + ":"
            ENDIF
            ?
            ***Now do body of letter.***
            TYPE &FNAME
            SET PRINT OFF
            EJECT
            RETURN
        ENDIF
SKIP
ENDDO
CLEAR
@ 5,5 SAY "Sorry... no remaining records on file by that name."
WAIT "     Press a key to return to menu..."
RETURN
*End of Letter.PRG*
```

The program finds an applicable record in the database and uses the DIR command to show all files. (In this case, files with .TXT extensions are used for consistency.) The user enters the name for the file to be used as the body of the form letter. After an IF .NOT. FILE command is used to test for the existence of the file, various print statements print the date and the name and address of the recipient. After a salutation is printed, the TYPE &FNAME command types the contents of the chosen form letter. Since a SET PRINT ON command is in effect, the results of the TYPE command are echoed to the printer.

This program assumes that your form letter consists of a page or less of text; an example of such a form letter appears below. Note that nothing in the program guarantees that the margin of the body text will align with the margin in the headings; you may want to add a SET MARGIN TO *numeric expression* command in the program to control the left margin.

```
        Thank you for your recent inquiry concerning the
possibility of employment with Johnson, Johnson, Johnson
and Fennerson.  While we regularly strive to fill our
ranks with candidates of exceptional qualifications like
yourself, we regret that at this time we are not looking
to fill any new positions.

We will keep your application on file for a period of not
less than one year.  If any opportunities should arise
during this time, we will give your application the
utmost consideration.

Sincerely,


Mary Doe
Recruiting Director
Johnson, Johnson, Johnson, & Fennerson
```

If you use the dBASE word processor to provide the body text for the form letters, you can also add a simple program, called from the appropriate menu option, that allows editing of a chosen form letter body text. Such a program might resemble the following:

```
* Program..: EditForm.PRG
*
CLEAR
@ 2,5 SAY [ CHOOSE A FORM LETTER ]
RUN DIR *.TXT /W/P
?
ACCEPT "Name of letter to create or edit (no extension)? " TO FNAME
CLEAR
IF LEN(FNAME) > 8
        CLEAR
        @ 5,5 SAY "Filenames MUST be 8 characters or less!"
        @ 6,5 SAY "Do NOT include the TXT extension in the name!"
```

```
        WAIT
        RETURN
ENDIF
STORE FNAME + ".TXT" TO FNAME
IF .NOT. FILE('&FNAME')
        CLEAR
        ACCEPT "This is a new letter.  Create it? Y/N:" TO MAKEIT
        IF UPPER(MAKEIT) = "N"
                RETURN
        ENDIF
ENDIF
MODIFY COMMAND &FNAME
RETURN
* End of EditForm.PRG
```

If you prefer to use a different word processor than the built-in dBASE word processor (or if you plan to compile the application with a compiler, in which case the dBASE word processor will not be available in the compiled version), you can use the RUN command in place of MODIFY COMMAND to call the external word processor (assuming that your system has sufficient memory to run the word processor and the application at the same time). Also, the file created by your word processor must be saved in ordinary ASCII format. Many native word processor files will not print with the TYPE command within dBASE unless the files have been saved as ASCII text. If your word processor lacks this capability, you can use the dBASE word processor as a substitute, provided your letters are short and you can do without features like search-and-replace and being able to move blocks of text.

This program works rather cleanly when you have variable fields making up a heading (as in the foregoing example, with a name, address, and salutation) followed by an unchanging block of text. Matters become considerably more complex, however, if you want to include selected fields as integral parts within the body of the letter. For example, in a letter requesting payment of an overdue account, you might want a past due amount or the date that a payment was due to appear within the text as a part of the letter. You could store text strings in combination with the contents of the fields to build a form letter, but you may decide that using your word processor's mail merge option with a foreign file exported from dBASE is less trouble.

Transferring Files from dBASE III PLUS
to MailMerge and Other Database Managers

To export the data in Delimited format, use the DELIMITED option of the COPY command. Delimited formats are routinely used to create files that can be used by WordStar's MailMerge option, by some word processors that can work with the MailMerge format, and by most other database managers. The normal format of the COPY command when used for transferring files with the delimited option is

```
COPY TO (filename) (SCOPE) (FIELDS<field list>) TYPE (DELIMITED)
```

When you specify the DELIMITED option, dBASE assumes an extension of .TXT for the file unless you specify otherwise. As an example, the commands

```
USE MAILER
COPY TO DATAFILE FIELDS LASTNAME, FIRSTNAME, ADDRESS,;
CITY TYPE DELIMITED
```

might create a file resembling the following format:

```
"Roarke","John","87899 Gallatin SW","Roanoke"
"Butler","Sarah","45 Macedonia Road","Raleigh"
"Randolph","Charles","894 Crigsby Road","Knoxville"
"Campbell","Chester","2716 Etoile Way","LaFayette"
"Neuhoff","Luann","8653 Rita Drive","Bloomington"
"Lakeland","Lionel","4902 Bluffside Road","Muskegon"
"Cooke","Jonathan","568 East Westbourn","Mission Ridge"
"Lyman","William","78 Rye Street","Topeka"
"Lakeland","Albert","2312 Medina Lane","Dallas"
"Greystoke","Arthur","8897 Plaines Lane","Cheyenne"
"Lock","Joseph","5788 Certified Way","Carson City"
"Jones","Edward","2411 Seedling Lane","Dallas"
"Smith","Larry","2314 Shaker Heights","Chicago"
```

A file like the foregoing example works well with most other database managers, including PC-File III, R:BASE 4000, and R:BASE 5000. You can also use this type of file in Wordstar's MailMerge option to create form letters.

When you specify the DELIMITED option without adding an optional delimiter, you get the default delimiter, which is the quotation marks around fields and the fields separated by apostrophe. As an option, you can specify the type of delimiter by using the WITH *character* along with the DELIMITED option in the command. For example, the command

```
COPY TO DATAFILE FIELDS LASTNAME, FIRSTNAME, ADDRESS,;
CITY DELIMITED WITH /
```

will produce a file with fields separated by slashes instead of the quotation mark-comma combination.

For database managers and other programs that accept data in the DIF format, use the DIF option with the COPY and APPEND commands, as shown in the following examples:

```
COPY TO STOCKS.VC1 FIELDS LASTNAME, FIRSTNAME, CITY, STATE TYPE DIF

APPEND FROM A:MAILER.DIF TYPE DIF
```

In the first example, the contents of the named fields within a database in use are copied to a file named STOCKS.VC1 in DIF format. In the second example, records will be copied from a DIF file on the "A" drive named MAILER into the database in use. Remember that when you are importing data into dBASE III PLUS with the APPEND command, the database structure must match the structure of the records within the file that contain the data.

CREATING FILES FOR USE
WITH MAIL MERGE OPTIONS

If your word processor supports some type of mail merge or merge print operation, you may prefer to create a foreign file and use that file with your word processor to generate form letters. The approach differs from word processor to word processor. Three of the more popular approaches are covered in some detail here.

WordStar

If you are using WordStar and its companion product MailMerge, create a delimited file using the default delimiters. For example, if you use commands like these

```
USE MAILING
COPY TO WSFILE FIELDS LAST, FIRST, GREETING, ADDRESS,;
CITY, STATE, ZIP, TYPE DELIMITED
```

to create the following foreign file

```
"Sampson","Jerry","Mr.","1412 Wyldewood Way","Phoenix","AZ","78009"
"Williamson","Paris","Ms.","P.O. Box 1834","Herndon","VA","22070"
"Smith","Mary","Dr.","37 Mill Way","Great Neck","NY","12134"
"McNiell","Nancy","Ms.","345 Pinetops Highway","Pinetops","NC","27404"
```

you can then proceed to create a form letter within WordStar with two lines of text at the top of the file. These lines of text will denote the name of the foreign file that will provide the data, and the names that should be assigned to the fields when in WordStar. As an example, a WordStar letter to use the above foreign file might resemble the following:

```
.df wsfile.txt
.rv last,first,greeting,address,city,state,zip

                    Johnson, Johnson,
                    Fennerson & Smith
                    303 Broadway South
                    Norfolk, VA 56008


&greeting& &first& &last&
&address&
&city&, &state& &zip&

Dear &greeting& &last&:
          In response to your letter received, we are
pleased to enclose a catalog of our latest products.  If
we can answer any questions, please do not hesitate to
call.

Sincerely,


Mike Rowe
Sales Manager
```

The fieldnames assigned the fields in WordStar are independent of those used in dBASE; WordStar uses the text that follows the .rv command to assign the names to the fields in the order they appear in the foreign file. The line of the WordStar document that starts with .df tells WordStar the name of the foreign file containing the data.

Microsoft Word

The process followed by Microsoft Word is similar to the one used by WordStar. Again, you can create a delimited file with the default delimiters. Microsoft Word, however, does not expect to see the names of the fields defined within the form letter; instead, it expects the names of the fields to appear as the very first line of text in the foreign file, with the fields separated by commas. Using the prior example, the foreign file that Microsoft Word would need to use would resemble this:

```
last,first,greeting,address,city,state,zip
"Sampson","Jerry","Mr.","1412 Wyldewood Way","Phoenix","AZ","78009"
"Williamson","Paris","Ms.","P.O. Box 1834","Herndon","VA","22070"
"Smith","Mary","Dr.","37 Nill Way","Great Neck","NY","12134"
"McNiell","Nancy","Ms.","345 Pinetops Highway","Pinetops","NC","27404"
```

A quick and painless way to create this file is to build a file that contains the heading and then use the DOS COPY command to combine the heading file with the foreign file to produce a file ready for use by Microsoft Word. This could be done entirely within dBASE with commands like these:

```
SET TALK OFF
SET ALTERNATE TO HEADS
SET ALTERNATE ON
? "Last,First,Greeting,Address,City,State,Zip"
?
CLOSE ALTERNATE
COPY TO WFILE FIELDS LAST, FIRST, GREETING, ADDRESS,;
CITY, STATE, ZIP, TYPE DELIMITED
RUN COPY HEADS.TXT + WFILE.TXT WORDFILE.TXT
```

The resultant file, called WORDFILE.TXT in this case, would resemble the foreign file shown above, with the header containing the fieldnames for use by Microsoft Word as the first line in the foreign file.

When designing the form letter within Microsoft Word, use a CTRL-left bracket keypress combination to mark the start of each field and a CRTL-right bracket combination to mark the end of each field. The CTRL-[key combination produces a symbol that resembles a double less-than sign, while pressing CTRL-] produces a symbol that resembles a double greater-than sign. Using these characters, you can create a form letter like the example here:

```
<<data wordfile.txt>>



                        Johnson, Johnson
                        Fennerson & Smith
                        3C3 Broadway South
                        Norfolk, VA 56008


<<greeting>> <<first>> <<last>>
<<address>>
<<city>>, <<state>> <<zip>>

Dear <<greeting>> <<last>>:

            In response to your letter received, we are
pleased to enclose a catalog of our latest products.  If
we can answer any questions, please do not hesitate to
call.

Sincerely,


Mike Rowe
Sales Manager
```

You can then generate the form letters using the PRINT MERGE command from within Microsoft Word.

An Export Algorithm for WordPerfect

If you want to use the Mailing Merge feature of WordPerfect, you must do things a little differently than with most other programs. WordPerfect expects to see data on individual lines, all flush left, with the ends of fields marked by a CTRL-R followed by a hard return. The end of a record is indicated by a CTRL-E followed by a return. A data file loaded within WordPerfect would resemble the following:

```
Jerry^R
Sampson^R
Mr.^R
1412 Wyldewood Way^R
Phoenix^R
AZ^R
78009^R
^E
Paris^R
Williamson^R
Ms.^R
P.O. Box 1834^R
Herndon^R
VA^R
22070^R
^E
Mary^R
Smith^R
Dr.^R
37 Mill Way^R
Great Neck^R
NY^R
12134^R
```

To generate such a file, simply write each desired field out to a line of a file, and end that line with a CTRL-R (ASCII 18). After the last field of the record, write a line containing only CTRL-E (ASCII 5). You can use the SET ALTERNATE TO and SET ALTERNATE ON commands to turn on the output to a foreign text file and write each desired line until done; then close the foreign file with the CLOSE ALTERNATE command. The following program would perform such a task:

```
*CREATES Word Perfect MAIL MERGE FILES.*
USE MAILER
STORE CHR(18) TO ENDFIELD
STORE CHR(5) TO ENDREC
SET TALK OFF
SET ALTERNATE TO PERFECT
SET ALTERNATE ON
GO TOP
DO WHILE .NOT. EOF()
    ? TRIM(FIRSTNAME) + ENDFIELD
    ? TRIM(LASTNAME) + ENDFIELD
    ? TRIM(GREETING) + ENDFIELD
    ? TRIM(ADDRESS) + ENDFIELD
```

```
        ? TRIM(CITY) + ENDFIELD
        ? STATE + ENDFIELD
        ? ZIP + ENDFIELD
        ? ENDREC
        SKIP
ENDDO
CLOSE ALTERNATE
RETURN
```

The result of such a program would be a foreign file similar to the one shown above, with each field on a separate line, terminated by the ASCII character CTRL-R, with CTRL-E on lines between the records. To use the files in a WordPerfect form letter document, first make note of the order of the fields as output by your program (the first field after an end-of-record indicator is field 1, the next is field 2, and so on). When creating the form letter in WordPerfect, use the ALT-F9 key combination to define the field numbers desired. For example, when you press ALT-F9, then enter F followed by 3 (to indicate field #3), and then press the RETURN key, WordPerfect will enter a symbol ($^\wedge$F3$^\wedge$) indicating that the contents of the third field in the sequence will appear in that position when the form letters are generated. The WordPerfect form letter might resemble the following:

```
                    Johnson, Johnson
                    Fennerson & Smith
                    303 Broadway South
                    Norfolk, VA 56008


^F3^ ^F1^ ^F2^
^F4^
^F5^, ^F6^ ^F7^

Dear ^F3^ ^F2^:

        In response to your letter received, we are
pleased to enclose a catalog of our latest products.  If
we can answer any questions, please do not hesitate to
call.

Sincerely,


Mike Rowe
Sales Manager
```

Save the letter using the usual save commands for WordPerfect. To generate the form letters in WordPerfect, first get into a blank document. Press CTRL-F9, choose Merge and enter the name of the form letter, then enter the name of the foreign file created by dBASE. WordPerfect will proceed to create the letters, which can then be printed in the usual manner.

If you work with WordPerfect and dBASE on a regular basis, you may want to examine third-party offerings that ease the problems of transfer between the two relatively incompatible packages. One such offering is a "shareware" product called WPMERGE, available from the supplier listed in Appendix D.

Two programs this section did not deal with are IBM's DisplayWrite software and MultiMate International Corporation's MultiMate. IBM's DisplayWrite uses a complex data tranfer language called DCA (Document Content Architecture). This format does not transfer easily between any of the dBASE formats, so if you are faced with trying to do a mail merge of sorts and DisplayWrite is your word processor of choice, consider using the pure dBASE approach to form-letter generation described earlier in this chapter. MultiMate users who are using recent versions of the software should refer to the MultiMate documentation; these recent versions of MultiMate can directly read dBASE files, so no conversion is necessary.

BUILDING FOREIGN FILES UNDER PROGRAM CONTROL

Users of an application will often want to move files between a dBASE application and a spreadsheet or word processor. You can include the COPY TO command with the appropriate options to write files that can be used under the control of a menu. For a rather painless way of limiting the records during an export, establish a filter condition first with a SET FILTER command, followed by a GO TOP and a COPY

using the desired options. You might want commands like the
following:

```
START = CTOD("01/01/65")
END = DATE()
a 5, 5 SAY "Beginning date for transactions?" GET START
a 6, 5 SAY "Ending date for transactions?" GET END
READ
SET FILTER TO TDATE >= START .AND. TDATE <= END
GO TOP
COPY TO 123FILE.WKS TYPE WKS
```

If you build a filter program that sets a choice of filters from a menu
(similar to the example named FILTERS.PRG in Chapter 4), you might
also provide your application with a menu choice labeled Write Lotus
Worksheet, which when run calls a program (in this example,
LOTUS.PRG). The program might contain code like the following:

```
*LOTUS.PRG
CLEAR
TEXT
NOTE: A LOTUS 1-2-3 WORKSHEET USUALLY CANNOT CONTAIN ALL RECORDS
IN A SIZEABLE DBASE DATABASE. LOTUS IS LIMITED TO 2,048 RECORDS
(OR ROWS) IN A WORKSHEET. YOU SHOULD SELECT DATA THAT RESULTS IN
A FILE WITH NO MORE THAN 2,048 RECORDS.
ENDTEXT
WAIT "PRESS A KEY TO SPECIFY RECORDS THROUGH A FILTER."
CLEAR
DO FILTERS
CLEAR
a 5, 5 SAY "INSERT FORMATTED DISK TO RECEIVE LOTUS FILE."
a 6, 5 SAY "IN DRIVE A, THEN PRESS ANY KEY."

WAIT
CLEAR
a 5, 5 SAY "CREATING LOTUS WORKSHEET CALLED REPORT.WKS..."
GO TOP
COPY FIELDS LASTNAME, FIRSTNAME, CITY, STATE, TRADED, SHARES,;
ACTION, PRICE TO A:REPORT.WKS TYPE WKS
CLEAR
SET FILTER TO
GO TOP
RETURN
```

When the program is run, the user will be prompted through the steps
to create the desired foreign file.

DEALING WITH LOTUS-FORMAT
SPREADSHEET FILES

As noted, dBASE III PLUS has an important ability that earlier versions of dBASE lacked: it can directly read and write files in Lotus 1-2-3 format. dBASE III PLUS can exchange data between 1-2-3 Release 1.1A, and between the newer 1-2-3 Release 2 and Symphony. To transfer data to and from Lotus 1-2-3 or Symphony, use the APPEND and COPY commands with the worksheet file type, as shown in this example:

```
APPEND FROM LOTUSFIL TYPE WKS
COPY TO LOTUSFIL TYPE WKS
```

The APPEND FROM command, when used in this manner, will read the contents of an existing 1-2-3 or Symphony spreadsheet and add those contents to a database that is in use. (If no database exists to store the data, you must first create a database with a structure that matches the column layout of the spreadsheet.) The COPY TO command will copy the contents of an existing database to a file that can be read by Lotus 1-2-3 or by Symphony. The file created by these commands will contain a 1-2-3 spreadsheet with each row containing one record. The individual columns of the spreadsheet represent the fields that were transferred, as specified by the list of fields in the example.

To read Lotus 1-2-3 files into dBASE III PLUS, no special preparation in 1-2-3 is needed. Simply store a 1-2-3 file in the usual manner and use the APPEND command of dBASE III PLUS to add the contents of the file into a dBASE III PLUS database. To import a 1-2-3 spreadsheet called FINANCE created by 1-2-3 Release 1A, you could use the following command:

```
APPEND FROM FINANCE TYPE WKS
```

To import a spreadsheet called FINANCE created by Lotus 1-2-3 Release 2, you would use this command:

```
APPEND FROM FINANCE.WK1 TYPE WKS
```

And to import a Symphony worksheet called FINANCE, you would use the following command:

```
APPEND FROM FINANCE.WR1 TYPE WKS
```

The only difference between the commands shown is the addition of the .WK1 extension to the filename in the second example and the .WR1 extension to the filename in the third example. These are the extensions used by Release 2 of 1-2-3 and by Symphony, respectively. dBASE III PLUS, however, expects the extension of a file loaded with the WKS type specified to be .WKS unless told otherwise.

TRANSFERRING FILES BETWEEN dBASE AND OTHER SOFTWARE

Users of Microsoft Multiplan can transfer a dBASE III PLUS database to a Multiplan spreadsheet by using the SYLK option of the COPY command. The SYLK file format is used for transfer of data to Multiplan and other Microsoft products. The normal format for the COPY command, when used with this option, is

```
COPY TO <filename> (SCOPE) (FIELDS<field list>) TYPE SYLK
```

As an example, the following commands could be used to create a spreadsheet that could be read by Microsoft's Multiplan:

```
USE RENTALS
COPY TO MPFILE2 FIELDS LASTNAME, CITY, STATE, RENTAMT, SIZE TYPE SYLK
```

The spreadsheet would contain columns for each of the fields named.

Multiplan users should note that when loading the file into Multiplan, the Transfer Options choice should be selected from the main Multiplan menu, and Symbolic should then be chosen from the menu that appears, which will tell Multiplan to load Symbolic Link type, or SYLK, files.

Transferring Files from Other Spreadsheets to dBASE III PLUS

Most spreadsheets provide an option for printing a file to disk, and the resultant file matches the SDF format. Different spreadsheets use different commands to create such files, so when in doubt check your software's documentation. Listed in Figure 11-1 are methods for creating dBASE-compatible files with some of the more popular spreadsheets.

Before transferring an SDF file into a database, be sure that the database field types and field widths match the SDF format precisely. You can use the APPEND FROM command with the SDF option to transfer the data into dBASE. The fields in the database must be as wide as the fields in the SDF file. If the database fields are narrower, the incoming data will be truncated. An alternate method for transferring an SDF file, although one that requires some work, is to convert the SDF file into a delimited file. This can be done by using your word processor to remove the spaces and adding delimiters (such as the quotes and comma) to separate the fields. You can then use the DELIMITED option of the APPEND FROM command to transfer the data, but this time you need not be concerned with precise matching of the field widths.

Transferring Information from dBASE III to Word Processors

Most word processors can read files of unformatted ASCII text, and such files can be created with the SET ALTERNATE command. Use the command

Lotus 1-2-3 Users:

1. Press the slash key (/) to display Lotus 1-2-3 commands.
2. Press F (for "file").
3. Press S (for "save").
4. Specify a name for the file you will create.
5. Press the slash key.
6. Press Q (for "quit").

Note: Lotus 1-2-3 Release 2 saves all files with an extension of .WK1. You must include this extension when naming the file in the dBASE III PLUS APPEND TO command.

Multiplan Users:

1. Press ESC to highlight Multiplan commands.
2. Press T (for "transfer").
3. Press O (for "options").
4. Press S (for "symbolic"), then RETURN.
5. Press T (for "transfer").
6. Press S (for "save").
7. Specify a name for the file you will create.

Note: Use the SYLK option of the APPEND command to read a Multiplan file into a dBASE III PLUS database.

SuperCalc 2 and 3 Users:

1. Press the slash key (/) to display SuperCalc commands.
2. Press O (for "output").
3. Press D (for "display option").
4. Specify a range of the spreadsheet to be transferred to the file.
5. Press D (for "disk").
6. Specify a name for the SDF file.

Note: SuperCalc saves all non-SuperCalc files with an extension of .PRN. You must include this extension when naming the file in the dBASE III PLUS APPEND TO command.

Figure 11-1.

Procedures for creating dBASE III
PLUS-compatible files for Lotus 1-2-
3, Multiplan, and SuperCalc 2 and 3

```
SET ALTERNATE TO <filename>
SET ALTERNATE ON
```

to begin saving everything that appears on the screen to a disk file with the exception of full screen operations and the results of @...SAY commands. This can be quite helpful for storing the text of reports, listings of data, and so forth, to a disk file. Once the disk file has been opened with the SET ALTERNATE TO *filename* command, you can alternately use the SET ALTERNATE ON and SET ALTERNATE OFF commands to begin and end the adding of information to the text file. To close the file, use the CLOSE ALTERNATE command.

Unless you specify a different extension along with the filename, dBASE adds an extension of .TXT to the file created by SET ALTER-NATE. As an example, if you had a stored report form called HOMES, you could create a disk file named HOUSE.TXT containing the information produced by that report by using the following commands:

```
SET ALTERNATE TO HOUSE.TXT
SET ALTERNATE ON
REPORT FORM HOMES
CLOSE ALTERNATE
```

The resultant file, HOUSE.TXT, would contain the ASCII text of the entire report. The only difference is that instead of being routed only to the screen or the screen and printer, the output also gets stored in a disk file. You can then load that disk file with your word processor in the usual manner for loading ASCII files.

Note that at the bottom of the file that was transferred with dBASE there may be an ASCII end-of-file marker (a left-pointing arrow) that dBASE produces when it closes the ASCII file. If you are using WordStar, this character may appear as one or more control-@ symbols (^@) at the end of the file, and it can be deleted using the word processors's usual delete keys.

Transferring Files Between
dBASE III PLUS and PFS:File

Databases from PFS:File can be converted to dBASE III PLUS format, and dBASE III PLUS databases can be converted to PFS:File format. PFS:File is a special case and does not use the COPY TO and APPEND FROM commands used with other software packages. Instead, dBASE III PLUS provides two commands, IMPORT and EXPORT, to perform the task of sharing files with PFS:File.

The IMPORT command reads a PFS:File database and creates a dBASE III PLUS database with a matching database structure. The IMPORT command also creates a screen format file that matches the screen format of the PFS:File database. And a view file is created that, when used, will link the database and screen format file. The format of the IMPORT command is

```
IMPORT FROM D:filename TYPE PFS
```

For example, to import a PFS:File database called PATIENTS you would use a command like

```
IMPORT FROM B:PATIENTS TYPE PFS
```

You can use the converted database separately or with the view file or screen format file created along with the database by the IMPORT command. All field types contained in the converted database will be character fields because PFS:File treats all fields as character fields.

The EXPORT command performs a function opposite to the IMPORT command, converting a dBASE III PLUS database to a PFS:File database. The format of the EXPORT command is

```
EXPORT TO D:filename TYPE PFS
```

As an example, to export to a database called CLIENTS as a PFS:File database, you would use a command like this one:

```
EXPORT TO B:PATIENTS TYPE PFS
```

All fields in the database are converted to character fields in the

PFS:File database. If a screen format file is in use when the conversion takes place, that format will be used as a screen design within the PFS:File database. If no screen format is used, the file structure of the dBASE database will be used as the screen design within PFS:File.

Sending Information from Other Programs to dBASE III

Transferring data from other programs to dBASE takes just a little more work than the process of sending dBASE data to other programs because files brought into dBASE must meet a specific format: SDF or Delimited. dBASE doesn't work with standard ASCII text in any random order, so it would seem that a transfer of a file from your word processor to dBASE would not be possible. In actuality, however, you can send data from your word processor to dBASE; you must simply be careful to create a file that looks like a Delimited file or an SDF file. If you use your word processor to create or edit files that resemble either of these formats, you can use the APPEND command of dBASE to load those files. Note that if you use the SDF format, you must keep track of the exact number of spaces between the beginning of the first field and the beginning of the next field. You must then set up the dBASE III database so that there are similarly-sized fields available to contain the data exactly as it is stored in the document that was created with your word processor.

Transferring Data Between Other Database Software and dBASE III

Other database software packages can often share data with dBASE III. (dBASE II files are a special case, made easy by some special conversion programs that will be discussed in Chapter 14.) Again, the possibilities of being able to transfer data depends on whether the other database package can use files in a delimited or SDF format. Different databases vary greatly in the specific commands used, so a look at the particular software package's operating manual will enable you to determine whether or not you can transfer files.

Whenever you are transferring a file from another program such as a word processor or spreadsheet into dBASE III, a database structure must already exist (or be created) that matches the design of the data you wish to transfer. In real life, the format of your foreign file may not precisely match the format of your database structure. When your existing categories of data in the two programs (dBASE and the other program) do not match, you will need to perform whatever work is necessary to make them match. You can do this in one of two ways: either change the order of the data in the other program or design a new database in dBASE that matches the order of the data in the other program. Once the new database is designed, use the APPEND command to add the data from the delimited or SDF file to the new database. Concentrate first on getting the data from the other file into dBASE. Once the data is contained in an acceptable dBASE database file, you can then use various dBASE commands to move that data into other dBASE database files that have different structures.

12: Optional
Equipment

A major advantage of dBASE that can't be found anywhere in the software itself is the support network of add-on products and other resources that are made to be used with dBASE. The enduring popularity of this software package has resulted in dozens of vendor offerings aimed at more effectively using dBASE. They include report writers, program generators, program utilities, compilers, and even dBASE work-alike clones at a lower cost than the original product. Anyone who is serious about realizing the full powers of dBASE should look at these packages, which can take you beyond the limitations of dBASE itself. Finding time to determine what is genuinely useful among the hundreds of offerings may be a problem, however. This chapter will help by describing a few of the useful add-ons and related software for the dBASE market. Addresses and (where available) phone numbers for the suppliers of these products can be found in Appendix D.

COMPILERS

Any serious power user of dBASE who develops applications using the dBASE programming language will use a compiler for the speed and protection it offers. dBASE in its native form is an interpreted language; when run with the DO command, programs are run one line at a time by the interpreter. This operating procedure is normal for the dBASE interpreter, whether a part of the program has been performed once or a thousand times, but it makes repetitive code of the type often used in sequential processes very inefficient. For example, a program like

```
X = 2
SET VIEW TO PATIENTS
DO WHILE .NOT. EOF()
  @ X, 5 SAY PATIENT
  @ X, 25 SAY DIAGNOSED
  @ X, 35 SAY ADMITTED
  @ X, 45 SAY DOCTORS->DRNAME
  @ X+1,5 SAY "Comments: " + COMMENTS
  X = X+3
  IF X > 52
     EJECT
     X = 2
  ENDIF
  SKIP
ENDDO
```

(which prints a report based on a simple sequential access of a database, along with one field in a related file) is inefficient under an interpreter like dBASE because dBASE must read each line in sequence and translate each command, function, and expression into internal instructions. It must do this each time the loop repeats, despite the fact that dBASE is performing the identical step, only with a different record, for each line that falls between the DO WHILE and the ENDDO.

By comparison, compilers perform this type of interpretation only once, when the code is compiled into a form of object code. The object code is then "linked" with a run-time library containing routines that tell the program how to perform common dBASE operations like opening files, selecting records, and routing output to a screen or printer. The resultant compiled program, because it is not repeating a translation process for each line of code in a program, is much faster in many operations.

Compilers also offer security and cost-effectiveness for multiple users. Users cannot modify your program files once they are compiled; an application becomes about as secure as possible. And compiled applications can be legally duplicated and handed out to as many users as desired, making considerable cost savings possible.

Drawbacks of Compilers

Like so many things in life, compilers represent a trade-off. You gain speed, security, and low cost, but you give up the ability to perform interactive dBASE tasks and full dBASE compatibility.

Clipper

Clipper from Nantucket is (at the time of this writing) the most popular compiler on the market. It has enjoyed a sizable following, perhaps because it was the first true dBASE compiler with speed to appear on the market. Clipper creates a free-standing dBASE program through a two-step process. First you create an object file by running the program file through the Clipper compiler. You need to provide only the name of the main program in the command string passed to Clipper. Clipper automatically links all associated program files, format files, and report and label forms. The result is a file with an .OBJ extension. You then perform the second step, which is to run the object file through the linker. The linker links the object file with the routines stored in Clipper's run-time library and produces an executable file.

One minor annoyance is that Clipper does not support index files in native dBASE format. Clipper uses its own index files, which use a default extension of .NTX. Although building the required index files in your compiled programs with the INDEX ON *expression* TO *filename* command is a simple matter, the incompatibility can be annoying when you have an application that exists in dBASE for development and debugging and in Clipper for everyday use. Each time you move changes in the application between dBASE and Clipper, you must rebuild your index files.

A more significant annoyance you will have to grow accustomed to when using Clipper is that some dBASE commands and functions are either supported differently or not at all. All compilers exhibit differences between how they work and how interpreted dBASE works, and Clipper is no exception. For example, the usual full-screen commands like EDIT, APPEND, and BROWSE are not supported, which is not a serious drawback because most programmers agree that full-screen commands should not be used in dBASE programs. In some cases, however, Clipper treats macros differently, and this can be more than a minor annoyance if you make extensive use of macros. For example, Clipper cannot use a macro to represent a command. In dBASE, you can include in a program statements like

```
STORE "USE NAMES" TO DOIT
&DOIT
```

and the dBASE interpreter will execute the code without any difficulty. Clipper, on the other hand, will have a real problem trying to compile this code. This particular example may look like a useless exercise, but it shows that you cannot use a command word as a part of a macro in Clipper. When you want to do this sort of task, you will have to find another way. Many valid dBASE commands and functions are not supported in Clipper, and a large number of commands and functions are supported differently. Among the more commonly used commands in dBASE that Clipper does not support are the following:

```
APPEND
ASSIST
BROWSE
CREATE <filename>
CREATE LABEL
CREATE QUERY
CREATE REPORT
CREATE SCREEN
CREATE VIEW
CREATE VIEW FROM ENVIRONMENT
DISPLAY FILES
DISPLAY MEMORY
DISPLAY STATUS
DISPLAY STRUCTURE
EDIT
ERROR()
EXPORT TO
GETENV()
IMPORT FROM
INSERT
ISALPHA()
```

```
ISCOLOR()
ISLOWER()
ISUPPER()
LEFT()
LIST MEMORY
LIST STATUS
LIST STRUCTURE
MAX()
MESSAGE()
MIN()
MOD()
MODIFY COMMAND
MODIFY LABEL
MODIFY QUERY
MODIFY REPORT
MODIFY SCREEN
MODIFY STRUCTURE
MODIFY VIEW
ON ERROR
ON ESCAPE
ON KEY
RESUME
RETRY
RETURN TO MASTER
SET CARRY
SET CATALOG
SET COLOR
SET DATE
SET FIELDS TO
SET HEADING
SET HISTORY TO
SET MEMOWIDTH
SET ORDER TO
SET PRINTER TO
SET SAFETY
SET VIEW TO
SUSPEND
```

Among the commands that are supported differently are the following:

```
&               -cannot include command words or commas.
AVERAGE         -a memory variable list is required.
COUNT TO        -a memory variable list is required.
DISPLAY         -a fields list is required.
INKEY()         -different in operation.
LIST            -a list of fields is required.
SET FORMAT TO   -format files can include commands.
SET FUNCTION    -support for 39 function keys.
SET INDEX       -the command cannot be used as a single
                 macro.
SET RELATION    -up to 8 relations out of one file.
SUM TO          -a fields list is required. No FOR or
                 WHILE allowed.
```

Like most compilers, Clipper adds some nice touches that are not possible in dBASE by providing new commands (or "extensions") for the dBASE language. A notable addition is that Clipper handles memo fields with the flexibility that should be in dBASE. Not only does Clipper let you search memo fields, you can create windows for editing the contents with relative ease, and you can move the contents of a memo field back and forth between the memo field file and a memory variable. (Clipper also supports memory variables as large as 16K.) The limits on memory variables are increased from the 256 permitted in dBASE to a maximum of 2048 in Clipper.

In addition, Clipper bypasses the dBASE limit of 128 fields per database with a new maximum of 1024, although why anyone with good design skills would want 1024 fields in a single database is hard to imagine. Clipper lets you use the SET RELATION command to set relations out of the same file into as many as eight other related files. And a combination of @ . . . PROMPT and MENU TO commands let you create moving light-bar menus with relative ease. Clipper supports single-dimensional arrays, a feature dBASE lacks, to the irritation of sophisticated programmers. The SAVE SCREEN and RESTORE SCREEN commands can be used to save a screen in memory temporarily and later redraw that screen. This tool is invaluable for displaying help screens because you can use the commands to save an existing screen, clear the screen and display help text, and then clear the screen and redisplay the original screen when you are finished reading the help text. Clipper also supports user-defined functions, which can be thought of as custom subroutines that return a value. Clipper is priced at $695 and is produced by Nantucket Corporation.

QuickSilver

QuickSilver is Wordtech's latest version of its dBASE compiler. Like Clipper, QuickSilver creates executable programs that run without the aid of dBASE. QuickSilver rates high in terms of true compatibility with dBASE: roughly 90% of existing dBASE programs will run without modifications when compiled with QuickSilver. QuickSilver also uses dBASE index, label, report form, memory variable, and screen format files without modification. And QuickSilver offers a set of tools for creating custom windows that may obviate the need for other screen generators.

One feature missing from QuickSilver is the VALID command (supported by Clipper), which lets you validate data entry more precisely than the dBASE RANGE and PICTURE clauses of the GET command in dBASE.

Compiling a program in QuickSilver is a three-step process. First, you use a compiler to compile the program into p-code. The file created by this step is then run through QuickSilver's optimizer, which generates an object code (.OBJ) file. A linker is then used to link the object file with the run-time libraries, creating an executable (.EXE) file that runs as a stand-alone program. You can use a -Q option within the command line to tell QuickSilver to perform all necessary steps in succession to generate the final program. Like other compilers, QuickSilver does not support full-screen commands like APPEND, EDIT, and BROWSE. And, as with other compilers, some commands are supported differently in QuickSilver.

Among the more commonly used commands in dBASE that Quick-Silver does not support are the following:

```
APPEND
ASSIST
BROWSE
CREATE <filename>
CREATE LABEL
CREATE QUERY
CREATE REPORT
CREATE SCREEN
CREATE VIEW
CREATE VIEW FROM ENVIRONMENT
DISPLAY STATUS
DISPLAY USERS
EDIT
EXPORT TO
IMPORT FROM
INSERT BEFORE
LIST STATUS
LOGOUT
MODIFY COMMAND
MODIFY LABEL
MODIFY QUERY
MODIFY REPORT
MODIFY SCREEN
MODIFY STRUCTURE
MODIFY VIEW
RESUME
SET CARRY
SET CATALOG
SET FIELDS TO
SET HEADING
```

```
SET HISTORY TO
SET MEMOWIDTH
SET PRINTER TO
SET SAFETY
SET VIEW TO
SUSPEND
```

Among the commands supported differently are the following:

```
&                  -cannot include reserved words or commas.
a...SAY            -an expression and mem. var. list is required.
a...GET            -picture template of 'Y' not permitted.
AVERAGE            -an expression and mem. var. list is required.
COUNT TO           -a memory variable list is required. FOR & WHILE
                    not allowed.
ERROR()            -the error codes are different.  This can lead
                    to bizarre results if error-trap routines are
                    not modified.
RETRY              -restarts at beginning of program instead of
                    at line which caused error.
SET FORMAT TO      -format files can include commands.
SET FUNCTION       -support for 39 function keys.
SET INDEX          -the command cannot be used as a single macro.
SET RELATION       -up to 8 relations out of one file.
SORT ON            -uses plus signs with multiple field names, not
                    commas.
SUM TO             -a fields list is required. No FOR or WHILE
                    allowed.
```

Among QuickSilver's nicer additions to the dBASE language are about a dozen window functions, which let you open multiple windows on the screen in various sizes, positions, and colors. QuickSilver is priced at $599 and is available from Wordtech Systems.

FrontRunner

FrontRunner, from Apex Software, is not an ordinary type of compiler; it has been placed in this category simply because it does not fit well in any other. FrontRunner lets you build memory-resident applications using dBASE programming code, even if you have never written a shred of assembly-language programs before. Memory-resident programs, also known as TSRs (for "terminate and stay-resident"), are those programs that appear and disappear at the touch of a key. Borland's SideKick made such programs famous in the DOS world, and since the success of SideKick hundreds of other memory-resident programs have come along to offer users convenience and a form of multitasking on a hardware design that was never intended to support such a concept.

FrontRunner can convert a dBASE program to a memory-resident application. To do so, you insert a user-defined command in a special configuration file named FR.INI and specify the hot-key sequence that will be used to bring up the program. You then load FrontRunner, and whenever the chosen hot key is pressed, your application pops up over whatever other program is running at the time. There are limitations, of course. The entire application and database do not load into RAM, since there is no physical way that an application and database files that might total 2 megabytes would fit into 640K of memory. FrontRunner sets aside memory caches and loads portions of your database and program files into memory as it needs them, so you will see some disk interaction. Also, since you are using FrontRunner and not dBASE to execute your programs, you will encounter incompatibilities with some commands that FrontRunner will not support. FrontRunner uses dBASE database, index, report form, and most program files. FrontRunner is not, however, compatible with QuickSilver or Clipper language enhancements or with Clipper's own index files.

While you might not want to use FrontRunner to replace entirely a complex application written in dBASE or under a dBASE compiler, the program can be a significant addition to an existing system. A time-and-billing system, for example, could have a memory-resident front end developed so that a large number of office workers could add records to a database while running a memory-resident adder routine at individual workstations. At the end of each month, the contents of those databases could be imported into a master file in the accounting department; the accounting application, written entirely in dBASE or under a compiler, would then generate the bills based on the month's entries. FrontRunner lists for $295 and is available from Apex Software. Also available at a nominal cost is a run-time license that lets you freely distribute your memory-resident applications with the necessary library and configuration files provided with FrontRunner.

dBASE CLONES

The dBASE look-alikes are relatively new aftermarket products for dBASE users. They are advertised as providing dBASE compatibility as well as added features for a lower price than dBASE itself. Some of these products also offer the partial benefits of a compiler. Two popular ones are FoxBASE+ and dBXL.

FoxBASE+

FoxBASE+ is thought of by some as a compiler, which is to shortchange the product somewhat because FoxBASE+ is in fact a complete replacement for dBASE, although it does differ in the treatment of some commands. FoxBASE+ uses its own index file format; all other dBASE files can be brought over to FoxBASE+ with no changes. Like dBASE, FoxBASE+ offers an interpreter that runs your programs written in the dBASE syntax. Unlike dBASE, FoxBASE+ also provides a fast compiler that compiles programs, although they are not linked to become fully executable, stand-alone programs. You will still need FoxBASE+ to run the programs. You can purchase an optional run-time module that lets you distribute applications on a royalty-free basis.

A major advantage of FoxBASE+ is speed. Most benchmark tests of FoxBASE+ and competitive products (including dBASE III PLUS, Clipper, and QuickSilver) show that FoxBASE+ runs its compiled applications faster than any of the others. And since FoxBASE+ uses an interpreter, you need not give up those full-screen commands if you prefer using them.

FoxBASE supports the VALID command for greater data validation than the dBASE RANGE and PICTURE clauses, and you can easily build light-bar menus. And you can set multiple relations from one parent database in FoxBASE+. The commands that dBASE supports and FoxBASE+ does not are relatively few. They include the following:

```
ASSIST
CREATE QUERY
CREATE SCREEN
CREATE VIEW FROM ENVIRONMENT
EXPORT TO
IMPORT FROM
```

Commands that execute differently in FoxBASE+ are also few. They include the BROWSE command, which lets you edit memo fields in FoxBASE+, and the MODIFY COMMAND command, which is not limited to 5K files.

FoxBASE+ uses a novel approach in providing both an interpreter and a compiler. When you are working from the dot prompt, you are using the FoxBASE interpreter. The first time you run a program, it is compiled and saved to a file with the .FOX extension. If you do not change the program, each successive time that you run it FoxBASE+ runs the compiled version, at blinding speeds. If you later change the program, the editor automatically erases the compiled version, and thus the next time you run the program it again gets compiled. FoxBASE+ is priced at $395 and is available from Fox Software.

dBXL

dBXL is from WordTech Systems, the same people who produce the QuickSilver compiler. While QuickSilver is designed to cover an area that dBASE is not designed to cover, dBXL's purpose is to perform the same functions as dBASE III PLUS, but at a significantly lower cost. dBXL is fully file and language-syntax compatible with dBASE III PLUS. Because it is an interpreter, dBXL does not have the incompatibilities between commands that the compilers have. dBXL does offer some new commands and features that are not present in dBASE III PLUS; you can create multiple windows with ease, and dual help levels make dBXL friendly for novice users. The most notable feature of the program is its low price: at $169, dBXL provides reasonable dBASE power at a cost lower than some nonrelational file managers.

REPORT GENERATORS

The limitations of the dBASE Report Generator have been known for some time, so it is no surprise that report generators are among the more popular add-on products. Two well-known packages are R&R from Concentric and QUICKREPORT from Fox & Geller.

R&R (an abbreviation for "relate and report") is a free-standing report generator that utilizes dBASE files to generate a variety of reports. R&R uses a series of Lotus-style menus and the concept of a page layout screen to design reports. You can designate any number of lines for page titles, headers, and footers, and you can position text items like headings or a system date by painting them anywhere on the screen. R&R can create reports based on a relational merge of multiple files, and it can draw more than one relation at a time out of a single database. Like most add-on report writers, R&R runs from DOS, outside of dBASE. A major plus of this program is the run-time license, which lets you package a program with your applications so users can generate the reports with R&R. You can access any R&R report through dBASE with the RUN command, and you can pass parameters from dBASE to R&R to selectively control which records are printed.

R&R includes its own filter selection screen to designate which records should be printed in a report. You can group up to eight levels, sort on up to eight levels, include totals or subtotals with any groups, and add user-defined calculated fields that are a part of the report. R&R lists for $149, and is available from Concentric Systems.

If you prefer the Ashton-Tate style of pull-down menus, you may prefer QUICKREPORT, a report writer from Fox & Geller. The user interface of QUICKREPORT bears a strong resemblance to numerous other Ashton-Tate products, with a series of menus outlining each available choice. If you are comfortable with the menus in the dBASE Report Generator and Screen Painter utility, you will find QUICKREPORT a familiar product.

As with R&R, you design a report in QUICKREPORT by painting a page with report headers, page headers, a report body, page footers, and report footers. Various menu options let you select the names of the databases and fields that will be used in the report. You can also set the relations and the sort and select order for the records that appear in the completed reports. Since QUICKREPORT does not produce a dBASE program file but instead runs the report from within the QUICKREPORT program, you must use QUICKREPORT each time you want to produce the report. If you want to supply the results of the report to multiple users of your application, you can do so by including the QUICKREPORT Runtime program, included with QUICKREPORT, on the disk along with the rest of the application. QUICKREPORT is priced at $295, and is available from Fox & Geller.

PROGRAM GENERATORS

Program generators have always been an intriguing part of the dBASE aftermarket, undoubtedly because writing a program is so much work. Any product that does that kind of work for you is bound to be appealing. The one drawback of program generators is that because they are written by programmers, they tend to generate code in the programmer's chosen style. If you don't like programs in that particular style, having to modify them can present a real problem because so many of today's program generators write complex code that can be a task to decipher. Also, the output of program generators is sometimes not fully compatible with compilers, and thus you may have considerable work to do if the program is to be compiled for efficiency.

Genifer

Genifer from Bytel is a powerful, detailed application generator that can crank out programs more complex than many dBASE programmers would care to write. Genifer produces the main menu, detailed data entry and editing screens with built-in validation, and complex reports. Relational applications are no problem to Genifer. Describe the fields to Genifer's data dictionary, paint the entry screens, menus, and reports, and provide any validation rules and relations, and then let Genifer crank out the lines of code to perform the common adding, editing, inquire, and reporting tasks. Even if you prefer the complete control over your applications that writing your own code affords, you may discover Genifer to be worth the cost because of the quality of the reports the program can create. And the code that Genifer produces is well written, well documented, and bug free. On the minus side, Genifer is not cheap, and the code it produces may not be compatible with the compiler you are using. The program is also so flexible in terms of the choices it offers for building an application that it may take a while to decide how to use effectively all the choices available. Genifer lists for $395 and is available from Bytel Corporation.

QUICKCODE

QUICKCODE PLUS is Fox & Geller's latest implementation of QUICKCODE, a program generator that has been around almost as long as dBASE. QUICKCODE PLUS builds custom applications with well-written code that can be modified by a person without a degree in advanced programming.

QUICKCODE PLUS uses Lotus 1-2-3-style menus to access its various commands. To create an application, you must design a form that contains the fields in your database. The fields can be from multiple databases, and you can include text, graphics, and color. QUICKCODE lets you link as many as four related files to the primary database, and full data validation can be defined within the design screen (although this feature is poorly explained in the manual). One excellent feature of this program is its QCBUILD option, which lets you take a default form and generate a complete application without going through the trouble of designing a screen form. Sometimes this kind of "quick and dirty" approach is all that is wanted. You can generate applications with professional screens and Lotus 1-2-3-style menus in a matter of minutes.

There are two notable disadvantages to QUICKCODE PLUS. First, the program relies entirely on the dBASE Report Generator for reports, and the limitations of the Report Generator are well known. You can get additional reporting capability by using QUICKCODE along with Fox & Geller's QUICKREPORT, an add-on program that generates report code, but this brings an extra $300 or so into the picture. The second disadvantage exists only when you stray outside of the pure Ashton-Tate environment. QUICKCODE was written to take full advantage of Ashton-Tate's dBASE III PLUS, and it makes use of commands that the compilers do not support in achieving its goals. If you try to compile an application created with QUICKCODE PLUS in Clipper or in Quick-Silver, expect to do a fair share of fine-tuning the code to get it to run without errors. As if anticipating this problem, Fox & Geller include in the documentation tips for users who need to compile their applications. QUICKCODE lists for $295.

PROGRAMMING UTILITIES

A number of programs falling under the general heading of utilities try to make the job of designing complex dBASE applications easier by checking your program code for improper use of commands or by writing detailed screens and add and edit routines for use within your programs.

dANALYST

dANALYST from TranSec Systems is a programmer's utility, similar in design to dFLOW, that can test for program errors and document your code. dANALYST checks for incorrect syntax in commands and missing closing statements, produces cross-referenced listings of your memory variables, and can produce diagrams indicating program flow within the application. Some features of dANALYST set it apart from the more established dFLOW. First, dANALYST is "multi-user capable" in that the program can take a single-user application and generate a network-ready application that contains network file-locking commands. The commands that dANALYST adds may not be the most efficient ones possible, and the resulting program may lock entire files more often than it needs to, but using dANALYST is still far better than taking a single-user application over to a network version of dBASE and running it with no modifications.

The network-ready programs produced by dANALYST are also Clipper- and QuickSilver-compatible, assuming that the original programs fed into dANALYST would have worked with these compilers. A second feature of note is that dANALYST can produce a DOS batch file that, when run, backs up onto floppy disks all program and data files used by the application. This feature means one less piece of code for you to write. Finally, at $94.95, the program is competitively priced. dANALYST is available from TranSec Systems, Incorporated.

dBASE Tools for C

For those useful functions that you sorely wish dBASE had, like building an array or amortizing a loan, there are the dBASE Tools For C, available from Ashton-Tate. These contain a library of very useful routines that you can access through a binary program (provided that it calls the functions). To run the program, called CFunc, you load it into memory with the CALL command within dBASE, and you pass on the name of the desired function or module as a part of the command statement. For example, the dBASE Tools For C include a random number generator that, when supplied with two numbers, will return a random number between the two. Assuming that you have the Tools For C modules installed on your hard disk, you could obtain a random number between 1 and 10 with the commands

```
LOAD CFUNC
CALL CFUNC WITH 'RAND 1,10'
```

Note that the LOAD command needs to be executed only once within a program; it loads the binary file into memory, and any of the routines within the Tools package can then be accessed with similar commands.

The Tools For C include functions and modules for creating arrays, calculating loan amortization, finding the present value, net present value, and future value of an investment, and determining the internal rate of returns for cash flows. A full set of scientific functions is provided, including SIN, COS, TAN, ASIN, ACOS, and ATAN. And various functions for manipulating the data stored within an array are provided. Ashton-Tate also offers a package called dBASE Tools For C, The Graphics Library that uses the same LOAD and CALL commands to access various tools for creating and manipulating graphics. Tools are provided for drawing arcs, circles, and boxes and pie, bar, and line charts. You can also save and restore graphics screens with the GSAVE and GRESTORE tools. Various charts can be produced based on the values stored in an array created with the Tools For C array functions. Both dBASE Tools For C and dBASE Tools For C, The Graphics Library are available from Ashton-Tate.

dFLOW

dFLOW by Wallsoft Systems is probably the most popular dBASE debugging utility on the market as of this writing. Its maker, Wallsoft Systems, has a deep knowledge of dBASE; the same company originally developed a screen painter utility, called SED, for use with dBASE III. Ashton-Tate later acquired the rights to the utility and packaged it with dBASE III; the useful screen-design tool evolved into the current Screen Painter system that is a part of dBASE III PLUS.

dFLOW effectively checks your program statements for mistakes in control logic, including missing ENDIF, ENDCASE, and ENDDO statements. dFLOW also checks for missing end quotes. (How often have you run a program, only to see the annoying "unterminated string" message at a half-dozen different locations in the code?) dFLOW tests for unbalanced parentheses, and provides cross-referenced listings that show you when and where a program calls other programs. Documentation of your program and reports of errors can be printed or written to a disk file or displayed on the screen. One helpful feature of dFLOW is that it can print a "T" (for "true") or "F" (for "false") inside of all IF...ENDIF statements while the program is being analyzed, indicating whether that portion of the program falls between IF and ELSE (true), or between ELSE and ENDIF (false). dFLOW creates cross-references that show which memory variables are used in the program's submodules. dFLOW can also produce flowcharts that visually show how the modules of the program interact.

If you write large, complex systems, a program like dFLOW is invaluable. Even if you prefer to do most or all of your own debugging as you go along, dFLOW is worth the cost simply as a way of producing effective documentation for other programmers to refer to if they ever need to modify your work. Simply get into dFLOW, provide the name of your main program file, and turn on line numbering, diagram program flow, and the modules' cross-reference options. Select printer as an output device, go get a cup of coffee, and when you return, add the printed sheets to the application's user manual. Some other programmer may someday think highly of you for your 30 seconds of work in creating such detailed documentation. dFLOW costs $229, and is available from Wallsoft Systems, Inc.

dSCAR

dSCAR is a debugging aid similar in design to dFLOW and dANALYST. It is worth noting because the product is shareware and can be obtained at a very reasonable cost. Like its commercial brethen, dSCAR performs structured indentations of existing code, produces flow diagrams and cross-reference statements, displays structural errors, and adds line numbering to source code. The program is menu-driven and simple to use. dSCAR does not catch as many errors as dFLOW or dANALYST, but dSCAR is priced at a fraction of the cost of the others. The author of dSCAR asks a contribution of $20, and the program can be obtained from the address listed in Appendix D.

dUTIL III PLUS

dUTIL III PLUS by Fox & Geller is designed to catch errors in your code and generally clean up your programs, like most utilities of this type. dUTIL III PLUS checks all statements that need a matching statement —such as IF with ENDIF and DO WHILE with ENDDO—and lets you know when matching statements are missing. dUTIL will also indent all commands between the DO WHILE and ENDDO statements and between the IF and ENDIF statements. You can set the levels of indentation to your preferences. dUTIL III PLUS will, if desired, capitalize all reserved words while converting all fieldnames, fields, and variables to lowercase. And as an option, you can create a map showing the relationship between the routines of a program. A menu with well-detailed options makes using the program a relatively simple task. And dUTIL III PLUS can combine the main menu file and all of the associated files into one large program file. However, this option should be used with care: if you write tight procedure code that is used effectively in multiple places in a program, having dUTIL III PLUS convert it into a single program may create a program that is much larger in disk space than the sum of its parts.

Tom Rettig's Library

Following the lead of Ashton-Tate in marketing functions that would have been nice to see in dBASE, Tom Rettig, an old hand at dBASE and a former manager of Ashton-Tate's software support group, has produced a library of useful functions quite simply titled Tom Rettig's Library. This library contains nearly 150 functions for business and scientific use, for manipulating database information, for performing specialized conversions, and for making complex DOS calls. You will find functions in this library for the most bizarre and challenging little tasks, like converting days to months or years to hours, for handling depreciation, for performing Soundex conversions, for saving and restoring screens, for switching printer ports, and for dozens of other uses. The library is offered in two versions: one for dBASE, which works with dBXL, QuickSilver, and FoxBASE, and another version for Clipper. Tom Rettig's Library is supplied by Tom Rettig Associates, and is priced at $99.95.

FINALLY, DON'T REINVENT THE WHEEL...

One type of product not examined in this chapter, primarily because the available products are far too numerous to mention, are the templates, or ready-made program files, that exist for various common applications. These are complete applications, written in the dBASE language, available on numerous bulletin boards and on library disks supplied by user groups. Someone has already spent dozens or hundreds of hours writing these programs, and finding the right one may save you just as many hours of work. Now, if your application requires monitoring incoming data from deep-space exploration probes, you're probably going to have to write your own application from scratch. But don't spend weeks writing a standard program (like accounting or a parts inventory) when you can spend a few days or a few hours modifying something that is already either in the public domain or for sale commercially.

13: Network Tips

The use of local-area networks calls for a whole new mind-set when you are working with dBASE and other software packages. Unless your application is a very unusual one that provides read/write capabilities to only one user, you must face the unpleasant reality that sooner or later two users will attempt an edit on the same record at the same time. When that happens, users should be prepared for what results; if you have written a program to handle an application, your program must be prepared to deal with this eventuality.

Effective use of dBASE on a net assumes that the dBASE Administrator, the network version of dBASE III PLUS, has been installed on a network, and the PROTECT program has been used (if desired) to create logon names, passwords, and read/write access levels. Under no circumstances should the single-user version of dBASE III PLUS be copied to a network hard disk and used by multiple users. This has been known to happen, usually in overly cost-conscious organizations trying to save the incremental cost of purchasing dBASE LAN Packs. The reasoning is that the network operating software can be used to lock files to prevent user collisions. Such a step could have disastrous consequences, however, because the single-user version of dBASE III PLUS is not designed to guard against corruption of files resulting from multiple-user access. The reality is that network users probably won't execute the necessary commands from the system level to lock the files they use, and databases will get trashed. If cost is a major consideration, compile the application using Clipper or QuickSilver and add the necessary file and record-locking commands to the application to avoid user collisions.

THE USEFUL NETWORK COMMANDS

The dBASE Administrator's most commonly used commands that guard against potential problems are SET EXCLUSIVE, which controls file availability, UNLOCK, which unlocks locked files or records, and the LOCK( ), RLOCK( ), and FLOCK( ) functions, which are used to lock records and files on demand. Additional security controls can be added with the PROTECT utility described in Chapter 10. Using PROTECT, you can assign user access levels that can be read by the ACCESS( ) function, and you can designate whether specific fields within files should be read-only or read/write. Varying capabilities can be granted to different users; see Chapter 10 or your dBASE documentation for more details on the use of PROTECT.

EXCLUSIVE VERSUS SHARED ACCESS

dBASE III PLUS lets you open files in exclusive or in shared mode. In shared mode, all users on the net can read and write to files, assuming that any write capabilities are not restricted through the use of PROTECT or the network operating system. In exclusive mode, only one user can work with the file; all other users must wait until the file is released from exclusive use by that user. dBASE III PLUS protects users who work in the dot prompt mode by opening files in exclusive mode whenever a write operation could be performed by multiple users. Most dBASE commands open files in an exclusive mode by default. You can change this default with the SET EXCLUSIVE OFF command, which will make the file available for shared use. To reverse the command, use the SET EXCLUSIVE ON command.

These commands control whether files opened after the use of SET EXCLUSIVE are opened in the exclusive or shared mode. If you use SET EXCLUSIVE ON, all files opened after that command has been executed will be opened for exclusive use. Even if you later change the status of the exclusive mode with the SET EXCLUSIVE OFF command, files that were opened in exclusive mode remain that way until closed. An alternative way of opening a file in exclusive mode is to add the EXCLUSIVE clause to the USE command. A command like

```
USE MAILER INDEX NAMES EXCLUSIVE
```

will open both the named database and index files in exclusive mode.

If another user tries to open a file while it is open in exclusive mode, dBASE displays the message, "file is in use by another" in the message area below the status bar. For dot prompt users on a net, the SET EXCLUSIVE command, along with writing to files in exclusive mode by default, is dBASE's primary way of controlling who can write to a file and who cannot.

The exclusive and shared modes of file protection, although effective, are usually not the most efficient ways to work with dBASE in a network environment. Sometimes operations that must make extensive sequential reads and writes to a file, such as REPLACE, SORT, INDEX, and PACK commands, require that a file be locked from shared use until the operation has been completed. If you are examining or updating only a single record, however, locking the entire database is a selfish use of resources. When editing records, you should use the record-locking facilities of dBASE to lock individual records rather than the entire file. dBASE protects network users by attempting to lock a file whenever an operation that requires a locked file is attempted. (It cannot lock the file if someone has locked it already.) These operations include the following commands:

```
APPEND
AVERAGE
BROWSE
COPY
COUNT
DELETE ALL
INDEX
JOIN
RECALL ALL
REPLACE ALL
SORT
SUM
TOTAL
UPDATE
```

If the file was automatically locked by dBASE as a result of one of these commands, the file will be automatically unlocked when dBASE completes the operation. This automatic file locking and unlocking is the major method of network file protection when dBASE is used from the dot prompt mode.

When programming, you should make use of the dBASE locking functions, LOCK( ), FLOCK( ), and RLOCK( ), and the unlocking command, UNLOCK. The LOCK( ) and RLOCK( ) functions perform the same task: they attempt to lock the current record, and they return a logical value of "true" if the attempt to lock was successful. The FLOCK( ) function performs the same task for an entire file; it attempts to lock the file, and returns a logical value of "true" if the lock is successful. With individual records, you can choose to leave the records unlocked if the program is performing an inquiry only, and you can attempt to lock the record with the LOCK( ) or RLOCK( ) functions if the program is attempting an update of the record.

The following is an example of the code needed to lock a record effectively:

```
COUNTER = 100
DO WHILE COUNTER > 0 .AND. .NOT. RLOCK()
     COUNTER = COUNTER - 1
ENDDO
IF .NOT. RLOCK()
     *record still locked.
     CLEAR
```

```
    WAIT "Record in use by another.  Try again later."
  RETURN
ELSE
    <...more commands to edit the record contents...>
  UNLOCK
ENDIF
```

This is more code than is actually needed to lock a record, but by adding the lines that increment a counter for a defined period of time and providing an automatic abort if the record remains locked, you avoid the dreaded "deadly embrace," that is, two machines attempting to lock the same record at the same time.

NETWORK PROGRAMMING

Programming for a network version requires thinking about what your program does with shared files during each routine. For example, the process of adding records requires a file lock; the APPEND BLANK command will automatically trigger a file lock if one has not been already established with a FLOCK( ) function or a SET EXCLUSIVE command. If the file cannot be locked when the APPEND BLANK command is encountered, dBASE will report an error code, and the program must be able to handle the error.

Even with commands that automatically lock files, you must think about more in the design process than simply error trapping. Do you wait until you have filled up a string of memory variables during an append routine and then perform an APPEND BLANK, only to find that the file is locked by another user who is performing a two-hour indexing job? If you perform an APPEND BLANK and then fill the variables, how do you deal with the user who brings up a screen for a new record, fills in the first two fields, and then decides to break for lunch, leaving the file locked and unusable by others? These are the kinds of programming considerations you will need to deal with. Experience will demonstrate what works best in your application, but some general hints will get you started.

Error Trapping

Of prime importance in a network program is an error-trapping routine
that handles errors generated by file access problems and other network
difficulties. The ON ERROR command at the start of the program
should be used to run the error-trapping routine when an error occurs.
Depending on the value returned by the ERROR( ) function, the error-
trapping program can take appropriate action. At the start of the
program, include a command like

```
ON ERROR DO RECOVER
```

and in the file, RECOVER.PRG, include tests to interpret and deal with
the error condition. The file may be similar to ones you already use to
trap errors; the only differences are the added conditionals to deal with
the network error codes. An example of such a program is shown here:

```
***RECOVER.PRG is error trapping.
**Last update 10/14/87
CLEAR
DO CASE

    CASE (ERROR() = 109 .OR. ERROR() = 128 .OR. ERROR = 129;
             .OR. ERROR() = 130 .OR. ERROR() = 142)
        COUNTER = 100
        DO WHILE .T.
            ? CHR(7)
            CLEAR
            a 5, 5 SAY "Record is locked.  Retrying access."
            DO WHILE COUNTER > 0
                a 7, 5 SAY "Retry number:"
                a 7, 21 SAY LTRIM(STR(100-COUNTER))
                IF RLOCK()
                    UNLOCK
                    EXIT
                ENDIF
                COUNTER = COUNTER - 1
            ENDDO
            IF RLOCK()
                RETURN
            ELSE
                a 12, 0
                WAIT "     Record in use by another. Try later."
                STORE .T. TO RECBUSY
                RETURN
            ENDIF
        ENDDO
```

```
CASE ERROR() = 108
     COUNTER = 50
     DO WHILE .T.
          ? CHR(7)
          CLEAR
          @ 5, 5 SAY "File is locked.  Retrying access."
          DO WHILE COUNTER > 0
               @ 7, 5 SAY "Retry number:"
               @ 7, 21 SAY LTRIM(STR(50-COUNTER))
               IF FLOCK()
                    UNLOCK
                    EXIT
               ENDIF
               COUNTER = COUNTER - 1
          ENDDO
          IF FLOCK()
               RETURN
          ELSE
               @ 12, 0
               WAIT "     File in use by another. Try later."
               STORE .T. TO FILEBUSY
               RETURN
          ENDIF
     ENDDO

CASE (ERROR() = 29 .OR. ERROR() = 111)
     ? "You are trying to update a file for which you"
     ? "have NO ACCESS.  Contact Network Administrator."
     WAIT
     CLEAR ALL
     RETURN TO MASTER

CASE ERROR() = 124
     ? "You are trying to reach a network printer"
     ? "which does not exist or is not reachable."
     WAIT
     RETURN TO MASTER

CASE ERROR() = 125
     ? "Printer not ready.  Reset printer, then"
     WAIT
     RETRY

CASE ERROR() = 148
     ? "WARNING: File Server Overload condition."
     ? "Contact your Network Administrator NOW."
     ? "Report this message."
     WAIT
     CLEAR ALL
     QUIT

CASE ERROR() = 1
     ? "Cannot find a file.  Record this message,"
     ? "and contact program developer for assistance."
     CLEAR ALL
     WAIT
     QUIT

CASE ERROR() = 20 .or. ERROR() = 26 .or. ERROR() = 114
     ? "The index file seems to be missing a record."
     ? "please wait while I repair the index."
     SET TALK ON
```

```
            INDEX ON LAST + FIRST TO NAMES
            SET TALK OFF
            CLEAR
            RETRY

    CASE ERROR() = 9 .or. ERROR() = 134 .or. ERROR() = 143
            ? CHR(7)
            ? "     The Filter you entered does NOT match the database"
            ? "     you are using, OR it contains an invalid term."
            ? "     Make sure you are using the right filter."
            ?
            WAIT
            CLEAR ALL
            RETURN TO MASTER

    CASE ERROR() = 6
            ? "Too many files open for this task.  Report this message"
            ? "to the Network Administrator or the DP department."
            WAIT
            QUIT

    OTHERWISE
            *haven't the foggiest idea what went wrong...
            ? "A program error has occurred.  Record the message,"
            ? "and inform your network administrator."
            ?
            ? MESSAGE()
            ?
            ? "After noting the above message, press any key."
            WAIT
            SET CONSOLE OFF
            SET ALTERNATE TO ERRORS.TXT
            SET ALTERNATE ON
            LIST MEMORY
            LIST STATUS
            ? "Error message reported was: "
            ?? MESSAGE()
            CLOSE ALTERNATE
            CLEAR ALL
            QUIT

    ENDCASE
    *End of Recover.PRG.
```

Adding Records: The Blank Records Approach

One method of adding records in the network environment without
placing demands on the files within the system is to add a large number
of blank records early in the day, perhaps right after the system is

initially brought online for that day's work. Since the APPEND command ties up files by requiring their exclusive use, you can cut down on such exclusive use by using APPEND to add as many blank records as you suspect you will need throughout the day, plus a few extra blank records for good measure. A simple counter program will perform the task with code like

```
USE MAILFILE EXCLUSIVE
COUNTER = 1
DO WHILE COUNTER < 25
    APPEND BLANK
    COUNTER = COUNTER + 1
ENDDO
CLOSE DATABASES
```

If users were making use of interactive commands at the dot prompt, they could be instructed to fill in the blank records first before trying to create any new records. If the data entry is under the control of your program, the program could be written to look for an existing blank record and add to that record with the @...SAY...GET and REPLACE commands. Assuming the database is indexed on any field, blank records would appear at the start of the file because of the nature of the index. As a person on the network attempted to add data to an existing blank record, dBASE would consider such an operation to be an EDIT (since the record already exists), and therefore a record lock would be performed instead of the more demanding file lock. Any unused blank records can easily be deleted at the end of the day.

Adding Records: The Batch Processing Approach

In a network environment, the benefits of using the batch processing approach to adding records outweigh the minor disadvantage of the time required to create the temporary files. Chapter 3 provides a general description of batch processing. A program for adding records might resemble the following:

```
USE Primary
COPY STRUCTURE TO tempfile
UNLOCK
USE Tempfile EXCLUSIVE
DO WHILE .T.
    CLEAR
    <...commands to create memory variables...>
    <...@...SAY...GET commands to get data & validate...>
    APPEND BLANK
    REPLACE <...data fields with memory variables...>
    CLEAR
    ACCEPT " Add another? Y/N: " TO ANS
    IF UPPER(ANS) = "N"
        EXIT
    ENDIF
ENDDO
USE Primary
APPEND FROM Tempfile
USE
RETURN
```

This program solves both possible problems mentioned earlier. A file lock by another user will prevent this routine from ever executing because the error condition that will result when the COPY STRUCTURE command executes will call the error-trapping routine, thus alerting the user that the file is in use. And a lengthy append process by the person running a program like this one will not cause problems for others because it is a temporary file that is locked and not the master file used by everyone else.

Three other problems must be handled if you use batch processing. First, you need a good error-trapping routine (but that should be assumed for any network application). The error-trapping routine can let the user decide whether to retry the operation or quit and come back later. Second, records will get stored in the temporary file, and there is always the possibility that when the user finishes the appending process and the program attempts to copy these records back to the primary file, the primary file has been locked by another user. If you use the batch processing method for data entry, the error-trapping routine should set a flag alerting the remaining lines of your append routine that the primary file has not yet been updated. No overwrites to the temporary file should be permitted until the update process has taken place.

The third problem, which is also a problem in other areas of network database management, is that you will need temporary files for each user. In the preceding program, we say "COPY STRUCTURE TO tempfile", and then we use Tempfile in an exclusive mode. But what happens if five people want to add records, and their programs all use Tempfile for a temporary name? What happens is that we are right back where we started from with a file-contention problem. To get around this problem, everyone needs a different name for his or her temporary files. File contention can haunt you anywhere in your application. In reporting, for example, it is common to create temporary files that are used for specialized reports in a certain order and later discarded. Once one user runs the routine that creates a temporary file that is being written to, another user is effectively locked out of using the file with the same name.

There are at least a couple of ways around this problem. One is to store a different extension (often a user's initials) to a memory variable; the user can be prompted for the extension when starting the system. You then use macros to create the filenames. In the above example, assuming the user stored three characters to a variable called INITS by answering a prompt at the start of the program, you could create the file with commands like

```
STORE "Tempfile." + INITS TO TNAME
COPY STRUCTURE TO &TNAME
```

When appending the records back to the primary file, you would again use the designated name with the commands

```
USE Primary
APPEND FROM &TNAME
```

A second method, considerably more elegant and just slightly more complex, is to use the logical station number as a part of the filename.

The logical station number is a four-digit number, from 0001 to 0255, that gets assigned by the network operating system to each workstation as it logs on to the network. If you are using Novell's Advanced NetWare, you will need to use the Novell SYSCON utility to add the following line to the system logon script before you can use the station number:

```
SET STA = %STATION
```

This line will create a variable in NetWare's environmental area called *STA*. The variable will contain the logical station number for that particular workstation.

When running a dBASE program, you can access the workstation number with the GETENV( ) function, used to get environmental variables from the operating system. For example, the following commands

```
STA = GETENV("STA")
STATION = LTRIM(STR(STA,4,0))
```

will get that four-digit numeric variable and convert it to a three-digit character string that can then be used as a part of the filename, with commands like

```
TNAME = "Temp" + STATION + ".DBF"
NNAME = "Temp" + STATION + ".NDX"
COPY STRUCTURE TO &TNAME
USE &TNAME EXCLUSIVE
INDEX ON CUSTID TO &NNAME
<...more commands...>
```

This method takes no more work than the first one, other than using your network's operating system configuration utility to make sure that station numbers are available as environmental variables.

If batch processing looks too complex for your application, or if you are running an application on a small network with less intensive demands, you may choose the more common method of adding to and editing the primary files. This method is acceptable as long as you test for file and record availability. One way to perform this test is to write individual file-locking and record-locking routines that can be called from your adder or editor or from your indexing and printing routines.

The versions of such routines shown in the two following examples use the locking functions to attempt to lock the files or records in question. The two programs are identical except for the use of the appropriate functions (FLOCK( ) for files, RLOCK( ) for records) and a different time-out value (the FileLock program spends twice as long trying to complete the lock). If the attempted lock is unsuccessful, the routines pass a logical variable (called *FileBusy* or *RecBusy*) containing a value of "false" back to the calling programs.

```
*FileLock.PRG*
FileBusy = .F.
IF FLOCK()
     *lock successful this time, so...
     RETURN
ELSE
a 12, 5 SAY "File is locked... retrying..."
COUNTER = 100
DO WHILE COUNTER > 0
     a 13, 5 SAY "Attempts remaining:" +
LTRIM(STR(COUNTER)+"    ")
     IF FLOCK()
          EXIT
```

```
        ENDIF
        COUNTER = COUNTER - 1
ENDDO
IF COUNTER = 0
    FileBusy = .T.
    RETURN
ELSE
    WAIT "   *File LOCKED for your exclusive use.*"
ENDIF
RETURN



*RecLock.PRG*
RecBusy = .F.
IF RLOCK()
    *lock successful this time, so...
    RETURN
ELSE
@ 12, 5 SAY "Record is locked... retrying..."
COUNTER = 50
DO WHILE COUNTER > 0
    @ 13, 5 SAY "Attempts remaining: " +
LTRIM(STR(COUNTER)+"   ")
    IF RLOCK()
            EXIT
    ENDIF
    COUNTER = COUNTER - 1
ENDDO
IF COUNTER = 0
    RecBusy = .T.
    RETURN
ELSE
    WAIT "    *Record LOCKED for your exclusive use.*"
ENDIF
RETURN
```

You can call routines like FileLock.PRG and RecLock.PRG inside of
your add, edit, delete, and print routines to lock records or files before
performing data entry or updates. The add record and edit record
routines shown below call the programs in the above examples.

```
*Adder.PRG adds records on a LAN*
*Last update 10/19/87*
DO WHILE .T.
    IF .NOT. FLOCK()
            DO FileLock
    ENDIF
    IF FileBusy
            FileBusy = .F.
            CLEAR
            WAIT " File locked by another.  Cannot add records now."
            RETURN
    ENDIF
    APPEND BLANK
    <...commands to create memory variables...>
    <...commands to get data from user...>
    <...commands to replace field contents with variables...>
            CLEAR
ACCEPT "Add another? Y/N: " TO ANS
IF UPPER(ANS) = "N"
    EXIT
ENDIF
```

```
ENDDO
UNLOCK
RETURN


*EDITOR.PRG EDITS RECORDS*
*LAN version*
*LAST UPDATE 10/19/87
SET EXCLUSIVE OFF
USE STOCKS INDEX STOCKS
CLEAR
MLAST = SPACE(40)
MFIRST = SPACE(40)
@ 5, 6 SAY [LAST NAME ?] GET MLAST
@ 6, 6 SAY [FIRST NAME ?] GET MFIRST
READ
FINDIT = MLAST + MFIRST
SEEK FINDIT
IF .NOT. FOUND()
     CLEAR
     @ 5, 5 SAY [CAN'T FIND THAT NAME. CHECK SPELLING.]
     WAIT
     USE
     RETURN
ENDIF
CLEAR
DO WHILE .NOT. EOF()
     STORE "N" TO EDITANS
     CLEAR
     @ 3, 2 TO 17,70
     @ 5, 5 SAY [LASTNAME] + LASTNAME
     @ 6, 5 SAY [FIRSTNAME] + FIRSTNAME
     @ 7, 5 SAY [ADDRESS] + TRIM(ADDR1)+ " " + ADDR2
     @ 8, 5 SAY TRIM(CITY)+ " "+TRIM(STATE)+ " " + ZIP
     @ 10, 5 SAY "IS THIS THE DESIRED RECORD TO EDIT? Y/N;
     or C to Cancel"
     @ 15, 62 GET EDITANS
     READ
     DO CASE
     CASE UPPER(EDITANS) = "C"
          EXIT

     CASE UPPER(EDITANS) = "Y"
          IF .NOT. RLOCK()
               DO RECLOCK
          ENDIF
          IF RECBUSY
               RECBUSY = .F.
               CLEAR
               WAIT "That record is in use by another. Try later."
               RETURN
          ENDIF
          CLEAR
          <...commands to create memory variables...>
          <...commands to get data from user...>
          <...commands to replace field contents with variables...>
          CLEAR
          EXIT

     CASE UPPER(EDITANS) = "N"
          SKIP
          IF FINDIT <> LASTNAME + FIRSTNAME
               CLEAR
               @ 5, 5 SAY "Sorry...no more records;
               by that name."
               WAIT "Press a key to return to menu."
               EXIT
          ENDIF
     ENDCASE
ENDDO
USE
RETURN
```

Handling the ESC Key

You may want to think about how you handle the ESC key on a network. Different users may mean different things when they press ESC. A novice user may be trying to say, "I'm confused." A seasoned pro may be saying, "Give me the dot prompt so I can code a quick report using MODIFY COMMAND." How do you handle both requests in the same program? (If you are leaning towards the use of the ACCESS( ) function, that is one good solution.) Decide which access level should allow users the privilege of the dot prompt. Then, add an ON ESCAPE command at the start of the program that transfers control to a subroutine or procedure when ESC is pressed, something like

```
ON ESCAPE DO BACKOUT
```

In the called program, you can choose whether or not to provide a dot prompt, using code that executes based on the access level set with the PROTECT utility. You could use commands like the following:

```
*Backout.PRG*
IF ACCESS > 6
      CLEAR ALL
      CANCEL
ELSE
      CLEAR ALL
      CLEAR
      a 5, 5 SAY "Aborting operation at your request."
      RETURN TO MASTER
ENDIF
*end of Backout.PRG*
```

NETWORK-SPECIFIC HINTS

The hints in this section apply to different networks and are based on general experience in working with networks. One of these hints may save you trouble some day.

Desperately Seeking Records: Avoid The LOCATE Trap

In your code for finding an appropriate record, there are strong reasons for avoiding the use of LOCATE when running on a network. The problem with LOCATE under the dBASE Administrator is that the LOCATE command stops on *all* locked records because dBASE cannot evaluate a LOCATE condition for a record that has been locked. If a record has been locked by one user and another user carries out a LOCATE command that is searching for a record that falls after the locked record, the dBASE Administrator will halt at the locked record and display a "record is in use by another" message. There are at least two ways around this problem. The obvious solution is to abandon the use of LOCATE in favor of FIND and SEEK. The second solution is to use the file-locking function (FLOCK) or the SET EXCLUSIVE command to lock the file, perform the LOCATE command, and then unlock the file and lock the record.

Running ACCESS on a File Server

The dBASE documentation says that you can use ACCESS on a File Server to make the File Server do double duty as both a server and a workstation. In theory perhaps, but in practice using ACCESS on the server usually does not work out. If you are using Novell NetWare, do *not* attempt to install a copy of ACCESS on the server, no matter what the manual says. If you are running on AT&T's STARLAN, you will find that once the STARLAN O/S fully loads into memory, there is not enough free RAM left to run the dBASE Administrator through ACCESS on a File Server. And on an IBM PC Network, the dBASE Administrator supports only dedicated servers. If you need another workstation, buy another workstation; don't severely lower network performance by attempting to make a server do double duty as a workstation.

Memory Constraints

If your workstations do not have at least 384K of memory, get them upgraded. File servers should have no less than 640K. If you are running into memory conflicts, make sure the CONFIG.SYS files contain the recommended numbers of files and buffers. On an AT&T Starlan, the CONFIG.SYS file should contain FILES = 51 and BUFFERS = 17. On an IBM PC Network, use FILES = 45 and BUFFERS = 30 at the servers; the normal nonnetwork files and buffers statements will do fine at the workstations.

A large number of problems due to the inability to find desired files are often the result of improper mapping of your network drives. Make sure that directories that need to be public are public. If properly set up, the batch files that take your users into dBASE can create the necessary paths or maps to the logical drives on the network. An example of a batch file for starting dBASE on a Novell network is shown here.

```
echo off
map h:=sys:dbase
map i:=sys:dbase\personnl
map j:=sys:dbase\accounts
if exist c:\dbase\access.com goto Ready
goto NoGood
:Ready
path c:\dbase;z:.;y:.;x:.;
c:
cd\dbase
access m=g:
goto Finis
:NoGood
echo Access missing, Contact System Admin. to use dBASE.
:Finis
cls
```

Of course, your batch file may differ, depending on where you keep your public and private files, and on which network operating system you are using. Nevertheless, all network systems have their own commands for designating available files; the appropriate commands should be used so that users don't get the idea that something is missing when it isn't.

14: Uncommon Techniques

This chapter covers a variety of advanced topics that you may find useful as you work with dBASE:

- Using RUN and external data

- Enhancing dBASE power with LOAD and CALL

- Drawing bar charts

- Searching memo fields

- External editors

- Using INKEY( ) and READKEY( )

- dBASE II conversions

USING RUN AND EXTERNAL DATA

Sometimes when you are working with an unusual application, your first thought after a need becomes evident in the design stage is, "How am I going to do that?" For many tasks that either strain the limits of dBASE or that can't be done in dBASE at all, a favored command is RUN. It stands to reason that dBASE can't be expected to do everything, no matter how flexible its programming language may be. dBASE is still a database manager, and therefore you run into major design constraints when you try to make it imitate a spreadsheet, word processor, or communications program. At times you must have a door to the outside world, and you must be able to move information through that door. One effective way to do so, without being a whiz at assembler, is to write external programs using the tool of your choice, be it Turbo Pascal, Quick BASIC, C, or simply SuperKey or ProKey macros.

The external process performs an operation that builds an external data file. Once the external application has been performed, APPEND the data from the external file into a dBASE database, and perform whatever manipulations are needed to put the data into manageable form. If the external data contains text downloaded from a mainframe, a widely used approach is a temporary database containing one field, 254 characters in length. Use ZAP to get rid of any current records in the temporary file, and then use the APPEND FROM *filename* SDF command to append the lines of text from the external file into the temporary database. You can then use the appropriate substring and other functions to convert the data into something you can use.

If the external process produces a file that appears as columnar data, you can create a temporary database with a structure matching the external file, and then use the APPEND FROM *filename* SDF command to get the data directly into the dBASE file in manageable form. Your program can then isolate the usable records, delete unwanted headings that come across as records, and move the qualified records from the temporary file into the permanent database.

In one application, this design was used to query an online service for historical data on stock purchases, capture the response (as one month's prices for a given stock) to a text file, and convert the text file to a database containing the stock prices. In this particular application, the dBASE command that started the external process happened to be

```
RUN KEY /ML STOCKS.MAC
```

This command loaded a SuperKey macro. (SuperKey is a commercial keyboard enhancer with a simple programming language of its own that can be used to simulate keystrokes that call and run other programs outside the dBASE environment.) In this application, the command line passed on to SuperKey (/ML STOCKS.MAC) caused a self-executing SuperKey macro to load. The macro then simulated the keystrokes necessary to load PC-TALK (a communications program), dial Compu-Serve, and request one month's historical data on a given stock. While the data was being retrieved, it was also stored to a text file opened by the SuperKey macro.

Once the query from the online service is completed, the SuperKey macro closes the text file, disconnects the modem, and returns control to the dBASE program. The dBASE program then appends the text file into a database of multiple-character fields, deletes the first five and last three records (which contain unneeded headers and footers from the online service), does string manipulation to convert character strings like "123 1/2" to values like 123.5, and moves the converted data into a permanent file containing a history of stock trades.

Obviously, unless your task matches this one precisely, your approach must be different, but this example shows how dBASE can be used with other programs to perform the complete job. One caveat to keep in mind is that you may need plenty of memory for schemes like this one. In this case, dBASE III PLUS, Borland's SuperKey, and PC-TALK III were all in memory during the download from CompuServe, thus necessitating the use of a 640K machine.

ENHANCING dBASE POWER
WITH LOAD AND CALL

Two dBASE commands that do much toward tapping power not normally present in dBASE are the LOAD and CALL commands, used to access assembly-language programs written in binary (.BIN) format. You can transfer control to an assembly-language routine, and, assuming the program is written to move data, you can pass data from the routine back to dBASE. The LOAD command is used to tell dBASE that the assembly-language routine exists and is to be loaded into memory for future use. The syntax for the command is

```
LOAD <binary filename.ext>
```

and the extension is optional; if omitted, it is assumed to be .BIN. Up to five binary files can be loaded into memory at once, and each can be up to 32K. (Unneeded modules that have been loaded into memory can be released with the RELEASE MODULE *module name* command.)

Once the binary file has been loaded into memory, it can be executed at any time by using the CALL command, the syntax of which is

```
CALL <module name> [WITH <expression>/<memory variable>]
```

where the *module name* is the name of the binary file (the extension is omitted). The optional WITH clause lets you specify a character expression or a memory variable that is passed to the assembly-language routine. When your dBASE program processes the CALL command, control is passed to the binary routine, and execution begins at the first byte of the routine. Once control passes to the routine, the data segment (DS and BX registers) will contain the address for the first byte of the memory variable or character expression that was passed from dBASE.

dBASE treats binary files loaded and executed with the LOAD and CALL commands differently from external program files executed with RUN. When you use RUN, dBASE creates a DOS shell and transfers control to the program called with RUN. Because you are building a duplicate of COMMAND.COM in memory and loading the external program, RUN can eat significant amounts of memory. With LOAD and CALL, however, dBASE treats the binary files as subroutines or "modules" and not as external programs. As a result, dBASE needs considerably less additional memory to use LOAD and CALL. You may encounter problems on a 256K machine, but any system with 384K or more should allow dBASE and your external assembly-language routines to coexist without difficulty. One caveat: if you are writing programs that must work in dBASE III as well as dBASE III PLUS environments, you may have to find other ways to handle the job because dBASE III does not support the LOAD and CALL commands.

An Example: How LOAD and CALL Can Be Used

A simple example demonstrates the ease with which LOAD and CALL can be used, and for this simple example you will need nothing more than your DOS diskettes and dBASE. Find your DOS Supplemental Diskette and copy the program DEBUG.COM onto your working disk or into a directory accessible through your PATH commands or into your dBASE directory.

This binary routine, which changes the shape of the cursor, performs the same task as the fine example on page 5-122 of the dBASE III PLUS documentation. If you refer to that example in your documentation, you can use the IBM Macro Assembler (assuming you own a copy) to assemble the routine shown on that page; however, a program to do this sort of job is so short that it would be easier to create it using the mini-assembler present in DEBUG (and everyone who owns a copy of

DOS already has DEBUG). To try creating the program, get to the DOS prompt and enter **DEBUG**. The DEBUG prompt (a hyphen) will appear. Enter the following:

```
A               (press Return)
MOV CX,[BX]     (press Return)
MOV AH,1        (press Return)
INT 10          (press Return)
RETF            (press Return)
                (press Return again; hyphen will appear.)
RCX             (press Return; colon will appear.)
7               (press Return; hyphen will appear.)
NCURSOR.BIN     (press Return)
W               (press Return; file will be saved to disk.)
Q               (press Return to get back to DOS.)
```

This book is not meant to serve as an introduction to assembler; there are enough texts on the market serving that purpose. It is sufficient to say that the above commands used the mini-assembler built into DEBUG to create a binary assembly-language routine. With the program CURSOR.BIN saved on disk, get into dBASE and from the dot prompt enter

```
LOAD CURSOR
```

to load the BIN file into memory. Then enter

```
CALL CURSOR WITH CHR(18)
```

to change the shape of the cursor to a flashing block. This simple example performs an admittedly simple function, but all binary routines, no matter how complex, can be accessed from within dBASE in the same manner.

Sources of Assembler Routines

For those who are thinking, "This is just fine for those assembly-language hackers, but I have no intention of writing code in assembler," the good news is that you don't have to if you don't want to. There is no shortage of assembly-language .BIN files on publicly available disks, from software vendors and user groups, and advertised on bulletin boards. Many of the utilities provided with commercial products such as dBASE Tools For C and Tom Rettig's Library (described in Chapter 13) are .BIN files, executable with the LOAD and CALL commands.

Assembler Guidelines and a Warning

Certain guidelines must be followed if you are designing your own binary files to be accessed from dBASE with the LOAD and CALL commands. If you write your own binary files, the guidelines that follow will make sense. If you don't, the guidelines that follow become someone else's problem; however, that person should be aware of them.

1. Your binary routine must begin (ORG) its first executable instruction at offset zero.

2. Leave the stack pointer and the contents of the stack *alone.* Violating this rule is a sure way to wreak havoc when you are attempting to return from the binary routine back to dBASE. At worst, you will crash your system, requiring a complete reboot. If you must play around with the stack within your routine, you should restore both the stack segment (SS) and code segment (CS) registers to their

original states before returning control to dBASE.

3. Do not design routines that consume additional RAM beyond the size of the program. The LOAD command uses the file size to allocate memory, and you may overwrite portions of dBASE in RAM if the program dramatically increases its memory needs.

4. Make sure that the binary routine ends with a FAR RETURN to ensure that program control will return to the address that was pushed onto the stack before the routine began its execution, particularly if someone else is writing a .BIN routine for use in dBASE for you. Many binary routines are written to end with an EXIT rather than a FAR RETURN. Assembly-language programs that end with an EXIT should be assembled into fully executable files and called with RUN rather than with LOAD and CALL.

Finally, a warning: if you usually use both binary routines accessed with LOAD and CALL and external programs accessed with RUN, you can paint yourself into a corner with memory-allocation conflicts that are very, very difficult to debug. If you use LOAD to load a series of binary files and then use RUN to run an external program before you get around to using the binary files with CALL commands, the effects of the RUN command may overwrite the binary files in memory. Then your program later tries a CALL command and jumps to a point in memory where the expected routine no longer exists. To avoid such a bizarre occurrence, change the MAXMEM value in the CONFIG.DB file to a value above the default of 256K.

DRAWING BAR GRAPHS

Bar graphs can be drawn using the CHR( ) and REPLICATE functions to plot representative columns on the screen. If your printer supports the extended character set, you can route the output to the printer and achieve similar results. A database containing the following data:

```
Record#   SALESREP       REPNUMB AMTSOLD

   1     Jones, C.       1003      350.00
   2     Artis, K.       1008      110.00
   3     Johnson, L.     1002      675.00
   4     Walker, B.      1006     1167.00
   5     Keemis, N.      1007       47.00
   6     Williams, E.    1010      256.00
   7     Smith, A.M.     1009      220.00
   8     Allen, L.       1005      312.00
   9     Smith, A.       1001      788.50
  10     Jones, J.       1011      875.00
  11     Shepard, F.     1004     1850.00
  12     Robertson, C.   1013      985.50
```

results in the display shown in Figure 14-1 when plotted with the
following program:

```
*Bars.PRG is bar graph program.
SET TALK OFF
Divisor = 30
*See note in text on calculating Divisor.
*AmtSold is field in database to be graphed.
CLEAR
USE SALES2
@ 2, 1
DO WHILE .NOT. EOF()
     BarLength = INT(AMTSOLD/DIVISOR)
     @ ROW(), 2 SAY REPLICATE(CHR(177),BarLength)
     @ ROW()+1, 2 SAY "Name: " + SALESREP
     @ ROW() + 2, 0
     IF ROW() > 18
          @ 20, 2 SAY "--------300-------600-------900--;
          ----1200------1500------1800"
          @ 1, 0 TO 21, 79 DOUBLE
          WAIT "Press a key for next screen..."
          CLEAR
          @ 2, 1
     ENDIF
     SKIP
ENDDO
IF ROW() > 2
     @ 20, 2 SAY "--------300-------600-------900--;
     ----1200------1500------1800"
     @ 1, 0 TO 21, 79 DOUBLE
     WAIT
ENDIF
RETURN
```

The program takes the contents of a field that is to be graphed (in
this case, AMTSOLD), divides it by a set amount (Divisor), and uses the
INT( ) function to return a whole number based on that figure. This
number, stored to the memory variable *BarLength,* is then used as an

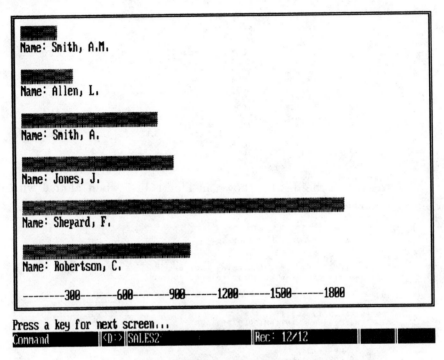

Figure 14-1.

Bar graph

argument in the REPLICATE( ) function to determine the length of the bar.

The calculation of the best value for Divisor is a simple matter: assuming you want to use almost a complete screen width for the longest bar, the value of Divisor must be no less than the value of the highest amount to be graphed, divided by the available screen width. In this example, the highest sales amount ($1850) divided by a screen width of 76 (which leaves room for the starting position and the borders) suggests a value no less than 24. The example uses a value of 30, partly to make the scale simple to construct and partly to leave room for increases in sales performance. You will need to adjust the scope of your scale accordingly.

SEARCHING MEMO FIELDS

A complaint often heard regarding the memo field, the poor stepchild of dBASE III/III PLUS, is that you can't search such fields for a string of text. Anyone who has stored items like bibliographic summaries, personnel reviews, or legal case notes in memo fields probably realizes that this limitation can come back to haunt you. This chapter is not going to reveal some sure-fire, heretofore unknown way to search memo fields in dBASE, if such a way exists. What will be described is an excellent, low-cost alternative that can solve the search problem for you.

The publishers of *Data Based Advisor,* a popular magazine aimed at users of PC database software, offer a low-cost program called Memo Searcher. The program costs $29 and uses a fast search routine written in Turbo Pascal to scan the .DBT file for text that matches a search string you supply. Memo Searcher can be run from within dBASE with the RUN command or from DOS. In its default mode, the program displays a menu that the user can respond to by answering a series of prompts for items like the database name and the string of text to search for. As the program finds matching records, the contents of the memo fields are displayed on the screen, along with the record numbers. (You can also store the matching memos and their record numbers to a file for printing at a later time.)

In an application, you can also include a single logical field as the first field in the database, and you can run Memo Searcher from dBASE, with an optional parameter that tells the program to set the logical field to true for each record that matches a search term. You can then create reports based on records containing a value of true in the logical field. In the following program, designed around the use of Memo Searcher,

```
*Searcher.PRG searches memo fields for text string.*
CLEAR
ACCEPT "Enter search term: " TO FINDER
CLEAR
a 5,5 SAY "please wait while I scan the records."
*make sure file is closed with use command first.
USE
RUN MEMOFILE LITIGATE &FINDER 1
CLEAR
USE LITIGATE INDEX LITIGATE
SET MEMOWIDTH TO 40
?
?    "Control-S starts and stops the display."
WAIT "    Press a key to see the found records..."
DISPLAY ALL BEGINNUMB, DATEOFDOC, SUMMARY FOR MEMOMARK
WAIT
RETURN
*end of Searcher.PRG.*
```

the command line RUN MEMOFILE LITIGATE &FINDER 1 tells the Memo Searcher to scan the database file (LITIGATE) for a character string stored to the variable *FINDER*. (The database must be closed before using the Memo Searcher.) In the database, the first field is a logical field named MEMOMARK. That field gets flagged as true for every record in which the search term is found. Then the database is again opened in dBASE, and the command DISPLAY ALL BEGIN-NUMB, DATEOFDOC, SUMMARY FOR MEMOMARK causes selected fields from all flagged records to be shown. There is a sacrifice of speed in this process because Memo Searcher must make one pass through the database to flag the records, and your report printing program must make another pass to display the records meeting the criteria. Still, this method is far better than being unable to search the memo fields at all. And if you are a developer, you will welcome the fact that the purchase of the software includes the rights to bundle it as a part of your application.

EXTERNAL EDITORS

Among the first things serious dBASE users do is to discard the built-in editor in favor of something with a little more heft. dBASE was not designed to be a word processor, but Ashton-Tate continues to provide an editor partly out of thoughtfulness and partly because it would be difficult to edit memo fields without one. Nevertheless, the editor is a limited imitation of WordStar (which is arguably not a state-of-the-art text editor). The 5000-character limit and the inability to do a block copy are usually enough to send serious users looking for another text editor. There is no shortage of choices; most word processors can successfully double as program editors. Integrating the editor into the dBASE environment so that it functions efficiently as a program editor may require some work, but the work will be worth the effort.

You can run editors with the RUN command, but an easier way is to modify the CONFIG.DB file so that it contains the commands

```
WP = <editor name>
TEDIT = <editor name>
```

where *editor name* is the name of your text editor, such as ED.EXE (PC-Write), PE.EXE (the WordPerfect program editor), or WS.EXE (WordStar). The WP command assigns the editor you designate as the text editor that appears when you create or edit entries in memo fields. The TEDIT command assigns the editor that appears when you use MODIFY COMMAND. You can include a path along with the name of the program if you want to.

Second, the editor you use must be able to load and save files as ASCII text; with most word processors, this is not a problem. For editing programs, it helps to set the program's default margins as long as possible so that word wraps do not become hard returns when program files are written as ASCII text. Although it is wasteful of disk space, it may be more convenient to duplicate the program to your dBASE directory and change the margins in that version of the program.

At least four programs are recommended as text editors because they all read and write text as ordinary ASCII files, thus saving you the trouble of remembering to save in a special "unformatted" or "nondocument" mode. The four that work well with dBASE (and there are probably others) are SideKick, PC-Write, the WordPerfect Program Editor, and the Norton Editor.

When loaded, all external editors consume some RAM. If you are tight on memory, consider the Norton Editor from Peter Norton Enterprises. The Norton Editor is small (taking about 45K to load), yet it gives you full editing features, including split screen and multiple-file editing, full search-and-replace, and block operations.

If you like extreme speed along with a product that never feels like it is in your way, consider the Notepad within Borland's SideKick. Since it is memory-resident, it gets loaded before dBASE rather than with the RUN command or with any variations in the CONFIG.DB file. The program's RAM-resident nature gives it advantages that non-RAM-resident programs can't offer; you can call up SideKick while the error message from a program bug is still on the screen, quickly make the change, and save it. The SideKick Notepad uses editing commands that duplicate those of WordStar, but you can use function keys, or you can change the keys to imitate some other word processor. SideKick will consume moderate amounts of memory, but you can reduce the memory requirements by loading limited versions of SideKick. (See the SideKick manual for details.)

If you prefer a full-featured word processor that is fast, can afford to give up a significant amount of memory, and want to spend as little money as possible, PC-Write will be hard to beat. Because PC-Write is a shareware product, its authors ask for a voluntary contribution if you use the product; it can be obtained from bulletin boards and user groups or by sending $10 to the program's supplier, Quicksoft. PC-Write has grown larger over the years and will easily chew up 128K of RAM by the time you load a good-sized program for editing. But it is still very fast, still writes files as unadulterated ASCII, and has about every feature you could want in a word processor.

The final choice mentioned is the WordPerfect Program Editor, provided as a part of the WordPerfect Library (and *not* to be confused with the standard version of WordPerfect). The WordPerfect Program Editor reads and writes files as ASCII text in its default mode; the standard WordPerfect word processor, on the other hand, writes files as something very different from unadulterated ASCII. In most other respects, the features and keystroke sequences of the WordPerfect Program Editor are the same as in the other version of WordPerfect. If you use either WordPerfect's Program Editor or PC-Write as your program editor, you may want to change the default right margin to a value of around 80 or 100 characters so that you can enter long lines in programs without forced word wrapping.

USING INKEY( ) AND READKEY( )

The INKEY( ) function can detect a single keystroke. "So does the WAIT command," you say; "What's so special about INKEY( )?" There are two significant differences. First, the WAIT command halts the execution of the program; it can do nothing else while awaiting a response. The INKEY( ) function, on the other hand, can monitor the keyboard as a part of a loop, during which time other commands can be carried out. You could, for example, have something like

```
STORE 0 TO KEYS
@ 5, 5 SAY "Printing.  Press any key to halt."
DO WHILE .NOT. EOF() .AND. KEYS = 0
     ? PATIENT, ROOMNO, DIAGNOSED, ADMITTED, INSURED
     KEYS = INKEY()
     SKIP
ENDDO
<...more commands...>
```

Any key that is pressed gets stored in the keyboard buffer, and the INKEY( ) function will act on it when the statement containing INKEY( ) next executes.

The second important difference is that INKEY( ) can be used to test for keys that aren't normally monitored by ACCEPT, INPUT, or WAIT. The cursor keys, control-key combinations, and function keys fall into this category. When a key is pressed, the INKEY( ) function returns an integer matching the ASCII value of that key if it is an alphanumeric key, and a special value if it is a function or cursor key. For example, the value of the F10 key is −9. If you wanted to encourage the use of F10 as a universal "quit" key, you could rewrite the prior example to look like this:

```
STORE 0 TO KEYS
@ 5, 5 SAY "Printing. Press F10 to abort and exit."
DO WHILE .NOT. EOF() .AND. KEYS # −9
     ? PATIENT, ROOMNO, DIAGNOSED, ADMITTED, INSURED
     KEYS = INKEY()
     SKIP
ENDDO
<...more commands...>
```

In a similar fashion, the INKEY( ) function could be used to trap function keys used to execute menu options or UP-ARROW and DOWN-ARROW keys used to move between screens. The values returned by the INKEY() function for the more unusual keys are listed in Table 14-1.

Table 14-1.

Values Returned by INKEY ( )

F1	28	CTRL-F1	94	ALT-F1	104
F2	−1	CTRL-F2	95	ALT-F2	105
F3	−2	CTRL-F3	96	ALT-F3	106
F4	−3	CTRL-F4	97	ALT-F4	107
F5	−4	CTRL-F5	98	ALT-F5	108
F6	−5	CTRL-F6	99	ALT-F6	109
F7	−6	CTRL-F7	100	ALT-F7	110
F8	−7	CTRL-F8	101	ALT-F8	111
F9	−8	CTRL-F9	102	ALT-F9	112
F10	−9	CTRL-F10	103	ALT-F10	113

PGUP	18	CTRL-PGUP	31
PGDN	3	CTRL-PGDN	30
HOME	1	CTRL-HOME	29
END	6	CTRL-END	23
RIGHT ARROW	4	CTRL-RIGHT ARROW	2
LEFT ARROW	19	CTRL-LEFT ARROW	26
UP ARROW	5		
DOWN ARROW	24		
DEL	7		
INS	22		
TAB	9		
BACKSPACE	127		

The READKEY( ) function is useful in the same way. It can be used
to tell a program which key was used to exit from a full-screen operation
such as READ or EDIT. You can use READKEY( ) to detect noncharacter keys such as CTRL-END and ESC or CTRL-Q, PGUP, PGDN, and the
other keys that will let you exit from a full-screen operation. READ-

KEY( ) also has a split personality in that it returns different values depending on whether changes were made to the record or not. As an example, when using the REPLACE command to replace the contents of fields with the contents of memory variables, you may want to perform a long, time-consuming string of REPLACE commands only if the user did not try to abort the process by pressing ESC or the CTRL-Q key combination. You could do so with commands like these in your edit routine:

```
<...@...SAY...GET commands to get data...>
READ
IF READKEY() <> 268 .AND. READKEY() <> 12
   *Escape not pressed.
   REPLACE LAST WITH M_LAST, FIRST WITH M_FIRST
   <...more REPLACE commands...>
ENDIF
```

The replacements would take place as long as the ESC or equivalent CTRL-Q keys were not used to exit the full-screen operation. Table 14-2 shows the values returned by the READKEY( ) function for frequently used keys.

Note that the F1 function key can return a value to the READKEY( ) function. This can come in handy if you believe that F1 should always be used for access to help screens. You could structure a conditional expression that would determine if F1 had been pressed in an attempt to exit from a full-screen operation. If F1 had been pressed, you could then proceed to display appropriate help screens as a response.

dBASE II CONVERSIONS

As hard as it is to believe, a substantial number of people still use dBASE II on 16-bit, MS-DOS compatible machines. If you are faced with the unenviable task of moving a dBASE II application over to dBASE III PLUS, help is available in the form of the dCONVERT program, supplied on the Sample Programs and Utilities Disk in the dBASE

Table 14-2.

READKEY ( ) Values

Key Combination	Value Returned (No Data Change)	Value Returned (Data Change)
CTRL-END or CTRL-W	14	270
ESC or CTRL-Q	12	268
CTRL-S, CTRL-H, or BACKSPACE	0	256
CTRL-D or RIGHT ARROW	1	257
CTRL-A or HOME	2	258
CTRL-F or END	3	259
CTRL-E or UP ARROW	4	260
CTRL-X or DOWN ARROW	5	261
CTRL-R or PGUP	6	262
CTRL-C or PGDN	7	263
CTRL-Z or CTRL-LEFT ARROW	8	264
CTRL-B or CTRL-RIGHT ARROW	9	265
CTRL-U	10	266
CTRL-N	11	267
CTRL-M (or type past end of field)	15	271
RETURN	16	272
CTRL-HOME	33	289
CTRL-PGUP	34	290
CTRL-PGDN	35	291
F1	36	292

package. The dCONVERT program is designed to convert databases, screen and report format, memory variables, and command (or program) files from dBASE II format to dBASE III/III PLUS format. The program can also convert dBASE III/III PLUS databases back to dBASE II format, within certain limits: databases of more than 32 fields will not convert from dBASE III/III PLUS to dBASE II because dBASE II does not support databases of more than 32 fields. Also, any memo fields will be lost because dBASE II has no support for memo fields.

To use the program, copy the file, DCONVERT.EXE, to your dBASE subdirectory, and run it from the DOS prompt by entering DCONVERT. Figure 14-2 shows the choices available under dCONVERT.

The use of dCONVERT is straightforward: simply select the type of file to be converted by highlighting the choice and pressing ENTER, and then respond to the prompts for the names of the input (old) and output (new) files. When a conversion is completed, dCONVERT renames the old file by adding a letter "B" as the last letter of the extension and names the new file with the same original name as the old file.

The only true conversion not offered by dCONVERT is with index files. What dCONVERT provides instead is a small program containing the commands necessary to rebuild the indexes. You may choose to run this program with a DO *filename* command, or you may decide to rebuild the indexes manually with the usual INDEX commands.

You can also use dCONVERT while bypassing the menus by sending filenames or wildcards to the program as a part of the command line. For example, the command

```
DCONVERT A:MAILER.DBF
```

would convert the dBASE II database called MAILER.DBF on drive A to dBASE III PLUS format and store it on the default drive. In a similar fashion, the command

```
DCONVERT A:*.DBF
```

could be used to convert all database files on the disk in drive A and store the newly converted files on the default drive.

```
┌─────────────────────────────────────────────────────────────────────┐
│                                                                       │
│      dBASE CONVERT - dBASE III File Conversion Aid  v2.01  11/19/85    │
│            (c) 1984 By Ashton-Tate   All Rights Reserved              │
│                                                                       │
│                      dBASE II --> dBASE III                          │
│                                                                       │
│              1 - Database File        <.DBF> _                        │
│              2 - Memory Variable File <.MEM>                          │
│              3 - Report Format File   <.FRM>                          │
│              4 - Command File         <.PRG>                          │
│              5 - Screen Format File   <.FMT>                          │
│              6 - Index File Help      <.NDX>                          │
│              7 - Un-dCONVERT III->II  <.DBF>                          │
│                                                                       │
│              9 -         Instructions                                │
│              0 -             EXIT                                     │
│                                                                       │
│                                                                       │
│                                                                       │
│                                                                       │
│      < Use cursor arrows to move between choices;  hit RETURN to select choice >   │
│                                                                       │
└─────────────────────────────────────────────────────────────────────┘
```

Figure 14-2.

Main menu for dCONVERT
program

Converting Command Files

Converting command files from dBASE II to later versions of dBASE
can prove troublesome because dBASE III and dBASE III PLUS are so
different from dBASE II. Menu choice number 4 of dCONVERT will do
its best to perform a conversion that will run without errors, but you
will probably need to do some fine-tuning before the program will run

properly. Once a program file has been converted from dBASE II to dBASE III PLUS, examine the new program code carefully. Any lines in the program prefixed by an asterisk (*) and two exclamation points (!!) are lines so syntactically different that dCONVERT could not perform the conversion accurately. Some other areas in the program may also cause problems, but dCONVERT will be unable to warn you that those areas exist, often because of subtle differences in operation between dBASE II and later versions of dBASE. The only way to completely debug converted code is to run the code under the dBASE III PLUS environment and test all of the program options thoroughly.

15: Modular
Programming

Don't get the impression that this chapter is going to take you through a textbook discussion of the benefits of system analysis and modular design. You can find that kind of a discussion in more than enough basic programming textbooks. Instead, this chapter will demonstrate ways to design dBASE applications in modular form so that you can easily use the same code repeatedly. Assuming you write programs in dBASE (and if you don't, you probably would not be reading this chapter), chances are you are spending time developing more than one program. If all your dBASE work does center on a single application (like that monster sales-tracking system that keeps tabs on things at your office), then writing modular programs may not bring you much more than a warm feeling for having developed efficient code. But if you have to develop or maintain a number of different applications at your work location or for others, you will save a good deal of time by writing programs in modules and reusing those modules (with appropriate modifications) for different tasks.

The first step in adopting a system of modular dBASE coding is to recognize that the tasks in most dBASE applications fall into the same kinds of groups. Applications provide a main menu, leading to choices stored in individual programs or as procedures. Among those other tasks handled within the submodules, or individual procedures of the dBASE application, are the tasks of adding records, editing records, and deleting unwanted records. You can break many of the subtasks into similar parts. As an example, consider the task of editing records in a database. Well-written routines for editing records perform at least six tasks within the editing module:

1. Finding the desired record to edit

2. Storing the contents of the fields into memory variables

3. Displaying the prompts and the memory variables on the screen

4. Allowing editing of the memory variables with GET statements

5. Performing any data validation desired, and allowing corrections when necessary

6. Moving the validated data into the database

Most programs written to edit records are written as a complete submodule that handles all six tasks listed above. But if you are going to use and reuse your code for multiple applications, strict adherence to the concepts behind modular programming suggests that you go a step farther and create individual modules for the individual steps. This may seem like a lot of work, but the first time you need to use the existing code in another application, you will be glad that you chose this method of design.

A general approach to consider following in designing highly modular code for a dBASE application is to write the following routines for each database file and enclose the routines within a procedure file that can be accessed through the SET PROCEDURE TO *filename* command:

- A "display" routine for adding borders and graphic designs in a consistent format

- A "makevars" routine for creating memory variables

- A "fillvars" routine for moving the contents of a field into a memory variable

- A "sayer" routine to display the prompts and memory variables

- A "getter" routine for getting memory variables

- A "validate" routine for performing any desired data validation

- A "movevars" routine to move the contents of the memory variables into the database fields

- A "finder" routine to locate records based on FIND or SEEK commands using available index files

As an example of the preceding routines, consider the procedures described within a procedure file:

```
*Procedrs.PRG
Procedure Border
@ 0, 0 TO 19, 79 DOUBLE
@ 0, 1 TO 4, 78 DOUBLE
Draw = 1
Do While Draw < 4
    @ Draw, 2 SAY REPLICATE(chr(176),76)
    Draw = Draw + 1
Enddo
```

```
Return
**********************
Procedure Finder
DO MAKEVARS
@ 5, 5 SAY "Last name? " GET M_LAST
@ 6, 5 SAY "First name? " GET M_FIRST
STORE M_LAST + M_FIRST TO FINDIT
SEEK FINDIT
RETURN
**********************
Procedure Sayer
@ 5, 10 SAY "Last Name:"
@ 5, 22 SAY M_LAST
@ 6, 10 SAY "First name:"
@ 6, 22 SAY M_FIRST
@ 7, 10 SAY "Address:"
@ 7, 22 SAY M_ADDRESS
@ 8, 15 SAY "City:"
@ 8, 22 SAY M_CITY
@ 9, 15 SAY "State:"
@ 9, 22 SAY M_STATE
@ 10, 15 SAY "Zip:"
@ 10, 22 SAY M_ZIP
RETURN
**********************
Procedure Getter
@ 5, 22 GET M_LAST
@ 6, 22 GET M_FIRST
@ 7, 22 GET M_ADDRESS
@ 8, 22 GET M_CITY
@ 9, 22 GET M_STATE
@ 10, 22 GET M_ZIP
RETURN
**********************
Procedure MakeVars
PUBLIC M_LAST, M_FIRST, M_ADDRESS, M_CITY,;
M_STATE, M_ZIP
M_LAST = space(20)
M_FIRST = space(20)
M_ADDRESS = space(30)
M_CITY = space(20)
M_STATE = space(2)
M_ZIP = space(10)
RETURN
**********************
Procedure FillVars
M_LAST = LAST
M_FIRST = FIRST
M_ADDRESS = ADDRESS
M_CITY = CITY
M_STATE = STATE
M_ZIP = ZIP
RETURN
**********************
Procedure MoveVars
REPLACE LAST WITH M_LAST, FIRST WITH M_FIRST,;
ADDRESS WITH M_ADDRESS, CITY WITH M_CITY,;
STATE WITH M_STATE, ZIP WITH M_ZIP
RETURN
**********************
Procedure Validate
IF M_LAST = SPACE(20)
   WAIT " Name required!"
   VALID = .F.
ENDIF
RETURN
```

By putting all of these tasks in a procedure file and using DO commands to call the procedures from your add, edit, and delete subroutines, you can repeatedly use the same procedures in all of the routines. A program for adding records, using the above procedures, can be visually laid out in a block diagram (see Figure 15-1). The resultant code that might be used follows.

```
*Adder.PRG adds records*
VALID = .T.
DO WHILE .T.
    DO MAKEVARS
    DO BORDER
    @ 3, 10 SAY "DATA ENTRY SCREEN ADD NEW RECORDS"
    DO SAYER
    DO GETTER
    READ
    DO VALIDATE
    IF .NOT. VALID
        LOOP
    ENDIF
    APPEND BLANK
    DO MOVEVARS
    ACCEPT "Add another record? Y/N:" TO ANS
    IF UPPER(ANS) = "N"
        EXIT
    ENDIF
ENDDO
```

Create Dummy Variables	Display Borders	Display Prompts	Get Variables
Validate Data	Append Blank Record	Store Data in Database	

Figure 15-1.

Block diagram of add routine

The beauty of taking program modularization down to this level is
that you can use the same code that is already in the procedures for the
edit and delete routines. An editing routine that assumes the database is
indexed on a combination of last and first names is illustrated in Figure
15-2. The resultant code that might be used follows.

```
*Editor.PRG edits records
DO WHILE .T.
    CLEAR
    DO MAKEVARS
    DO FINDER
    VALID = .T.
    IF FOUND()
        CLEAR
        DO BORDER
        DO FILLVARS
        DO SAYER
        DO GETTER
        READ
        DO VALIDATE
        IF .NOT. VALID
            EXIT
        ENDIF
        DO MOVEVARS
        CLEAR
        ACCEPT "Edit another? " TO ANS
        IF UPPER(ANS) = "N"
            EXIT
        ENDIF
    ELSE
        CLEAR
        @ 5, 5 SAY "No record by that name!"
        WAIT
        EXIT
    ENDIF
ENDDO
```

Prompt User for SEEK Expression	Find Desired Record	Display Borders	Move Existing Data into Variables	Display Prompts
Get Variables	Validate Data	Store Data in Database		

Figure 15-2.

Block diagram of edit routine

Your routine for deleting records would use much of the same code, like that illustrated in Figure 15-3 and shown in the code that follows.

```
DO WHILE .T.
   CLEAR
   STORE "Y" TO ANS
   DO FINDER
   DO MAKEVARS
   IF FOUND()
      CLEAR
      DO BORDER
      DO FILLVARS
      DO SAYER
      @ 20, 5 SAY "Delete record, are you SURE? Y/N:"
      @ 20,40 GET ANS
      READ
      IF UPPER(ANS) = "Y"
         DELETE
      ENDIF
   ELSE
      CLEAR
      @ 5, 5 SAY "No record by that name!"
      WAIT
      EXIT
   ENDIF
ENDDO
```

Since the routines that perform the adding, editing, and deleting of records are generic (containing little or nothing specific to that particular application), when you need to rewrite an application for a different database design you will need to make most changes only in the procedure file.

| Prompt User for SEEK Expression | Find Desired Record | Display Borders | Move Existing Data into Variables | Display Prompts |
| Display Variables on Screen | Prompt User to Verify Deletion | Delete Record | | |

Figure 15-3.

Block diagram of delete routine

When do you modularize? It's easy to get carried away and modularize virtually every task in an application, but this can and probably will result in a loss of speed because you may need to swap multiple procedure files in and out of memory since each procedure file is limited to a maximum of 20 procedures. A major objective of this approach is to save you time by duplicating code in more than one location, and therefore a general rule to follow becomes rather obvious. If the task is likely to be repeated at more than one place in your application, code that task as a procedure, and call it from the procedure file. If the task will only be performed once, you may want to leave it as program code integral to that particular routine, since calling it as a procedure won't provide you with any visible benefits.

16: A Complete
Database System

This chapter includes a complete database system written in dBASE. This system manages accounts receivable, and it makes use of two database files: INVOICES, which contains a record of each invoice sent out by the company, and CUSTOMER, which contains a record of each customer who gets billed for a product or service. The application makes extensive use of procedures to minimize the amount of code that must be duplicated, in a fashion similar to that described in Chapter 15. Figure 16-1 illustrates the overall design of the program. The database structures and the programs themselves that make up the system begin after the diagram. Appendix C contains generic user documentation that applies to the accounts receivable system; the documentation can be used with no changes for the system described in this chapter, or it can be modified to serve as an example of user documentation for your customized applications.

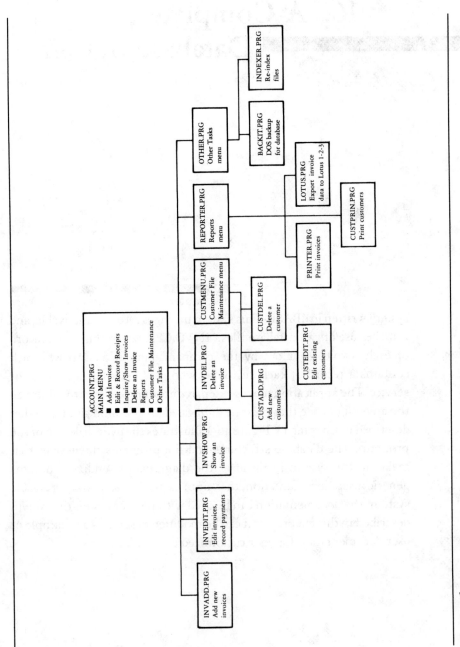

Figure 16-1.

Overall design of accounts receivable system

The command files for the system consist of a main menu that calls one of seven programs. Three of those programs (CUSTMENU.PRG, REPORTER.PRG, and OTHER.PRG) serve as secondary menus that call additional routines. The other four programs (INVADD.PRG, INVEDIT.PRG, INVSHOW.PRG, and INVDEL.PRG) are used for adding, editing, displaying, and deleting invoices. Note that the system makes use of SET DELETED ON and does not provide a PACK option, leaving the use of the PACK command up to the programmer. If a PACK option is desired, it could easily be added as an option in the OTHER.PRG menu, which currently provides reindexing and backup options.

The database files use four index files. The CUSTOMER database is indexed on the CUSTID field to CUSTID.NDX, and on the CUSTNAME field to CUSTNAME.NDX. The INVOICES file is indexed on the INVNUMB field to INVOICES.NDX, and on the CUSTID field to INVCUST.NDX. The presence of the index files makes it a simple matter to set relations for reports that can be generated in alphabetical order by customer group. When the program is run for the first time, the Reindex All Files option under the Other Tasks menu should be chosen in order to create the needed index files.

The system also uses a numeric variable named *NEXTINV* as a counter that controls which invoice number is assigned to each new record. When the Add Invoice routine is selected, the current value LASTINV is retrieved from the disk. As new invoices are added, the variable is incremented upward by one. When the user exits from the Add Invoices routine, the latest value of the variable is saved back to disk. Before using the program for the first time, you must create the variable and save it to disk under the name *DEFAULTS.MEM*. You can do so with commands like

```
STORE 10001 TO NEXTINV
SAVE TO DEFAULTS
```

The Report Generator portion of the system produces reports based on invoices by customer group and a report displaying all customers. The report provides some selectivity by storing portions of a command line to a variable called *CONDITION,* depending on the choice made in the Reports menu. The actual report code, contained in PRINTER.PRG, then uses that variable to determine which invoices are to be included in the report.

In its existing form, the program is close to being, but is not fully, Clipper-compatible. To compile under Clipper, the option to write Lotus 1-2-3 files must be rewritten or eliminated because Clipper (Autumn 86) does not support the SET FIELDS command or the COPY TO command with the TYPE WKS option. You would also need to find and delete the SET MESSAGE TO commands because they are written in dBASE format in a syntax that the Clipper compiler will not accept. Once these changes are made, the program will compile and link under Clipper.

```
Structure for database: C:customer.dbf
Number of data records:        6
Date of last update    : 01/04/80
Field  Field Name  Type       Width   Dec
    1  CUSTID      Character      3
    2  CUSTNAME    Character     30
    3  CUSTATTN    Character     20
    4  CUSTADDR    Character     30
    5  CUSTCITY    Character     15
    6  CUSTSTATE   Character      2
    7  CUSTZIP     Character     10
    8  CUSTPHONE   Character     12
** Total **                    123
```

```
Structure for database: C:invoices.dbf
Number of data records:        7
Date of last update    : 01/03/80
Field  Field Name  Type       Width   Dec
    1  INVNUMB     Numeric        5
    2  CUSTID      Character      3
    3  INVDESC     Character     40
    4  AMOUNTDUE   Numeric        9     2
    5  DATEDUE     Date           8
    6  DEPTCODE    Character      4
    7  SERVICETYP  Character      4
    8  DATEPAID    Date           8
    9  AMOUNTPAID  Numeric        9     2
   10  PAIDINFULL  Logical        1
   11  EXPLAIN     Character     20
   12  COMMENTS    Character     40
** Total **                    152
```

```
* Program..: ACCOUNT.PRG
* Date.....: 10/26/87
* Copyright, 1987, Osborne/McGraw Hill, Edward Jones
*****************************************************
* NOTE: store 5-digit starting no. of your choice   *
* to NEXTINV and SAVE TO DEFAULTS before running    *
* this program for the first time.  The value will  *
* be used as self-incrementing invoice numbers.     *
*****************************************************
SET TALK OFF
SET BELL OFF
SET CONFIRM ON
SET SAFETY OFF
SET DELETED ON
SET PROCEDURE TO PROCFILE
ON ERROR DO RECOVER
ON ESCAPE DO BACKOUT
PUBLIC NEXTINV, FOUNDIT
PUBLIC MCUSTID, MCUSTNAME, MCUSTATTN, MCUSTADDR,;
MCUSTCITY, MCUSTSTATE, MCUSTZIP, MCUSTPHONE
PUBLIC MINVNUMB, MCUSTID, MINVDESC, MAMOUNTDUE, MEXPLAIN,;
MDATEDUE, MDEPTCODE, MSERVICE, MDATEPAID, MAMOUNTPAY, MCOMMENTS
SELECT 1
USE INVOICES INDEX INVOICES, INVCUST
SELECT 2
USE CUSTOMER INDEX CUSTID, CUSTNAME
Do While .T.
   Do Borders
   @  1,25 SAY [YOUR COMPANY NAME HERE]
   @  2,22 SAY [INVOICES/RECEIVABLES SYSTEM]
   @  5,16 Say [1. ADD New Invoices]
   @  6,16 Say [2. EDIT or RECORD RECEIPTS for Existing Invoice]

   @  8,16 Say [3. INQUIRE: Show Data On An Invoice]
   @  9,16 Say [4. Delete An Invoice]
   @ 10,16 Say [5. Produce Reports]
   @ 12,16 Say [6. Customer File Maintenance]
   @ 13,16 Say [7. Other Tasks (Backup, Index Maintenance)]
   @ 18,16 Say [0. Quit This System and Return to DOS]

   Store 0 to SelectNum
   @ 20,0
   Input "     [Selection?] " TO SelectNum

   Do Case
      Case SelectNum = 1
         Do InvAdd
      Case SelectNum = 2
         Do InvEdit
      Case SelectNum = 3
         Do InvShow
      Case SelectNum = 4
         Do InvDel
      Case SelectNum = 5

         Do Reporter
      Case SelectNum = 6
         Do CustMenu
      Case SelectNum = 7
         Do Other

      Case SelectNum = 0
         Clear All
         QUIT
```

```
        Case SelectNum = 999
                *for programmer's use only!
                *is back door to dot prompt
                Clear All
                Close Procedure
                cancel
    EndCase
EndDo
Return
* End of Main Menu


*PROCFILE.PRG is procedure file.*
****************************************
PROCEDURE BORDERS
CLEAR
a 0,0 TO 19,79 DOUBLE
a 0,1 TO 4,78 DOUBLE
Draw = 1
DO WHILE Draw < 4
    a Draw,2 SAY REPLICATE(chr(176),76)
    Draw = Draw+1
ENDDO
RETURN
****************************************
PROCEDURE FINDINV
MEMNUMB = 10001
CLEAR
a 5, 5 SAY "Invoice number? " GET MEMNUMB
READ
SEEK MEMNUMB
IF FOUND()
    FOUNDIT = .T.
ENDIF
RETURN
****************************************
PROCEDURE FINDCUST
MEMCUST = SPACE(3)
CLEAR
a 5, 5 SAY "Customer Code? " GET MEMCUST
READ
SEEK MEMCUST
IF FOUND()
    FOUNDIT = .T.
ENDIF

RETURN
****************************************
PROCEDURE SAYCUST
a  3,  8  SAY "Customer ID:"
a  3, 20  SAY   MCUSTID
a  5,  6  SAY "Customer Name:"
a  5, 20  SAY   MCUSTNAME
a  6,  5  SAY "Attn. Of:"
a  6, 14  SAY   MCUSTATTN
a  8,  6  SAY "Address:"
a  8, 14  SAY   MCUSTADDR
a 10,  9  SAY "City:"
a 10, 14  SAY   MCUSTCITY
a 10, 28  SAY "State:"
a 10, 34  SAY   MCUSTSTATE
a 10, 38  SAY "Zip:"
a 10, 42  SAY   MCUSTZIP
a 12,  6  SAY "Phone:"
a 12, 12  SAY   MCUSTPHONE   PICTURE "999-999-9999"
a 14, 27  SAY "CUSTOMERS VERIFICATION SCREEN"
a  1,  4  TO 15, 73
RETURN
```

```
**************************************
PROCEDURE GETCUST
@  3,  8  SAY "Customer ID:"
@  3, 20  SAY   MCUSTID PICTURE "!!!"
@  5,  6  SAY "Customer Name:"
@  5, 20  GET   MCUSTNAME
@  6,  5  SAY "Attn. Of:"
@  6, 14  GET   MCUSTATTN
@  8,  6  SAY "Address:"
@  8, 14  GET   MCUSTADDR
@ 10,  9  SAY "City:"
@ 10, 14  GET   MCUSTCITY
@ 10, 28  SAY "State:"
@ 10, 34  GET   MCUSTSTATE PICTURE "!!"
@ 10, 38  SAY "Zip:"
@ 10, 42  GET   MCUSTZIP PICTURE "99999-9999"
@ 12,  6  SAY "Phone:"
@ 12, 12  GET   MCUSTPHONE  PICTURE "999-999-9999"
@ 14, 24  SAY "CUSTOMERS DATA ENTRY/EDIT SCREEN"
@  1,  4  TO 15, 73
RETURN
**************************************
PROCEDURE MAKECVAR
MCUSTID = SPACE(3)
MCUSTNAME = SPACE(30)
MCUSTATTN = SPACE(20)
MCUSTADDR = SPACE(30)
MCUSTCITY = SPACE(15)
MCUSTSTATE = SPACE(2)
MCUSTZIP = SPACE(10)
MCUSTPHONE = SPACE(12)
RETURN
**************************************
PROCEDURE FILLCVAR
MCUSTID = CUSTID
MCUSTNAME = CUSTNAME
MCUSTATTN = CUSTATTN
MCUSTADDR = CUSTADDR
MCUSTCITY = CUSTCITY
MCUSTSTATE = CUSTSTATE
MCUSTZIP = CUSTZIP
MCUSTPHONE = CUSTPHONE
RETURN
**************************************
PROCEDURE MOVECVAR
REPLACE CUSTNAME WITH MCUSTNAME, CUSTATTN WITH MCUSTATTN,;
CUSTADDR WITH MCUSTADDR, CUSTCITY WITH MCUSTCITY
REPLACE CUSTSTATE WITH MCUSTSTATE, CUSTZIP WITH MCUSTZIP,;
CUSTPHONE WITH MCUSTPHONE, CUSTID WITH MCUSTID
RETURN
**************************************
PROCEDURE SAYINV
@  3, 22  SAY "INVOICE INFORMATION"
@  5,  5  SAY "Invoice No:"
@  5, 16  SAY   MINVNUMB
@  5, 29  SAY "Customer Code:"
@  5, 43  SAY   MCUSTID  PICTURE "!!!"
@  5, 49  SAY "Dept. Code:"
@  5, 60  SAY   MDEPTCODE  PICTURE "!!!!"
@  7,  5  SAY "Description of Service:"
@  7, 29  SAY   MINVDESC
@  9,  5  SAY "Amount Due:"
@  9, 17  SAY   MAMOUNTDUE
@  9, 31  SAY "Date Due:"
@  9, 40  SAY   MDATEDUE
@  9, 50  SAY "Service Type:"
@  9, 63  SAY   MSERVICE
@ 12, 22  SAY "PAYMENT INFORMATION"
```

```
a 14,  5  SAY "Date Paid:"
a 14, 15  SAY   MDATEPAID
a 14, 27  SAY "Amount Paid:"
a 14, 39  SAY   MAMOUNTPAY
a 16,  5  SAY "If less than full amount paid, why?"
a 16, 41  SAY   MEXPLAIN
a 18,  5  SAY "Comments:"
a 18, 14  SAY   MCOMMENTS
a 19, 23  SAY "INVOICE DATA ENTRY/EDIT SCREEN"
a  1,  3  TO 10, 70
a 11,  3  TO 20, 71
RETURN
**************************************
PROCEDURE GETINV
a  3, 22  SAY "INVOICE INFORMATION"
a  5,  5  SAY "Invoice No:"
a  5, 16  SAY   MINVNUMB
a  5, 29  SAY "Customer Code:"
a  5, 43  GET   MCUSTID  PICTURE "!!!"
a  5, 50  SAY "Dept. Code:"
a  5, 61  GET   MDEPTCODE  PICTURE "!!!!"
a  7,  5  SAY "Description of Service:"
a  7, 29  GET   MINVDESC
a  9,  5  SAY "Amount Due:"
a  9, 17  GET   MAMOUNTDUE
a  9, 31  SAY "Date Due:"
a  9, 40  GET   MDATEDUE
a  9, 50  SAY "Service Type:"
a  9, 63  GET   MSERVICE
a 12, 22  SAY "PAYMENT INFORMATION"
a 14,  5  SAY "Date Paid:"
a 14, 15  GET   MDATEPAID
a 14, 27  SAY "Amount Paid:"
a 14, 39  GET   MAMOUNTPAY
a 16,  5  SAY "If less than full amount paid, why?"
a 16, 41  GET   MEXPLAIN
a 18,  5  SAY "Comments:"
a 18, 14  GET   MCOMMENTS
a 19, 23  SAY "INVOICE DATA ENTRY/EDIT SCREEN"
a  1,  3  TO 10, 70
a 11,  3  TO 20, 71
RETURN
**************************************
PROCEDURE MAKEIVAR
MINVNUMB = 10001
MCUSTID = SPACE(3)
MINVDESC = SPACE(40)
MAMOUNTDUE = 0.00
MDATEDUE = (DATE() + 30)
MDEPTCODE = SPACE(4)
MSERVICE = SPACE(4)
MDATEPAID = CTOD("  /  /  ")
MAMOUNTPAY = 0.00
MEXPLAIN = SPACE(20)
MCOMMENTS = SPACE(40)
RETURN
**************************************
PROCEDURE FILLIVAR
MINVNUMB = INVNUMB
MCUSTID = CUSTID
MINVDESC = INVDESC
MAMOUNTDUE = AMOUNTDUE
MDATEDUE = DATEDUE
MDEPTCODE = DEPTCODE
MSERVICE = SERVICETYP
MDATEPAID = DATEPAID
MAMOUNTPAY = AMOUNTPAID
```

```
MEXPLAIN = EXPLAIN
MCOMMENTS = COMMENTS
RETURN
************************************
PROCEDURE MOVEIVAR
REPLACE INVNUMB WITH MINVNUMB, CUSTID WITH MCUSTID,;
INVDESC WITH MINVDESC, AMOUNTDUE WITH MAMOUNTDUE,;
DATEDUE WITH MDATEDUE, DEPTCODE WITH MDEPTCODE
REPLACE SERVICETYP WITH MSERVICE, DATEPAID WITH MDATEPAID,;
AMOUNTPAID WITH MAMOUNTPAY, EXPLAIN WITH MEXPLAIN,;
COMMENTS WITH MCOMMENTS
RETURN
************************************
*End of ProcFile.PRG*


*Routine to add INVOICES.*
RESTORE FROM DEFAULTS ADDITIVE
SELECT 2
SET ORDER TO 1
SELECT 1
DO WHILE .T.
     CLEAR
     STORE SPACE(3) TO MEMCUST
     @ 3,2 TO 9,40 DOUBLE
     @ 5,5 SAY "   Customer ID? " GET MEMCUST
     @ 7,5 SAY "(enter BLANKS to exit.)"
     READ
     IF (LEN(TRIM(MEMCUST)) = 0)
          EXIT
     ENDIF
     SELECT 2
     SEEK MEMCUST
     IF .NOT. FOUND()
          CLEAR
          ? CHR(7)
          @ 5, 5 SAY "No such customer ID on file!"
          WAIT
          EXIT
     ENDIF
     SELECT 1
     CLEAR
     DO MAKEIVAR
     MCUSTID = MEMCUST
     MINVNUMB = NEXTINV
     DO GETINV
     READ
     APPEND BLANK
     NEXTINV = NEXTINV + 1
     DO MOVEIVAR
     IF AMOUNTPAID >= AMOUNTDUE
          REPLACE PAIDINFULL WITH .T.
     ENDIF
     CLEAR
     ACCEPT "  Add another? Y/N:" TO ANS
     IF UPPER(ANS) = "N"
          CLEAR
          @ 5, 5 SAY "One moment please..."
          SAVE TO DEFAULTS ALL LIKE NEXTINV
          EXIT
     ENDIF
ENDDO
RETURN
*End of CustAdd.PRG*
```

```
*InvEdit.PRG edits Invoice file.*
SELECT 1
DO WHILE .T.
     FOUNDIT = .F.
     CLEAR
     DO FINDINV
     IF FOUNDIT
          CLEAR
          DO FILLIVAR
          DO GETINV
          READ
          IF MAMOUNTPAY >= AMOUNTDUE
               REPLACE PAIDINFULL WITH .T.
          ELSE
               REPLACE PAIDINFULL WITH .F.
          ENDIF
          DO MOVEIVAR
          CLEAR
          ACCEPT " Edit another? Y/N:" TO ANS
          IF UPPER(ANS) = "N"
               EXIT
          ENDIF
     ELSE
          CLEAR
          @ 5, 5 SAY "That invoice number is NOT on file!"
          @ 6, 5 SAY "Use reports menu to see all invoices"
          @ 7, 5 SAY "for a given customer."
          WAIT
          EXIT
     ENDIF
ENDDO
RETURN
*End of InvEdit.*



*InvDel.PRG deletes records from customer file.*
SELECT 1
DO WHILE .T.
     FOUNDIT = .F.
     CLEAR
     ANS = "N"
     DO FINDINV
     IF FOUNDIT
          CLEAR
          DO FILLIVAR
          DO SAYINV
          ? CHR(7)
          @ 20, 5 SAY "Delete invoice, are you SURE? Y/N:"
          @ 20, 42 GET ANS
          READ
          IF UPPER(ANS) = "Y"
               DELETE
          ENDIF
          CLEAR
          ACCEPT "   --Delete different invoice? Y/N:" TO AGAIN
          IF UPPER(AGAIN) = "N"
               EXIT
          ENDIF
     ELSE
          CLEAR
          @ 5, 5 SAY "That invoice is NOT on file!"
          @ 6, 5 SAY "Use reports menu to see all invoices"
          @ 7, 5 SAY "for a given customer."
          WAIT
          EXIT
     ENDIF
ENDDO
*End of InvDel.*
```

```
*InvShow.PRG shows data from Invoice file.*
SELECT 1
DO WHILE .T.
     FOUNDIT = .F.
     CLEAR
     DO FINDINV
     IF FOUNDIT
          CLEAR
          DO FILLIVAR
          DO SAYINV
          @ 20, 78
          WAIT
          CLEAR
          ACCEPT " View another? Y/N:" TO ANS
          IF UPPER(ANS) = "N"
               EXIT
          ENDIF
     ELSE
          CLEAR
          @ 5, 5 SAY "That invoice number is NOT on file!"
          @ 6, 5 SAY "Use reports menu to see all invoices"
          @ 7, 5 SAY "for a given customer."
          WAIT
          EXIT
     ENDIF
ENDDO
RETURN
*End of InvShow.*


* Program..: CustMenu.PRG
* Date.....: 10/26/87
*
Do While .T.
  Do Borders
  @ 1,23 SAY [INVOICES/RECEIVABLES SYSTEM]
  @ 2,24 SAY [CUSTOMER MAINTENANCE MENU]
  @ 6,16 Say [1. ADD New Customers]
  @ 8,16 Say [2. EDIT Existing Customers]
  @ 10,16 Say [3. DELETE A Customer]
  @ 18,16 Say [0. Return To Prior Menu]

  Store 0 to SelectNum
  @ 20,0
  Input "      [Selection?] " TO SelectNum

  Do Case

     Case SelectNum = 1
          Do CustAdd
     Case SelectNum = 2
          Do CustEdit
     Case SelectNum = 3
          Do CustDel
     Case SelectNum = 0
          Return

  EndCase
EndDo
* End of CustMenu


*Routine to add CUSTOMERS.*
SELECT 2
DO WHILE .T.
     CLEAR
```

```
       STORE SPACE(30) TO MEMNAME
       STORE SPACE(3) TO MEMID
       @ 3,2 TO 10,60 DOUBLE
       @ 5,5 SAY " Customer Name? " GET MEMNAME
       @ 7,5 SAY "    Customer ID? " GET MEMID
       @ 9,5 SAY "(enter BLANKS to exit.)"
       READ
    IF (LEN(TRIM(MEMNAME)) = 0 .OR. LEN(TRIM(MEMID)) = 0)
           EXIT
       ENDIF
       SET ORDER TO 2
       SEEK MEMNAME
       IF .NOT. EOF()
           CLEAR
           DO FILLCVAR
           DO SAYCUST
           ? CHR(7)
           @ 16,20 SAY "This customer is already on file!"
           @ 17,2
           ACCEPT "Add new customer anyway? Y/N:" TO ADDANS
           IF UPPER(ADDANS) = "N"
               EXIT
           ENDIF
       ENDIF
       CLEAR
       SET ORDER TO 1
       SEEK MEMID
       IF FOUND()
           CLEAR
           @ 5, 5 SAY "You are attempting to use a customer code"
           @ 6, 5 SAY "which ALREADY EXISTS.  You MUST pick a new;
           code."
           WAIT
           EXIT
       ENDIF
       DO MAKECVAR
       MCUSTNAME = MEMNAME
       MCUSTID = MEMID
       DO GETCUST
       READ
       APPEND BLANK
       DO MOVECVAR
       CLEAR
       ACCEPT "  Add another? Y/N:" TO ANS
       IF UPPER(ANS) = "N"
           EXIT
       ENDIF
ENDDO
RETURN
*End of CustAdd.PRG*


*CustEdit.PRG edits customer file.*
SELECT 2
DO WHILE .T.
    FOUNDIT = .F.
    CLEAR
    DO FINDCUST
    IF FOUNDIT
        CLEAR
        DO FILLCVAR
        DO GETCUST
        READ
        DO MOVECVAR
        CLEAR
        ACCEPT " Edit another? Y/N:" TO ANS
        IF UPPER(ANS) = "N"
            EXIT
        ENDIF
```

```
        ELSE
            CLEAR
            @ 5, 5 SAY "That customer ID is NOT on file!"
            WAIT
            EXIT
        ENDIF
ENDDO
RETURN
*End of CustEdit.*




*CustDel.PRG deletes records from customer file.*
SELECT 2
DO WHILE .T.
    FOUNDIT = .F.
    CLEAR
    ANS = "N"
    DO FINDCUST
    IF FOUNDIT
        CLEAR
        DO FILLCVAR
        DO SAYCUST
        ? CHR(7)
        @ 20, 5 SAY "Delete customer, are you SURE? Y/N:"
        @ 20, 42 GET ANS
        READ
        IF UPPER(ANS) = "Y"
                DELETE
        ENDIF
        CLEAR
        ACCEPT "    --Delete different customer? Y/N:" TO AGAIN
        IF UPPER(AGAIN) = "N"
                EXIT
        ENDIF
    ELSE
        CLEAR
        @ 5, 5 SAY "That customer ID is NOT on file!"
        WAIT
        EXIT
    ENDIF
ENDDO
*End of CustDel.*


* Program..: Reporter.PRG
* Date.....: 10/26/87
*
DO WHILE .T.
    DO BORDERS
    @ 1,22 SAY [INVOICES/RECEIVABLES SYSTEM]
    @ 2,27 SAY [REPORTS MENU]
    @ 6,16 Say [1. List All Unpaid Invoices]
    @ 7,16 Say [2. List All Paid Invoices]
    @ 9,16 Say [3. List All Unpaid Invoices For A Company]
    @ 10,16 Say [4. List All Paid Invoices For A Company]
    @ 12,16 Say [5. List All Customers]
    @ 14,16 Say [6. Export to Lotus, All Unpaid Invoices]
    @ 15,16 Say [7. Export to Lotus, All Paid Invoices]
    @ 18,16 Say [0. Return To Prior Menu]
    STORE 0 TO SELECTNUM
    @ 20,0
    INPUT "      [Selection?] " TO SELECTNUM
    DO CASE

        CASE SELECTNUM = 1
            CONDITION = " .NOT. PAIDINFULL"
            HEADER = "*All Unpaid*"
            DO PRINTER
```

```
        CASE SELECTNUM = 2
            CONDITION = " PAIDINFULL"
            HEADER = "*All Paid*"
            DO PRINTER

        CASE SELECTNUM = 3
            PUBLIC MEMCUST
            SELECT 2
            FOUNDIT = .F.
            DO FINDCUST
            IF .NOT. FOUNDIT
                CLEAR
                ? CHR(7)
                WAIT "  Customer number is invalid!  Press a key..."
                RETURN
            ENDIF
            SELECT 1
            CONDITION = " .NOT. PAIDINFULL .AND. CUSTID = MEMCUST"
            HEADER = "*Unpaid*"
            DO PRINTER

        CASE SELECTNUM = 4
            PUBLIC MEMCUST
            SELECT 2
            FOUNDIT = .F.
            DO FINDCUST
            IF .NOT. FOUNDIT
                CLEAR
                ? CHR(7)
                WAIT "  Customer number is invalid!  Press a key..."
                RETURN
            ENDIF
            SELECT 1
            CONDITION = " PAIDINFULL .AND. CUSTID = MEMCUST"
            HEADER = "*Paid*"
            DO PRINTER

        CASE SELECTNUM = 5
            DO CUSTPRIN

        CASE SELECTNUM = 6
            CONDITION = " .NOT. PAIDINFULL"
            DO LOTUS

        CASE SELECTNUM = 7
            CONDITION = " PAIDINFULL"
            DO LOTUS

        CASE SELECTNUM = 0
            SELECT 2
            SET ORDER TO 1
            SELECT 1
            SET ORDER TO 1
            RETURN

    ENDCASE
ENDDO
* End of Reporter


*Printer.PRG
CLEAR
? " Printer should be turned on and ready."
```

```
WAIT " Press C to cancel, or any other key to begin." TO PANS
IF UPPER(PANS) = "C"
     RETURN
ENDIF
CLEAR
@ 5, 5 SAY "Printing... please wait..."
STORE 6 TO LINES
STORE 1 TO PAGES
SELECT 1
SET ORDER TO 2
SELECT 2
SET ORDER TO 1
SELECT 1
SET RELATION TO CUSTID INTO CUSTOMER
GO TOP
SET DEVICE TO PRINT
@ 2, 30 SAY "INVOICE  REPORT"
@ 2, 60 SAY Header
@ 3,  5 SAY REPLICATE("=",68)
@ 4,  5 SAY "Inv. No.      Customer Name"
@ 4, 56 SAY "Amt. Due Date Due"
@ 5,  5 SAY REPLICATE("=",68)
DO WHILE .NOT. EOF()
     IF &CONDITION
          @ LINES, 5 SAY INVNUMB
          @ LINES, 20 SAY CUSTOMER->CUSTNAME
          @ LINES, 55 SAY AMOUNTDUE
          @ LINES, 65 SAY DATEDUE
          STORE LINES + 1 TO LINES
     ENDIF the condition
     IF LINES > 50
          @ LINES + 2, 40 SAY "PAGE " + TRIM(STR(PAGES))
          EJECT
          STORE PAGES + 1 TO PAGES
          STORE 6 TO LINES
          @ 2, 30 SAY "INVOICE REPORT"
          @ 2, 60 SAY Header
          @ 3, 10 SAY REPLICATE("=",68)
          @ 4,  5 SAY "Inv. No.      Customer Name"
          @ 4, 56 SAY "Amt. Due Date Due"
          @ 5,  5 SAY REPLICATE("=",68)
     ENDIF
     SKIP
ENDDO
SUM AMOUNTDUE TO TOTAMT FOR &CONDITION
@ LINES+1, 5 SAY "TOTAL:"
@ LINES+1, 51 SAY TOTAMT
IF LINES > 5
     EJECT
ENDIF
SET DEVICE TO SCREEN
RETURN
*End of Printer.*


*CustPrin.PRG
CLEAR
? " Printer should be turned on and ready."
WAIT " Press C to cancel, or any other key to begin." TO PANS
IF UPPER(PANS) = "C"
     RETURN
ENDIF
```

```
CLEAR
a 5, 5 SAY "Printing... please wait..."
STORE 5 TO LINES
STORE 1 TO PAGES
SELECT 2
SET ORDER TO 2
GO TOP
SET DEVICE TO PRINT
a 2, 30 SAY "CUSTOMER REPORT"
a 2, 53 SAY "As of date:"
a 2, 65 SAY DATE()
a 3,  5 SAY REPLICATE("=",68)
DO WHILE .NOT. EOF()
    a LINES,  5 SAY "Name: " + CUSTNAME
    a LINES, 45 SAY "Attn: " + CUSTATTN
    a LINES+1,  5 SAY "Add: " + CUSTADDR
    a LINES+1, 38 SAY "City: " + CUSTCITY
    a LINES+1, 62 SAY "State: " + CUSTSTATE
    a LINES+2,  5 SAY "ZIP: " + CUSTZIP
    a LINES+2, 25 SAY "Phone: " + CUSTPHONE
    a LINES+2, 50 SAY "CUST ID: " + CUSTID
    STORE LINES + 5 TO LINES
    IF LINES > 50
        a LINES + 2, 40 SAY "PAGE " + TRIM(STR(PAGES))
        EJECT
        STORE PAGES + 1 TO PAGES
        STORE 5 TO LINES
        a 2, 30 SAY "CUSTOMER REPORT"
        a 2, 53 SAY "As of date:"
        a 2, 65 SAY DATE()
        a 3,  5 SAY REPLICATE("=",68)
    ENDIF
    SKIP
ENDDO
IF LINES > 5
    EJECT
ENDIF
SET DEVICE TO SCREEN
SET ORDER TO 1
SELECT 1
RETURN
*End of CustPrin.*


*Lotus.PRG exports 1-2-3 worksheets of invoices.*
CLEAR
? " Insert a formatted disk in Drive A."
WAIT " Press C to cancel, or any other key to begin." TO LANS
IF UPPER(LANS) = "C"
    RETURN
ENDIF
CLEAR
a 5, 5 SAY "Creating Lotus 1-2-3 file... please wait..."
SELECT 1
SET ORDER TO 2
SELECT 2
SET ORDER TO 1
SELECT 1
SET RELATION TO CUSTID INTO CUSTOMER
SET FIELDS TO CUSTID, CUSTOMER->CUSTNAME, INVNUMB, AMOUNTDUE,;
DATEDUE, AMOUNTPAID, DATEPAID, PAIDINFULL
GO TOP
COPY FIELDS CUSTNAME, CUSTID, INVNUMB, AMOUNTDUE, DATEDUE, AMOUNTPAID,;
DATEPAID, PAIDINFULL TO A:123FILE.WKS TYPE WKS FOR &CONDITION
SET FIELDS OFF
SET ORDER TO 1·
RETURN
*End of Lotus.*
```

```
*OTHER.PRG is Other Tasks menu.*
DO WHILE .T.
   CLEAR
   DO BORDERS
   @  2,28 Say [OTHER TASKS MENU]
   @  8,16 Say [1. BACKUP The Database]
   @ 10,16 Say [2. REBUILD Database Indexes]
   @ 18,16 Say [0. Quit This Menu]
   @ 20,0
   INPUT "       [Selection?] " TO SELECTNUM

   DO CASE
      CASE SELECTNUM = 1
           DO BACKIT

      CASE SELECTNUM = 2
           DO INDEXER

      CASE SELECTNUM = 0
           RETURN
   ENDCASE
ENDDO
* End of Other.PRG


***BACKIT.PRG***
**Backup program using DOS backup function.
**Last update 10/21/87
CLEAR
? "This menu option backs up your database."
? "You will need sufficient FORMATTED floppy disks to proceed."
? "Press C to CANCEL this option, or any other key to proceed."
WAIT "" TO JUNK
IF UPPER(JUNK) = "C"
     RETURN
ENDIF
**Change to DOS subdirectory if necessary.**
RUN CD\DOS
ACCEPT "Would you like to format floppy disks first? (Y/N): " TO ANS
IF UPPER(ANS) = "Y"
     RUN FORMAT A:
ENDIF
RUN BACKUP *.DBF A: /S
**Re-set your directory here, if you changed it.**
CLEAR
? "Backup process complete.  Remove last disk from Drive A."
?
? "To return to main menu,"
WAIT
RETURN
*End of BACKIT.PRG*


*Indexer.PRG rebuilds indexes.
CLEAR
@ 5, 5 SAY "Please wait... this may take a while."
SET MESSAGE TO "***DO NOT INTERRUPT COMPUTER!***"
SET TALK ON
SELECT 1
USE INVOICES
INDEX ON INVNUMB TO INVOICES
INDEX ON CUSTID TO INVCUST
SET INDEX TO INVOICES, INVCUST
SELE 2
USE CUSTOMER
INDEX ON CUSTID TO CUSTID
INDEX ON CUSTNAME TO CUSTNAME
```

```
SET INDEX TO CUSTID, CUSTNAME
SELECT 1
SET TALK OFF
SET MESSAGE TO DTOC(DATE())
RETURN
*End of Indexer.


*BackOut.PRG handles Escsape key.*
SET TALK OFF
SELECT 2
SET ORDER TO 1
SELECT 1
SET ORDER TO 1
RETURN TO MASTER
*End of BackOut.*


***RECOVER.PRG is error trapping.
**Last update 10/26/87
CLEAR
DO CASE
    CASE ERROR() = 1
        ? "Cannot find a file.  Record this message,"
        ? "and contact program developer for assistance."
        CLEAR ALL
        WAIT
        QUIT
    CASE ERROR() = 20 .or. ERROR() = 26 .or. ERROR() = 114
        ? "The index file seems to be missing a record."
        ? "please wait while I repair the index."
        DO INDEXER
        RETRY
    CASE ERROR() = 56
        ? "Disk full!  Exit this system and erase uneeded files"
        ? "from the disk."
        WAIT
        CLEAR ALL
        RETURN
    CASE ERROR() = 125
        ? "Printer not ready.  Reset printer, then"
        WAIT
        RETRY
    CASE ERROR() = 6
        ? "Your system was not started from the hard disk."
        ? "Press a key to exit dBASE, and restart the computer."
        WAIT
        QUIT
    OTHERWISE
        ? "A program error has occurred.  Record the message,"
        ? "and inform your program developer."
        ?
        ? MESSAGE()
        ?
        ?
        ? "  After noting the above message, press any key."
        WAIT
        ? "  One moment please..."
        SET CONSOLE OFF
        SET ALTERNATE TO BOMBED.TXT
        SET ALTERNATE ON
        ? "Error message reported was: "
        ?? MESSAGE()
        LIST STATUS
        LIST MEMORY
        CLOSE ALTERNATE
        CLEAR ALL
        QUIT
ENDCASE
*End of Recover.PRG.
```

A: Glossary of dBASE III PLUS Commands

This appendix contains a listing of dBASE III PLUS commands. Each command name is followed by the syntax of the command and a description of how the command works. Examples of applications are provided for some commands. Most of them you will recognize from the tutorial section; others will be introduced here.

GLOSSARY SYMBOLS AND CONVENTIONS

1. All commands are printed in UPPERCASE, although you can enter them in either uppercase or lowercase letters.

2. All parameters of the command are listed in *italics*.

3. Any part of a command or parameter surrounded by left and right brackets — [and] — is optional.

4. When a slash separates two choices in a command, such as ON/OFF, you specify one choice but not both.

5. Ellipses (...) following a parameter or command mean that the parameter or command can be repeated "infinitely" — that is, until you exhaust the memory of the computer.

6. The parameter *scope,* which is always an option, can have four different meanings depending on the command: ALL, for all records; NEXT *n,* for *n* number of records beginning at the current position of the record pointer; REST, for remaining records; and RECORD, for only one record beginning at the current position of the record pointer.

COMMANDS

Command: ? or ??

Syntax: *? expression* or *?? expression*

The ? command displays the value of a dBASE III PLUS expression. If a single question mark (?) is used, the cursor executes a carriage return and linefeed, and then the value of the expression is displayed. If the double question mark (??) is used, the cursor does not move before the value of the expression is displayed.

Command: @

Syntax: @ *<row,col>* [SAY *expression*] [GET *variable*] [PICTURE *expression*] [RANGE exp, exp][CLEAR][SINGLE][DOUBLE]

The @ command places the cursor at a specific screen location, which is identified by *row,col.* The @ command can be used with one or more of the following options. The SAY option displays the expression following the word SAY. The GET option allows full-screen editing of *variable*. The PICTURE option allows the use of templates, which specify the way data will be displayed or accepted in response to the GET option. The RANGE option is used with the GET option to specify a range of acceptable entries.

Example: To place the message "Enter shareholder name:" at screen location 12,2 and to allow full-screen editing of the value contained in the variable SHN, enter

```
@ 12,2 SAY "Enter shareholder name:" GET SHN
```

When used with the SINGLE or DOUBLE options, the @ command draws single or double lines or borders (or a combination) on the screen. The first value represents the upper-left screen coordinate, and the second value represents the lower-right screen coordinate. If both coordinates share a horizontal or vertical coordinate, a line is drawn; otherwise, a rectangular border is drawn. The CLEAR option can be used to clear a line or border that was drawn previously.

Example: To draw a single line from row 3, column 5 to row 3, column 50, enter the following:

```
@ 3,5 TO 3,50 SINGLE
```

To draw a double-line box, with the upper-left corner at row 4, column 1, and the lower-right corner at row 18, column 70, enter

```
@ 4,1 TO 18,70 DOUBLE
```

To erase the border drawn in the previous example, enter

```
@ 4,1 CLEAR TO 18,70
```

Command: ACCEPT

Syntax: ACCEPT [*prompt*] TO *memvar*

The ACCEPT command stores a character string to the memory variable *memvar*. ACCEPT can be followed by an optional character string. If this string is included, it will appear on the screen when the ACCEPT command is executed.

 Example: To display the prompt "Enter owner name:" and store to the memory variable *OWNER* the character string that the user enters in response to the prompt, enter

```
ACCEPT "Enter owner name: " TO OWNER
```

Command: APPEND

Syntax: APPEND [BLANK]

The APPEND command appends records to a database. When the APPEND command is executed, a blank record is displayed, and dBASE III PLUS enters full-screen editing mode. If the BLANK option is used, a blank record is added to the end of the database, and full-screen editing mode is not entered.

Command: APPEND FROM

Syntax: APPEND FROM *filename* [FOR/WHILE *condition*]
   [SDF/DELIMITED]

APPEND FROM copies records from *filename* and appends them to the active database. The FOR/WHILE option specifies a condition that must be met before any records will be copied. If the *filename* containing the data to be copied is not a dBASE III PLUS database, the SDF or Delimited options must be used.

Command: ASSIST

Syntax: ASSIST

The ASSIST command lets you operate dBASE III PLUS with a series of menus. You enter dBASE III PLUS commands by selecting menu choices. To select menus from other menus within ASSIST, press the LEFT-ARROW or RIGHT-ARROW key until the desired menu is highlighted and then press ENTER.

Command: AVERAGE

Syntax: AVERAGE *field-list* [*scope*][FOR/WHILE *condition*] [TO *memvar-list*]

The AVERAGE command computes an average of a specified numeric field listed in *field-list*. If the TO option is not used, the average is displayed on screen. If TO is used, the average of the first field is assigned to the first memory variable, the average of the second field to the second memory variable, and so on down the list; and the average is stored as the memory variable specified. If the *scope* option is not used, the quantifier of ALL is assumed, meaning all records in *field-list* will be averaged. The FOR/WHILE option can be used to specify a condition that must be met for the fields to be averaged.

Command: BROWSE

Syntax: BROWSE [FIELDS *field-list*]

The BROWSE command displays a database on screen. If the database is too large for the screen, BROWSE displays only the fields that will fit on the screen. More fields can be viewed by scrolling to the left or right, by holding the CTRL key and pressing the LEFT-ARROW or RIGHT-ARROW key. The contents of any field can be edited while in BROWSE mode. To save changes made during BROWSE, press CTRL-END; to exit BROWSE, press CTRL-ESC. The FIELDS option will display only the fields listed in *field-list*.

Command: CALL

Syntax: CALL <module name> [WITH <*expression*>]

The CALL command executes a binary (assembly-language) program that was previously loaded into memory with the LOAD command (see LOAD). If the optional [WITH <*expression*>] clause is included, the value of the expression is passed to the binary program, and the data segment (DS and BX registers) will contain the address for the first byte of the memory variable or character expression that was passed from dBASE. The CALL command should be used only with external programs designed as binary modules. Normal executable programs should be accessed with the RUN command.

Command: CANCEL

Syntax: CANCEL

The CANCEL command halts execution of a command file and returns dBASE III PLUS to the dot prompt.

Command: CHANGE

Syntax: CHANGE [*scope*][FIELDS *field-list*][FOR/WHILE *condition*]

The CHANGE command permits full-screen editing of fields listed in *field-list*. If the *scope* option is absent, the quantifier ALL is assumed. The FOR/WHILE option allows editing to only those records satisfying the *condition*.

   Example: To edit the RENTAMT and EXPDATE fields in the ABC1 database, enter

```
CHANGE FIELDS RENTAMT,EXPDATE
```

Command: CLEAR

Syntax: CLEAR

The CLEAR command erases the screen and returns the cursor to location 0,0 (the upper-left corner). CLEAR can also be used as an option of the @ command to clear the screen below and to the right of the location specified by the @ command.

Examples: To erase the entire screen, enter

```
CLEAR
```

To erase the screen below and to the right of the cursor at 12,20, enter

```
@12,20 CLEAR
```

Command: CLEAR ALL

Syntax: CLEAR ALL

The CLEAR ALL command closes all open database, memo, index, and format files. The current work area is set to 1.

Command: CLEAR FIELDS

Syntax: CLEAR FIELDS

Clears the list of fields specified by the SET FIELDS command. The CLEAR FIELDS command has no effect if SET FIELDS was not previously used to specify fields (see SET FIELDS).

Command: CLEAR GETS

Syntax: CLEAR GETS

The CLEAR GETS command clears values from variables provided by the GET that were accessed with a READ command.

Example: The following CLEAR GETS command would permit

the user to clear previous responses to various GET commands.

```
ACCEPT "Enter Y to store entries, N to delete" TO ANS
IF ANS = "N"
        CLEAR GETS
ENDIF
```

Command: CLEAR MEMORY

Syntax: CLEAR MEMORY

The CLEAR MEMORY command erases all current memory variables.

Command: CLEAR TYPEAHEAD

Syntax: CLEAR TYPEAHEAD

The CLEAR TYPEAHEAD command clears the contents of the type-ahead buffer (see SET TYPEAHEAD).

Command: CLOSE

Syntax: CLOSE *file-type*

The CLOSE command closes all file types listed in *file-type*. *File-type* can be one of five: ALTERNATE, DATABASES, FORMAT, INDEX, or PROCEDURE.

Command: CONTINUE

Syntax: CONTINUE

The CONTINUE command resumes a search started by LOCATE. After LOCATE finds the record matching the criteria specified in the command, you can find additional records that meet the same criteria by entering CONTINUE. Using CONTINUE saves you from having to reenter the LOCATE command (see LOCATE).

Command: COPY

Syntax: COPY TO *filename* [*scope*] [FIELDS *field-list*] [FOR/WHILE *condition*][SDF/DELIMITED [WITH *delimiter*]]

The COPY command copies all or part of the active database to *file-name*. If *scope* is not listed, ALL is assumed. The FIELDS option is used to pinpoint the fields to be copied. The FOR/WHILE option copies only those records meeting the *condition*. Specifying SDF will copy the file in System Data format; specifying DELIMITED will copy the file in Delimited format.

Example: To copy LASTNAME, RENTAMT, and EXTRAS fields from the active database ABC1 to WORLDWIDE, enter

`COPY TO WORLDWIDE FIELDS LASTNAME, RENTAMT, EXTRAS`

Command: COPY FILE

Syntax: COPY FILE *source-file* TO *destination-file*

The COPY FILE command creates an identical copy of a file. You must supply the extension in both *source-file* and *destination-file*.

Example: To copy a file named REPORTER.FRM, to a new file named TESTER.FRM, enter

`COPY FILE REPORTER.FRM TO TESTER.FRM`

Command: COPY STRUCTURE

Syntax: COPY STRUCTURE TO *filename* [FIELDS *field-list*]

The COPY STRUCTURE command copies the structure of an active database to *filename*. Specifying FIELDS with *field-list* will copy only those fields to the structure.

Command: COUNT

Syntax: COUNT [*scope*][FOR/WHILE *condition*][TO *memvar*]

The COUNT command counts the number of records in the active database that meet a specific condition. The *scope* option quantifies the records to be counted. The FOR/WHILE option can be used to specify a condition that must be met before a record will be counted. The TO option can be used to store the count to the memory variable *memvar*.

Example: To count the number of records containing the letters MD in the STATE field and to store that count as the memory variable MTEMP, enter

```
COUNT FOR STATE = "MD" TO MTEMP
```

Command: CREATE

Syntax: CREATE *filename*

The CREATE command creates a new database file and defines its structure. If CREATE is entered without a filename, dBASE III PLUS will prompt you for one. If CREATE is followed by a filename, a database with that filename will be created. The filename extension .DBF is added automatically to the filename unless you specify otherwise.

Command: CREATE LABEL

Syntax: CREATE LABEL *filename*

The CREATE LABEL command creates a label form file. This file can be used with the LABEL FORM command to produce mailing labels.

Command: CREATE QUERY

Syntax: CREATE QUERY *filename*

CREATE QUERY creates or modifies a query file to filter a database of records that do not meet specified conditions. The specified filename is assigned an extension of .QRY. Upon entry of the command, the Query menu appears on the screen. Options within the Query menu allow design of the filter. If a catalog is open when CREATE QUERY is used, the resultant query file will be added to the catalog.

Example: To create a query file named PAST DUE, enter

```
CREATE QUERY PASTDUE
```

Command: CREATE REPORT

Syntax: CREATE REPORT

The CREATE REPORT, or as an alternative MODIFY REPORT, command creates or allows the user to modify a report form file for producing reports. Once the report has been outlined with the CREATE REPORT command, the report can be displayed or printed with the REPORT FORM command.

Command: CREATE SCREEN

Syntax: CREATE SCREEN *filename*

CREATE SCREEN creates or modifies a custom screen form that is used for the display and editing of records. Two files are created by the CREATE SCREEN command. One file is assigned the .SCR extension, and the other file is assigned the .FMT extension. Upon entry of the command, the Screen Painter menu appears. Options within the Screen Painter allow design of the custom screen form. If a catalog is active when CREATE SCREEN is used, the resultant .FMT and .SCR files will be added to the catalog.

Example: To create a custom screen format named PARTS, enter

`CREATE SCREEN PARTS`

Command: CREATE VIEW

Syntax: CREATE VIEW *filename*

CREATE VIEW creates or modifies a view file to group related databases and associated index, format, and filter files into what appears to be a single file. View files can contain database files open in chosen work areas along with associated index files, one format file, and one filter file. Relations between the open databases are also contained within the view file. The view file is assigned the .VUE extension. Upon entry of the CREATE VIEW command, the View menu appears. Options within the menu allow the selection of databases and associated files that will be contained within the view file. If a catalog is active when CREATE VIEW is used, the view file and its contents will be added to the catalog.

Example: To create a view file named CLIENTS, enter

```
CREATE VIEW CLIENTS
```

Command: CREATE VIEW FROM ENVIRONMENT

Syntax: CREATE VIEW *filename* FROM ENVIRONMENT

The CREATE VIEW FROM ENVIRONMENT command creates a view file based upon the databases, index files, relations, and associated format file in use at the time the command is entered. The view file created by this command will contain all open database files and associated index files; all existing relations between databases; and one format file, if a format file is open. The current work area number and field list (if a field list is active) are also saved within the view file.

Command: DELETE

Syntax: DELETE [*record-number*][*scope*][FOR/WHILE *condition*]

The DELETE command marks specific records for deletion. If DELETE is used without a record number, the current record is marked for deletion. The *scope* option is used to identify the records to be deleted. The FOR/WHILE option can be used to specify a condition that must be met before a record will be deleted. DELETE marks a file for deletion; the PACK command actually removes the record.

Example: To mark 24 records for deletion beginning with the current record and specifying that they have an entry of VA in the STATE field in order to be deleted, enter

```
DELETE NEXT 24 FOR STATE = "VA"
```

Command: DIR

Syntax: DIR [*drive:*][*filename*]

The DIR command displays the directory of all database files or files of a specific type if a file extension is specified. *Drive* is the drive designator (A:, B:, or C: for hard-disk users), and *filename* is the name of a file with or without an extension. Wildcards, which are asterisks or question marks, can be used as part of or as a replacement for *filename*. In the case of database files, the display produced by DIR includes the number of records contained in the database, the date of the last update, and the size of the file (in bytes).

Example: To display all index files from the current default drive, enter

```
DIR *.NDX
```

Command: DISPLAY

Syntax: DISPLAY [*scope*][*field-list*][FOR/WHILE *condition*][OFF]

The DISPLAY command displays a record from the active database. You can display more records by including the *scope* option. The FOR/WHILE option limits the display of records to those satisfying *condition*. Only the fields listed in *field-list* will be displayed; if *field-list* is absent, all fields will be displayed. The OFF option will prevent the record number from being displayed.

Example: To display the LASTNAME, FIRSTNAME, RENTAMT, and EXPDATE fields for ten records beginning with the current record, enter

```
DISPLAY NEXT 10 LASTNAME, FIRSTNAME, RENTAMT, EXPDATE
```

Command: DISPLAY HISTORY

Syntax: DISPLAY HISTORY [LAST *number*][TO PRINT]

The DISPLAY HISTORY command displays all commands stored in HISTORY unless the LAST option (where *number* equals the number of commands to display) is used to specify a certain number of commands. The TO PRINT option will cause the displayed commands to be printed on the printer.

Example: To print the last ten commands entered, enter the following:

```
DISPLAY HISTORY LAST 10 TO PRINT
```

Command: DISPLAY MEMORY

Syntax: DISPLAY MEMORY [TO PRINT]

The DISPLAY MEMORY command displays all active memory variables, their sizes, and their contents. From a total of 256 variables, the number of active variables and available variables are listed along with the number of bytes consumed and bytes available. These statistics will be displayed on the printer as well as the screen if **TO PRINT** is included.

Command: DISPLAY STATUS

Syntax: DISPLAY STATUS

The DISPLAY STATUS command displays the names and aliases of all currently active work areas and active files. Any key fields used in index files, the current drive designator, function-key settings, and settings of SET commands are also displayed.

Command: DISPLAY STRUCTURE

Syntax: DISPLAY STRUCTURE

The DISPLAY STRUCTURE command displays the structure of the active database. The complete filename is listed, along with the current drive designator, number of records, date of last update, and names of fields, including their statistics (type, length, and decimal places).

Command: DISPLAY USERS

Syntax: DISPLAY USERS

The DISPLAY USERS command, present in the network version of dBASE, displays a list of all users who are logged onto the network. Those users who are currently active are indicated by a $>$ symbol preceding their name.

Command: DO

Syntax: DO *filename* [WITH *parameter-list*]

The DO command starts execution of a dBASE III PLUS command file. The filename extension of .PRG is assumed unless otherwise specified. If the WITH option is specified and followed by a list of parameters in *parameter-list*, those parameters are transferred to the command file.

Command: DO CASE

Syntax: DO CASE

    CASE *condition*

      commands...

    [CASE *condition*]

      commands...

    [OTHERWISE]

      commands...

    ENDCASE

The DO CASE command selects one course of action from a number of choices. The conditions following the CASE statements are evaluated until one of the conditions is found to be true. When a condition is true, the commands between the CASE statement and another CASE, or

OTHERWISE and ENDCASE, will be executed. If none of the conditions in the CASE statements is found to be true, any commands following the optional OTHERWISE statement will be executed. If the OTHERWISE statement is not used and no conditions are found to be true, dBASE III PLUS proceeds to the command following the END-CASE statement.

Example: In the following DO CASE commands, dBASE chooses from among three possible alternatives: (1) executing a command file named MENU; (2) appending the database; or (3) exiting from dBASE III PLUS.

```
DO CASE
    CASE SELECT = 1
    DO MENU
    CASE SELECT = 2
    APPEND
    CASE SELECT = 3
    QUIT
ENDCASE
```

Command: DO WHILE

Syntax: DO WHILE *condition*

　　　　　　commands...

　　　　ENDDO

The DO WHILE command repeatedly executes commands between DO WHILE and ENDDO as long as *condition* is true. When dBASE III PLUS encounters a DO WHILE command, the condition following the command is evaluated: if *condition* is false, dBASE III PLUS proceeds to the command following the ENDDO command; but if *condition* is true, dBASE III PLUS executes the commands following the DO WHILE command until the ENDDO command is reached. When the ENDDO command is reached, the condition following the DO WHILE command is again evaluated. If it is still true, the commands between DO WHILE and ENDDO are again executed. If the condition is false, dBASE III PLUS proceeds to the command below the ENDDO command.

Example: To print LASTNAME, CITY, STATE, RENTAMT, and

EXPDATE fields for each record until the end of the database, enter

```
DO WHILE .NOT. EOF()
          ? LASTNAME, CITY, STATE, RENTAMT, EXPDATE
          SKIP
ENDDO
```

Command: EDIT

Syntax: EDIT [RECORD *n*]

The EDIT command allows full-screen editing of a record in the database. If no record number is specified by RECORD (*n* being the record number), the current record, which is identified by the current position of the record pointer, will be edited.

Command: EJECT

Syntax: EJECT

The EJECT command causes the printer to perform a formfeed.

Command: ERASE

Syntax: ERASE *filename.ext*

The ERASE command erases the named file from the directory. The name must include the file extension. You can also use the command DELETE FILE *filename.ext* to erase a file. If the file is on a disk that is not in the default drive, you must include the drive designator.

Command: EXIT

Syntax: EXIT

The EXIT command exits a DO WHILE loop and proceeds to the first command below the ENDDO command.

Example: The following command-file portion uses the EXIT to exit the DO WHILE loop if a part number of 9999 is entered.

```
? "Enter part number to add to inventory."
? "Enter 9999 to exit."
DO WHILE .T.
INPUT TO PARTNO
IF PARTNO = 9999
     EXIT
ENDIF
```

Command: EXPORT

Syntax: EXPORT TO *filename* TYPE PFS

The EXPORT command creates a PFS:File database file and PFS-compatible screen format, based on a dBASE III PLUS database in use. If a format file is active, that format file will be used as the screen format within the PFS:File database.

Example: To export a file, PARTS, to a PFS:File database to be named INVPARTS, enter

```
USE PARTS
EXPORT TO INVPARTS TYPE PFS
```

Command: FIND

Syntax: FIND *"character-string"*

The FIND command positions the record pointer at the first record containing an index key that matches *"character-string"*. If there are leading blanks in *character-string*, *character-string* must be surrounded by single or double quotes; otherwise no quotes are necessary. If the specific character string cannot be found, the EOF() value is set to true and a "no find" message is displayed on the screen (if dBASE III PLUS is not executing a command file). An index file must be open before you use the FIND command.

Command: GO or GOTO

Syntax: GO or GOTO BOTTOM/TOP/*expression*

The GO (or GOTO) command positions the record pointer at a record. GO TOP will move the pointer to the beginning of a database, GO BOTTOM will move it to the end of a database.

Command: HELP

Syntax: HELP *command-name*

The HELP command provides instructions on using dBASE III PLUS commands and functions as well as other information. If you enter HELP without specifying a command or function, a menu-driven system of Help screens allows you to request information on various subjects. If HELP is followed by a command or function, information about it will be displayed.

Command: IF

Syntax: IF *condition*

   commands...

   [ELSE]

   commands...

   ENDIF

IF is a decision-making command that will execute commands when certain conditions are true. If *condition* for the IF statement is true, the commands between the IF and ENDIF will be executed. Should *condition* be false and there is an ELSE, the commands will be executed between ELSE and ENDIF. On the other hand, if *condition* for IF is false and there is no ELSE, dBASE III PLUS will drop to the ENDIF statement without executing any commands.

Command: IMPORT

Syntax: IMPORT FROM *filename* TYPE PFS

The IMPORT command creates a dBASE III PLUS database, format file, and view file from a PFS:File database. The format file created will mimic the design of the PFS:File screen form. The resultant dBASE III PLUS database can be used separately from the format file, or both files can be used, with or without the accompanying view file. The imported file will be assigned the same filename as the PFS file.

Example: To create a dBASE III PLUS database from a PFS:File
database called ILLNESS, enter

```
IMPORT FROM ILLNESS TYPE PFS
```

Command: INDEX

Syntax: INDEX ON *field-list* TO *filename*

The INDEX command creates an index file based on a field from the
active database. Depending on the field, the index file will be indexed
alphabetically, numerically, or chronologically. If the index based on the
first field has duplicate entries, the duplicates are indexed according to
the second field in *field-list*, provided a second field has been listed.

Example: To create an index file called RENTS based on the values
in the RENTAMT field, enter

```
INDEX ON RENTAMT TO RENTS
```

Command: INPUT

Syntax: INPUT [*prompt*] TO *memvar*

The INPUT command stores a numeric entry assigned to a memory
variable by the user. An optional *prompt* can display a message to the
user during keyboard entry. *Prompt* can be a memory variable or a
character string.

Example: To display the prompt "Enter name to search for:" and
store the response to the memory variable NEWNAME, enter

```
INPUT "Enter name to search for:" TO NEWNAME
```

Command: INSERT

Syntax: INSERT [BLANK][BEFORE]

The INSERT command adds a new record below the record pointer's
position and renumbers the records below the insertion. Specifying

BEFORE causes the record to be inserted at the record pointer; thus, if the pointer is at record 3, the new record will be 3 and the records below it renumbered. If the BLANK option is omitted, dBASE III PLUS allows full-screen editing of the new record; otherwise the record will be blank.

Example: To insert a new record at position 10 in the active database, enter

```
GO 10
INSERT BEFORE
```

Command: JOIN

Syntax: JOIN WITH *alias* TO *filename* FOR *condition* [FIELDS *field-list*]

The JOIN command creates a new database by combining specific records and fields from the active database and the database listed as *alias*. The combined database is stored in *filename*. You can limit the choice of records from the active database by specifying a FOR *condition*. All fields from both files will be copied if you do not include a *field-list*; but if you do, only those fields specified in *field-list* will be copied. Specify fields from the nonactive database by supplying *filename, -> fieldname*.

Example: To join ABC1 and ABC2 to create a new file named NEWFILE including only the LASTNAME field from ABC2 and records from ABC1 with RENTAMT less than $400, enter

```
JOIN WITH ABC2 TO NEWFILE FOR RENTAMT < 400 FIELDS ABC2-> LASTNAME
```

Command: LABEL FORM

Syntax: LABEL FORM *label-filename* [*scope*][SAMPLE][TO PRINT] [FOR/WHILE *condition*][TO FILE *filename*]

The LABEL FORM command is used to print mailing labels from a label form file (extension .LBL). The SAMPLE option allows a sample label to be printed. The FOR/WHILE option can be used to specify a condition that must be met before a label for a record will be printed. The TO PRINT option sends output to the printer, and the TO FILE option sends output to a named disk file.

Example: To print mailing labels, using the label form named MAILERS, for records with STATE fields containing NM and to restrict printing to the next 25 records beginning at the current record-pointer position, enter

```
LABEL FORM MAILERS NEXT 25 FOR STATE = "NM" TO PRINT
```

Command: LIST

Syntax: LIST [OFF][*scope*][*field-list*][FOR/WHILE *condition*][TO PRINT]

The LIST command provides a list of database contents. The *scope* option is used to quantify the records to be listed. If *scope* is absent, ALL is assumed. The FOR/WHILE option specifies a condition that must be met before a record will be listed. The OFF option will prevent the record number from being listed. If the TO PRINT option is used, the listing will be printed on the printer.

Command: LIST HISTORY

Syntax: LIST HISTORY [LAST *number*][TO PRINT]

The LIST HISTORY command operates in a manner identical to the DISPLAY HISTORY command (see DISPLAY HISTORY) except for one difference: the screen will not pause every 24 lines, as it does with the DISPLAY HISTORY command.

Command: LIST MEMORY

Syntax: LIST MEMORY [TO PRINT]

The LIST MEMORY command lists the names, sizes, and types of memory variables. If the TO PRINT option is used, the listing will be printed on the printer.

Command: LIST STATUS

Syntax: LIST STATUS [TO PRINT]

The LIST STATUS command lists information on currently open work areas, the active files, and system settings. All open files and open index filenames are displayed, along with work area numbers, any key fields used in index files, the default disk drive, function-key settings, and settings of the SET commands. If the TO PRINT option is used, the listing will be printed on the printer. LIST STATUS does not pause during the listing, which is the only difference between LIST STATUS and DISPLAY STATUS.

Command: LIST STRUCTURE

Syntax: LIST STRUCTURE [TO PRINT]

The LIST STRUCTURE command lists the structure of the database in use, including the name, number of records, all names of fields, and the date of the last update. If the TO PRINT option is used, the listing will be printed on the printer. LIST STRUCTURE does not pause during the listing, which is the only difference between LIST STRUCTURE and DISPLAY STRUCTURE.

Command: LOAD

Syntax: LOAD *<binary filename.ext>*

The LOAD command is used to load binary (assembly-language) programs into memory for future use. The extension is optional; if omitted, it is assumed to be .BIN. Up to five binary files can be loaded into memory at once, and each can be up to 32K in size.

Command: LOCATE

Syntax: LOCATE [*scope*] FOR *condition*

The LOCATE command finds the first record that matches *condition*. The *scope* option can be used to limit the number of records that will be searched. If *scope* is omitted, ALL is assumed. The LOCATE command

ends when a record matching *condition* is found, after which dBASE III
PLUS prints the location of the record but not the record itself.

Example: To locate a record containing the character string Smith
in the LASTNAME field, enter

```
LOCATE FOR LASTNAME = "Smith"
```

Command: LOGOUT

Syntax: LOGOUT

The LOGOUT command, present in the network version of dBASE,
will close all files and clear all variables, close the current procedure file
if one is running, and present the user with the dBASE Administrator
Login screen. The user must then enter a valid password to use the
dBASE Administrator.

Command: LOOP

Syntax: LOOP

The LOOP command causes a jump back to the beginning of a DO
WHILE loop. The LOOP command is normally executed conditionally
with the IF statement.

Example: The following portion of a command file uses the LOOP
command to return to the start of the DO WHILE loop if the RENT-
AMT field equals 800.

```
DO WHILE .NOT. EOF()
    IF RENTAMT = 800
        SKIP
        LOOP
    ENDIF
    SET PRINT ON
    LIST LASTNAME,FIRSTNAME,RENTAMT
    SKIP
    SET PRINT OFF
ENDDO
```

Command: MODIFY COMMAND

Syntax: MODIFY COMMAND *filename*

MODIFY COMMAND starts the dBASE III PLUS word processor,

which can be used for editing command files or any ASCII text files. *Filename* will be given the extension .PRG.

Command: MODIFY LABELS

Syntax: MODIFY LABELS *filename*

The MODIFY LABELS command creates or allows editing of a label form file. This file can be used with the LABEL FORM command to produce mailing labels. *Filename* will be given the extension .LBL.

Command: MODIFY QUERY

Syntax: MODIFY QUERY *filename*

MODIFY QUERY modifies an existing query file to filter a database of records that do not meet specified conditions. (To create a new query file, use CREATE QUERY.) Upon entry of the command, the Query menu appears on the screen. Options within the Query menu allow changes to the filter design. If a catalog is open when MODIFY QUERY is used, the modified query file will be added to the catalog.

Command: MODIFY REPORT

Syntax: MODIFY REPORT *filename*

The MODIFY REPORT command allows you to use a menu-assisted, full-screen editor to create or modify a report form file for producing reports. *Filename* will be given the extension .FRM.

Command: MODIFY SCREEN

Syntax: MODIFY SCREEN *filename*

The MODIFY SCREEN command modifies an existing custom screen form. (To create a new custom screen form, use the CREATE SCREEN command.) Upon entry of the command, the Screen Painter menu appears. Options within the Screen Painter allow modifications to the design of the custom screen form. If a catalog is active when MODIFY SCREEN is used, the modified .FMT and .SCR files will be added to the catalog.

Command: MODIFY STRUCTURE

Syntax: MODIFY STRUCTURE *filename*

The MODIFY STRUCTURE command allows you to alter the structure of a database. The filename extension .DBF is given to *filename* unless specified otherwise.

A backup copy is created to store the data from *filename*. The data is later returned to the modified file; the backup file remains on disk with the same *filename* but with a different extension of .BAK.

Command: MODIFY VIEW

Syntax: MODIFY VIEW *filename*

MODIFY VIEW modifies an existing view file that groups related databases and associated index, format, and filter files into what appears to be a single file. (To create a new view file, use the CREATE VIEW command.) Upon entry of the MODIFY VIEW command, the View menu appears. Options within the menu allow changes to the selection of databases and associated files that will be contained within the view file. If a catalog is active when MODIFY VIEW is used, the modified view file will be added to the catalog.

Command: NOTE or *

Syntax: NOTE or *

The NOTE or * command is used to insert comments in a command file. Text after the * or the word NOTE in a command file will be ignored by dBASE III PLUS.

Command: ON
Syntax: ON ERROR *command*

ON ESCAPE *command*

ON KEY *command*

The ON command causes a branch within a command file, specified by *command*, to be carried out when the condition identified by ON (an error, pressing the ESC key, or pressing any key) is met. If more than one

ON condition is specified, the order of precedence is ON ERROR, then ON ESCAPE, then ON KEY. All ON conditions remain in effect until another ON condition is specified to clear the previous condition. To clear an ON condition without specifying another condition, enter ON ERROR, ON ESCAPE, or ON KEY without adding a command.

Examples: To cause program control to transfer to another program called ERRTRAP if an error occurs, enter

```
ON ERROR DO ERRTRAP
```

To cause the program to display a customized error message if an error occurs, enter the following:

```
ON ERROR ? "A serious error has occured.  Call J.E.J.A. Tech
Support for instructions."
```

To cause the program to call another program, named HELPER.PRG, and containing customized help screens, if the ESC key is pressed, enter

```
ON ESCAPE DO HELPER
```

To halt processing within a program and transfer program control to a program named HALTED.PRG if any key is pressed, enter

```
ON KEY DO HALTED
```

Use of the ON KEY syntax of the command will result in the key that is pressed being stored in the keyboard buffer. The routine that is called by the ON KEY command should use a READ command or INKEY( ) function to clear the buffer.

Command: PACK

Syntax: PACK

The PACK command removes records that have been marked for deletion by the DELETE command.

Command: PARAMETERS

Syntax: PARAMETERS *parameter-list*

The PARAMETERS command is used within a command file to assign variable names to data items that are received from another command file with the DO command. The PARAMETERS command must be the first command in a command file; the parameter list is identical to the list of parameters included with the WITH option of the DO command that called the command file.

Example: The following portion of a command file shows the use of the PARAMETERS command to receive four parameters—SALARY, FEDTAX, STATETAX, and FICA—sent from the command file that called this command file.

```
NOTE This is the calculations command file.
PARAMETERS SALARY, FEDTAX, STATETAX, FICA
STORE SALARY - (FEDTAX + STATETAX + FICA) TO NET
RETURN
(...rest of program...)
```

Command: PRIVATE

Syntax: PRIVATE [ALL[LIKE/EXCEPT*skeleton*]][*memory variables list*]

The PRIVATE command sets named variables to private, hiding the values of those variables from all higher-level parts of a program. *Skeletons* are the acceptable DOS wildcards of asterisk (*) and question mark (?). Memory variables are private by default.

Examples: To hide all variables, excluding BILLPAY, from higher-level parts of the program, enter

```
PRIVATE ALL EXCEPT BILLPAY
```

To hide all variables with eight-character names that end in TEST from higher-level parts of the program, enter

```
PRIVATE ALL LIKE ????TEST
```

To hide only the variable named PAYOUT from higher-level parts of the program, enter

```
PRIVATE PAYOUT
```

Command: PROCEDURE

Syntax: PROCEDURE

The PROCEDURE command identifies the start of each separate procedure within a procedure file.

Although using a one-line procedure is inefficient (procedures should be at least three lines long), the following example demonstrates a simple procedure.

Example:

```
PROCEDURE ERROR1
@2.10 SAY "That is not a valid date.  Please try again."
RETURN
```

Command: PUBLIC

Syntax: PUBLIC [*memory variables list*]

PUBLIC sets named variables to public, making the values of those variables available to all levels of a program.

Example: To make the variables named BILLPAY, DUEDATE, and AMOUNT available to all modules of a program, enter

```
PUBLIC BILLPAY, DUEDATE, AMOUNT
```

Command: QUIT

Syntax: QUIT

The QUIT command closes all open files, leaves dBASE III PLUS, and returns you to the DOS prompt.

Command: READ

Syntax: READ [SAVE]

The READ command allows full-screen data entry from an @ command with GET option. Normally, a READ command clears all GETs when all data entry or editing is completed. The SAVE option is used to avoid clearing all GETs after completion of data entry or editing.

Command: RECALL

Syntax: RECALL [*scope*] [FOR/WHILE *condition*]

The RECALL command unmarks records that have been marked for deletion. If *scope* is not listed, ALL is assumed. The FOR/WHILE option can be used to specify a condition that must be met before a record will be recalled.

Command: REINDEX

Syntax: REINDEX

The REINDEX command rebuilds active index files. If any changes have been made to the database while its index file was closed, you can update the index with REINDEX.

Command: RELEASE

Syntax: RELEASE [*memvar*][ALL [LIKE/EXCEPT *wildcards*]]

The RELEASE command removes all or specified memory variables from memory. Wildcards, which are asterisks or question marks, are used with the LIKE and EXCEPT options. The asterisk can be used to represent one or more characters, the question mark to represent one character.

Example: To release all memory variables except those ending with the characters TAX, enter

```
RELEASE ALL EXCEPT ???TAX
```

Command: RENAME

Syntax: RENAME *filename.ext* TO *new-filename.ext*

The RENAME command changes the name of a file. The name must include the file extension. If the file is on a disk that is not in the default drive, the drive designator must also be included.

Command: REPLACE

Syntax: REPLACE [*scope*] *field* WITH *expression* [,...*field2* WITH *expression*] [FOR/WHILE *condition*]

The REPLACE command replaces the contents of a specified field with new values. You can replace values in more than one field by listing more than one *field* WITH *expression*; be sure to separate each field replacement with a comma. The FOR/WHILE option can be used to specify a condition that must be met before a field in a record will be replaced. If the *scope* or FOR/WHILE options are not used, the current record (at the current record-pointer location) will be the only record replaced.

Example: To replace the contents of the field RENTAMT at the current record with a new amount equal to the old amount multiplied by 1.05, enter

```
REPLACE RENTAMT WITH RENTAMT * 1.05
```

Command: REPORT FORM

Syntax: REPORT FORM *filename* [*scope*][FOR *expression*][PLAIN] [HEADING *character-string*][NOEJECT][TO PRINT][TO FILE *filename*]

The REPORT FORM command uses a report form file (previously created with the CREATE REPORT command) to produce a tabular report. A *filename* with the extension .FRM is assumed unless otherwise specified. The FOR *condition* option can be used to specify a condition that must be met before a record will be printed. If *scope* is not included, ALL is assumed. The PLAIN option omits page numbers and the system date. The HEADING option (followed by a character string) provides a header in addition to any header that was specified when the report was created with CREATE REPORT. The NOEJECT option cancels the initial formfeed.

Command: RESTORE

Syntax: RESTORE FROM *filename* [ADDITIVE]

The RESTORE command reads memory variables into memory from a memory variable file. RESTORE FROM assumes that *filename* ends with .MEM; if it does not, you should include the extension. If the ADDITIVE option is used, current memory variables will not be deleted.

Command: RESUME

Syntax: RESUME

The RESUME command is a companion to the SUSPEND command. RESUME causes program execution to continue at the line following the line containing the SUSPEND command (see SUSPEND).

Command: RETRY

Syntax: RETRY

The RETRY command returns control to a calling program and executes the same line that called the program containing the RETRY command. The function of RETRY is similar to the function of the RETURN command; however, where RETURN executes the following line of the calling program, RETRY executes the same line of the calling program. RETRY can be useful in recovering errors when action can be taken to clear the cause of an error and the command repeated, as shown in the following example:

```
*Main Menu program
ON ERROR DO FIXIT
USE ABC1 INDEX NAMES
<...rest of program follows...>


*FIXIT.PRG
CLEAR
? "Cannot find ABC database and index files on disk."
? "please insert the disk with the databases in drive B."
? "and press a key to continue."
WAIT
RETRY
```

Command: RETURN

Syntax: RETURN [TO MASTER]

The RETURN command ends execution of a command file or procedure. If the command file was called by another command file, program control returns to that command file. If the command file was not called by another command file, control returns to the dot prompt. If the TO MASTER option is used, control returns to the highest-level command file.

Command: RUN

Syntax: RUN *filename*

The RUN command executes a non-dBASE III PLUS program from within the dBASE III PLUS environment. The program must have an extension of .COM or .EXE. When the program completes its execution, control is passed back to dBASE III PLUS. You can also execute DOS commands with RUN, provided there is enough available memory.

Command: SAVE

Syntax: SAVE TO *filename* [ALL LIKE/EXCEPT *wildcard*]

The SAVE command copies memory variables to a disk file. Wildcards, which are asterisks or question marks, are used with the LIKE and EXCEPT options. The asterisk can be used to represent one or more characters, the question mark to represent one character.

Example: To save all existing six-letter memory variables ending in the letters TAX to a disk file named FIGURES, enter

```
SAVE TO FIGURES ALL LIKE ???TAX
```

Command: SEEK

Syntax: SEEK *expression*

The SEEK command searches for the first record in an indexed file whose field matches a specific *expression*. If *expression* is a character string, it must be surrounded by single or double quotes. If *expression* cannot be found and dBASE III PLUS is not executing a command file, the EOF( ) value is set to true and a "No find" message is displayed on the screen. An index file must be open before you can use the SEEK command.

Command: SELECT

Syntax: SELECT *n* or SELECT *alias*

The SELECT command chooses from among ten possible work areas for database files. When dBASE III PLUS is first loaded into the computer, it defaults to work area 1. To use multiple files at once, you must select other work areas with the SELECT command; other files can then be opened in those areas. Acceptable work areas are the letters A through J for *alias* and the numbers 1 through 10 for *n*.

   Example: To open a file named TAXES in work area 5, enter

```
SELECT 5
USE TAXES
```

Command: SET

Syntax: SET

The SET command causes Set Menus to be displayed. Set Menus can then be used to select most available SET parameters within dBASE III PLUS.

Command: SET ALTERNATE

Syntax: SET ALTERNATE ON/OFF and SET ALTERNATE TO
      filename

The SET ALTERNATE ON command creates a text file with extension .TXT, and when actuated by SET ALTERNATE ON stores all keyboard entries and screen displays to the file. The SET ALTERNATE OFF command halts the process.

   Example: To store the actions of the LIST command to a text file, enter

```
SET ALTERNATE TO CAPTURE
SET ALTERNATE ON
LIST LASTNAME, FIRSTNAME
SET ALTERNATE OFF
```

Command: SET BELL

Syntax: SET BELL ON/OFF

The SET BELL command controls whether audible warnings will be issued during certain operations.

Command: SET CARRY

Syntax: SET CARRY ON/OFF

The SET CARRY command controls whether data will be copied from the prior record into a new record when APPEND or INSERT is used.

Command: SET CATALOG

Syntax: SET CATALOG ON/OFF

The SET CATALOG command causes or does not cause files that are opened to be added to an open catalog (see SET CATALOG TO).

Command: SET CATALOG TO

Syntax: SET CATALOG TO *catalog filename*

SET CATALOG TO either opens a catalog, or if the named catalog does not exist, creates a new catalog. Any catalog previously opened will be closed when the SET CATALOG TO command is used.

Command: SET CENTURY

Syntax: SET CENTURY ON/OFF

The SET CENTURY COMMAND either causes or does not cause the century to be visible in the display of dates. For example, a date that appears as 12/30/86 will appear as 12/30/1986 after the SET CENTURY ON command is used.

Command: SET COLOR

Syntax: SET COLOR TO *standard* [,*enhanced*][,*border*]

The SET COLOR command is used to select screen colors and display attributes (see Chapter 15 for more on SET COLOR).

Command: SET CONFIRM

Syntax: SET CONFIRM ON/OFF

The SET CONFIRM command controls the behavior of the cursor during full-screen editing.

Command: SET CONSOLE

Syntax: SET CONSOLE ON/OFF

The SET CONSOLE command turns output to the screen on or off. SET CONSOLE does not control output to the printer.

Command: SET DATE

Syntax: SET DATE
AMERICAN/ANSI/BRITISH/ITALIAN/FRENCH/
GERMAN

SET DATE sets the display format for the appearance of dates. American displays as mm/dd/yy; ANSI displays as yy.mm.dd; British displays as dd/mm/yy; Italian displays as dd-mm-yy; French displays as dd/mm/yy; and German displays as dd.mm.yy. The default value is American.

Command: SET DEBUG

Syntax: SET DEBUG ON/OFF

The SET DEBUG command routes the output of the SET ECHO command to the printer instead of the screen.

Command: SET DECIMALS

Syntax: SET DECIMALS TO n

The SET DECIMALS command, which applies only to division, SQRT( ), LOG( ), and EXP( ), changes the minimum number of decimal places normally displayed during calculations.

Command: SET DEFAULT

Syntax: SET DEFAULT TO *drive:*

The SET DEFAULT command changes the default drive used in file operations. Usually, *drive:* is A or B; it is usually C for hard-disk drives.

Command: SET DELETED

Syntax: SET DELETED ON/OFF

With SET DELETED ON, all records marked for deletion will be displayed when commands such as LIST are used. With SET DELETE OFF, delete markers are turned off, even though they are still present.

Command: SET DELIMITER

Syntax: SET DELIMITER TO [*character-string*][DEFAULT]
SET DELIMITER ON/OFF

The SET DELIMITER command assigns characters other than the default colon (:) to be used to mark the field area. Once they are assigned, SET DELIMITER ON activates the delimiters, and SET DELIMITER OFF deactivates the delimiters. DEFAULT restores the colon (:) as the delimiter.

Example: To mark the beginning of a field with a left curly bracket ({) and end the field with a right bracket (}), enter

```
SET DELIMITER TO "{}"
```

Command: SET DEVICE

Syntax: SET DEVICE TO PRINTER/SCREEN

The SET DEVICE command controls whether @ commands are sent to the screen or printer. SET DEVICE is normally set to SCREEN, but if PRINTER is specified, output will be directed to the printer.

Command: SET DOHISTORY

Syntax: SET DOHISTORY ON/OFF

The SET DOHISTORY command causes or does not cause the commands executed by a command file to be stored within HISTORY (see SET HISTORY).

Command: SET ECHO

Syntax: SET ECHO ON/OFF

The SET ECHO command determines whether instructions from command files will be displayed or printed during program execution. It is mostly used with SET DEBUG. The default for SET ECHO is OFF.

Command: SET ENCRYPTION

Syntax: SET ENCRYPTION ON/OFF

The SET ENCRYPTION command, present in the network version of dBASE, will cause all database files created by copying existing files to be encrypted, assuming PROTECT is in use within the dBASE Administrator. The encryption affects only files created with commands like SORT and COPY TO. Existing files and new files created with the CREATE command are not directly encrypted by the use of SET ENCRYPTION; such encryption must be performed with the Protect utility. Note that SET ENCRYPTION must be OFF before you can write foreign files with TYPE options of the COPY TO command or with the EXPORT command.

Command: SET ESCAPE

Syntax: SET ESCAPE ON/OFF

The SET ESCAPE command determines whether the ESC key will interrupt a program during execution. The default for SET ESCAPE is ON.

Command: SET EXACT

Syntax: SET EXACT ON/OFF

The SET EXACT command determines how precisely two-character strings will be compared. With SET EXACT deactivated, which is the default case, comparison is not strict: a string on the left of the test is equal to its substring on the right if the substring acts as a prefix of the larger string. Thus, "turnbull"="turn" is true even though it is clearly not. SET EXACT ON corrects for this lack of precision.

Command: SET EXCLUSIVE

Syntax: SET EXCLUSIVE ON/OFF

The SET EXCLUSIVE command, present in the network version of dBASE, controls whether files are opened in exclusive mode or in shared mode. Once the SET EXCLUSIVE ON command is used, all files opened are opened in exclusive mode until the SET EXCLUSIVE OFF command is used. An alternative way to open a database file in exclusive mode is to use the EXCLUSIVE clause along with the USE command when opening the file.

Command: SET FIELDS

Syntax: SET FIELDS ON/OFF

The SET FIELDS command respects or overrides a list of fields specified by the SET FIELDS TO command.

Command: SET FIELDS TO

Syntax: SET FIELDS TO [*list of fields* [ALL]]

The SET FIELDS TO command sets a specified list of fields that will be available for use. The ALL option causes all fields present in the active database to be made available.

Command: SET FILTER

Syntax: SET FILTER TO *condition*

The SET FILTER command displays only those records in a database that meet a specific condition.

    Example: To display only those records in a database that contain the name Culver City in the CITY field during a DISPLAY or LIST command, enter

```
SET FILTER TO "Culver City" $ CITY
```

Command: SET FIXED

Syntax: SET FIXED ON/OFF

The SET FIXED command activates the SET DECIMAL command for all calculations; thus, when used with SET DECIMAL, SET FIXED specifies the number of decimal places to be displayed with all numeric output.

Command: SET FORMAT

Syntax: SET FORMAT TO *filename*

The SET FORMAT command lets you select *filename* for the format of screen displays. If *filename* has the extension .FRM, you need not supply the extension.

Command: SET FUNCTION

Syntax: SET FUNCTION *n* TO *character-string*

The SET FUNCTION command resets a function key to a command of your choice (30 characters maximum). You can view the current settings with the DISPLAY STATUS command.

    Example: To change the function of the F5 key to open a file named ABC1 and enter APPEND mode, enter

```
SET FUNCTION 5 TO "USE ABC1;APPEND;"
```

The semicolon (;) executes a carriage return.

Command: SET HEADING

Syntax: SET HEADING ON/OFF

The SET HEADING command determines whether column headings appear when the LIST, DISPLAY, AVERAGE, or SUM command is used.

Command: SET HELP

Syntax: SET HELP ON/OFF

If SET HELP is ON, the "Do you want some help?" prompt appears if dBASE cannot understand the command you entered.

Command: SET HISTORY

Syntax: SET HISTORY TO *numeric expression*

SET HISTORY identifies the maximum number of commands that will be stored within HISTORY. The default value provided if the command is not used is 20.

Command: SET INDEX

Syntax: SET INDEX TO *filename*

The SET INDEX command opens the index file *filename*. If your file has the .NDX extension, you do not need to include it in the command. You can list more than one index file in the command line, but remember that only seven index files can be opened simultaneously.

Command: SET INTENSITY

Syntax: SET INTENSITY ON/OFF

The SET INTENSITY command determines whether reverse video is on or off during full-screen operations. SET INTENSITY is ON when you begin a session with dBASE III PLUS.

Command: SET MARGIN

Syntax: SET MARGIN TO *n*

The SET MARGIN command resets the left printer margin from the default of 0.

Command: SET MEMOWIDTH

Syntax: SET MEMOWIDTH TO *numeric expression*

The SET MEMOWIDTH command controls the width of columns containing the display or printed listings of contents of memo fields. The default value provided if this command is not used is 50.

Command: SET MENUS

Syntax: SET MENUS ON/OFF

The SET MENUS command determines whether cursor-key menus appear during full-screen commands. SET MENUS is ON when you being a session.

Command: SET MESSAGE

Syntax: SET MESSAGE TO *character-string*

The SET MESSAGE command identifies a user-definable message that appears on the message line at the bottom of the screen.

Example: To display the message "Press F1 for assistance" on the message line, enter

```
SET MESSAGE TO "Press F1 for assistance."
```

Command: SET ORDER

Syntax: SET ORDER TO *index file name*

The SET ORDER command makes the named index file the active index without changing the open or closed status of the other index files.

Example: If three index files, NAME, CITY, and STATE, are open and STATE is the active index, to keep the three index files open while changing the active index to CITY, enter

```
SET ORDER TO CITY
```

Command: SET PATH

Syntax: SET PATH TO *pathname*

The PATH command identifies a DOS path that will be searched for files if a file is not found in the current directory.

    Example: To change the path from the default or root path to a path named DBASE on drive C, enter

```
SET PATH TO C:\DBASE
```

For more information on pathnames, read your DOS manual (version 2.0 or later).

Command: SET PRINT

Syntax: SET PRINT ON/OFF

The SET PRINT command directs output to the printer as well as the screen. The default for SET PRINT is OFF.

Command: SET PRINTER

Syntax: SET PRINTER TO *LPT1, COM1, COM2,...other DOS device*

Reroutes printer output to the DOS device specified.

Command: SET PROCEDURE

Syntax: SET PROCEDURE TO *procedure-filename*

The SET PROCEDURE command opens the procedure file named. SET PROCEDURE is placed in the command file that will reference the procedures in a procedure file. Only 1 procedure file can be open, and up to 35 procedures can be in a procedure file.

Command: SET RELATION

Syntax: SET RELATION [TO *key-expression/numeric-expression*]
INTO *alias*

The SET RELATION command links the active database to an open
database in another area. If the *key-expression* option is used, the active
file must contain that key, and the other file must be indexed on that key.

Example: To set a relation between the active database and a database named PARTS, using a key field named CUSTNO, enter

    SET RELATION TO CUSTNO INTO PARTS

Command: SET SAFETY

Syntax: SET SAFETY ON/OFF

The SET SAFETY command determines whether a confirmation message will be provided before existing files are overwritten. SET
SAFETY is normally set to ON.

Command: SET STATUS

Syntax: SET STATUS ON/OFF

The SET STATUS command turns on or turns off the display of the
dBASE III PLUS status line.

Command: SET STEP

Syntax: SET STEP ON/OFF

SET STEP is a debugging command that determines whether processing will stop each time a command in a command file is executed. The
default of SET STEP is OFF.

Command: SET TALK

Syntax: SET TALK/ON/OFF

The SET TALK command determines whether responses from dBASE
III PLUS commands are displayed on the screen. The default for SET
TALK is ON.

Command: SET TITLE

Syntax: SET TITLE ON/OFF

The SET TITLE command turns on or turns off the prompt for file titles that appears when files are added to an open catalog.

Command: SET TYPEAHEAD

Syntax: SET TYPEAHEAD TO *numeric expression*

SET TYPEAHEAD sets the size, in number of keystrokes, of the typeahead buffer. The default value provided if this command is not used is 20. The size of the typeahead buffer can be increased to prevent fast typists from outrunning the keyboard. Acceptable values are any number between 0 and 32,000.

Command: SET UNIQUE

Syntax: SET UNIQUE ON/OFF

The SET UNIQUE command is used with the INDEX command to create lists of items with no duplicates. The list may not be indexed adequately if there are duplicates. The default setting for SET UNIQUE is OFF.

Command: SET VIEW

Syntax: SET VIEW TO *filename*/[?]

The SET VIEW command selects the view (.vue) file specified by *filename*. If the question mark option is used in place of a valid filename, a menu of all available view files will appear. If a catalog is open, the named view file will be added to the catalog.

Command: SKIP

Syntax: SKIP *expression*

The SKIP command moves the record pointer. SKIP moves one record forward if no value is specified. Values can be expressed as memory variables or as constants.

Example: To skip two records back, enter

```
SKIP -2
```

Command: SORT

Syntax: SORT TO *filename* ON *fieldname* [A/D] [*fieldname* [A/D]][*scope*]

The SORT command creates a rearranged copy of a database. The order of the new copy depends on the fields and options specified.

Example: To sort a database on the LASTNAME and then FIRST-NAME fields for duplicate entries in LASTNAME, both in descending order, and output the sorted file to a file named NEWNAME, enter

```
SORT TO NEWNAME ON LASTNAME/D, FIRSTNAME/D
```

Command: STORE

Syntax: STORE *expression* TO *memvar-list*

The STORE command creates a memory variable and stores a value to that variable.

Example: To multiply the field RENTAMT value, for the current record, by 1.05 and store it in the new memory variable named NEWAMT, enter

```
STORE RENTAMT*1.05 TO NEWAMT
```

Command: SUM

Syntax: SUM [*scope*][*field-list*][TO *memvar-list*] [FOR/WHILE *condition*]

The SUM command provides a sum total of *field-list* involving numeric fields. If the TO option is not used, the sum is displayed. If the TO option is used, the sum is stored as the memory variable specified. If the *scope* option is not used, ALL is assumed by dBASE III PLUS. The FOR/WHILE option can be used to specify a condition that must be met before an entry in a field can be summed.

Example: To total the contents of two specified fields (SALARY and TAXES) and store those sums to the memory variables A and B, enter

```
SUM SALARY, TAXES TO A,B
```

Command: SUSPEND

Syntax: SUSPEND

The SUSPEND command suspends execution of a command file or procedure and returns program control to the dot prompt while leaving current memory variables intact. Execution of the command file or procedure can be restarted where it was interrupted with the RESUME command.

Command: TEXT

Syntax: TEXT

> *text to be displayed*

ENDTEXT

The TEXT command displays blocks of text from a command file.
> *Example:*

```
TEXT
Press the RETURN key to run the payroll.
Or press the ESCAPE key to exit.
ENDTEXT
```

Command: TOTAL

Syntax: TOTAL TO *filename* ON *key* [*scope*] [FIELDS *field-list*]
    [FOR/WHILE *condition*]

The TOTAL command adds the numeric fields in a database and creates a new database containing the results.
    Example: To total the SALARY, FEDTAX, STATETAX, and FICA fields in a database named PAYROLL, and store those totals to a second database named RECORDS, enter

```
USE PAYROLL
TOTAL TO RECORDS ON SALARY, FEDTAX, STATETAX, FICA
```

Command: TYPE

Syntax: TYPE *filename.ext* [TO PRINT]

The TYPE command displays the contents of a disk file on screen. If the TO PRINT option is used, the file will be printed.

Command: UNLOCK

Syntax: UNLOCK [ALL]

The UNLOCK command, present in the network version of dBASE, releases the last lock placed on a record or on a file in the current work area. If UNLOCK is used, any lock that applies to the active file is released. If UNLOCK ALL is used, all existing locks in all work areas are released.

Command: UPDATE

Syntax: UPDATE [*RANDOM*] ON *key-field* FROM *alias* REPLACE
field WITH *expression* [,*field2* WITH *expression2*...]

The UPDATE command uses data from a specified database, *alias*, to make changes to the database in use.

Example: To update the RENTAMT field in a database named WORLDWIDE, based on the contents of the RENTAMT field in a database named CURRENCY, enter

```
SELECT 2
USE CURRENCY
SELECT 1
USE WORLDWIDE
UPDATE ON LASTNAME FROM CURRENCY REPLACE RENTAMT
   WITH CURRENCY -> RENTAMT
```

Both files must be sorted or indexed on the key field unless RANDOM is included, in which case only *alias* need be indexed. *Alias* must be in a work area.

Command: USE

Syntax: USE [*filename*] [INDEX *file-list*][ALIAS *alias*]

The USE command opens a database file and related index files in a work area.

Command: WAIT

Syntax: WAIT [*prompt*] [TO *memvar*]

The WAIT command halts operation of a command file until a key is pressed. If a prompt is included, it will be displayed on the screen. If the TO option is used, the key pressed will be stored as a memory variable.

Command: ZAP

Syntax: ZAP

The ZAP command removes all records from the active database file. The ZAP command is equivalent to a DELETE ALL command followed by a PACK command.

B: Functions

T he following table provides you with the dBASE III PLUS functions and their uses.

Function	Use
&	Macro substitution; used with character variables to replace the contents of the variable with a literal
ABS(<exp.>)	Finds the absolute value of a numeric expression
ASC(<exp.>)	Returns the ASCII value for the leftmost character in the string stored as the expression
AT(<exp.1>, <exp.2>)	Performs a substring search and returns a number indicating the starting position of a substring *exp.1* within a string *exp.2*
BOF( )	Returns logical true (.T.) when an attempt is made to move the record pointer backward beyond the first record
CDOW(<exp.>)	Returns the day of the week for a date expression
CHR(<exp.>)	Returns the ASCII value represented by the numeric expression

Function	Use
CMONTH(<exp.>)	Returns the name of the month for a date expression
COL( )	Returns the current column cursor position
CTOD(<exp.>)	Returns a date expression based on a character expression supplied in valid date format
DATE( )	Returns the date indicated by the system clock
DAY(<exp.>)	Returns a numeric value indicating the day of the month as represented by a date expression
DBF( )	Returns the name of the active database file
DELETED( )	Returns a logical true (.T.) when the current record is marked for deletion
DISKSPACE( )	Returns a numeric value indicating the amount of free space on the default drive
DOW(<exp.>)	Returns a numeric value indicating the day of the week as represented by a date expression
DTOC(<exp.>)	Returns a character expression based on a date expression
EOF( )	Returns logical true (.T.) when record pointer is at end of a file, beyond the last record in the file
ERROR( )	Returns a numeric value that corresponds to the error flagged by the ON ERROR command
EXP(<exp.>)	Returns a numeric value that is the value of the exponent (x) in e to the X power
FIELD(<exp.>)	Returns a fieldname that corresponds to the order represented by the numeric expression supplied (for example, FIELD(3) returns the name of the third field)
FILE(<filename>)	Returns a logical true (.T.) if the named file exists on the default drive
FKLABEL(<exp.>)	Returns a character indicating the function key whose number corresponds to the number supplied as *expression*
FKMAX( )	Returns a numeric variable indicating the number of available function keys
FOUND( )	Returns a logical true (.T.) if a prior FIND, SEEK, LOCATE, or CONTINUE command was successful

Function	Use
GETENV(<exp.>)	Returns a character string indicating the DOS environmental variable named by the expression
IIF(<logical exp.>, <exp.1>,<exp.2>)	Returns expression 1 if the logical expression is true, and expression 2 if the logical expression is false
INKEY( )	Reads the keyboard and either returns a numeric variable indicating the ASCII value of the depressed key or zero if no key is pressed
INT(<exp.>)	Returns an integer based on the numeric variable supplied. Performs the conversion by stripping values after the decimal point, not by rounding
ISALPHA(<exp.>)	Returns a logical true (.T.) if the character expression named begins with an alpha character
ISCOLOR( )	Returns a logical true (.T.) if dBASE is operating in color mode
ISLOWER(<exp.>)	Returns a logical true (.T.) if the character expression named begins with a lowercase character
ISUPPER(<exp.>)	Returns a logical true (.T.) if the character expression named begins with an uppercase character
LEFT(<char. exp.>, <no. of chars>)	Returns the number of characters specified in *no. of chars* from the string named in *char. exp.*
LEN(<exp.>)	Returns the numeric value indicating the number of characters in the expression
LOG(<exp.>)	Returns the logarithm of the number supplied in *expression* in base e
LOWER(<exp.>)	Returns the lowercase equivalent of a string of uppercase characters
LTRIM(<exp.>)	Trims leading blanks from the specified character expression
LUPDATE( )	Returns the date of the last update of the current database file
MAX(<exp.1>, <exp.2>)	Returns the higher of two numeric values
MESSAGE( )	Returns the error message in the form of a character string

Function	Use
MIN(<exp.1>, <exp.2>)	Returns the lower of two numeric values
MOD(<exp.1>, <exp.2>)	Returns the modulus, or remainder, of a division where *exp.1* is divided by *exp.2*
MONTH(<exp.>)	Returns the numeric value indicating the month of the year as represented by a date expression
NDX(<exp.>)	Returns the name of active index file, corresponding to the number in *exp.*
OS( )	Returns the name of the present operating system
PCOL( )	Returns the current printer column cursor position
PROW( )	Returns the current printer row cursor position
READKEY( )	Returns a numeric value representing which key was pressed to exit from a full-screen command
RECCOUNT( )	Returns the number of records in the active database
RECNO( )	Returns the current record number in the active database
RECSIZE( )	Returns the size of a record in the active file
REPLICATE(<char. exp.>,<num. exp.>)	Repeats the specified character expression by the number of times specified by the numeric expression
RIGHT(<char. exp.>, <no. of chars>)	Returns the number of characters specified in *no. of chars* starting from the rightmost character in the string named in *char. exp.*
ROUND(<exp.1>, <exp.2>)	Returns the number that is a rounded number where *exp.1* is the value to be rounded, and *exp.2* is the number of decimals specified
ROW( )	Returns the current row cursor position
RTRIM(<exp.>)	Trims trailing blanks from the character expression specified in *exp.* Identical to TRIM function
SPACE(<exp.>)	Generates a character expression consisting of the number of spaces specified in the expression
SQRT(<exp.>)	Returns the square root of a positive expression
STR(<exp.>, [<length>], [<decimal>]	Converts a numeric value into an equivalent character string. With [<length>] omitted, the length defaults to 10. With [<decimal>] omitted, the number is rounded to an integer

Function	Use
STUFF(<char. exp.1>,<starting position>,<no. of chars.>,<char. exp.2>)	Inserts, or stuffs, a character string into an existing character string. *char.exp.1* is the substring to be changed, and *char.exp.2* is the replacement string
SUBSTR(<char. exp.>,<starting position>,<no. of chars.>)	Extracts a portion (substring) of a character string
TIME( )	Returns the time indicated by the system clock
TRANSFORM(<exp.1>, <exp.2>)	Returns the character expression defined by *exp.1*, formatted by the PICTURE format described in *exp.2*
TRIM(<exp.>)	Trims trailing blanks from the character expression specified in *exp.*
TYPE(<exp.>)	Returns a C (Character), N (Numeric), L (Logical), D (Date), M (Memo), or U (Undefined) indicating the type of the expression defined in *exp.*
UPPER(<exp.>)	Returns the uppercase equivalent of a string of lowercase characters
VAL(<exp.>)	Converts a character string composed of digits into an equivalent numeric value
VERSION( )	Returns the version number of dBASE III PLUS
YEAR(<exp.>)	Returns the numeric value indicating the year as represented by a date expression

C: User
Documentation

User documentation is a sore point with many users and is regarded as an unwanted necessity by many system developers. This appendix provides a sample of detailed user documentation that can be used as a model and modified to fit your applications. It describes the operation of the Invoices/Receivables System described in Chapter 16.

If you look for user documentation for custom applications written in dBASE, you will discover some documentation that is well done and some that is not so well done. And sometimes you will find no documentation at all. Poorly written or nonexistent user documentation is a particular problem with systems developed by staff members inside companies for internal use. The staff member charged with setting up the system under dBASE usually decides that she or he has better things to do than sit around writing user manuals. This sort of decision can quickly return to haunt the person who made it, however, when users start phoning to ask questions that they should have found answered in a manual.

The problem is not limited to in-house applications; many programming and consulting houses provide poor end-user documentation. Most programmers are not writers, and many consulting shops are too small to keep a full-time writer on the staff. As a result, the client gets a loosely organized stack of notes humorously referred to as "documentation." The poor image that this presents to the end users (the people who are ultimately paying for the system) can be avoided if some time is spent on developing adequate end-user documentation.

What is adequate documentation? At the very least, user documentation should include coverage of the following topics:

1. An explanation of how to get the system started, from turning the power on, all the way through DOS, and into the main menu of the application

2. A short description of what the application does

3. A description of the main menu, with a listing of what options are available in that menu

4. A detailed explanation of each main menu option

5. Illustrations of all the data-entry screens, with examples of data filled into the fields

6. An explanation of any data validation the system performs, and instructions to users on how to reenter an item that is not accepted by the system

7. An explanation of how to generate reports, along with examples of the reports

8. Instructions for backing up the system files

Any additional features provided by the system should also be described in the documentation. In the example documentation provided in Figure C-1, a section describes the exporting of invoice data to Lotus 1-2-3 because that feature is provided within the system. This may seem like a lot of work, but in the long run the benefits of good user documentation are significant. The end users will appreciate it, and your application will have a more professional appearance.

GENERIC DOCUMENTATION

INVOICES/RECEIVABLES SYSTEM

designed for

Generic Clients, Ltd.

by

Generic Consultants
101 Main Street
Los Angeles, CA 90020

Figure C-1.

Documentation for the Generic
Invoices-Receivables System

Table of Contents

Figure C-1.

Documentation for the Generic
Invoices-Receivables System
(*continued*)

_____

INTRODUCTION

The Invoices / Receivables System (IR System) is a
database management system designed to handle payment of
invoices to your firm, or the "accounts receivables"
function. The system is written using dBASE III PLUS, a
popular database manager for the IBM-PC and
compatible computers. This manual details the operation
of the IR System.

STARTING THE SYSTEM

To start the system, turn on the IBM-PC/XT or AT on
which the system is installed. Do NOT insert any floppy
disk in the computer; the system is designed to start
from the built-in "hard disk." The screen will appear
dark (with the exception of a single flashing cursor at
the upper left side) until the computer completes its
memory test. Within one to two minutes, the red lamp on
the disk drive will light, and the computer may display
a prompt asking you to enter the date. The prompt looks
like this:

        Enter new date (mm/dd/yy):

Enter today's date in the format shown (example:
10/15/86) and press the Return key; if prompted, also
enter the time, in military format (example: 13:15:30).
The DOS prompt should appear (unless your system uses a
custom menu design). Next, enter the following:

        CD\name

(where "name" is the name of the subdirectory where
dBASE III PLUS and the IR System are installed). Then
press the Return key. The system will switch to the
proper directory. Enter DBASE ACCOUNT and press Return.
Within a moment, a copyright screen for dBASE will
appear. Press the Return key to get past this screen,
and into the IR System. The IR System Main Menu will
appear (Figure 1).

3

_____

Figure C-1.

Documentation for the Generic
Invoices-Receivables System
(*continued*)

```
┌──────────────────────────────────────────────────────────┐
│                 YOUR COMPANY NAME HERE                     │
│               INVOICES/RECEIVABLES SYSTEM                  │
├──────────────────────────────────────────────────────────┤
│                                                            │
│       1. ADD New Invoices                                  │
│       2. EDIT or RECORD RECEIPTS for Existing Invoice      │
│                                                            │
│       3. INQUIRE: Show Data On An Invoice                  │
│       4. Delete An Invoice                                 │
│       5. Produce Reports                                   │
│                                                            │
│       6. Customer File Maintenance                         │
│       7. Other Tasks (Backup, Index Maintenance)           │
│                                                            │
│                                                            │
│                                                            │
│       0. Quit This System and Return to DOS                │
│                                                            │
└──────────────────────────────────────────────────────────┘
```

[Selection?]

| Command | <C:> CUSTOMER | Rec: 2/6 | | |

Enter a dBASE III PLUS command.

Figure 1

4

Figure C-1.

Documentation for the Generic
Invoices-Receivables System
(*continued*)

There are eight choices, numbered zero through seven,
provided on the Main Menu. The most often-used choices
are (1) for adding new invoices, (2) for editing
existing invoices or for recording the payment of an
invoice, and (5) for printing reports. Other choices
provided include (3) for displaying the data for an
invoice, (4) for deleting an invoice that is no longer
desired, (6) for maintaining the list of customers and
adding new customers, and (7) for other tasks such as
backing up the database and reindexing of the files.
The IR System is menu-driven, meaning you will be
presented with numbered options for various tasks
throughout the system. Choice (0) will exit the system
and return you to the DOS prompt. You can then turn off
the computer if it will not be used for some time.

ADDING NEW INVOICES

To add new invoices to the database, select Option #1,
"Add New Invoices" from the Main Menu, and press Return.
You will be asked for the Customer ID code. Enter the
unique three-character code assigned to that customer,
and press Return. (To add a customer code and new
customer data, see Page 9.) Once you have entered a
valid Customer ID code, the Invoice Data Entry/Edit
Screen will appear (Figure 2).

5

Figure C-1.

Documentation for the Generic
Invoices-Receivables System
(*continued*)

```
┌───────────────────────────────────────────────────────┐
│                  INVOICE INFORMATION                  │
│                                                       │
│  Invoice No:    10001   Customer Code: JEJ   Dept. Code: SER  │
│                                                       │
│  Description of Service: Service 660 copier           │
│                                                       │
│  Amount Due:        250.00 Date Due: 02/03/00  Service Type: XCS  │
└───────────────────────────────────────────────────────┘
┌───────────────────────────────────────────────────────┐
│                  PAYMENT INFORMATION                  │
│                                                       │
│  Date Paid:  / /     Amount Paid:          0.00       │
│                                                       │
│  If less than full amount paid, why?                  │
│                                                       │
│  Comments:                                            │
│            INVOICE DATA ENTRY/EDIT SCREEN             │
└───────────────────────────────────────────────────────┘
```

```
Command       <C:> INVOICES          Rec: 2/8
```

Enter a dBASE III PLUS command.

Figure 2

6

Figure C-1.

Documentation for the Generic
Invoices-Receivables System
(*continued*)

The data entry screen contains the various fields for
the invoices database, as shown in the illustration.
Pressing Return when in the last field of the screen
automatically stores the information, and the system
asks if you wish to enter an additional record. The up
and down arrow (cursor) keys let you move from one field
to another, if necessary. You will normally fill the
screen by entering the desired information for each
field, and by pressing the Return key. When you press
Return, the cursor automatically moves to the next
field.

Note that when you add a new invoice, the computer
automatically assigns a new invoice number for you.
This invoice number remains with that invoice and cannot
be changed. The Customer ID code can be any three-digit
code which you choose when assigning customers; often,
the initials of a firm's name serve as satisfactory
Customer ID codes. (Whatever identification system you
choose must use unique codes. The system will not
permit you to enter the same code twice for two
different customers.)

You can complete the data entry process in one of two
ways: by pressing Return after entering the data for the
final field, or by pressing either the Page Down or the
Control-End key combination while in any field. Either
technique will cause the IR System to ask,

           Add another? Y/N:

And you can either enter the letter "Y," to add another
record, or the letter "N," to return to the IR System
Main Menu. Press Return after entering the letter of
your choice. If you choose "Y" to add another record,
you will again be asked for the Customer ID. After
entering a valid Customer ID, the same Data Entry Screen
will again appear, with a new invoice number and a blank
set of fields. If you choose "N" in response to the
"Add another?" prompt, you will return to the Main Menu.

EDITING EXISTING INVOICES

To edit existing records, choose Option #2 from the Main
Menu. The IR System will display a "Search Screen"
asking for the invoice number. Enter the invoice number
for the desired invoice, and press Return.

The IR System will search for the record in the database
that matches the invoice number supplied. It will show
you that record in a screen resembling the one shown
earlier in Figure 2. Make the desired changes, and use

7

Figure C-1.

Documentation for the Generic
Invoices-Receivables System
(*continued*)

the Control-End key combination to save the changes.
You will be asked if you wish to edit another record.
Enter "Y" if you wish to repeat the editing process, or
"N" to return to the Main Menu.

DISPLAYING AN INVOICE

Main Menu Option #3, INQUIRE, is used to display the
contents of a record. It works in a fashion similar to
that of editing a record, but you do not have to move
through any fields or press Control-End to exit. It
simply shows you the data, and is useful for displaying
information in response to customer queries.

When you select this option, the IR System will display
a "Search Screen" asking for the invoice number. Enter
the invoice number for the desired invoice, press
Return, and the desired invoice will be displayed. When
done viewing the record, press any key. You will be asked
if you wish to view another record. Enter "Y" if you wish
to see another record, or "N" to return to the Main Menu.

IF YOU CAN'T SEEM TO FIND AN INVOICE...

It may help to print a report of all invoices for the
company you are interested in; then, look at that report
to find the desired invoice, and verify the invoice
number. (See the "Printing Reports" section for
information on how to do this.)

DELETING AN INVOICE

Main Menu Option #4, "Delete An Invoice", lets you
remove invoices from the database if they are no longer
desired. Such a process is final; once you delete a
record, you cannot retrieve it. (The system will ask
for confirmation before it will delete any record.)

To delete the invoice, choose Option #4 from the Main
Menu, and press Return. You will be presented with a
Search Screen similar to the one which was used to find
invoices to edit.

Enter the invoice number, and press Return. The IR
System will search for the invoice in the database that
matches the supplied invoice number. It will show you
that invoice, in a screen resembling the one shown
earlier in Figure 2. Once the invoice appears, the
system will ask for confirmation by beeping and
displaying this message at the bottom of the screen:

        DELETE invoice-- Are you SURE? (Y/N):

8

Figure C-1.

Documentation for the Generic
Invoices-Receivables System
(*continued*)

And you must enter "Y," then press Return, for the
invoice to be deleted. Once the invoice has been
deleted, you will be asked if you wish to delete another
invoice. Enter "Y" if you wish to delete another
record, or "N" to return to the Main Menu.

If you enter "N" in response to the "DELETE invoice"
prompt, the invoice will not be deleted, and you will be
returned to the Main Menu.

ADDING CUSTOMERS

The IR System maintains a list of your firm's customers.
To add, edit, and delete customers in this list, choose
Option #6 from the Main Menu, "Customer File
Maintenance." When you do this, a new menu will appear,
shown in Figure 3.

9

Figure C-1.

Documentation for the Generic
Invoices-Receivables System
(*continued*)

```
                   INVOICES/RECEIVABLES SYSTEM
                   CUSTOMER MAINTENANCE MENU


          1. ADD New Customers

          2. EDIT Existing Customers

          3. DELETE A Customer




          0. Return To Prior Menu
```

[Selection?]
Command   <C:> INVOICES   Rec: 9/9

Enter a dBASE III PLUS command.

Figure 3

10

Figure C-1.

Documentation for the Generic
Invoices-Receivables System
(*continued*)

The Customer Maintenance Menu contains choices for
adding new customers, editing existing customers, and
for deleting a customer from the customer list.

Enter 1 and press Return to add a new customer. The
system will ask you for the name of the customer, and
for a unique 3-character Customer ID code. You can use
any letter or numbering scheme which you are comfortable
with, but each customer must have a unique code. The
system will reject any attempt to enter a code for a new
customer if that code has already been used for an
existing customer.

Once you have entered the name and ID, the system will
check to see that another identical customer name does
not exist. If another firm by the same name exists, the
system will show that firm, and ask for confirmation
before creating a new entry. This safeguards against
accidental additions of duplicate customer names, while
still permitting two or more customers with the same
names (for example, you might have branch offices of one
company as multiple customers).

With the name and new Customer ID code entered, the
Customers Data Entry Screen will appear, as illustrated
on the next page.

11

Figure C-1.

Documentation for the Generic
Invoices-Receivables System
(*continued*)

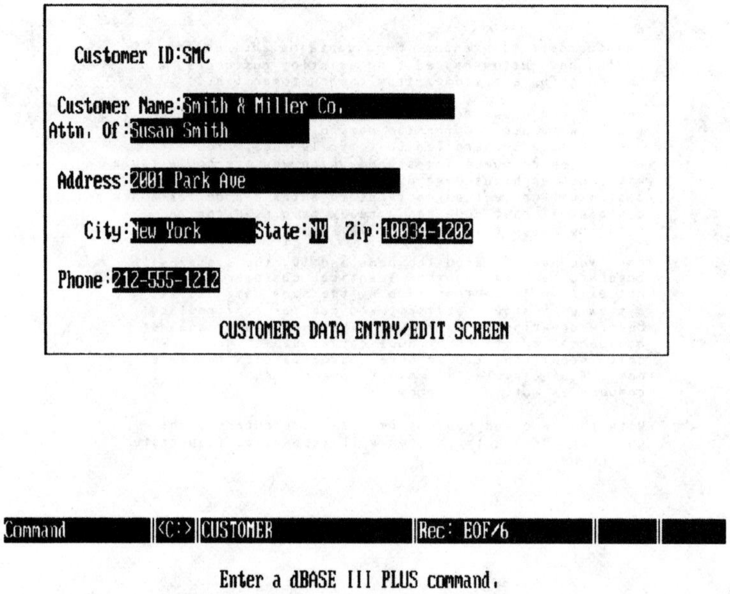

Figure 4

12

Figure C-1.

Documentation for the Generic Invoices-Receivables System (*continued*)

The Customer ID code and customer name which you previously entered will automatically appear in the new record. You can proceed to enter the remaining data, pressing Return to move to the next field when done. Press Return at the last field, or press Control-End while in any field, to store the addition. Either technique will cause the IR System to ask,

Add another? Y/N:

And you can either enter the letter "Y," to add another record, or the letter "N," to return to the IR System Main Menu. Press Return after entering the letter of your choice. If you choose "Y" to add another record, you will again be prompted for a customer name and customer ID code, and the process will be repeated. If you choose "N," you will return to the Main Menu.

EDITING CUSTOMERS

To edit a customer record, choose Option #6 from the Main Menu to get to the Customer File Maintenance Menu, then choose Option #2, "Edit Existing Customers." You will be prompted for a valid customer code. Enter the desired code, and the record will appear, in a screen similar to the one shown in Figure 4.

You can make changes to every field EXCEPT the Customer ID field. Because invoices may have been generated based upon the Customer ID, the system will not let you change the Customer ID at random; to do so could create havoc with the printing of existing invoices. Make the desired changes with the cursor, backspace, and delete keys; then, use Control-End to save the changes. You will be asked if you wish to edit another customer record. Enter "Y" if you wish to repeat the editing process, or "N" to return to the Main Menu.

DELETING CUSTOMERS

WARNING: exercise care when deleting a customer. Even if a customer is inactive, you probably should not delete that customer until all invoices for that customer are off the books. If you delete a customer and later generate reports containing invoices for that customer, the reports will not contain the customer name.

To delete a customer, choose Option #6 from the Main Menu to get to the Customer File Maintenance Menu, then choose Option #3, "Delete A Customer." You will be

13

Figure C-1.

Documentation for the Generic
Invoices-Receivables System
(*continued*)

prompted for a valid Customer ID code. Enter the
desired code, and the record will appear, in a screen
similar to the one shown in Figure 4. Once the invoice
appears, the system will ask for confirmation by
beeping, and displaying this message at the bottom of
the screen:

DELETE customer, are you SURE? (Y/N):

And you must enter "Y," then press Return, for the
customer to be deleted. Once the customer has been
deleted, you will be asked if you wish to delete
another; answer "Y" or "N" as desired. If you enter "N"
in response to the "DELETE customer" prompt, the
customer will not be deleted, and you will be returned
to the Main Menu.

PRINTING REPORTS

Main Menu Option #5, "Produce Reports", is used to print
a variety of reports. To print a report, enter 5 from
the Main Menu, and press Return. The Reports Menu will
appear (Figure 5).

14

Figure C-1.

Documentation for the Generic
Invoices-Receivables System
(*continued*)

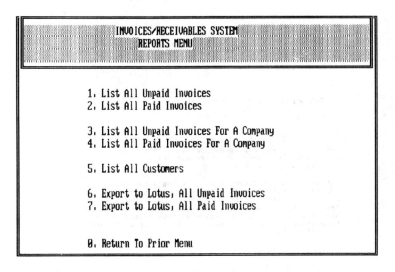

```
              INVOICES/RECEIVABLES SYSTEM
                    REPORTS MENU


          1. List All Unpaid Invoices
          2. List All Paid Invoices

          3. List All Unpaid Invoices For A Company
          4. List All Paid Invoices For A Company

          5. List All Customers

          6. Export to Lotus, All Unpaid Invoices
          7. Export to Lotus, All Paid Invoices


          8. Return To Prior Menu
```

```
[Selection?]
Command        <C:> CUSTOMER              Rec: ?/?
```

Enter a dBASE III PLUS command.

Figure 5

15

Figure C-1.

Documentation for the Generic
Invoices-Receivables System
(*continued*)

Five types of reports are currently available from the
system. They are:

1. All Unpaid Invoices

2. All Paid Invoices

3. All Unpaid Invoices For A Company

4. All Paid Invoices For A Company

5. List All Customers

The Reports Menu also provides two options for creating
Lotus 1-2-3 worksheets. These options are described in
the following section.

Choose the desired report by entering a number and
pressing Return. You will be asked to verify that your
printer is ready and to press a key. (You can press "C"
for Cancel, to cancel the report.) Once you press any
key other than "C", the report will be printed. If you
have chosen one of the invoice reports, it will resemble
the following:

```
                        INVOICE   REPORT
                                            All Unpaid
==============================================================================
   Inv. No.        Customer Name            Amt. Due  Date Due
==============================================================================

   10004           J.E. Jones Associates
                                            120.50    02/03/87

   10009           JES Financial Services
                                            220.00    09/27/87

   10008           JES Financial Services
                                            150.00    10/19/87

   10007           Osborne-McGraw Hill
                                             65.00    10/20/87


   TOTAL:                                   555.50
```

If you have chosen the customer list, you will be
provided with a list of all customers currently in the
system, with complete names, addresses, and phone
numbers.

CREATING LOTUS 1-2-3 SPREADSHEETS

16

Figure C-1.

Documentation for the Generic
Invoices-Receivables System
(*continued*)

CREATING LOTUS 1-2-3 SPREADSHEETS

The IR System has the ability to create files that can
be loaded into Lotus 1-2-3 as a spreadsheet. This
feature gives you the ability to graph trends in billing
activity, using the graph features of Lotus 1-2-3. To
create a Lotus spreadsheet, choose Option #6 or #7 from
the Reports Menu.

Note that earlier versions of Lotus 1-2-3 cannot handle
more than 2000 rows in any single spreadsheet. Keep
this limitation of Lotus in mind as you create files for
use with Lotus 1-2-3.

Enter the number for the desired option, and press
Return. You will then see a message which says,

        Insert formatted disk in Drive A.
        Press C to cancel, or any other key to begin.

Place a formatted disk which will receive the 1-2-3
worksheet in drive A of the computer, then press any
key. The system will create the Lotus 1-2-3
spreadsheet, and it will be named 123FILE.WKS. When
this process is completed, the Main Menu for the IR
System will reappear.

The spreadsheet is created in Lotus 1-2-3, Release 1A
format. If you are using Lotus 1-2-3 Release 2, just
load the spreadsheet in the usual manner. It will
automatically be converted to Release 2 format by Lotus
as it is loaded.

USING dBASE III PLUS FOR OTHER WORK

As noted earlier, the IR System is written using the
industry-standard database manager, dBASE III PLUS. You
may want to use dBASE III PLUS for any other database
related work, from tracking the office football pool to
keeping a phone list of fellow workers and contacts.
ONE NOTE OF WARNING: The IR System uses databases and
index files which are stored in the IR System
subdirectory. Under NO circumstances should you attempt
to change the design or contents of these files while
using dBASE III PLUS. If you do so, you may damage the
files, or cause them to be changed so that the IR System
cannot reliably operate.

For more information on how you can use dBASE III PLUS,
see the tutorial booklet, "Getting Started", which
accompanies your dBASE III PLUS documentation.

17

Figure C-1.

Documentation for the Generic
Invoices-Receivables System
(*continued*)

BACKING UP THE IR SYSTEM

All information that is stored on a "hard disk" should
be backed up for emergency purposes from time to time.
How often backup should be done varies with the case
load, but a good rule of thumb is this: if you can't
stand the thought of losing all the data you've entered
since the last backup, then it is time to do another
backup.

Performing backup of the IR System is simple. All you
need are formatted floppy disks. You will need
approximately one formatted floppy disk for every 700
invoices in the system. This is a rough estimate; it is
better to have extra floppy disks available because once
the backup process starts, you cannot interrupt it to
format a floppy disk. You can, however, format disks
from within the IR System just before the backup process
begins. An option will appear after you select the
"Backup" choice, asking you if you wish to format any
disks at this time.

To back up the IR System, get your disks ready, and
choose Option #7 from the Main Menu. You will see a new
menu for "Other Tasks." Currently included on this menu
are two choices: file backup (Option #1), and reindexing
of files (Option #2). Enter 1 and press Return. The
system will warn you to have disks available. You are
given the option of pressing "C" to cancel the process,
or any other key to continue.

Once you press a key (other than "C"), a message appears
at the bottom of the screen, asking:

        Would you like to format floppy disks first? (Y/N):

You can enter "Y," and the system will ask you to insert
a disk in drive A. The disk will be formatted, and you
will be asked if you want to format another. This
process will continue until you enter "N" in response to
the "format another" question.

If you choose "N" in response to the "format disks"
question, you will next be asked to "insert source disk
if appropriate; strike any key when ready." Press a key,
and you will be asked to place the BACKUP disk #1 (the
first disk that files will be backed up onto) in drive
A. Place the disk in drive A, and press a key.   The
backup process will begin automatically.

LEAVE THE COMPUTER ALONE UNTIL IT ASKS FOR ANOTHER DISK.
The computer will proceed to place as much information

18

Figure C-1.

Documentation for the Generic
Invoices-Receivables System
(*continued*)

as it can fit on a single disk. When it has filled that
disk, it will ask for another. REMOVE the first disk,
and place a label with the number 1 on that disk. Label
another disk 2, and place that disk in drive A; then,
press any key to continue the backup process.

Continue labeling and inserting disks until the backup
process is completed. (The computer will let you know
by displaying a message when it is done.) Place the
disks in a safe place. You might want to consider
making an extra set of backups and sending them out with
your other off-site storage of valuable documents, if
the data is important enough to warrant such care.

??? QUESTIONS ???

Contact Mary Doe or John Doe at Generic Consultants,
(metro phone 555-1212) for any questions regarding the
IR System.

19

Figure C-1.

Documentation for the Generic
Invoices-Receivables System
(*continued*)

D: Resources

The following provides you with the resources available to dBASE III PLUS users.

PROGRAM GENERATORS

Genifer
Supplier: Bytel Corp.
1029 Solano Ave., Berkeley, CA 94706
(415) 527-1157

QUICKCODE
Supplier: Fox & Geller
604 Market Street
Elmwood Park, NJ 07407
(201) 794-8883

REPORT GENERATORS

R&R Relational Report Writer
Supplier: Concentric Data Systems, Inc.
18 Lyman Street, P.O. Box 4063
Westboro, MA 01581-4063
(800) 325-9035

QUICKREPORT
Supplier: Fox & Geller
604 Market Street
Elmwood Park, NJ 07407
(201) 794-8883

COMPILERS

Clipper
Supplier: Nantucket Software
12555 W. Jefferson Blvd.
Los Angeles, CA 90066
(213) 390-7923

dBRUN and RUNTIME +
Supplier: Ashton-Tate
20101 Hamilton Ave.
Torrance, CA 90502
(800) 437-4329 ext. 2831

QuickSilver
Supplier: WordTech Systems, Inc.
P.O. Box 1747
Orinda, CA 94563
(415) 254-0900

FrontRunner
Supplier: Apex Software Corp.
4516 Henry Street
Pittsburgh, PA 15213
(412) 681-4343

dBASE WORK-ALIKES

dBXL
Supplier: WordTech Systems, Inc.
P.O. Box 1747
Orinda, CA 94563
(415) 254-0900

FoxBASE+
Supplier: Fox Software, Inc.
27493 Holiday Lane
Perrysburg, OH 43551
(419) 874-0162

PROGRAMMER'S UTILITIES & OTHER UTILITIES

dANALYST
TranSec Systems
220 Congress Park Drive, Suite 200
Delray Beach, FL 33445
(800) 423-0772

dBASE Tools For C
Ashton-Tate
20101 Hamilton Ave.
Torrance, CA 90502
(800) 437-4329 ext. 2831

dFLOW
WallSoft Systems, Inc.
233 Broadway
New York, NY 10279
(800) 233-3569

dSALVAGE
Comtech Publishing, Ltd.
P.O. Box 456
Pittsford, NY 14534
(716) 586-3365

dSCAR
Supplier: Ryan Kitri (shareware)
2575 Drake Hill Road
Fortuna, CA 95440

dUTIL III PLUS
Supplier: Fox & Geller
604 Market Street
Elmwood Park, NJ 07407
(201) 794-8883

MEMO Searcher
Data Based Solutions
1975 Fifth Avenue, Suite 105
San Diego, CA 92101
(800) 336-6060 ext. 341
(800) 833-2700 ext. 341 (in CA)

Tom Rettig's Library
Tom Rettig Associates
9300 Wilshire Blvd., #470
Beverly Hills, CA 90212-3237
(213) 272-3784

WPMERGE (software product for transferring dBASE data to Word-
Perfect)
Supplier: Stuart Ozer (shareware)
1249 7th Avenue
San Francisco, CA 94122
(415) 566-6923

PUBLICATIONS OF INTEREST

Data Based Advisor
1975 Fifth Avenue, Suite 105
San Diego, CA 92101

TechNotes
Ashton-Tate
20101 Hamilton Ave.
Torrance, CA 90502

BOOK SOURCE CODE
The programs and generic user documentation in this text are available
on disk. See the page following the introduction of this book for details.

OTHER PROGRAM LISTINGS
AND SOURCE CODE DISKS

Data Based Solutions
1975 Fifth Avenue, Suite 105
San Diego, CA 92101
(800) 336-6060 ext. 341
(800) 833-2700 ext. 341 (in CA)

The Boston Computer Society
One Center Plaza
Boston, MA 02108
(617) 367-8080

Capitol PC Users' Group
4520 E. West Highway, Suite 550
Bethesda, MD 20814
(703) 750-7809

Trademarks

Advanced NetWare®	Novell, Inc.
Ashton-Tate®	Ashton-Tate Corporation
Clipper™	SPSS, Inc.
CompuServe®	CompuServe, Inc.
CP/M®	Digital Research, Inc.
dANALYST®	TranSec Systems
dBASE®	Ashton-Tate Corporation
dBASE II®	Ashton-Tate Corporation
dBASE III®	Ashton-Tate Corporation
dBASE III PLUS™	Ashton-Tate Corporation
dBRUN™	Ashton-Tate Corporation
dBXL™	WordTech Systems, Inc.
dFLOW®	WallSoft Systems, Inc.
DIF®	Lotus Development Corporation
dSALVAGE™	Comtech Publishing
dUTIL™	Fox & Geller, Inc.
Epson®	Seiko Epson Corporation
FoxBASE™	Fox Software, Inc.
FoxBASE+™	Fox Software, Inc.
Framework®	Ashton-Tate Corporation
FrontRunner™	Apex Software Corp.
Genifer®	Bytel Corp.
Hilco Software®	Hilco Software

IBM®	International Business Machines Corporation
IBM PC AT®	International Business Machines Corporation
IBM PC XT™	International Business Machines Corporation
Jet/Setter® (laser printer)	C. Itoh
LaserJet™	Hewlett-Packard Company
Lotus® 1-2-3®	Lotus Development Corporation
Macintosh™	Apple Computer, Inc.
MailMerge®	MicroPro International Corp.
Microsoft®	Microsoft Corporation
Microsoft® File™	Microsoft Corporation
Microsoft® Multiplan™	Microsoft Corporation
MultiMate®	MultiMate International Corporation
Norton®	Peter Norton Computing
PC's Limited 386™	PC's Limited
PC-File III®	ButtonWare, Inc.
PC-TALK III®	The Headlands Press, Inc.
PC-Write®	Quicksoft
PFS:®File™	Software Publishing Corp.
PFS:®First Choice®	Software Publishing Corp.
PFS:®Professional File™	Software Publishing Corp.
ProKey™	RoseSoft, Inc.
PS/2™	International Business Machines Corporation
QUICKCODE™	Fox & Geller, Inc.
QUICKREPORT™	Fox & Geller, Inc.
QuickSilver™	QuickSilver Software, Inc.
Quicksoft®	Quicksoft
R&R Relational Report Writer™	Concentric Data Systems, Inc.
RapidFile™	Ashton-Tate Corporation
R:BASE®	Microrim, Inc.
RunTime+™	Ashton-Tate Corporation
SideKick®	Borland International, Inc.
SuperCalc®	Computer Associates International, Inc.

Index

The manuscript for this book was prepared and submitted to
Osborne/McGraw-Hill in electronic form. The acquisitions editor
for this project was Nancy Carlston, the technical reviewer was
Stuart Ozer, and the project editor was Dusty Bernard.

Text design by Judy Wohlfrom using Garamond for text body and
display.

Cover art by Bay Graphics Design Associates. Color separation by
ColourImage. Cover supplier, Phoenix Color Corp. Book printed
and bound by R.R. Donnelley & Sons Company, Crawfordsville,
Indiana.

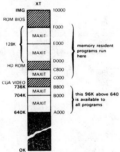
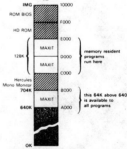